The Art of Recognition
in Wolfram's *Parzival*

The Art of Recognition
in Wolfram's *Parzival*

D. H. GREEN
*Schröder Professor of German
in the University of Cambridge and
Fellow of Trinity College, Cambridge*

Cambridge University Press

Cambridge
London   New York   New Rochelle
Melbourne   Sydney

Published by the Press Syndicate of the University of Cambridge
The Pitt Building, Trumpington Street, Cambridge CB2 1RP
32 East 57th Street, New York, NY 10022, USA
296 Beaconsfield Parade, Middle Park, Melbourne 3206, Australia

© Cambridge University Press 1982

First published 1982

Printed in Great Britain at the University Press, Cambridge

Library of Congress catalogue card number: 82–1283

British Library Cataloguing in Publication Data
Green, D. H.
The art of recognition in Wolfram's Parzival.
1. Wolfram, *von Eschenbach*. Parzival
I. Title
831'.2   PT1688
ISBN 0 521 24500 1

Contents

		page	
Preface			vii
Abbreviations			viii

1	Possibilities	1
2	Gahmuret (Books I and II)	38
3	Parzival's youth (Books III and IV)	60
4	Parzival's failure (Books V and VI)	89
5	Gawan (Books VII–VIII and X–XIII)	133
6	Parzival and Trevrizent (Book IX)	176
7	Parzival's success (Books XIV–XVI)	226
8	Conclusions	264
Appendix A	The recognition of Parzival at Munsalvæsche and by Trevrizent	320
Appendix B	Trevrizent's 'lie'	337

Bibliography	342
Index	351

Preface

It is a pleasure to record the various debts of gratitude I have incurred in writing this book. Ideal conditions for uninterrupted work and for stimulating discussion were provided by two institutions to whose far-sighted generosity many others are likewise indebted: the Humanities Research Centre of the Australian National University, which invited me to Canberra in 1978, and the Herzog August Bibliothek in Wolfenbüttel, which likewise made it possible for me to work in Germany in 1979. Without the facilities provided at both these centres the completion of this book would have taken immeasurably longer.

I also acknowledge my gratitude to the support received from the British Academy and its Small Grants Research Fund as well as to the Deutscher Akademischer Austauschdienst, both of whom made it possible to undertake working visits to a number of German libraries.

Two personal expressions of warm thanks are no less deeply felt for being the last to be mentioned. Peter Johnson of Cambridge has devoted much time to reading the manuscript and has given me the benefit of his own knowledge of Wolfram, not least when we were unable to reach agreement. Maria von Katte of Wolfenbüttel has likewise given up much of her time to discussion and to providing the stimulus which arises from the conviction of shared concerns.

Trinity College, Cambridge　　　　　　　　　　　　　　D. H. G.
May, 1981

Abbreviations

ABÄG	Amsterdamer Beiträge zur älteren Germanistik
CCM	Cahiers de Civilisation Médiévale
DU	Der Deutschunterricht
DVjs	Deutsche Vierteljahrsschrift für Literaturwissenschaft und Geistesgeschichte
FMSt	Frühmittelalterliche Studien
FS	Festschrift
GLL	German Life and Letters
GQ	German Quarterly
GR	Germanic Review
GRLMA	Grundriss der romanischen Literatur des Mittelalters
GRM	Germanisch-romanische Monatsschrift
JHGG	Jahrbuch der heraldisch-genealogischen Gesellschaft 'Adler'
KHM	Kinder- und Hausmärchen (Brüder Grimm), ed. F. Panzer, Munich, 1913
MLN	Modern Language Notes
MLR	Modern Language Review
MPL	J. P. Migne, *Patrologiae cursus completus. Series Latina*
OL	Orbis Litterarum
PBB	Paul und Braunes Beiträge. *(T)* stands for the Tübingen series.
RG	Recherches Germaniques
RJb	Romanistisches Jahrbuch
ZfdA	Zeitschrift für deutsches Altertum
ZfdPh	Zeitschrift für deutsche Philologie

1
Possibilities

If this is a difficult book to read my plea must be that it deals with a difficult text. Wolfram was quite conscious of the difficulties he created for many of his listeners, for he said of those he dismissed as *tumbe liute* that *sine mugens niht erdenken* (1,17). If we accept the implied flattery that we belong with the *wîser man* rather than the *tumbe liute*, then we cannot avoid the obligation of *erdenken*, of thinking through Wolfram's *Parzival* to its ultimate conclusions. In doing this we may rightly ask, as did Wayne Booth of the search for irony,[1] just how far we can take this process. Certainly not as far as did the late Mergell, for whom not one detail in the whole work was out of place in a fine mesh which connected it with everything else,[2] for this would mythologise Wolfram as much as in the *Wartburgkrieg*, where even the magician Klingsor attributes supernatural assistance to the poet: *Ich wil gelouben, daz den list / ein engel vinde, oder daz der tiufel in dir ist*.[3] Yet the danger of such an extreme, as long as we are aware of it, need not stop us following the poet's invitation, seeing how far he provides us with the means to *erdenken* his work, how far his clues take us in this intellectual quest.

As might be expected of a poet who sets great store by his own ability (cf. 4,2ff.) and who composes primarily for the *wîsen* in his audience, Wolfram makes considerable demands of his listeners. Some may doubt whether a German audience around 1200 could live up to such demands and may therefore suspect that we are imposing on the work a degree of complexity foreign to the literary situation in which the poet worked. Such doubts have been voiced about the ability of a medieval German audience to cope with the

---

1. Booth, *Irony*, p. 190.
2. Cf. the critical comments of Henzen, *Parzival*, pp. 192 and 214, and Schröder, *GRM* 40 (1959), 330.
3. Cf. Ragotzky, *Studien*, p. 53, and Johnson, *Beauty*, p. 273.

difficulties of irony,[4] and an ability to respond to complicated aesthetic demands of any kind has even been denied to medieval German listeners on principle.[5] The best reply to such arguments is to ignore a dogmatic *parti pris* and to pay attention to the text.[6] If the poet builds into his text points which demand a complex response, then we must assume such a response, as a possibility catered for if not always as a fact realised, on the part of the medieval audience. If a sophisticated artistry presupposes a wish or hope to train at least some members of the audience to appreciate it, we must recognise that the medieval courtly poet did not regularly compose in the abstract, without any chance of contemporary appreciation.[7] How much he hoped for close attention to his words is shown in Chrétien's *Yvain*, where Calogrenant addresses his audience in a way we should have expected from the narrator in his prologue, appealing for more than just perfunctory listeners (150: *Cuer et oroilles me randez! / Car parole oïe est perdue, / S'ele n'est de cuer antandue*).[8] That Chrétien is speaking for more than himself alone is confirmed by the adoption of the same appeal in Hartmann's *Iwein* (249: *man verliuset michel sagen, / man enwellez merken unde dagen. / maneger biutet diu ôren dar: / ern nemes ouch mit dem herzen war, / sone wirt im niht wan der dôz, / und ist der schade alze grôz: / wan si verliesent beide ir arbeit, / der dâ hœret und der dâ seit*).[9] To listen not just with the ears, but with the heart or mind is the precondition of Wolfram's invitation to *erdenken*, to think out the implications of his narrative.

The way in which I have chosen to follow up these implications involves combining five different approaches. These are the

---

4. Mertens has expressed doubts about this on the grounds of the sophistication of contemporary response it presupposes (*ZfdA* 106 (1977), 350, fn. 5). The question to ask, however, is not whether we are prepared to attribute this in theory to a medieval audience or not, but whether the evidence of a medieval text takes us towards that conclusion.
5. E.g., Huby, *RG* 6 (1976), 17. On Huby's whole approach and his dogma of the *adaptation courtoise* see my review, *MLR* 65 (1970), 666ff., and especially the demolition performed by Wolf, *GRM* 27 (1977), 257ff.
6. Cf. Wolf, *GRM* 27 (1977), 262.
7. See Hellgardt's justified criticism of what, in the case of numerical symbolism, he calls 'literarische Bauhüttengeheimnisse', *Grundsätzliches*, p. 27.
8. On the function of Calogrenant's 'prologue' as an unexpected replacement for the poet's see Gallais, *CCM* 7 (1964), 491.
9. Cf. Ragotzky and Weinmayer, *Identitätsbildung*, pp. 215 and 226. On *herze* as the seat of the intellectual faculties in Hartmann's *Büchlein* see Gewehr, *Frühscholastik*, pp. 112ff. See also Kaiser, *Textauslegung*, pp. 19f., on a passage from Gottfried's *Tristan*.

Possibilities

narrator's use of a point of view technique, one specific problem concerning the medieval reception of his work, a procedure best described as 'revealing while concealing',[10] the technique used in naming characters, and the theme of recognition in *Parzival*. A brief survey of what is meant by these approaches will show that each has come up for discussion before, but not always taken far enough or free of misinterpretation, and nowhere in combination with one another, as the following chapters attempt to do.

The narrator's point of view technique

Although much work has recently been done on Wolfram's narrator, none of it answers the questions raised by a combination of the five approaches just mentioned. Pörksen restricts his analysis to *Willehalm* alone, Curschmann discusses the function of the narrator in *Parzival*, but goes no further than the first six Books, whilst the usefulness of Nellmann's survey lies more in his factual presentation of material than in interpretation.[11] Moreover, each of these scholars tells us simply about the information which the narrator passes on to his listeners, whereas what will concern us more is the rate of instalments by which this information is fed to us, allowing us sometimes to share the narrator's omniscience, but sometimes forcing upon us the relative or total ignorance of a character in the narrative. This shifting technique thus operates with a shift in the point of view from which we are allowed to behold events.

How this point of view technique enables the listeners to recognise the facts of a situation which may escape the characters can be seen in the preliminaries to Keii's joust with Parzival when lost in his love rêverie. Keii judges by externals: since this knight is visible with upright spear (290,12: *mit ûf gerihtem sper*), this must represent a challenge to combat (290,7: *der gerte tjoste reht als ê*). That Keii is wrong in going by appearances, however, is made clear to us by the narrator's comment that Parzival is lost to the world outside (290,26: *der truoc der minne grôzen last*), so that a wish for combat is far from his thoughts and the way in which he grasps his spear must be purely fortuitous.[12] Yet this very gesture, wrongly interpreted

---

10. Cf. Poag, *Mære*, p. 72.
11. Cf. Pörksen, *Erzähler*, p. 235, *s.v.*; Curschmann, *DVjs* 45 (1971), 627ff; Nellmann, *Erzähltechnik*, *passim* (for a criticism of two details of his interpretation, see below, pp. 28ff., and for a third, Christ, *Rhetorik*, pp. 47ff.).
12. On the full implications of this gesture, see below, pp. 126f.

by Keii but explained to us by the narrator, can also illustrate how careful we must be in assuming a difference in point of view between ourselves and a character. When Gawan looks in the magic *sûl* at Schastel Marveile and sees a knight approaching (592,21ff.) we are shown things from Gawan's point of view,[13] but are then given a detail about the distant knight's intentions (592,30: *nâch im diu reise wart getân*; 593,6: *tjostieren was sîn ger*) which apparently cannot be known to Gawan and must therefore come from the narrator. But the reversion to Gawan's point of view after this[14] shows us that he can indeed see enough to be able to judge of the other knight's intentions: from the fact that he rides *mit ûf gerihtem sper* (593,24) Gawan surmises that Lischoys is seeking combat (593,27), so that, as the new ruler of Schastel Marveile, Gawan regards such an armed approach as a direct personal challenge (594,15ff.; 595,3f.). Unlike Keii, Gawan interprets appearances correctly, so that what appeared to be a narrator's interpolation about Lischoys is in fact a reflection of Gawan's thought processes in which his reading of the signs, unlike Keii's, in no way differs from the narrator's omniscient view of things.

The use of a point of view technique by Wolfram's narrator is nothing new in the medieval romance, for we also find it employed by his German predecessor, Hartmann,[15] and in his French source, Chrétien's *Perceval*. Indeed, the difference in this respect between Chrétien and Wolfram has been regarded as a major formal distinction between their two works. With very few exceptions[16] Chrétien has organised his narrative on an inductive principle, beginning *in medias res* in the forest scene so that we know as little of Perceval's origins as he does himself and leading us, together with the hero, by gradual stages from the unknown to the known.[17] This narrative principle is fully adequate to the theme of an inexperienced youth to whom the world presents a sequence of discoveries which he has to make, but by presenting events from Perceval's initially restricted, but slowly widening point of view Chrétien has ensured that his audience's progressive enlightenment largely keeps pace with the

13. Cf. 592,22 (*sach*), 24 (*schouwen*) and 25 (*dûht in*).
14. 593,10 (*sach*), 22 (*sach*) and 23 (*her*).
15. Harms, *Kampf*, pp. 124 and 129, has shown how in the case of Erec's second combat with Guivreiz and of Iwein's with Gawein the narrator informs his listeners who the combatants are, whilst they themselves remain in ignorance about their opponent.
16. One example is adduced by Bertau, *Literatur*, p. 775.
17. Cf. Frappier, *Chrétien*, p. 174, and *Graal*, pp. 64ff.

hero's. By contrast, Bertau suggests that Wolfram has abandoned this technique in favour of a narrative in the natural (chronological) order, in which the questions raised by Chrétien's opening scene have already been answered in Wolfram's preceding narrative and in which, as far as possible, everything is named at its first appearance.[18] I think that Bertau sees Wolfram's technique too much as an absolute contrast with Chrétien's, for in taking over this subject-matter the German poet was partly bound to a similar technique of progressively enlightening both hero and audience, even though he complicates the structure of his work in that the audience's progress towards enlightenment need not always be at the same pace as Parzival's, there are occasional vantage-points from which they can see further ahead than the hero.[19] We shall have ample occasion to discuss such cases, but for the moment it may suffice to register that the point of view technique plays a central rôle in how we are to view things in the German romance.

This last point needs to be stressed, if only because the importance of point of view has not always been realised in interpretation. Sometimes this is because a failure to distinguish between what the narrator tells us and the information available to a character can lead to a straightforward error, as Weigand has shown in the case of Fourquet at one point.[20] The French scholar criticises Wolfram for concluding the combat between Parzival and Orilus in Book V without having his hero reproach his defeated foe for being the killer of Schionatulander and the enemy of his dynasty, and draws far-reaching conclusions from this omission. Weigand rightly rejects these conclusions and the hypothesis on which they rest, for although in the course of the episode we learn from the narrator that the hero's opponent is none other than Orilus,[21] it is nowhere suggested that Parzival too was apprised of this. Nowhere in the dialogue between Parzival, Jeschute and Orilus which is reported to

---

18. Cf. Bertau, *Literatur*, pp. 779f.
19. How far Bertau's statement (p. 779: 'Alle Dinge werden möglichst gleich bei Namen genannt') is from being true, even just in the literal sense, I hope to have shown in *Namedropping*, pp. 116ff., where I discuss the interval between the introduction of several characters in *Parzival* and their naming. When Bertau also refers in the same context to the complex kinship relationships of the work (p. 780), it needs to be stressed that these are made clear to the audience only very gradually. On the kinship affiliations of Gawan and Parzival and on the listeners' slow enlightenment on these see below, pp. 151ff. and 214ff.
20. Weigand, *Parzival*, pp. 88, fn. 18. Fourquet's argument occurs in his *Wolfram*, p. 128.
21. See below, pp. 118ff.

us is this opponent's name actually mentioned, and if Parzival comes to recognise Jeschute and therefore to realise that his opponent must be her husband, this takes him no further since the name Orilus was not mentioned by Jeschute in her earlier meeting with Parzival or mentioned elsewhere as that of Jeschute's husband.[22] Parzival has therefore no occasion to link what he has learned of the knight called Orilus with the knight he has just defeated, they are connected only for us because the name is used by the narrator in his comments on each scene, so that the correct interpretation of the combat depends on our realising that what is revealed to us is concealed from the protagonist.

On other occasions failure to take this kind of distinction into account leads rather to an emphasis which can give rise to a false impression, as with Parzival's first visit at the Grail-castle. Schröder says of the atmosphere of grief and suffering here that it could not possibly have remained concealed from the visitor, and quotes several details to substantiate this,[23] but these details are comments made by the narrator to his listeners and as such unavailable to Parzival.[24] The hero can see the grass in the courtyard (227,10), but is not privy to the explanation given us (227,9 + 11: for grief no tournaments are held here).[25] Grief is conveyed to us by the narrator's choice of descriptive adjective in the case of Anfortas (230,30: *der wirt jâmers rîch*) and his retinue, of whom it is expressly said that they concealed this by putting on a front of courtly rejoicing (228,26: *die trûregen wâren mit im vrô*). Even the most emphatic remark about Anfortas's sickness (230,20: *er lebte niht wan töude*) is again made by the narrator to us, at a point before Parzival has even been received by his host,[26] so that on two scores it is withheld from him. This is not to say that no hints at all are given to the hero, for that would make his understanding of the situation impossibly difficult, but what is suggested to him is much less than what we are expressly told.[27] By means of these narratorial com-

---

22. Jeschute thus refers to Orilus simply as *mîn man* (132,12), whilst Sigune's reference to Orilus by name (141,9) is silent about his being the husband of Jeschute.
23. Schröder, *ZfdA* 100 (1971), 121.
24. See below, pp. 93ff., and also Hirschberg, *Untersuchungen*, pp. 128 and 160.
25. Even the later explanation (242,4ff.) quoted by Schröder is given by the narrator to his listeners and, since it bypasses Parzival, is strictly irrelevant.
26. Only in 230,21ff. does Parzival enter the hall in which he joins his host. See below, p. 110.
27. The first explicit hint to Parzival of the suffering at Munsalvæsche (229,17) is carefully given little emphasis (cf. below, p. 95), so that 231,23ff. is the first explicit and emphatic indication which he receives.

ments the listeners are enabled to recognise the vital fact of the situation earlier and more emphatically than can Parzival. This technique confirms what Bertau suggests about the difference between Wolfram and Chrétien, but such an insight is blurred if we argue that Parzival is just as well apprised of the facts as we are in our privileged position.[28]

Elsewhere the different amounts of information available to listeners and character are clear only when we pay heed not just to the information itself, but to the sequence in which it is gradually released. In her discussion of Orgeluse[29] Zimmermann interprets Cundrie's hint in Book VI that the adventure awaiting Gawan at Schastel Marveile will be a 'Minneabenteuer' (318,15ff.) as suggesting to the listeners that the reward of love will be granted him by Orgeluse rather than by any of the queens at that castle, because each of these queens is closely related to Gawan. This argument correctly states the facts of the narrative, but it is based on a retrospective knowledge supplied by later stages of the action, it is not knowledge on which the listeners can call when they first hear the Cundrie episode recited.[30] Soon after Cundrie's announcement Gawan in fact learns who these four queens are by name (334,16ff.) and realises how closely related they are to him, but at this point these names mean nothing to the listeners, who learn only very much later that they are relatives of Gawan.[31] In short, Zimmermann's statement is correct as an assessment of the total course of Gawan's quest for the adventure of Schastel Marveile, but invalid if it is meant to recapture the audience's reaction on first hearing a recital of the Cundrie episode. But this example also suggests the limitations to Bertau's absolute contrast between Chrétien's and Wolfram's techniques, for whereas in the episode of Parzival at Munsalvæsche the listeners were supplied with infor-

28. Hirschberg, *Untersuchungen*, p. 123, has also criticised Curschmann's suggestion that the scene of Parzival at Munsalvæsche is depicted 'ganz aus der Perspektive des Helden' (*DVjs* 45 (1971), 636). Although Curschmann rightly goes on to talk of another perspective which the narrator opens up for the listeners, his examples confine this to a view of the narrator (Abenberg, Wildenberg, his poverty), he nowhere suggests that the perspective revealed to the audience also concerns the events at the Grail-castle, thus putting them in a superior position to Parzival.
29. Zimmermann, *Euphorion* 66 (1972), 141.
30. This is not to say that the position may not be drastically different at a second recital, but Zimmermann is not considering this possibility at this point. On the way in which a subsequent recital can alter the audience's reception of a particular episode or detail see Green, *Irony*, pp. 259ff.
31. See below, pp. 151ff.

mation withheld from the hero, now in the case of Gawan's adventure they are denied vital information which is available to him almost from the outset.

Another example of the need to pay close attention to the point in the narrative where an informative statement is made by the narrator is provided by Cundrie's second appearance before the Round Table, when she announces that Parzival has been called to kingship of the Grail. Schroedel has drawn attention to some of the links between this scene and the occasion when Cundrie first appears, to denounce Parzival before the same company.[32] He mentions verbal links such as *noch* and *dennoch* (780,15: *si fuorte och noch den selben lîp*; 780,19: *ir ougen stuonden dennoch sus*) and a detail which echoes her appearance when she first appeared by the Plimizœl (780,24: *si fuorte ân nôt den tiuren huot / ûf dem Plimizœles plân*). All such parallels are quite correct, but what they leave out of account is the fact that these explicit links are made by the narrator only after Cundrie has cast aside her hood and been recognised (780,7ff.), whereas before this point other parallels have been made only implicitly,[33] so that it is left to the listeners to recognise their force, to suspect a connection between the two scenes and to see that Cundrie has entered the scene again. As with Chrétien's overall technique, the narrator expressly mentions Cundrie's name only at the point when the Round Table realise her identity (780,11), but unlike Chrétien he also gives us hints, however concealed, to recognise her before this point.

These illustrations of the narrator's point of view technique suggest that we have to ask not merely how much we in the audience know by contrast with a character in the action, but also at what points in the narrative sequence such information is released to us by the narrator. This last point is also particularly important in connection with the medieval reception of Wolfram's work.

The medieval reception of 'Parzival'

Under this heading I wish to take up a point once made in passing by S. M. Johnson, but nowhere developed to the extent which it merits.[34] He observes, when discussing the carefully orchestrated surprise which Gawan organises in Book XIII, that this surprise is

---

32. Schroedel, *Erzählen*, p. 106.
33. See below, pp. 250ff.
34. Johnson, *GR* 33 (1958), 285f.

Possibilities

largely spoilt for the modern reader by the detailed information and explanations given by present-day editors. We thus learn from footnotes the identity of a new character and the salient points in his biography as soon as he appears in the text, whilst the medieval listener received his information in carefully controlled instalments, dependent on how much the narrator was prepared to let him know at any point. The medieval listener therefore received his rations of enlightenment from the narrator, acting as the poet's mouthpiece, so that he was under the poet's indirect control and was brought by stages towards full awareness only as the poet thought fit, whereas we today are subjected to the whims of an editor who blurts out all at once what was originally meant for gradual release. Two examples may show how the editor's concern with factual helpfulness can conflict with what the poet has in mind.

Towards the end of Book III, when Gurnemanz recounts the fate of his three sons to Parzival, he mentions the circumstances under which Schenteflurs met his end (177,30: *dâ Cundwîr âmûrs / lîp unde ir lant niht wolte gebn, / in ir helfer flôs sîn lebn / von Clâmidê und von Kingrûn*). At this point the Bartsch-Marti edition has a footnote commentary on the first line, telling us that *dâ* refers to the place where Condwiramurs rejected her suitor and specifying this place as the city of Pelrapeire, soon to be the site of the action in the following Book.[35] Being thus apprised in advance by the editor, the modern reader knows when he comes to 180,24f. in Book IV (*dô vander / die stat ze Pelrapeire*) that the city reached by Parzival belongs to Condwiramurs. By contrast, neither the medieval listener nor Parzival himself can have realised this at this early stage. This can be shown by the fact that no mention was made at the close of Book III of Brobarz or Pelrapeire (either by the narrator or by Gurnemanz), so that their early mention in Book IV (180,18 and 25) is not enough to provide a link back to what had been recounted by Gurnemanz. Conversely, whereas the name of Condwiramurs had been mentioned by Gurnemanz, she is not at first referred to by name when Parzival arrives at Pelrapeire.[36] By withholding any explicit link between these two scenes the narrator ensures that his medieval listeners are not just provided with information, but are

35. Bartsch–Marti, fn. to 177,30.
36. On the anonymity in which the narrator initially keeps Condwiramurs in Book IV see below, p. 73, and on the careful avoidance of any informative link between Gurnemanz's words and the start of the Pelrapeire episode see below, *ibid.*, but also p. 84.

invited to *erdenken* the implications of the clues he does give them
and to reach their conclusion independently. I do not of course wish
to deny the relevance and helpfulness of such explanatory editorial
footnotes, but would stress that they constitute a difference
between our reception of the work and that which the poet had
in mind for his contemporary audience. As with Zimmermann's
remark about Gawan's 'Minneabenteuer' with regard to Orgeluse
rather than the four queens at Schastel Marveile, we can only assess
what the narrator has in mind with his audience at any point if we
disregard what we learn retrospectively from a reading of the whole
work, whether our own or the editor's.

Orgeluse also plays a rôle in my second example. When in Book
IX Trevrizent explains how Anfortas was wounded he relates that
this was a punishment for transgressing the rule of chastity by
involving himself in a love-affair, but takes care not to mention the
name of the Grail-king's mistress, saying only that he *kôs im eine
friundîn, / des in dûht, mit guotem site. / swer diu was, daz sî dâ mite*
(478,18ff.).[37] The hermit may have his own reason for silence over
this (he shows courtly tact in not mentioning the lady's name in this
kind of context and since her identity is unimportant he sees no
point in unnecessary scandal), but so has the narrator in keeping his
listeners as ignorant as Parzival. By releasing this information three
Books later (616,11ff.: Orgeluse tells Gawan that she had once
sought to gain vengeance for the death of Cidegast by accepting the
love-service of Anfortas, who was wounded as a result) the narrator
has carefully placed this delayed piece of information in close
conjunction with another revelation (618,19ff.: still seeking vengeance, Orgeluse had later also set her cap at Parzival, but met with
failure). This conjunction of two revelations brings it forcefully
home to us how different Anfortas and Parzival are in this respect,
how easily Parzival avoided the temptation to which Anfortas succumbed, in other words in how much better and safer hands Grail-
kingship will be with him than it was with Anfortas. The force of
this contrast is conveyed to us by the close conjunction of these two
revelations in Book XII, so that here we can observe the narrator
serving his own ulterior purpose by having Trevrizent keep silent
about the lady's name for reasons of courtesy in Book IX. But all

---

37. The narrator, too, preserves discretion when he later refers to Anfortas sending
a gift to Orgeluse (519,27: *dô sande der süeze Anfortas, / wand er et ie vil milte
was, / Orgelûsen de Lôgroys / disen knappen kurtoys*) by attributing this innocu-
ously to generosity, rather than to the special nature of their relationship.

this is jeopardised by the kind of footnote we find in the Bartsch–Marti edition, where the hermit's tactful reticence is commented on by the revelation that this is a reference to Orgeluse de Logroys.[38] This may be factually correct and helpful for the beginner, but why should this consideration take priority over the poet's intentions with his audience? Only by disregarding what the editor thrusts upon us can we learn to appreciate the poet's technique.[39]

Revealing while concealing

Under both the previous headings we have come across cases where the narrator equips his listeners with some information, but not enough for them to grasp the whole situation at once, so that he may be said to be 'revealing while concealing', a phrase which I take from Poag.[40] Something similar has been suggested at greater length by Harroff,[41] who makes the point that the underinformed hero is accompanied by the underinformed listeners who must attempt to interpret the narrative as it unfolds without at first grasping that the narrator has placed certain vital facts in inconspicuous positions, thereby concealing them.[42] By making the listeners privy to certain events as they occur, whilst withholding from them their overall significance, the narrator creates for them a tension between knowing and not knowing as real as it is for Parzival himself.[43]

38. Bartsch–Marti, fn. to 478,20.
39. Other examples which can be illustrated from the Bartsch–Marti edition include the following: fn. to 257,4 (the editors disclose the identity of Jeschute in advance, cf. below, pp. 119ff.), fn. to 333,30 (they reveal that Parzival descends from the Grail-dynasty on his mother's side, cf. below, p. 217), fn. to 334,19f. and 21f. (they tell us in detail of Gawan's kinship with the four queens at Schastel Marveile, cf. below, p. 153), fn. to 574,5 (we are reminded that Arnive is Gawan's grandmother, contrary to the narrator's technique of keeping this still concealed from us, cf. below, p. 154), fn. to 778,13 (the anonymity of the new arrival before the Round Table is broken by our being told that it is the Grail-messenger, cf. below, pp. 252f.). In the same edition Book XV is headed 'Parzival und Feirefiz', so that the identity of the unknown knight whom Parzival soon encounters is revealed to us in advance, again in contradiction to the narrator's technique (cf. below, pp. 246ff.).
40. Poag, *Mære*, p. 72.
41. Harroff, *Wolfram, passim*.
42. *Ibid.*, pp. 2f.
43. *Ibid.*, p. 61. When making the same point elsewhere (pp. 2f.) Harroff also effectively quotes Booth, *Fiction*, p. 293: 'Leave the reader to choose for himself, force him to face each decision as the hero faces it, and he will feel much more deeply the value of the truth when it is attained, or its loss if the hero fails.' I have made a similar point in connection with *Parzival* when discussing the pedagogic implications of irony (*Irony*, p. 388).

How careful we must be in applying this insight is demonstrated unwittingly by Harroff when he argues that the listeners are deliberately put in the same position as the hero in his encounter with Ither, so that they too are ignorant of the red knight's blood-kinship with Parzival.⁴⁴ This is certainly true of Parzival, for he learns that he has unwittingly killed a kinsman only in the course of his conversation with Trevrizent, but it cannot be claimed that this is also a revelation for any but the less attentive listeners. Although he makes demands on their memory and perspicacity, the narrator certainly makes it possible for them to realise, at the time of the encounter, that the contestants are related to each other.⁴⁵ The significance of the references making this conclusion possible is not just that the narrator carefully establishes this kinship between Parzival and Ither (*via* Arthur), but that he gives his audience the means of realising this at the time when these two meet. Admittedly, this can only have been clear to the percipient and retentive listeners, but it was for them that the poet ultimately intended his work and it was they whom he wished to train to an even greater degree of critical receptiveness.

Our knowledge that Parzival and Ither are kinsmen is not given us by the narrator bluntly and emphatically all at once, but the facts on which it is built are conveyed discreetly in various stages which we have to correlate with one another if we are to grasp the significance of this encounter.⁴⁶ As with the narrator's point of view

---

44. Harroff, in both the instances just quoted (pp. 2 and 61), illustrates his point by a reference to the Ither episode. Cf. also *ibid.*, p. 43: '... throughout the entire Ither episode Wolfram has given his audience only that information which was available to his hero, concealing from them any information about the blood relationship involved'.
45. See below, p. 83.
46. This interpretation of the encounter between Parzival and Ither differs from the approach of Velten, *Plan*, who uses such scattered references in the romance to throw light on its piecemeal genesis and the inner chronology of the separate Books. He argues in terms of a change in overall conception as the work progressed, deducing, for example, from the narrator's early silence on Parzival's kinship with the Grail-dynasty that the poet had not conceived this idea and from the later revelation of this relationship that he had by Book IX begun to operate with it. Significantly, Velten nowhere discusses the 'Bogengleichnis' or other passages in which the narrator alludes to his technique of consciously deferring the release of full information until a predetermined point (see below, pp. 27ff.). His thesis also suffers from the fact that, written in 1956 before work on the narrator in *Parzival* had been done (see above, p. 3, fn. 11), he makes no distinction between Wolfram the poet and the narrator. In the light of this distinction it is impermissible to suggest that, because the narrator is silent on a point, this means that Wolfram himself is ignorant of it (e.g.

technique we have to consider not merely what information is passed on to us by the narrator, but also the fact that it is released by stages or in instalments.

The importance of such a piecemeal revelation can be seen in the way in which it is made clear to us that Parzival is the beneficiary of preternatural guidance at the start of his journey, from Soltane to Munsalvæsche, and on a different level even afterwards. The poet's methods have been analysed in detail by Wynn,[47] who sees them comprising suggestions that the hero's single-minded effort, the haste and speed of his travel, take him along the correct path, as well as the use of gradation to strengthen the impression that he heads unfailingly for the next event that awaits his coming. For Wynn, who is concerned to establish no more than the fact of preternatural guidance, it is perfectly legitimate to collect all the evidence that points in this direction, without further differentiation, but for anyone who is analysing the narrative technique by which this impression of guidance is given to the listeners it will instead be necessary to realise that the narrator suggests guidance by remarks which are deliberately ambiguous and only later allows us to grasp their full implications.[48]

If the different problem with which she is concerned justifies Wynn in the use of a method which ignores the stages in which information is progressively released, the same cannot be claimed of what Mergell has said of the 'Blutstropfenszene' in which Parzival is reminded of his wife and which he regards as a token of God's grace extended to him (282,30ff.). He describes these words by Parzival as a 'Verherrlichung der göttlichen Führung..., der sich Parzival auf allen Stufen seines Weges, vom Waldleben bis zur Gralsszene und zur zweiten Begegnung mit Jeschute, unterworfen weiß'.[49] This statement may be true of this particular episode where the hero expressly acknowledges divine intervention, but we cannot infer from this that he is equally aware of the divine assis-

Velten, *Plan*, p. 48) or that his knowledge of the source did not yet extend that far (*ibid.*, p. 64). When Velten says that Wolfram was not so much a conscious planner, but wrote rather as the spirit took him (pp. 130f.), he stands apart from all recent research. Rejecting this view does not commit us to the opposite extreme of Mergell's mythologising or even to the suggestion that Wolfram is nowhere guilty of self-contradiction.

47. Wynn, *Speculum* 36 (1961), 393ff.
48. I have discussed the nature of these ambiguous remarks, and the way in which they are progressively clarified, in different contexts on several occasions: *Weg*, pp. 11ff.; *Viator* 8 (1977), 174ff.; *Irony*, pp. 150ff.
49. Mergell, *Parzival*, p. 89.

tance granted him at all other stages since his departure from Soltane. The position is more complex than this, instead of Mergell's unchanging state we have a threefold pattern: a first stage in which the listeners know for certain as little as Parzival; a second stage in which they realise more than he does; and a third stage in which the hero once more draws level with them. The result of this shifting pattern is that the listeners, sharing ignorance with Parzival, are invited to make his experience their own, but are also given the superior knowledge with which to ascertain his ignorance. The narrator's technique of concealing and revealing information by instalments draws his listeners now closer to the fumbling Parzival, now closer to the poet's omniscience. It is a technique more complex than either Mergell's suggestion or Bertau's view that Wolfram's method is simply the direct opposite of Chrétien's technique of progressive enlightenment.[50]

The technique of naming

Under the second heading we saw that the narrator could sometimes withhold a piece of information by leaving the named identity of a character (Condwiramurs, Orgeluse) still in doubt. Whenever earlier scholarship was engaged with the problem of the names used in Wolfram's works, it was above all questions of etymology and sources which claimed most attention,[51] whilst more recently aesthetic questions lie behind the renewed interest in the poet's use of names,[52] as is also the case with recent work on the same problem with Chrétien and Hartmann.[53] Of special relevance to the question of revealing and concealing is the fact that the narrator in

50. Although the Bartsch–Marti edition (fn. to 333,30, commenting on 333,27: *schildes ambet umben grâl | wirt nu vil güebet sunder twâl | von im den Herzeloyde bar. | er was ouch ganerbe dar*) says quite simply that Parzival was descended from the Grail-family on his mother's side, this is by no means made unequivocally clear at this point, and in fact the listeners have to wait considerably longer for final clarification. See below, pp. 214ff.
51. Cf. Bartsch, *Germanistische Studien* 2 (1875), 114ff.; Heinzel, *Parzival*, pp. 1ff.; Martin, *Kommentar, passim*.
52. See Boesch, *DVjs* 32 (1958), 241ff.; Rosenfeld, *Gestaltung*, pp. 203ff. and *Herkunft*, pp. 36ff.; Fourquet in the FS for E. Hoepffner, pp. 245ff.; Lofmark, *Wolfram-Studien* IV, pp. 61ff. I have also discussed some of the functions of Wolfram's use of names in *Namedropping*, pp. 84ff. and in *Naming*, pp. 103ff.
53. On Chrétien see Kellermann, *Aufbaustil*, pp. 61ff.; Bezzola, *Sens*, pp. 33ff.; Ziltener, *Chrétien*, pp. 51ff.; Kelly, *Sens*, pp. 151ff.; Le Rider, *Chevalier*, pp. 94ff. Cf. also Duggan, *OL* 24 (1969), 112ff., and Schwake, *GRM* 20 (1970), 338ff. On Hartmann see Harms, *Kampf*, pp. 129f.; Mohr, *ZfdA* 100 (1971), 73ff.; Ruberg, *Schweigen*, pp. 187f., 193f., 216ff.; Steinle, *Kennzeichnen, passim*.

Possibilities

Parzival can name a character immediately he plays a part in the action or can withhold the name until a carefully chosen point, or can even carve out episodes in which the name of a previously identified character can be temporarily withdrawn from him.[54] All of this has an obvious bearing on the theme of recognition, especially when the narrator's choice of anonymity for a character means that the audience is as unable to recognise him as are others in the narrative. To illustrate the relevance of this technique of naming to our theme I choose the period of Parzival's youth in which he is at first ignorant of his own name and is accordingly presented to us in anonymous terms.

Here too it can be shown that our modern way of receiving a medieval work as a scholarly edition differs from the situation in which a medieval audience found themselves. When we pick up a modern edition of Wolfram's romance we know its title and hence that its hero is called Parzival, whereas in the narrative itself this detail is released only at 140,16,[55] well after the start of the Parzival action in Book III and over 4000 lines after the opening of the work. The poet has his own reason for synchronising this information given to us with Parzival learning his name from Sigune, for having our path from ignorance to recognition parallel his, but this is thwarted when a modern reader is given this crucial detail from the outset by the editor.

Yet to be sure that a modern reader is in a different position from a medieval listener we need to know where the latter stood as regards the title of a work he was about to hear recited for the first time. This situation we can reconstruct by having regard to the way in which the author of a romance, Chrétien, Hartmann or Wolfram, introduces his work to his listeners in the prologue.[56] In every case the naming of a hero in the prologue or the narrator's silence on this point ties up with the manner in which he introduces his hero in the narrative itself. Where he has a reason for leaving us in ignorance of the hero's identity for some initial span of the action he does not go against this decision by prematurely revealing his name in the prologue,[57] so that Wolfram follows Chrétien in preserving his

---

54. Cf. Green, *Namedropping*, pp. 114ff. and 127ff.
55. See below, pp. 72f. and 79.
56. On the ways in which Chrétien introduces the protagonists of his works see Green, *Namedropping*, pp. 90ff. For Hartmann Steinle, *Kennzeichnen*, devotes no special attention to this point.
57. Erec is referred to by name in the prologue because his name is likewise given when he first enters the action (82: *Uns chevaliers, Erec ot non*), but in the later

The Art of Recognition in Wolfram's *Parzival*

hero's anonymity from the prologue to the point where his name is divulged to him by Sigune.

Wolfram shrouds his hero in anonymity by using circumlocutions or uninformative epithets from the moment he enters the action until his encounter with Sigune,[58] but he does this also up to this same point whenever, as narrator, he has to comment on the nature of his story and its protagonist. This is already true in the prologue when the hero is referred to by anonymous epithets (4,18: *er küene, træclîche wîs, / (den helt ich alsus grüeze)*) and it is made clear that some considerable narrative time will lapse before the hero's story is begun in Book III (4,23: *den ich hie zuo hân erkorn, / er ist mæreshalp noch ungeborn, / dem man dirre âventiure giht*). Anonymity is similarly preserved in a comment on the hero's birth: he is referred to simply as *diss mæres sachewalte* (112,17) and his birth is presented in terms which still withhold his identity (112,11: *wand er ist alrêrst geborn, / dem diz mære wart erkorn*). This contrast between the narrator's reticence, sustained over three Books, and Sigune's revelation is then highlighted by the narrator's last anonymous reference immediately before Sigune's information (140,11: *nu hært in rehter nennen, / daz ir wol müget erkennen / wer*

---

romances Chrétien has realised the potential advantage of suspense by withholding the hero's name for some time after the narrative concerning him has begun. Accordingly, Lancelot enters the narrative at first without a name (271: *un chevalier*) and circumlocutions continue to be used of him for more than 3000 verses (i.e. for more than half of the completed work) before he is eventually named for us (3660: *Lanceloz del Lac a a non / li chevaliers, mien escïant*). In *Yvain* the position is slightly different since although the hero may be mentioned by name on the occasion when he is first brought into the narrative (53ff.), this is together with so many other knights at Arthur's court that we have no grounds for thinking that this one is to be the hero of the romance. Only after Calogrenant has finished his account is Yvain mentioned again by name (581), but from now on with such growing frequency that, with the focus now on him, we slowly realise, without any explicit remark by the narrator, that this must be the protagonist. Although the name itself is not withheld, our realisation that this is the name of the hero has been delayed until this point. Finally, as a reflection of Perceval growing up in ignorance of himself and therefore of his name he too, like Lancelot, enters the story in a perfect anonymity (74: *li filz a la veve dame*) which is maintained by a variety of circumlocutions for about as long a narrative span as in *Lancelot* until it is revealed to him and at the same time to us (3575: *Percevaus li Galois a non*).

It may well be, as has been suggested by Haidu, *Lion*, pp. 49ff., that there are symbolic or ironic reasons for Chrétien's change of technique between *Erec* and the later romances, but the above parallels suggest that we cannot afford to ignore the connection between the narrator's naming of the hero or silence in the prologue and the way in which he introduces the hero in the narrative.

58. See Green, *Naming*, *passim*.

Possibilities

dirre âventiur hêrre sî). Such deliberate uninformativeness on the part of the narrator in talking of his story is of a piece with his delay in naming Parzival in the depiction of narrative events.[59] It allows us to suspect that, if we can imagine Wolfram being impatiently asked what his story was going to be about by someone awaiting its first recital, he would not have destroyed his carefully contrived effects by blurting out the name which we now read on the title-page. Rather would he, I submit, have preserved anonymity and suspense by describing what was to come in something like the impersonal terms used in 452,30, referring to his story as *ein mære umben grâl*, thereby achieving for his version the same effect as had Chrétien for his romance by calling it *li contes del Graal* in his prologue (66).[60]

The implication that Wolfram's narrator keeps his listeners uninformed on this vital point for as long as Parzival himself, within the story, is unaware of his own identity can be strengthened by a counter-check which is called for. The statement that we are not told Parzival's name until he learns it from Sigune does not mean that the name is not mentioned in the work before this point. In fact, it is mentioned once before, but in such a manner that, as with the repeated mention of Yvain's name at the start of both the French and German romances, we can have no idea that this is indeed the name of the protagonist. This first mention occurs in Book I when the narrator qualifies his stress on Kaylet's beauty by the comment that it will be surpassed by that of two men not yet born, Beacurs, the son of Lot, and Parzival (39,22: *er bluome an mannes schœne! / sîn varwe an schœne hielt den strît, / unz an zwên die nâch im wuohsen sît, / Bêâcurs Lôtes kint / und Parzivâl, die dâ niht*

---

59. This narratorial reticence before the Sigune scene can be confirmed by the narrator's readiness to use Parzival's name in comments on his story and its hero after this turning-point. Whereas on the brink of Sigune's revelation the hero was referred to simply as *dirre âventiur hêrre* (140,13), a similar phrase is later used in conjunction with his name (338,7: *des mæres hêrren Parzivâl*). When the narrator first mentions his source Kyot he refers explicitly to *dise âventiur von Parzivâl* (416,26), whilst the anonymity of the circumlocution in 455,22 (*des disiu mære sint*) is only apparent, since it follows an allusion to the child of Herzeloyde and Gahmuret (455,20ff.) whom by this stage we cannot fail to recognise as Parzival, long since known to us by name. On other later occasions where the narrator refers to his *âventiure* or *mære*, the name of Parzival is explicitly mentioned (433,9 and 30; 734,15; 827,17).
60. Dewald, *Minne*, p. 141, makes the suggestive point that, at this hypothetical stage, the word *grâl* would have meant very little to the listeners before Book V or VI.

The Art of Recognition in Wolfram's *Parzival*

sint:/die wâren dennoch ungeborn,/und wurden sît für schœne erkorn). There is nothing about this remark which casts a special light on the unknown character named Parzival.[61] The detail that, like Beacurs, he is *dennoch ungeborn* is not enough to identify him as the protagonist of whom it was said in the prologue that he was *noch ungeborn* (4,24), the motif of the hero's outstanding beauty begins to play its part only from Book III on,[62] and if we are given the means to place Beacurs (he is the son of Lot, and therefore the brother of Gawan), we learn nothing here about Parzival's genealogy and have no chance to surmise that, as the son of the hero of the first two Books, he might indeed be destined to be the hero of the whole work. Nothing about this passage alerts us to the importance of this figure, just as the early references to Yvain failed to reveal that there was anything special about him, in no way is it hinted that we shall later come across this Parzival.

All we may conceivably remember of this early passing mention is that he is one of the two men who will one day surpass Kaylet in beauty. In this connection, assuming that we are nimble enough to recall a detail from Book I by the time we reach Book III, the first suggestion of the hero's outstanding beauty, given as he encounters the world outside Soltane for the first time and immediately arouses the admiration of Karnahkarnanz, assumes a special importance, for the hyperbole used to evoke his beauty (122,13: *Aller manne schœne ein bluomen kranz*)[63] implies that this wild young creature must be one of the two men mentioned in Book I. Wolfram can employ either *bluome* or *kranz* by itself figuratively to convey a superlative impression, meaning 'the flower of' or 'the crown of', but in this verse we find a pile-up of superlatives which is unique: *aller manne*, but also *bluome* as well as *kranz*. It has been rightly said that this phrase involves a double intensification, what it implies is not a simple hyperbole, but 'the highest of the highest'.[64] As such, this thumbnail sketch of the boy's beauty makes it stylistically clear that he must surpass Kaylet: whereas even Kaylet was no more than a *bluome an mannes schœne* (39,22), a flower of manly beauty, the hero is described as the crown of flowers of all manly beauty, he

---

61. Cf. Cucuel, *Eingangsbücher*, p. 7.
62. Johnson, *Beauty*, p. 279.
63. The implications of this verse have been worked out by a pupil of mine, D. N. Yeandle, who is at present working on a critical commentary on Book III of *Parzival*.
64. Cf. Boysen, *Gebrauch*, pp. 34f.

surpasses Kaylet's beauty by far.⁶⁵ If so, then this young boy must be one of the two exceptions named by the narrator in Book I when he praised Kaylet for his beauty. He cannot be Beacurs, since we were expressly told on that occasion that Beacurs was *Lôtes kint*, whereas we know from the Soltane episode that this young boy is in fact *Gahmuretes kint* (117,15). By a process of elimination the hero of the work whose story has started in Book III, the son of Gahmuret and Herzeloyde, must be called Parzival and this fact is made available to us at this early stage, before Parzival actually encounters Sigune. We are not told this as explicitly by the narrator as Parzival is by Sigune, but we are certainly provided with the requisite pointers to such a conclusion, as long as we learn to pay close attention to them and to the need to correlate them.

In that the narrator's hyperbole for Parzival's beauty (122,13) paradoxically suggests the name of Parzival in going out of its way to avoid it, it is a concise example of 'revealing while concealing' applied to the technique of naming. As with Chrétien, we are expressly told Parzival's name at the moment when he learns it himself from Sigune, but Wolfram differs from his French predecessor in also giving us advance information, however well concealed this might remain from the casual listener who only, in Hartmann's words, *biutet diu ôren dar* and pays no closer attention. It is an example which illustrates how much active work Wolfram expects from those of his listeners who can measure up to his demands. Like the hero on his path from *tumpheit* to *wîsheit*, they too are invited on a quest towards recognition in which they are supplied with apparently fortuitous information which they are expected to recall on later occasions whilst avoiding any judgment which may turn out to be based on still incomplete knowledge.⁶⁶ In developing such a narrative technique the poet has ensured that both his hero and his listeners are engaged on a progress towards recognition.

65. Bartsch–Marti, fn. to 122,13 ('... er ist nicht nur wie Kaylet (39,22) *bluome an mannes schœne*, sondern ein Blumenkranz in Beziehung auf alle Mannesschönheit, die Vereinigung davon') take *kranz* in the literal sense of garland. Against this, however, see Braune, *PBB* 24 (1899), 189f., who reads *kranz* as the equivalent of *krône* (e.g. 781,14). Braune is wrong in suggesting that *Aller manne schœne ein bluomen kranz* is the same here as *Aller manne schœne ein bluome*. This ignores the vital fact that the poet makes use of a double hyperbole through which alone we can perceive that the person so described must be Parzival.
66. Cf. Harroff, *Wolfram*, p. 87.

The Art of Recognition in Wolfram's *Parzival*

The theme of recognition

This theme underlies all the approaches we have been considering. The use of a point of view technique implies that what a person may recognise need not correspond to all the facts of the situation (Parzival comes to recognise Jeschute, but has no idea of the identity of Orilus), while acknowledgment that medieval listeners received the work in a manner quite different from modern readers forces us on to the path towards recognition which is blocked or covered up for us when an editor betrays the poet by giving us on a plate an insight for which we were meant to work. The procedure of revealing while concealing ensures that the listeners' task of recognition is a continuous and progressive one, just as the technique of naming can give us the means, if we learn to make use of it, of recognising the truth in advance of a character in the story.

There are other considerations, however, which bring the theme of recognition to the fore in the genre of the romance. To the extent that it is concerned with adventures and a quest the romance is characterised by a series of encounters,[67] but it only needs one party to be unaware of the other's identity, as is frequently the case, for the problem of recognition to become dominant.[68] Furthermore, this genre from the days of the Hellenistic romance made great play with separations and renewed encounters after a lapse of time where a failure in recognition, mutual or not, can often ensue.[69] But apart from such general considerations there are also particular reasons to account for the frequency of episodes in *Parzival* where a meeting between characters is informed by a failure in recognition. More pointedly than most romances, its plot contains both a wide circular movement back to its starting point (from possession through loss to recovery) and constant growth on the part of Parzival, a conjunction within which paradoxes of identity can easily arise.[70]

---

67. Cf. Bindschedler, *DVjs* 31 (1957), 100.
68. In *Irony*, p. 252, I made this point with regard to dramatic irony in the romance, but since this rests on the failure of a character to recognise the facts of a situation and on the audience's recognition of this failure (*ibid.*, pp. 250ff.), it can equally well be applied to the theme of recognition.
69. Cf. Perry, *Romances*, pp. 285ff. (on the Pseudo-Clementine *Recognitiones*) and pp. 294ff. (on *Apollonius of Tyre*).
70. Hanning, *Individual*, pp. 201f. On this conjunction in Chrétien's works see Warning, *Wolfram-Studien* v, pp. 79ff. and, in a different context, in *Formen*, pp. 25ff.

Possibilities

How this general observation works out in practice has been brought out well by Hirschberg's structural analysis of some chosen examples where the repetition involved by a circular movement plays an important part. She points out that between Parzival's visit at the Grail-castle and the start of the Gawan action the various episodes on the hero's way are repetitions of earlier encounters,[71] a sustained patterning which prompts the question whether recognition will or will not take place. How the theme of recognition can dominate one encounter and its later counterpart can be shown in the case of Parzival's two encounters with Jeschute. All the characters involved (Parzival, Jeschute and, later, Orilus) are equipped with features in each episode which establish continuity between them[72] – these parallels may not suffice for the listeners to be able to identify Jeschute or Orilus, but they constitute the basis on which the more telling clues in the second encounter rest, concerning Jeschute's appearance and her horse.[73] The repetition of this scene is therefore used by the narrator as a challenge to his listeners, inviting them to see if they can recognise who it is that they, accompanying Parzival on his travels, have come across again. But this task of recognition to which the audience are submitted cannot be separated from the recognition accomplished, or not, by the actors in these episodes, as we see when, with Hirschberg,[74] we look at both episodes in their totality from this point of view. In both encounters Jeschute recognises Parzival from the beginning for what he is: on the first occasion as a young fool (131,25) and on the second as the person responsible for her present plight (258,2ff.). The protagonist, on the other hand, superficially follows his mother's advice in the first episode and fails in his inexperience to recognise in Jeschute *daz minneclîche wîp* (130,24) which she manifestly is, whilst in the second encounter he is initially unable to recognise that he has met her before (258,15ff.). On the second occasion, however, Parzival does eventually recognise Jeschute and the link between the two episodes which this establishes for him leads him to a further insight, the acknowledgment of his past folly (269,24: *ich was ein tôre und niht ein man,/gewahsen niht pî witzen*), a recognition on his part which corresponds to the recognition which

---

71. Hirschberg, *Untersuchungen*, p. 98.
72. *Ibid.*, pp. 151f.
73. See below, pp. 119ff.
74. Hirschberg, *Untersuchungen*, p. 152.

the parallel between the two meetings allows the listeners to make, that the earlier *tôre* has now become a chivalric and courteous knight.[75]

It is hardly by chance, then, that the theme of recognition in *Parzival* has come up for discussion recently on a number of occasions. Salmon has compared Chrétien with Hartmann and Wolfram with regard to ignorance and awareness of identity, but confines himself in the case of *Parzival* to the second meeting with Jeschute.[76] As part of a much wider survey Harms has analysed those scenes in the work where kinsman unwittingly fights with kinsman, Johnson has considered a number of more general encounters from the point of view of dramatic irony, whilst I have briefly looked at the second Jeschute meeting with regard to irony and narrative technique.[77] Two recent articles by Hahn also touch on this theme: her discussion of the motif of Parzival's beauty bears the subtitle 'Zum Problem des Erkennens und Verkennens im "Parzival"', while her wider-ranging essay 'Zur Theorie der Personerkenntnis' touches briefly on *Parzival* from time to time.[78] If there appears to be a certain topicality about the theme, the approaches made up to now have all been highly selective, so that there is every justification in now tackling this problem in the context of the whole work, looking at all the encounters where recognition of one type or another plays a part.

Like Harms I distinguish in the following chapters between knowledge, recognition, non-recognition and mistaken identification ('Verkennen').[79] Non-recognition implies that a character does not understand the situation in which he finds himself, but that his actions do not in any way conflict with what he would have regarded as just and appropriate if he had comprehended his position. In those cases, however, where this behaviour conflicts with the true facts of the relationship between the parties involved, we are justified in talking of mistaken identification, rather than merely non-recognition. We can illustrate this with the two examples from *Parzival* adduced by Harms: the encounter (near or actual)

---

75. *Ibid.*
76. Salmon, *PBB(T)* 82 (1960), 95ff.
77. Harms, *Kampf*, pp. 144ff.; Johnson, *Ironie*, pp. 133ff.; Green, *Irony*, pp. 167ff.
78. Hahn, *Schönheit*, pp. 203ff. (especially pp. 217ff.) and *PBB(T)* 99 (1977), 395ff. Hagen, *Erkennen*, has also discussed the same theme in *Parzival*, but the limits of a 'Zulassungsarbeit' mean that he looks at only a selection of the possible episodes. On this problem with Gottfried's *Tristan* see Ries, *ZfdA* 109 (1980), 316ff.
79. Harms, *Kampf*, pp. 10f.

between Parzival and Gawan at Bearosche is an instance of non-recognition, whereas the combat between these two at Joflanze is due to mistaken identification. Recognition itself is only possible where what has preceded it is a case of non-recognition or mistaken identification. Where these are lacking, we are dealing with unchanging and unjeopardised knowledge.

Recognition and its cognates can be concerned with various persons, things or situations, as has been accepted since Aristotle's discussion of *anagnorisis*, whether or not we regard it as confusing that the same word should denote both recognition of a person and realisation of a situation.[80] But even the range of recognition of a person is widened significantly in the direction of self-recognition once we talk of *anagnorisis* implying the 'discovery of the true identity of other persons *in relation to oneself*'[81] (my italics) or describe it rather as the realisation of the situation in which one is placed and of which one has hitherto been ignorant.[82] Bearing this in mind we shall find that the theme of recognition in *Parzival* includes the following possibilities: (1) the recognition of someone whom one has met before (e. g. Parzival's second encounter with Jeschute); (2) the recognition of the truth from someone (Parzival learns about the Grail from Trevrizent); (3) the recognition of the truth about someone (Parzival's combat with Feirefiz and its conclusion); (4) the recognition of the truth about oneself (what Parzival learns about the Grail from Trevrizent largely concerns his own position within the Grail-dynasty). It is significant that at the close of the work, once Parzival has completed his progress from *tumpheit* to *wîsheit*, the task of recognition which had hitherto been his now gives way to the fact of knowledge: when he comes to Munsalvæsche for the second time he knows precisely what his goal is,[83] reaches it without difficulty and knows how to act once he is there,[84] whilst the death of Sigune, once Parzival has now successfully asked the question, has been interpreted as symbolising the fulfilment of the hero's quest, the fact that Sigune has nothing more to tell him.[85]

* * * *

80. Cf. Lucas, *Aristotle*, p. 131. I owe this reference and that in the next two footnotes to Hunt, *MLR* 74 (1979), 791ff. (especially pp. 799ff.).
81. See Rees, *Greece and Rome* 19 (1972), 1.
82. *Ibid.*
83. Wynn, *Speculum* 36 (1961), 414, and Hirschberg, *Untersuchungen*, p. 169.
84. Hirschberg, *Untersuchungen*, p. 161. See also below, p. 194.
85. See below, p. 36, fn. 143.

The Art of Recognition in Wolfram's *Parzival*

Before we consider the many encounters in Wolfram's romance in the light of the theme of recognition and the narrative devices employed to bring it to our attention, it would be helpful to consider a number of passages in which the narrator discusses explicitly, if not always with the clarity we might desire, something of his narrative technique. Although these passages include such difficult and contested ones as the prologue and the 'Bogengleichnis', we are fortunately not concerned with a total interpretation of them, but only with those details which have a direct bearing on the theme of recognition and its presentation. With this in mind I keep the following comments as short as possible, discussing what the narrator says of the qualities of his listeners, those passages in which he explicitly exercises a direct control over them, and the so-called 'Bogengleichnis'.

The narrator tells us about the qualities of his listeners on three occasions: chiefly in the prologue, but also at the start of Books VII and VIII. The part of the prologue beginning at 1,15 divides the listeners into two groups, the *tumbe liute* (1,16) and the *wîser man* (2,5), a conventional distinction which is given a novel twist by its asymmetry.[86] The narrator polemically shows his scorn for the *tumbe liute*, for their inability to follow him and realise the implications of what he says (1,17: *sine mugens niht erdenken*), thereby hinting at the demands he makes on his audience.[87] These demands are to be met by the *wîser man* who in addition to being accessible to what the story can teach him (2,8: *waz si guoter lêre wernt*) is aware of what he himself must contribute: a readiness to follow the twists and turns of the story, to grasp its changes of perspective and to undertake the *erdenken* which the *tumbe liute* cannot.[88] Equally important is the reason given for such listeners' readiness to pay close attention, for their wisdom lies precisely in recognising what they do *not* know and hence what they may still learn (2,5: *ouch erkante ich nie sô wîsen man, / ern möhte gerne künde hân, / welher stiure disiu mære gernt / und waz si guoter lêre wernt*). If such listeners are invited to progress from partial to greater *wîsheit*, they

---

86. Cf. Rupp, *Prolog*, p. 379, and Nellmann, *Erzähltechnik*, p. 5, fn. 23. The asymmetry of Wolfram's treatment has been stressed by Haas, *Tumpheit*, p. 32, and lies above all in the contrast between a plural and a (collective) singular, as well as one between those whose *tumpheit* is unqualified and the *wîser man* who is partly ignorant.
87. See Rupp, *Prolog*, pp. 380f.; Haug, *DVjs* 45 (1971), 702; Nellmann, *Erzähltechnik*, p. 9.
88. See Haug, *DVjs* 45 (1971), 703; Nellmann, *Erzähltechnik*, pp. 9f.; Schweikle, *ZfdA* 106 (1977), 183ff.

Possibilities

are moving along the same path as the hero, of whom it is soon said that he is *træclîche wîs* (4,18).[89] How close they are thereby brought to Parzival is made clear at the close of Book III where he says to Gurnemanz with newly awakened self-knowledge '*hêrre, in bin niht wîs*' (178,29)[90] at a point where the narrator tells us that he has already shed his earlier *tumpheit*.[91] If the hero is shown on the path from a *tumpheit* which he has put behind him to a *wîsheit* which he has not yet reached, he is paralleled by those listeners who are *wîs* because they are aware of what they still have to learn. By this means the narrator establishes a rhetorical link between the listeners he addresses and the protagonist, he wins them for his purpose at the outset by persuading them that Parzival's story is their own.[92]

In the prologue which introduces the Gawan action in Book VII the reciprocal relationship between poet and audience is emphasised at one point (338,11: *im wære der liute volge guot, / swer dicke lop mit wârheit tuot*). Here *der liute volge* means the approval or applause of the audience, but for this to be at all worthwhile it must be based on a correct understanding of what the poet says – far from being uninformed approval, it must proceed from a knowledgeable assessment of the work.[93] Without acceptance of this kind the poet's task is uncompleted (338,13: *wan, swaz er sprichet oder sprach, / diu rede belîbet âne dach*),[94] for words destined for another fail if they are not taken up in the sense in which they are meant. It is significant, however, that this correct acceptance is attributed to *die wîsen* (338,15: *wer sol sinnes wort behalten, / es enwelln die wîsen walten?*), in other words to those listeners whom the poet really addresses. They are the listeners on whose acumen he depends if his purpose is to be achieved, yet it is they who are also being trained by him in the exercise of their critical faculties in following his hints. So closely tied up with these critical and appreciative listeners is the success of the poet's task that he has no need to mention the others, the *tumbe liute* whom he dismisses in silence.[95]

---

89. Cf. Tax, *Kingdom*, p. 21: 'As a result, even the bold reader of Wolfram's *Parzival* becomes only slowly wise.'
90. Parzival's knightly judgment on himself is confirmed by what the narrator has recently said of him in the context of Gurnemanz's tournament (175,6: *er wart ouch sît an strîte wîs*).
91. Cf. 179,23 and 188,15ff.
92. Nellmann, *Erzähltechnik*, pp. 7f., especially p. 8.
93. Hirschberg, *Untersuchungen*, p. 343.
94. *Ibid.*, p. 345 (with a reference to Martin, *Kommentar*, note on 338,14), with an interpretation of *dach* as meaning both 'Obdach, Schutz' and 'Vollendung, Abschluß'.
95. Hirschberg, *Untersuchungen*, p. 346.

The Art of Recognition in Wolfram's *Parzival*

The third occasion for the audience to be referred to in terms of *wîsheit* and *tumpheit* comes at the start of Book VIII when the narrator, warning us of the trials awaiting Gawan, appeals to his listeners to grieve with him (399,4: *mîn wîser und mîn tumber, / die tuonz durch ir gesellekeit / und lâzen in mit mir [sîn] leit*). However we interpret this double formula, I do not think that we can accept Nellmann's suggestion (based on *Titurel* 170,3: *der tumbe und ouch der grîse*) that it refers to the audience at large as 'young and old'.[96] This assumes that what is true of one work (in a different context) is also true of another, and it also ignores the fact that whereas *grîs* explicitly means 'old', this is only partly true of *wîs*. Furthermore, if the narrator of *Parzival* refers to his listeners as *wîs* and *tump* we need to be told why we should read this differently from the opening of the whole work (*tumbe liute* and *wîser man*). Yet if these listeners are addressed with regard to their perceptiveness or lack of it, there are difficulties in assuming that the narrator here simply refers to the two parts of his total audience, asking both of them to share his grief, since the prologue to Book VII has already made it clear that when it comes to the point the *tumbe liute* are simply ignored and only *die wîsen* are taken into account.

As a tentative answer to this I suggest that the phrase 399,4 might be read as implying not two parts of the whole audience, but two aspects of the same listeners. If we recall what was said of the *wîser man* in the prologue, it is clear that his wisdom lies in the acknowledgment of ignorance, that he is, like Parzival, *træclîche wîs* and that in his progress from *tumpheit* to *wîsheit* he partakes of both qualities and could be fittingly described by an oxymoron. If that is so, then the black and white nature of the *agelster* (1,6) would be reflected not merely in Parzival[97] but also, in intellectual terms, in the listeners whom the narrator wishes to convince of the analogy of their position to his. When Antanor, for example, is described as a *witzehafter tôre* (153,11) the narrator implies by this oxymoron a contrast between appearances and reality[98] in that Antanor, like Cunneware, is *witzehaft* in grasping the hero's potential quality, but seems a *tôre* because of his silence. If this oxymoron were applied to Parzival at this point, then he really would be a *tôre*, so that the positive aspect (*witzehaft*) would hint at his future potential. The listeners addressed by the narrator are engaged on a simi-

---

96. Nellmann, *Erzähltechnik*, p. 4, fn. 17.
97. Cf. Wapnewski, *Parzival*, pp. 55ff. and 108f.
98. Freytag, *Oxymoron*, p. 58.

lar progress: they show *witze* (2,14) because of their readiness and ability to join in this progress, but are also *tump* in so far as this progress is at all necessary.

By addressing these listeners in particular the narrator establishes a special bond between himself and them (as is shown by the double use of *mîn* in 399,4), a bond which is quite different from the way in which *die tumben* are ignored at the start of Book VII. If what I suggest as a singular phrase describing two aspects of the same subject (*mîn wîser und mîn tumber*) is followed by a plural verb (399,5: *die tuonz*), this is because the subject is a collective singular, so that we have here a familiar tension between grammar and logic.[99] This is no different from the prologue, where the *wîser man*, as a collective singular, is the counterpart to the plural *tumbe liute*. That this singular is a collective is confirmed by the transition in this passage from singular (2,5)[100] to plural (*si* in 2,9ff., which I take to refer to the listeners able to follow the ins and outs of the narrative)[101] and then to generalised singular (*swer* in 2,13). By implying that he addresses only such *wîsen* and by flattering each individual listener into believing that he belongs to this category, the narrator wins his audience for himself as effectively as when he manipulates them rhetorically into accepting Parzival's story as very much their own.

Having said what he expects from the listeners' participation in his work and having established a favourable relationship with them, the narrator continues to exercise direct control over them by keeping up a teasing dialogue on the subject of their impatience with his withholding essential information from them. The point of his teasing is partly to heighten their impatience, partly to stimulate them to reflect upon what information they already have and, if possible, to draw their independent conclusions from the clues given them. This dialogue between narrator and listeners on delayed information is conducted on three occasions, in each case in connection with the mysteries of the Grail,[102] so that the listeners' impatience, rhetorically contrived, reflects the eagerness and quest for enlightenment which characterise Parzival.

99. See the examples listed in the Bartsch–Marti edition (vol. III, p. 336) under the heading 'Mehrzahl – auf kollektive Einzahl bezogen'.
100. Cf. also *er* in the following line.
101. This is not meant to exclude the possibility that *si* in these lines (like *si* in 5,8) also refers to *mære*, but rather to suggest that it includes these listeners as well. If the narrative takes many twists and turns, then so must the listeners who are able to follow it.
102. Harroff, *Wolfram*, p. 59.

The Art of Recognition in Wolfram's *Parzival*

On the first occasion, coming in Book V just before the 'Bogengleichnis', the narrator states how he proposes to deal with the Grail theme, telling his listeners that they will have to wait until later for information about different aspects of Munsalvæsche (241,1: *Wer der selbe wære, / des freischet her nâch mære. / dar zuo der wirt, sîn burc, sîn lant, / diu werdent iu von mir genant, / her nâch sô des wirdet zît, / bescheidenlîchen, âne strît / unde ân allez für zogen*). The occasion for this remark, placed just after Parzival catches a glimpse of an unnamed old man in an adjoining room as the Grail-procession leaves the castle hall, stresses the parallel between the hero's point of view and ours: his glimpse behind the scenes is converted for us into a passing view of the narrative perspective,[103] whilst we are also made to share his ignorance of what is involved. To the question this poses (when is this information conveyed to Parzival and to us?) the answer has usually been that this is done in Book IX,[104] but Nellmann has instead suggested that the timespan of information deferred is much shorter, reaching only as far as the following scene when Sigune divulges to the hero and to us the names of Titurel, Anfortas, Munsalvæsche and Terre de Salvæsche (251,1ff.).[105] This may be factually correct, but it is an impossibly literalist reading to take *nennen* as meaning only 'to give the name' and not also 'to explain' or 'to tell all about',[106] and thus to deny that the narrator's remark also extends to Book IX, where so much more about the Grail is said by Trevrizent than the names given by Sigune. To concentrate on the short-term, like Nellmann, to the exclusion of the long-term implications is to block off the perspective which this passage is meant to open up, it invites us to fall victim to the same kind of misunderstanding as Parzival: to assume that because we learn something about the Grail (the names mentioned by Sigune), we know all that there is to know. This is true even of the cluster of narrator's forecasts which, more frequently than anywhere before, tell us something of what escapes Parzival at this point[107] and are used by Nellmann to justify his short-term

---

103. Cf. Spitz, *Bogengleichnis*, p. 248.
104. On this consensus of opinion see the bibliographical references in Nellmann, *Erzähltechnik*, p. 89, fn. 67, and Spitz, *Bogengleichnis*, p. 249, fn. 10.
105. Nellmann, *Erzähltechnik*, pp. 90f.
106. Cf. Green, *Irony*, p. 148, fn. 4. This verb is used in *Parzival* to mean 'to talk about' in 545,19 (*ir nennet reht*), 'to explain or describe' in 414,21 (*des wâpen sol ich nennen*) and 'to tell all about' in 369,13 (*den nenne ich iu*).
107. These are listed by Nellmann, *Erzähltechnik*, p. 89.

Possibilities

reading of 241,1ff.[108] Each of these forecasts resembles what Sigune tells Parzival in 251,1ff. in giving only partial information and leaving questions unanswered which are cleared up only much later, all in Book IX.[109] All these forecasts, like the 'Bogengleichnis' and the narrator's address to his listeners which introduces it, operate with a tension of information withheld which stretches from Book V to Book IX.

Not surprisingly, given this span between the two Books, the narrator next addresses his listeners on this topic in Book IX, in lines which introduce his remarks on Kyot just before Parzival comes to Trevrizent (452,29: *an dem ervert nu Parzivâl / diu verholnen mære umben grâl. / Swer mich dervon ê frâgte / unt drumbe mit mir bâgte, / ob ichs im niht sagte, / umprîs der dran bejagte. / mich batez helen Kyôt, / wand im diu âventiure gebôt / daz es immer man gedæhte, / ê ez d'âventiure bræhte / mit worten an der mære gruoz / daz man dervon doch sprechen muoz*). As with the passage in Book V, these lines suggest a parallel between the listeners' position and Parzival's, for the narrator talks of his obligation to *helen* from his listeners details which are referred to as hitherto *verholen* from Parzival. Moreover, these two passages are linked together implicitly. Even though the earlier one made no mention of a listener actually objecting to the narrator's delaying tactics (*bâgte*), the present reference to not mentioning something at one point, but keeping it back until later, makes sense only in regard to what was said earlier of the treatment of the Grail theme.

The link between these two passages, however, is closer than this. Two of the details withheld in 241,1ff. concern the identity of two people (the old man in the adjoining room, the lord of the castle), about which Nellmann claims that the necessary information is provided shortly afterwards when Sigune names them as Titurel and Anfortas. What this bare identification by name in the Sigune scene leaves out of account is the fact that Sigune keeps silent about one essential detail, her own kinship with the Grail-family and hence, because Parzival is a kinsman of hers, his own kinship with this dynasty.[110] It is here that our Kyot passage is especially important, for the narrator concludes it by telling us for the first time

---

108. Nellmann's point is that, since the information withheld at 241,1ff. is released by Sigune only 300 lines later, this slight delay constitutes a negligible clash with the cluster of forecasts.
109. I have discussed this in further detail in *Irony*, pp. 165f.
110. See below. pp. 216f.

that Parzival's mother was a member of the same family, so that it is through Herzeloyde, rather than Sigune, that we eventually learn that the hero was born into the Grail-family (455,17ff.). This still does not provide complete clarification,[111] so that we still have something to learn, together with Parzival, from Trevrizent, but it does mean that what the narrator withheld from us in his earlier passage was not simply the names released soon afterwards by Sigune, but more essentially the significance of these names, the fact that these two Grail-kings are kinsmen of Parzival and the suspicion that he stands in a close and special relationship to the events at Munsalvæsche. We learn this from the narrator in Book IX slightly in advance of Parzival being told it by Trevrizent, but by deferring his revelation until this point, without making it clear beyond doubt even now, the narrator ensures that our previous ignorance should parallel Parzival's and invites us to give more searching thought to this question.

The suggestion made in the Kyot passage (that Parzival stands in a special, even unique[112] relationship to Anfortas) creates a tension which is reduced soon afterwards by the information provided by Trevrizent, but which can be completely resolved by nothing less than the climax of the narrative action. Accordingly, when at the start of Book XV Parzival's quest for the Grail enters upon its last decisive stage[113] the narrator justifies his technique to the audience for the third and last time (734,1: *Vil liute des hât verdrozzen, / den diz mær was vor beslozzen: / genuoge kundenz nie ervarn. / nu wil ich daz niht langer sparn, / ich tuonz iu kunt mit rehter sage, / wande ich in dem munde trage / daz slôz dirre âventiure; / wie der süeze unt der gehiure / Anfortas wart wol gesunt*). The position with narrator and listeners presupposed here is the same as in the preceding passages: the impatience of the audience (*verdrozzen*) is carried over from their earlier objections (*bâgte*, 453,2),[114] the previous delaying tactics are about to be abandoned in favour of the ultimate revelation of Anfortas's divine healing[115] (*niht langer* now replace *her nâch*, 241,2 and 5), what was formerly concealed (*verholen*, 452,30, and *helen*, 453,5) is still referred to as such (*vor beslozzen*),[116] but on the brink

---

111. See below, pp. 218ff.
112. On the unique nature of Parzival's relationship see below, pp. 220f. Cf. also the brief comment by Spitz, *Bogengleichnis*, p. 264.
113. Cf. Spitz, *Bogengleichnis*, pp. 265f.
114. On the further link with 241,1f. (and also 241,22) cf. Spitz, *ibid.*, p. 266.
115. Harroff, *Wolfram*, p. 60.
116. Spitz, *Bogengleichnis*, p. 266.

of final clarification (*kunt tuon*).[117] These verbal links are the outward confirmation of the unity of these three passages of narrator's dialogue with his listeners. All concern Parzival's relationship with the Grail-dynasty: the first comes at the close of his disastrous evening at Munsalvæsche, the second just before he learns from Trevrizent the meaning of what he earlier experienced there, and the third introduces the events which lead to Anfortas being healed and Parzival succeeding him as Grail-king. These are meaningful turning-points at which the narrator explains his dispositions to his listeners, the progressive revelation which they plot may begin with the names provided by Sigune, but continues well beyond this and concerns much more important issues than names, even though the careful deployment of names is one of the methods by which the narrator encourages his listeners to work independently towards the truth he has in mind for them.

What the narrator expects from his listeners and how he exercises control over them come to a head in the so-called 'Bogengleichnis'[118] (241,1–30), because these thirty lines deal with three topics: a dialogue in which the listeners are told that the necessary enlightenment will be given only later (241,1–7), a passage on the *bîspel* of the bow (241,8–20), and a discussion of the qualities of the poor listener, from which those expected of the good one can be deduced *ex contrario* (241,21–30).[119] We may therefore use this *bîspel* as a means of summing up what the narrator has to say of his narrative technique and its reception by his audience. The image of an arrow shot from a bow, standing for a work of poetry, is a conventional one in classical literature and rhetoric, and known also to the Middle Ages,[120] but the image of the bow and the string also recurs in medieval biblical exegesis.[121] Whatever the nature of

---

117. On the importance of this choice of verb see Ohly, *Bedeutungsforschung*, p. 152. On the teasing of the audience even in this passage, when all is apparently about to be revealed at last, see Schroedel, *Erzählen*, pp. 9 and 17.
118. Recent literature on this passage which I make use of includes: Curschmann, *DVjs* 45 (1971), 639f.; Groos, *MLN* 87 (1972), 391ff.; Schroedel, *Erzählen*, pp. 5ff.; Spitz, *Bogengleichnis*, pp. 247ff.; Hirschberg, *Untersuchungen*, pp. 308ff.
119. This discussion of the listener was omitted from the earlier group of three passages (see above, pp. 24f.), because within the 'Bogengleichnis' he is not presented explicitly in terms of *wîsheit* or *tumpheit*.
120. Cf. Spitz, *Bogengleichnis*, p. 269, and Hirschberg, *Untersuchungen*, p. 309, fn. 54.
121. Groos, *MLN* 87 (1972), 395ff.; Spitz, *Metaphorik*, pp. 219ff.; Spitz, *Bogengleichnis*, pp. 270ff.

these precedents, Wolfram gives a novel twist to the image by using it to justify his narrative technique of deferring the release of information to his audience.

Having just told his listeners that he will release facts to them in due course (241,1–7), the narrator sums up this intention in the form of an image (241,8: *ich sage die senewen âne bogen. / diu senewe ist ein bîspel*) where he concentrates on the string rather than the bow itself[122] and regards it as a *bîspel* fit to describe the narrative technique he has just announced. This contrast, telling in favour of the *senewe*, is continued in the next pair of lines, even though what is mentioned is the bow and the arrow, by the device of referring to the arrow as that which is sped forth by the string (241,10: *nu dunket iuch der boge snel: / doch ist sneller daz diu senewe jaget*). Again the bow is played down by comparison with the string, for if the listeners addressed should attribute the speed and power of penetration of the arrow to the strength of the bow, they are reminded that these qualities derive rather from the power of the string. A conventional and superficial view is here attributed to the listeners, but is then corrected in a way with which they will have no choice but to agree.[123] The next group of three lines provides the interpretation of the central image of the string (241,12: *ob ich iu rehte hân gesaget, / diu senewe gelîchet mæren sleht: / diu dunkent ouch die liute reht*). The bowstring is therefore equated with *mæren sleht*, where I take the adjective to refer not just to the poet's style, but more particularly, because of the context provided by 241,1–7, to his narrative technique, implying therefore a straightforwardly composed narrative. This is the type of story that is pleasing to people, so that narrator and listeners appear to occupy common ground. The next pair of lines (241,15: *swer iu saget von der krümbe, / der wil iuch leiten ümbe*) is best read as implying criticism of the narrator's technique by others[124] because of the 'crooked' nature of his narrative, jumping hither and thither. In view of Wolfram's usage of *sagen von*, analysed by Schroedel, we have no choice but to read the couplet in this way.[125] When the narrator rejects the reproach of *krümbe*, thereby implying his adherence to the narrative principle of *slehte*, he again suggests how far he is in agreement with his

---

122. Cf. Hirschberg, *Untersuchungen*, p. 311.
123. *Ibid.*, pp. 311f.
124. Schroedel, *Erzählen*, p. 8, draws attention to the criticism of the narrator implicit in 734,1ff. (see above, p. 30) and also admitted later in *Willehalm* 4,19ff.
125. *Ibid.*, pp. 6f.

audience's preferences. He argues that whoever accuses him of not narrating straightforwardly, but rather crookedly, is wrong and misleads the audience. After the rejection of such criticism we are brought back to the original image of the bow and string (241,17: *swer den bogen gespannen siht, / der senewen er der slehte giht*). *Gespannen* here does not mean that the bow is bent, put under tension, in the act of shooting an arrow (for this is the contrasting possibility discussed in the next couplet), but rather that it is stringed,[126] a condition in which the bow is slightly bent, but the string quite straight. In such a condition no one will deny *slehte* as an attribute of the string instead of the bow, so that the narrator's initial concern with the string rather than the bow (241,8f.) has now been brought together with his arguments in favour of narrative straightforwardness rather than *krümbe*.

Every stage in the narrator's argument from 241,8 to 241,18 is meant to be one which the listeners can follow without hesitation, hence the rhetorical tactics with which he stresses his common ground with them. These eleven lines add up to an acknowledgment of the principle of straightforward narrative, or so it seems. Doubts are raised by the very occasion when the narrator chooses to make this point, for he does so immediately after telling his listeners (241,1–7) that he will not give them all the information they need about the episode in Munsalvæsche and that he will be coming back to it later (*her nâch* is said twice).[127] Precisely at this point the narrative is anything but straightforward in its progress, it is instead circuitous and we have been explicitly warned that this is so.

The tacit contradiction between the narrative principle advocated and the occasion chosen for this is resolved only in the last two lines of the actual *bîspel* (241,19: *man welle si zer biuge erdenen / sô si den schuz muoz menen*). This is the point of the whole passage, for the narrator now reminds his listeners of something about which he kept silent in the preceding couplet. Even if the string of the stringed bow must be described as normally straight (unlike the bow), this is not the case whenever it is put to the use for which it is intended. Whenever the bow is used to shoot an arrow the string must be bent, or, in terms of the *bîspel*, whenever the narrative is to strike home with the listeners it will follow an indirect or circuitous path. By inviting his listeners into agreement step by step in his

---

126. See Martin, *Kommentar*, note on 241,17.
127. Schroedel, *Erzählen*, pp. 7f.

bîspel the narrator has used rhetoric in order to trap them into an admission that his use of narrative *krümbe* is justified.[128] The long detour, irritating by the frustration caused,[129] which his technique involves is revealed, with the help of this *bîspel*, as necessary and called for by the nature of this work. What at first seems a retrograde step (the bending of a bow by the bowstring) reveals its value when it imparts speed and straightforward accuracy to the arrow,[130] an argument for which Groos[131] has found a rhetorical parallel in the claim that the *ordo artificialis* does not disorganise the natural order of a text, but makes what is crooked straight: *facit ut fiat ... transversa directa.*[132]

The final point of the *bîspel* (the bow performs its function when it shoots an arrow, the work of poetry exists to have an effect on its audience) has prepared the way for the last section of the 'Bogengleichnis', concerning the listener (241,21–30). This theme was tacitly present in the *bîspel* when the narrator, by using the same adverb or adjective, suggested that his correct narrative method (241,12: *ob ich iu rehte hân gesaget*) was in agreement with what his audience wanted (241,14: *diu dunkent ouch die liute reht*).[133] But if the argument of the *bîspel* led the listeners to concede the narrator's point and recognise that they had been in the wrong,[134] it is not surprising that this last section should be devoted expressly to the negative type of listener. How unsatisfactory he is for the narrator is immediately made clear (241,21: *swer aber dem sîn mære schiuzet, / des in durch nôt verdriuzet*). The arrow is now explicitly equated with the poet's *mære*, the act of shooting an arrow with the act of recital, and the target with the listener.[135] If this listener is bored and finds the narrative too lengthy (*verdriuzet*) this probably refers in this context to his impatience at having to wait so long for the narrator to release deferred information,[136] which, in view of the argument in the *bîspel*, is a criticism more of the listener than of the narrator. This is confirmed by the sharper note in what follows

128. *Ibid.*, pp. 8f., and Hirschberg, *Untersuchungen*, p. 313.
129. As is implied by the use of *verdriezen* in 734,1 to describe the reaction of some of the listeners.
130. Cf. Groos, *MLN* 87 (1972), 400.
131. *Ibid.*, p. 395.
132. Geoffrey of Vinsauf, *Poetria Nova* 122f.
133. Cf. Spitz, *Bogengleichnis*, p. 259.
134. Cf. Schroedel, *Erzählen*, pp. 8f. In *Tristan* 4591ff. Gottfried is similarly critical of the expectations of his audience (cf. Green, *Irony*, p. 238).
135. Hirschberg, *Untersuchungen*, p. 314.
136. *Ibid.*

Possibilities

(241,23: *wan daz hât dâ ninder stat, / und vil gerûmeclîchen pfat, / zeinem ôren în, zem andern für*), for this listener's impatience is revealed as an unwillingness to pay close attention,[137] to grant a place in his memory to details already narrated which it will later be necessary to recall if the narrator's purpose is to be realised. How essential this attention to details and their later application is to Wolfram's work we have already seen in the case of Parzival's name and the clue present in 122,13 (*Aller manne schœne ein bluomen kranz*), but this is only one example out of many. Where such attentiveness and readiness to cooperate are lacking the narrator's labour is wasted (241,26: *mîn arbeit ich gar verlür, / op den mîn mære drunge: / ich sagte oder sunge, / daz ez noch paz vernæme ein boc / odr ein ulmiger stoc*). From this negative picture of the narrator's dependence on his listener we see what he hopes for from the positive listener: perceptiveness in detail coupled with an ability to recall such details and correlate them over wide spans of the narrative.[138]

Indeed, at a much later stage, towards the end of the narrative action, we are meant to recall the 'Bogengleichnis' when it is briefly resumed (805,14: *ez ist niht krump alsô der boge, / diz mære ist wâr unde sleht*).[139] This compressed repetition (again the *mære* is compared with the *slehte* of the bowstring and contrasted with the *krümbe* of the bow) comes after Parzival has rejoined Condwiramurs and made his younger son Kardeiz heir to his feudal territories. To do this he had briefly left Munsalvæsche and is now speedily returning there with his wife. Just as on the outward journey the poet had inserted another encounter between Parzival

---

137. Such a listener is therefore revealed as similar to the superficial ones criticised by Hartmann in *Iwein* 249ff. (see above, p. 2).
138. Spitz, *Bogengleichnis*, pp. 262f., also includes 112,9ff. as a passage in which the image of the bow is used by the narrator, but to do this he has to follow Leitzmann who in his edition reads *bogen* instead of *begin* in 112,10 (based on the MS fragment Gˢ). To follow this one fragment here, especially in view of the doubts expressed by Bonath, *Untersuchungen*, I 36, fn. 97, is more uncertain than Spitz appears to believe. It is even more uncertain to use this interpretation of the passage (with its concentration on the *bogen*, as opposed to the *senewe* elsewhere) as an argument for the presence of typology in Wolfram's narrative (Spitz, *Bogengleichnis*, pp. 271ff.). I am far from rejecting this possibility in principle (cf. Green, *Auszug*, pp. 75ff.), but cannot accept that, on the basis of an uncertain MS reading, Spitz has succeeded in establishing a signal to the presence of typology here (*Bogengleichnis*, p. 275, fn. 76). The importance which Spitz here attributes to the presence of a signal is undermined by Ohly's demonstration of typology without an explicit signal (e.g. *Skizzen*, p. 256).
139. On the link between the two passages see Schroedel, *Erzählen*, p. 168, n. 90.

and Trevrizent in order to round off this narrative strand, so does he have Parzival encounter Sigune, now dead, on his return journey.[140] Two encounters like these might well have struck a listener as unnecessary interludes, a digression from the action at the climax of Munsalvæsche, but the narrator defends himself by means of the same *bîspel* as before, inserting this repetition just after Parzival's last encounter with Sigune.[141] By his standards this meeting does have a function to perform at this stage, as has been shown by Hirschberg's structural analysis[142] and also by the symbolic fact of Sigune's death after Parzival's call to Grail-kingship, the suggestion that he now has no more to learn from her.[143] Convinced of the necessity of this interlude within the economy of his work, the narrator denies that it is a digression at all and refers to his narrative at this stage as still *sleht*.[144]

This *bîspel* occurs therefore at two crucial points in Parzival's career: first when the dimensions of his failure at Munsalvæsche are beginning to be clear to the listeners, thanks to the intervention of the narrator, and finally as the action draws visibly to its conclusion.[145] Groos has therefore asked how far the *bîspel*, used at these points, casts light not just on narrative technique, but on the purpose behind it.[146] He suggests that it is employed in these two important contexts as 'a symbol of the paradox that men are sometimes stricken with misfortune in order that being amended they may be later found more prepared'.[147] In this sense the narrator's direction of his hero's destiny (a direction at which he has hinted in his sustained dialogue with the listeners) is analogous to the direction of all men by God.[148]

★ ★ ★ ★

140. *Ibid.*, pp. 9f., and Hirschberg, *Untersuchungen*, pp. 317f.
141. By contrast, Curschmann, *DVjs* 45 (1971), 641, and others before him (cf. Schroedel, *Erzählen*, p. 169, n. 91) interpret these lines with reference to what immediately precedes them (805,11–13), rather than the wider context in which they stand.
142. Hirschberg, *Untersuchungen*, pp. 158ff.
143. Cf. Spitz, *Bogengleichnis*, p. 258 ('Parzival bedarf nicht mehr der Führung Sigunes') and Hirschberg, *Untersuchungen*, p. 167.
144. Hirschberg, *Untersuchungen*, p. 318.
145. Cf. Spitz, *Bogengleichnis*, p. 267.
146. *MLN* 87 (1972), 400f.
147. *Ibid.*, p. 400.
148. *Ibid.*, p. 401. If this suggestion of the God-like function of the narrator seems to smack too much of the position in the modern novel (for a discussion of this in the case of Muriel Spark see Lodge, *Novelist*, pp. 119ff.), it can be countered that at the close of *Parzival* the narrator himself explicitly draws a parallel between providential control and his own direction of his hero (827,17: ...

Possibilities

In what follows I apply the various points discussed and illustrated in this chapter to the narratives dealing with Gahmuret, Parzival and Gawan, organising my discussion around the various encounters in which recognition or non-recognition plays a part. Parzival, as *des mæres hêrre*, claims several chapters for himself, since his career is complex and variegated enough to deserve it, but to Gahmuret and Gawan I have allotted one chapter each. This creates a difficulty of organisation in the case of Gawan, since the Books concerned with him come before and after Book IX, devoted to Parzival. Placing the chapter on Gawan either before or after that treating Parzival's encounter with Trevrizent inevitably involves either an anticipation of the later narrative or a recapitulation of what has gone before. The interpreter cannot avoid this, since he has after all been warned (2,10f.) about the hither and thither of the course of the narrative.

Parzivâls, den ich hân brâht / dar sîn doch sælde het erdâht). I have also written on this parallel in the context of dramatic irony (Green, *Irony*, pp. 284ff.). See also below, pp. 317f.

2
Gahmuret
(Books I and II)

Unlike Parzival, Gahmuret proceeds from a fully social context when he sets out from Anschouwe at the start of Wolfram's narrative,[1] from a feudal world in which he has an acknowledged place and well-defined obligations to others. It follows from his position there that during the course of his travels abroad he may well encounter people whom he knows already and can therefore recognise, just as conversely others are in a position, theoretically at least, to recognise him. There are three such encounters between Gahmuret and others in the two Books devoted to his knightly career, but before we consider these it would be as well to look at a number of detailed points which illustrate the poet training his listeners for, or alerting them to, the degree of attentiveness he is to demand of them in the larger encounter scenes.

Long-term implications are present in the phrase used to describe Herzeloyde when she is first introduced into the action (60,15: *si was ein maget, niht ein wîp*) and again in 84,6.[2] The temptation is to regard such a phrase as a conventional stylistic filler, used because of the easy rhyme with *lîp*, especially since Wolfram is fond of the description of a detail in both positive *and* negative terms (e.g. 43,14: *den jungen, niht den alden*).[3] But to ignore the possible relevance of this early reference to Herzeloyde is ultimately self-defeating since the poet reveals to us only very much later (494,15ff.) that Herzeloyde's earlier marriage to Castis had remained unconsummated because of the latter's premature death. Her description as a *maget*, rather than a *wîp*, thus has a very precise

---

1. It is possibly for this reason that I have been able to suggest sociological reasons for Gahmuret's departure (Green, *Auszug*, pp. 62ff.), but parallels with the 'Märchen' in the case of his son (Green, *Departure*, pp. 352ff.).
2. Cf. the Bartsch-Marti edition, fn. to 84,6.
3. Other examples of this stylistic device in the two opening Books are 52,4 and 70,24.

Gahmuret (Books I and II)

function within the narrative economy of the whole work.[4] No listener, hearing a recital of Book II for the first time, could have appreciated the force of this phrase and it is doubtful whether it would have been recalled by the time when Book IX was recited, but its implications could well have been different for an attentive listener, hearing this romance recited for the second time or later.

We are also taught to consider how far a narratorial comment simply reflects the subjective thought processes of the character presented and how far it may stem from the narrator's omniscience and convey a point of which the character himself is ignorant. This difference can be illustrated from two of the encounters we shall later consider. In the encounter between Gahmuret and his kinsman Kaylet during the battle for Zazamanc the narrator tells us that the former deliberately avoided the latter, adding that Kaylet wore a particular crest on his helmet (39,16: *ein strûz er ûf dem helme truoc*) and that he was the son of Gahmuret's maternal aunt (39,13: *wand er was sîner muomen suon*). These two comments by the narrator clearly reflect what Gahmuret is thinking: he recognises his opponent by his crest, sees that he is a kinsman and because of this (*wand*) avoids combat with him.

The position is more complex, however, when Gahmuret recognises the heraldic device on the shield of a kinsman from Anschouwe during the tournament at Kanvoleis. The narrator first tells us that Gahmuret recognises the insignia granted by his brother as king of that realm (80,14: *si gap der stolze Gâlôes / fil li roi Gandîn, / der vil getriuwe bruoder sîn*), thereby reflecting the way in which Gahmuret recognises the origins of this prince. But what the narrator then tells us is something completely unknown to Gahmuret (80,17: *dâ vor unz im diu minne erwarp / daz er an einer tjost erstarp*), as is made clear by the subsequent reference to Gahmuret's ignorance of his brother's death (80,28f.).[5] In other words, whereas the first three lines of this narrator's commentary objectivise the thought processes of Gahmuret for us, the next two lines change their function in conveying knowledge to us still denied to him.[6] Between them these two functions of the narrator's

---

4. See below, p. 220, fn. 159.
5. It is true that Gahmuret already suspects that his brother may be dead (see below p. 57), but even his intuition cannot tell him of the precise circumstances of his death: that he died jousting and in the cause of love (cf. 91,16ff.; 134,23ff. and 346,16ff.).
6. We also know more than Gahmuret himself realises in 43,13ff., where he is shown awaiting further combats at Zazamanc, presumably because he does not

39

commentary plot the difference between knowledge given by the narrator to his listeners alone and knowledge which they may share with a character in the work.

How far the narrator is in rhetorical control of his listeners, feeding them information as he thinks fit, may be shown by an example where he conversely withholds certainty from us. When news is brought to Herzeloyde of the death of her husband in battle, she faints with the shock and the narrator now tells us of her pregnancy (109,10: *wan si truoc in ir lîbe / der aller ritter bluome wirt, / ob in sterben hie verbirt*). Here we are given a glimpse of the future denied to Herzeloyde herself and opposed to her later wishes (her son is to be a paragon of chivalry), but this is qualified by an uncertainty as to whether Herzeloyde will survive to reach the term of her pregnancy. The narrator is so involved in the present crisis that, like the characters in his narrative, he can claim not to see forward into the future. This is a technique which Wolfram may have learned from Hartmann[7] and even though in this case his listeners may see through the pretence (if Parzival is not to be born he can never become *diss mæres sachewalte*, 112,17), this does not alter the principle at issue, that the narrator not merely conveys superior information to his audience, but can also withhold it from them at times or leave them uncertain as to its significance.[8]

The contrast between information provided and information withheld goes much further than this, for it is part of the richness and complexity of the narrative world created by Wolfram that we are given repeated glimpses of the wider background to the events on which he mainly concentrates his focus. This background can be revealed in two ways: by continuous hints at details which may not actually be narrated to us, but which we know from the subsequent course of events must have taken place, and by a repeated explicit

    know that by defeating three princes and obtaining their *sicherheit* he has put an end to the whole battle (cf. the Bartsch–Marti edition, fn. to 43,15). For one man to have put an end to the battle is contrary to the realistic first impression conveyed by Gahmuret himself, denying that one man alone could make much difference (24,25ff.). But in his turn the narrator takes care to give convincing reasons for Gahmuret's accomplishment: 'one man alone' could very well be a good general or tactician (cf. *houbetman* in 24,30ff.); Gahmuret fights with many others in the battle (40,20; 40,26f.; 45,14ff.), not just with the three princes; with Hiuteger and Razalic good reason is given why Gahmuret could not fail to come up against them (32,7ff.; 41,9ff.).

7. See my comments on Hartmann's *Erec* 6351, 6355f. and 6357 in *Irony*, pp. 141f.
8. This is true of Kaylet (see below, p. 50): he is named for us as soon as he enters the action, but his precise significance is withheld for some time.

opening up of further narrative perspectives. In one case the narrator avails himself of his privilege not to narrate every detail to us (but allows us to assume it subsequently), whilst in the other he narrates more than the foreground action strictly requires.

The first possibility is made use of especially in such collective scenes as a pitched battle or tournament, if only because the narrator must aim at clarity by selectively focusing on what is really necessary for his narrative action. Thus, Belakane's marshal knows that Gahmuret is an *Anschevîn* because he has already come across him in the fighting for Alexandria (21,19ff.). Although this detail was not mentioned earlier (14,3ff.), its subsequent mention fills in this earlier scene and retrospectively shows us one of its implications. At the end of the fighting at Zazamanc, when Gahmuret is praised for his exploits, these are summed up for us as the capture of three princes (45,17) and the defeat of twenty-four knights (45,14ff.). Although the fate of the three princes has been narrated in detail (as being of greater importance), that of the knights is mentioned here for the first time, so that again a complex action is enriched by a retrospective detail which runs no risk of overloading the earlier battle scene. In the tournament at Kanvoleis, on the other hand, this allusion to further action not actually narrated comes in the tournament scene itself (72,11f.), but is made so briefly that the narrative thread is not lost. Finally, in a context other than combat, the rôle of Razalic in ensuring that the rich tent should fall to Gahmuret as the victor's trophy is mentioned in retrospect (64,15ff.), even though the earlier narrative explicitly mentioned the names only of the other two princes defeated by him (52,17ff.). In these cases the subsequent narrative brings home to us details which had not been given in their proper context,[9] so that the action is progressively revealed as richer in its ramifications than we first suspected.

Enrichment of the plot by the converse technique means that the narrator frequently traces through a minor action before returning to his main narrative thread, thereby alerting us at the time to the wider perspective in which we are to see foreground events. He tells us more of the action surrounding Vridebrant after he has passed beyond the immediate context of warfare in the Middle East (25,2ff.), he informs us through Belakane of the prehistory concerning Isenhart (26,10ff.) and of the tent which is to become

---

9. An exception is 72,11f.

Gahmuret's trophy (27,15ff.).[10] Similarly in Book II a wider view of events is opened up concerning the enmity between Kaylet and Hardiz (the recurrence of such references gives the theme a very convincing insistence)[11] and the ill-fated love-affair between Galoes and Annore, first mentioned in 80,17f. and 91,16ff., but then taken up again only in 134,23ff. and 346,16ff.

This last example, like the narrator's reference to Herzeloyde as *ein maget, niht ein wîp*, operates over a long narrative span for its resolution and presupposes, for its full effect, an audience acquainted with the work from more than one recital and aware of the need to correlate widely separated passages and to pay close attention even to the most unpromising details. The same can be said of a point in Herzeloyde's prophetic dream before she receives news of her husband's death, the intimation that she is to give birth and suck to a dragon (104,10ff.).[12] It would be an improbably perceptive listener who, on hearing these lines for the first time, would assume that the dragon's flight from her (104,14f.) must anticipate her son's departure from her. For certainty about this equation of the dragon with Parzival we have to wait much longer: either for the explicit confirmation given by Trevrizent in Book IX (476,27: *du wær daz tier daz si dâ souc, / unt der trache der von ir dâ flouc. / ez widerfuor in slâfe ir gar, / ê daz diu süeze dich gebar*) or for the more concealed detail that Parzival as a 'dragon' uncomfortably resembles the violence of a Lähelin or Orilus, both of whom bear a dragon in their heraldic device.[13] In either case, however, this detail is far-reaching in its operation and reveals an author concerned to train his listeners to realise such implications, even if not at the first hearing.

Information can be provided or withheld in yet another respect: the names with which Wolfram, in contrast to Chrétien, equips most of his characters can be given us immediately by the narrator or kept back for some length of time.[14] Characters who are named as soon as they are introduced into the narrative action include Gahmuret himself (he is first referred to by a descriptive phrase, 5,22, but in the next line his name is revealed), Belakane (16,6 refers to her first of all as *ein wîp*, but she is named in the following line)

---

10. This is taken up again in 52,23ff. and 64,13ff.
11. Cf. 48,6ff.; 65,5ff.; 67,23ff.; 89,7ff.; 100,21ff.
12. On the wider significance of this dream and its imagery see Deinert, *Ritter*, pp. 3ff.; Rosskopf, *Traum*, pp. 2ff.; Speckenbach, *Troimen*, pp. 181ff.
13. Cf. Bumke, *Forschung*, p. 288, fn. 337a.
14. I have discussed these two possibilities in *Namedropping*, pp. 114ff.

Gahmuret (Books I and II)

and the three princes defeated by Gahmuret on her behalf (Hiuteger 25,9, Gaschier 25,14, Razalic 41,9).[15] To name his defeated foes is the narrator's way of enhancing the renown of the hero of this prehistory,[16] whilst the individualising of Gahmuret and Belakane by naming them lets them stand out as the two figures dominant in Book I. Yet this last point is not so self-evident as it might seem: by contrast with his father, Parzival is not immediately presented to us by name and the same is true in Book II of Herzeloyde, as opposed to Belakane. It will pay us therefore to look at those cases in the first two Books where a character is not named when first brought into the narrative.

Such characters include Gahmuret's father Gandin (first referred to anonymously 5,25, but then named only in 8,19), his host at Zazamanc, the marshal of queen Belakane (first introduced 18,8, but given a name as late as 43,16)[17] and other figures such as Killirjacac (the timelag stretches from 31,21 to 46,25), Hardiz (from 48,10 to 67,25ff.),[18] Lambekin (from 67,23 to 73,30f.)[19] and Schafillor (from 67,14 to 79,2). By employing this technique of delayed naming Wolfram can focus our attention more effectively on Gahmuret and Belakane, individualised from the start by their naming; he can also rouse his listeners' attention by keeping them in some suspense as to the identity of certain characters; and he realistically introduces us by stages into his fictional universe, so that we get to know its inhabitants gradually and piecemeal, as we do other people in the real world.[20]

15. To these should be added the names of Isenhart (16,5) and Vridebrant (16,6), but these are less significant because they have been removed from the narrative action at this point, the former by death and the latter by his absence from Zazamanc.
16. That Gahmuret can be regarded in this light is suggested by the narrator's reference to him as *unser rîter* (16,19). On this see Nellmann, *Erzähltechnik*, p. 48.
17. Until he is named this figure is referred to by epithets descriptive of his various functions: as the queen's *marschalc* (18,8; 20,29; 22,29), as her *burcgrâve* (20,19; 29,27; 43,9), and as Gahmuret's host (20,7; 23,11; 29,27; 32,1; 32,27; 34,8; 35,9 + 12; 42,8). I take the two titles of *marschalc* and *burcgrâve* to refer to the same person, since 20,19 and 20,29 suggest that only one person is involved. When the name Lachfilirost is eventually released we can readily associate it with the figure hitherto referred to anonymously by these epithets because the narrator takes care to say *Lachfilirost / sîn wirt* (43,16f.) and *Lachfilirost schahtelakunt* (43,19), where the last term represents Wolfram's 'French' version of *burcgrâve*.
18. See Green, *Namedropping*, pp. 117f.
19. Cf. Schirok, *Aufbau*, p. 484.
20. Cf. Johnson, *MLR* 63 (1968), 612.

Yet there are other reasons for Wolfram to control the rate at which his listeners should learn the name of a character, as we see with the remaining examples of delayed naming in the Gahmuret story, where the timelag is noticeably longer than in the cases hitherto. Gahmuret's mistress Ampflise is referred to early in the narrative, before he has set out from Anschouwe (12,6 and 11), but if she is named only in Book II (76,7) this very effectively serves the function of acquainting us with her at the moment when she decisively enters the action, sending her messengers to Kanvoleis to remind Gahmuret of his obligations towards her and thus heightening the dilemma of his position between Belakane and Herzeloyde.[21] Gahmuret's brother plays a part in the opening situation from 6,2, but is referred to anonymously, in terms of the functions he performs, throughout this episode.[22] His name is not released to us until Book II (80,14), but again this is a highly significant point, for it is here that Gahmuret first suspects that a calamity must have overtaken his elder brother. That this is not fortuitous is brought out by the mention of the name Galoes again (91,18) when Gahmuret learns for certain of his death from Kaylet. It is also confirmed by Wolfram's employment of the same technique for the same purpose in the case of Gahmuret's mother, Schoette. She too is introduced anonymously at an early stage of the story (7,5) and is similarly referred to[23] until the same scene in Book II (92,24), when her name is revealed only at the point where the son learns of her death since his departure.

The other character to whom this technique of delayed naming is applied is Herzeloyde.[24] She is introduced without a name at the start of the action dealing with the tournament she has arranged at Kanvoleis (60,9)[25] and remains anonymous throughout the action which she has called into being[26] until 84,9f. In other words, we in

21. Cf. Harroff, *Wolfram*, pp. 22ff.
22. These anonymous functions are: *elter sun* (6,2), *bruoder* (7,19; 12,16); *künec* (6,14 + 22 + 29; 7,18; 8,27; 9,29; 10,6; 11,28) and *hêrre* (7,13; 7,19; 9,17).
23. Schoette is referred to as *muoter* (7,5; 9,20; 10,13; 12,16), *wîp* (10,17), *frowe* (11,2 + 8 + 23) and *küneginne* (11,9).
24. On the gradual revelation of her identity see also Harroff, *Wolfram*, pp. 21 and 26f.
25. She is not even mentioned where we might expect it (59,1), when we are first told of the tournament she has organised.
26. Herzeloyde is thus referred to as *maget* (60,15; 84,6), *Wâleisinne* (81,16; 83,12; 84,1), *wirtin* (64,11; 83,14), *frouwe* (81,20; 83,27), but for the rest as *künegîn* (60,9; 61,3 + 29; 62,25; 64,5 + 12; 67,10; 69,24; 70,10; 77,11; 81,24; 82,30; 83,25).

the audience learn her name at what is the decisive moment for Gahmuret, for this is the start of the scene in which these two meet in the relative privacy of Gahmuret's tent and which concludes with Gahmuret's acknowledgment that, as victor at the tournament, he has no choice but to marry Herzeloyde. This is a feature which all these four examples have in common: the names of Ampflise, Galoes, Schoette and Herzeloyde are not released haphazardly, but rather at points in the narrative which are subjectively important for Gahmuret, when erotic entanglements trap him and he is suddenly overwhelmed by news of the death of those closest to him. By ensuring that his listeners confront the individuality of these characters only at such carefully selected points the narrator has done his best to allow them to share something of Gahmuret's subjective experience. Our process of enlightenment about these characters is synchronised with his realisation of the position in which he finds himself with each of them.

Wolfram's technique with personal names also applies to some of the circumlocutions which he can use of his characters.[27] Two circumlocutions for Gahmuret in Books I and II are informative in this respect: one is exclusively true of him alone (after his marriage to Belakane and acquisition of her territory as ruler, 90,24, he can be known as the king of Zazamanc), but the other (referring to his origins in Anschouwe) is true of many besides himself, but at this stage of the work[28] is generally used of Gahmuret.

Since I have discussed the circumlocution *künec von Zazamanc* elsewhere,[29] I do not intend to repeat my argument here, but wish simply to point to the aesthetic effects achieved by this narratorial substitute for Gahmuret's name. We shall see later[30] that Gahmuret comes to Kanvoleis unknown and as an outsider, so that it is fitting that the narrator, recapturing something of the knight's anonymity, should largely avoid using his name during the course of the tournament. It is also fitting that this knight, fresh from his victory in the Middle East and with a number of pagans in his retinue (62,3f.), should be announced by his pages, using their lord's highest title gained so far, as the king of Zazamanc (62,16).

27. I have looked at some of these circumlocutions in *Namedropping*, pp. 127ff.
28. Later in the work the epithet *Anschevîn* can still be applied to Gahmuret, but also to his son Feirefiz, and once to both Feirefiz and Parzival. The evidence for this can be conveniently found in Hartl, *Verzeichnis*, p. 423, under *Anschevîn*.
29. *Namedropping*, pp. 139f.
30. See below, pp. 52f.

The Art of Recognition in Wolfram's *Parzival*

To those at Kanvoleis Gahmuret is therefore not known by name, but by this regal title which is used of him regularly in a public context during the tournament.[31] But, as we shall see, Gahmuret is recognised by his kinsman Kaylet, who had encountered him at Zazamanc and therefore knows him both as *künec von Zazamanc* and by his personal name. The name Gahmuret can therefore be used by the narrator when talking of the relationship between these two kinsmen at Kanvoleis, but also when referring to others who know Gahmuret personally, such as Belakane or Ampflise,[32] even if they are not physically present at the tournament.

The narrator thus uses a double technique in this scene. When talking of Gahmuret's public rôle, his appearance at Kanvoleis before those who do not know him, he calls him the anonymous ruler of Zazamanc, but feels free to use his name in a private setting, hollowed out from the social events of the jousting, when referring to those who know him as an individual. To Gahmuret's double position at this point in the narrative (to some he is known, but to others not) there corresponds the narrator's double technique of using his personal name or an anonymous circumlocution. It would lack all verisimilitude, however, if Gahmuret were to remain unknown after his victory in the jousting, so that he is fittingly first mentioned by name in the public context of Kanvoleis when Herzeloyde expresses her judgment that he is the victor (82,3: '*doch wæne et Gahmuretes tât / den hœsten prîs derworben hât*'). The release of his name only at this point (not to Wolfram's listeners, of course, but to the internal audience) has an added aesthetic advantage, since Gahmuret acquires a name and hence individuality for Herzeloyde immediately before the point where she conversely is given a name for the listeners as well as for Gahmuret (84,8). By carefully controlling his use of names the narrator has allowed these two, soon to be married, to approach one another from impersonal obscurity, relative in the case of Gahmuret, but absolute with Herzeloyde.

This narratorial technique of using names or circumlocutions to reflect the subjective and therefore not always fully informed point of view of characters in the work can also be observed with the references to Gahmuret's origins in Anschouwe. From the moment when his elder brother Galoes offers to share his feudal territory

---

31. I have discussed the relevant material in *Namedropping*, p. 139.
32. Ibid.

Gahmuret (Books I and II)

with him and grants him the possibility of naming himself by that territory (6,25: *'wan nennet ir den bruoder mîn / Gahmuret Anschevîn? / Anschouwe ist mîn lant: / dâ wesen beide von genant'*) this epithet can be used of him. Although Gahmuret rejects the offer of territory, the narrator uses the epithet *Anschevîn* of him throughout Book I, sometimes distinguishing him from Galoes by saying *der junge Anschevîn*,[33] but sometimes dispensing with this distinction, especially as Gahmuret's adventures proceed and his brother fades more into the background.[34]

This technique is abandoned, however, once we come to Kanvoleis in Book II. Of Gahmuret's retinue, as he arrives there, it is reported to Herzeloyde (62,5f.): *'etslîcher mag ein Anschevîn / mit sîner sprâche iedoch wol sîn'*, but the indefinite *etslîcher* need refer only to some of the followers, not necessarily to their feudal lord himself. In 76,20 Gahmuret may be *dem von Anschouwe*, but this occurs in a private interlude, remote from the public scene of jousting, to which Gahmuret has withdrawn to change horses and in which he comes across Ampflise's messengers. If this is the kind of personal setting in which the narrator feels justified in referring to Gahmuret by name (78,17),[35] it is equally apt to allude to his Anschouwe origins here, since the absent Ampflise is perfectly well acquainted with both these facts. When Gahmuret later refers to his brother as *von Anschouwe Gâlôes* (92,17) this obviously implies that he too comes from Anschouwe, but nonetheless the explicit statement is made only of Galoes.[36] Finally, with reference to the courtly training he had received from Ampflise in France, Gahmuret says of himself (94,22f.): *'ich brâht in Anschouwe / ir rât und mîner zühte site'*. By this he means that on completion of this training he returned to his homeland, but this is not so unambiguously clear to anyone ignorant of his origins, since it could equally suggest that he put his training into practice as a knight errant and that Anschouwe was the first stage on his travels.

None of these four references to Anschouwe in Book II makes it publicly clear beyond doubt that this is where Gahmuret comes from, which agrees with his anonymity at Kanvoleis and the general

---

33. 11,1; 14,8; 17,9.
34. Such unqualified references come significantly later in the narrative than those to *der junge Anschevîn*: 21,13; 23,24; 38,11; 40,2; 41,17; 56,1.
35. Green, *Namedropping*, p. 139.
36. Furthermore, Gahmuret makes this remark in the private setting of a conversation with his kinsman Kaylet.

view of him as simply *künec von Zazamanc*. This changes however when it is reported to some Anschouwe knights present who the victor of the contest is (98,17: '*frou Herzeloyd diu künegîn / hât behabt den Anschevîn*'), for this is the first time in Book II when this epithet, regularly used of him in the preceding Book, is applied to Gahmuret again. When these knights ask in return (98,19: '*wer was von Anschouwe dâ?*'), the meaning of *von Anschouwe*, by contrast with *in Anschouwe* (94,22), is clear beyond doubt, for they mean someone who comes from Anschouwe because he is an *Anschevîn* by birth (cf. later 108,9: *von Anschouwe erborn*). After this revelation of Gahmuret's origins, dramatically effective because it is made to knights from Anschouwe unaware of their lord's presence at Kanvoleis, the epithet *Anschevîn* is free to be used of him for the rest of Book II,[37] as it had been thoughout Book I, and it also recurs in subsequent Books.[38] If the narrator carves out a segment of his narrative in this way in which he refrains from his normal use of *Anschevîn* to describe Gahmuret, this is because he can thereby hope to suggest the failure of these Anschouwe knights to recognise that Gahmuret is present in their midst. The tournament at Kanvoleis therefore involves two separate processes by which those taking part come to recognise Gahmuret's identity: one concerns his personal name (this has to be learned by Herzeloyde and her retinue) and the other his epithet *Anschevîn* (this has to be learned by his compatriots from Anschouwe). The name or epithet is withheld by the narrator for as long as the party concerned remains in ignorance of the facts.

A knightly character in a medieval romance can be referred to not just by name or circumlocution, but by his heraldic insignia, which perform the same individualising function.[39] In Books I and II this is made clear with Gahmuret and his father, the parallel going so far that, corresponding to the technique of delayed naming, the details of Gandin's coat of arms are given to us belatedly, but at a carefully chosen point.[40] At the first mention of Gandin's heraldic device (when, on his travels, Gahmuret decides to replace it by another) it

37. 98,30; 101,6 (cf. also 108,9).
38. The evidence for this can be extracted from Hartl, *Verzeichnis*, p. 423, *s.v.*
39. On this topic see Timpson, *GLL* 13 (1959/60), 88ff. and Zips, *JHGG* 8 (1971/73), 155ff., who regards some of his examples as showing 'daß das Wappentier im Hochmittelalter Ausdruck eigensten Selbstverständnisses sein konnte, das gleichsam das innerste Wesen des Ritters enthüllte' (p. 174).
40. Etzler, *Komposition*, p. 36, sees this chosen point in Gahmuret's marriage to Herzeloyde, but I should rather stress Gahmuret's newly found dynastic responsibilities as a ruler. See also Harroff, *Wolfram*, pp. 15f.

Gahmuret (Books I and II)

is referred to 'anonymously' with no descriptive details (14,12: *nu erloubt im daz er müeze hân / ander wâpen denne im Gandîn / dâ vor gap, der vater sîn*). The same lack of individualising detail is true of the next two references, once when Kaylet claims that Gahmuret's present coat of arms was never borne by his father (50,1ff.) and once when Gahmuret, by now aware of his brother's death, acknowledges to his knightly compatriots that, if he is to become ruler of Anschouwe, he will have to revert to his father's coat of arms (99,13). It is in this full dynastic sense (he acknowledges his function as ruler over Anschouwe, as well as over Herzeloyde's land) that Gahmuret can now be called *Anschevîn* (101,6) and also shown wearing his father's heraldic device (101,7: *dez pantel, daz sîn vater truoc, / von zoble ûf sînen schilt man sluoc*). Only at the moment when Gahmuret comes into his own as ruler of Anschouwe is this panther coat of arms described to us by the narrator; it serves to individualise not Gandin, but his son, the hero of these first two Books.

Although the scene where Gahmuret first changes his coat of arms is silent about the heraldic device he temporarily lays aside, full details are given of his heraldic appearance on his travels (14,15ff.). It has been suggested that there may be a very real, concrete reason for the change itself (Gahmuret's service of the *baruc* as a mercenary may not have been demeaning to a knight, but may have been a cause of embarrassment for a prince),[41] but Wolfram stresses rather the symbolic function of the new coat of arms in which the anchor stands for the firm foothold which Gahmuret seeks on his wanderings[42] (14,29ff.; cf. also 99,13ff.). Also significant is the timing of Gahmuret's change, since this is related to us only after he has joined the *baruc* in the Middle East (14,8). This is the coat of arms by which he is known in the Middle East (Belakane's marshal recognises him by this device at Zazamanc, since he had seen him in action at Alexandria, 18,5ff.) and when he comes to Kanvoleis (98,26f.). But if Gahmuret can be recognised by people he now encounters on his travels by means of his anchor device, this also means that those from his home region will now fail to recognise him when clad in knightly armour. This is true of those who knew him in Anschouwe (we shall see this to be the case when he encounters Kaylet in Book I and the knights from Anschouwe in Book II), but also of Ampflise's messengers who

---

41. Cf. the Bartsch–Marti edition, fn. to 14,10.
42. The anchor is appropriate as a symbol, since it is attached to a ship (the token of Gahmuret's wanderings) and seeks a firm grip on land, which is what the knight also seeks.

knew him in France (at least to judge by the way in which the narrator finds it necessary to provide a special motivation for their recognising him at Kanvoleis).[43] This detail of Gahmuret changing his coat of arms, mentioned recurrently so that we are not allowed to forget it,[44] is thus the factual basis for the theme of recognition in the three encounter scenes, to the first of which we now turn.

Gahmuret and Kaylet

The name of this kinsman of Gahmuret's whom he encounters in the Middle East should strictly have been included amongst those characters who are named as soon as they are introduced into the narrative, but Kaylet represents a special case. His name may be given on the first possible occasion, when a prince of Belakane's, listing the leaders of the besieging army confronting her, mentions him (25,16: *noch hât hie rîter mêre / Kaylet von Hoskurast*), but this tells us nothing of his significance at this point. Although Gahmuret has now been told that a kinsman of his is fighting on the side of those opposing Belakane, the tact demanded of a guest in his dealings with his hostess means that Gahmuret has every reason not to mention this embarrassing fact of their kinship. Gahmuret's silence means equally that the audience are given no clue that Kaylet means anything to him – although the name has been revealed at the first opportunity, its significance is still withheld. The same is true of a second reference, when this time Belakane's burgrave gives the new arrival an account of the military situation and says that the defenders of Zazamanc have captured a count who is Kaylet's nephew (31,20ff.). This nephew (later revealed as Killirjacac, 46,25) is also related to Gahmuret, but this in turn is only made clear later on the same occasion (46,9: *'ich sæhe och gerne den neven mîn'*). From early in his stay at Zazamanc Gahmuret must be aware that two of his kinsmen are present in the enemy ranks outside the city, but at this stage neither his hosts nor Wolfram's audience are apprised of this.[45]

43. See below, p. 56.
44. Cf. Timpson, *GLL* 13 (1959/60), 88ff. and Etzler, *Komposition*, pp. 33ff.
45. Cf. Harroff, *Wolfram*, pp. 12f. Gahmuret's superior knowledge (vis-à-vis his hosts as well as the actual listeners) is comparable to Gawan's position at Schastel Marveile, for his knowledge of the situation likewise grants him an advantage not shared by the four queens there or by the audience at this point in the narrative (see below, pp. 151ff.). This similarity between Gahmuret and Gawan underlines Parzival's position of repeatedly not knowing what is clear to other persons in the narrative or to the listeners themselves.

Gahmuret (Books I and II)

The vital fact of Gahmuret's relationship with Kaylet is communicated to the listeners when the narrator tells us of their encounter in the battle and of the former's deliberate avoidance of any combat (39,11: *dô kom gevaren Kaylet. / von dem kêrte Gahmuret*).[46] Gahmuret is already forewarned of the risk of encountering a kinsman in battle (he has learned this twice from his hosts), but in addition, as we have already seen from a narrator's commentary as a reflection of Gahmuret's thought processes,[47] he is able to recognise Kaylet from the heraldic function of his crest (39,16: *ein strûz er ûf dem helme truoc*), as Gahmuret later makes quite clear, when the process of mutual recognition has been concluded (50,4: '*do rekante abr ich wol dînen strûz, / ame schilde ein sarapandratest: / dîn strûz stuont hôch sunder nest*').

Yet what is possible for Gahmuret (thanks to a double forewarning and recognition by means of a distinctive crest) is not available for Kaylet: we are not told of anyone on his side telling him that Gahmuret is one of the defenders of the besieged city and recognition has been rendered impossible by Gahmuret changing his coat of arms between leaving Anschouwe and arriving at Zazamanc. Accordingly, Kaylet fails to recognise his kinsman when their paths cross in the battle, and the narrator's words of him in this situation (39,15: *der Spânôl rief im nâch genuoc*) are probably meant to convey his angry frustration at being denied knightly combat or a jeering accusation of cowardice, in either case an eagerness for fighting which Gahmuret cannot share because of what he knows. Kaylet learns the truth from Gaschier, who tells him first where this knight who avoided combat comes from (40,2: *bestêt ir den Anschevîn*) and then his actual name (40,6), both of which details he had learned from the knight who defeated him and accepted his parole (38,11: '*ich pin Gahmuret Anschevîn*'). On learning this, Kaylet is now as ready to give up fighting a kinsman as Gahmuret had been earlier (40,11: *dô sprach der künec Kaylet / 'ist daz mîn neve Gahmuret / fil li roy Gandîn, / mit dem lâz ich mîn strîten sîn*').[48] The fact of kinship, once it has been grasped on either side, is enough to put an end to knightly combat, which is perhaps why the narrator, from the moment of Gahmuret's recognition of the truth (39,11ff.), equips

---

46. Harroff, *Wolfram*, p. 12.
47. See above, p. 39.
48. Even now Gaschier is reluctant to trust Kaylet's self-control (40,15ff.) after this demonstration of his manifest eagerness for combat.

all the scenes in which Gahmuret and Kaylet appear together with a reference to their kinship.[49]

Although the narrator in his depiction of this scene leaves it to us to deduce why Kaylet failed to recognise his kinsman, he later takes care to motivate this detail, so that this subsequent confirmation of our assumption is probably meant to encourage just this kind of critical questioning. We have seen in the case of Gahmuret how the narrator's observation about Kaylet's crest (39,16) reflects what passes through Gahmuret's mind, as is confirmed by this knight's later words to his would-be opponent (50,4ff.). In the converse situation an exact parallel is impossible: since Gahmuret's present coat of arms means nothing to Kaylet, it cannot prompt recognition. The explanation for Kaylet's failure in recognition is given later, in fact in the same dialogue in which Gahmuret says how he was able to recognise his adversary, for Kaylet says expressly that the cause lay in the unexpected coat of arms borne by his kinsman (50,1: *'da erkant ich niht den anker dîn: / mîner muomen man Gandîn / hât in gefüeret selten ûz'*).[50] That this changed coat of arms is capable of confusing others is also clear from Gahmuret's encounter with an Anschouwe knight at Kanvoleis.

With that we have been given a full explanation of how Gahmuret was able to recognise Kaylet, whilst the converse was impossible for Kaylet until he was enlightened by Gaschier. In this episode the narrator withholds the name of neither party, so that we are shown the position from Gahmuret's well-informed point of view. In this enjoyment of superior knowledge, and hence his ability to avoid tragic combat with a kinsman, Gahmuret resembles Gawan and is essentially different from his son Parzival.

Gahmuret at Kanvoleis

The narrator makes it clear that on his arrival Gahmuret was quite unknown to Herzeloyde and her followers (61,29: *vor der küngîn wart vernomn / daz ein gast dâ solte komn / ûz verrem lande, / den niemen dâ rekande*). In their eyes he is therefore a stranger from a remote country, unknown to them and leading a retinue, some of

49. Etzler, *Komposition*, p. 57.
50. Harroff, *Wolfram*, p. 16, sees in the encounter between Gahmuret and Kaylet an early recommendation to pay attention to details in this work, for they may be of importance later. By remembering and correlating such details the listeners may learn to avoid the pitfall into which Kaylet, as the first of many, falls.

Gahmuret (Books I and II)

whom may be French (or even from Anschouwe), but others pagan (62,3ff.). To this the listeners can add from their knowledge of the Kaylet encounter that Gahmuret must also have been unrecognisable because of his anchor coat of arms.[51] It is hardly surprising that people should therefore ask who this stranger is, the more so since he stands out by the luxury of his train (63,27: *Vil dicke aldâ gevrâget wart, / wer wære der ritter âne bart, / der fuorte alsölhe rîcheit*). In view of Gahmuret's anonymity it is understandable that he should be referred to by a circumlocution, just as similar circumlocutions and nameless epithets like *der fiere, der gast, der helt* should accompany him throughout this episode.[52] We are not given the precise reply to the general question as to this knight's identity (63,30: *vil schiere wart daz mære breit: / si sagetenz in für unbetrogn*). To judge by the narrator's two main types of reference to him at this stage (by name or by his function as king of Zazamanc), the answer could have been either *Gahmuret* or *der künec von Zazamanc*. However, the latter is more likely, if only because the narrator distributes these alternatives in such a way that the newcomer is referred to as Gahmuret only in the context of those who know him personally and as king of Zazamanc by those who know only that this realm was the scene of his latest exploits before he came to Kanvoleis.[53]

By contrast, one person at the tournament has the means of recognising Gahmuret and we are shown why this should be so. Kaylet, present at Kanvoleis as he had been at Zazamanc, can recognise his kinsman by his new coat of arms, but also by the splendidly luxurious tent which had been offered Gahmuret as a trophy in the Middle East (52,25ff.) and which, when reported to him at Kanvoleis, acts as an immediate spur to recognition (64,13: *dô vriesch der künec von Spâne, / daz ûf der Lêôplâne / stüend ein gezelt, daz Gahmurete / durch des küenen Razalîges bete / beleip vor Pâtelamunt*). Kaylet is in a position to recognise Gahmuret at

---

51. If it is later shown (98,15ff.) that even Gahmuret's own compatriots from Anschouwe fail to recognise him because of the change in his coat of arms, how much more difficult must it have been for strangers at Kanvoleis to see who he is.
52. The circumlocutions used of Gahmuret in this episode occur in 63,27f.; 69,27f.; 76,20; 79,15; 83,30f.; 98,23ff. He is also referred to as *der fiere* (61,28; 81,11), *gast* (61,30; 70,26), *man* (62,23; 76,9), *helt* (62,29; 64,10 + 28; 72,4 + 14), *hêrre* (63,11; 68,30; 76,16), *degen* (63,13; 64,7), *ritter* (63,28; 81,26) and *wirt* (83,7 + 13).
53. This assumption is also rendered more likely by the answer given by Gahmuret's pages to a similar question (62,14: '*von im vrâgt ich der mære: / dô sageten si mir sunder wanc, / ez wære der künec von Zazamanc*').

Kanvoleis because he had also come across him at Zazamanc, as is made clear by his messenger with regard not merely to the detail of the tent,[54] but also to the general luxury of his train on both occasions. When the messenger reports to Kaylet (64,22: *'iwer muomen sun ich sach / kumende als er ie was fier'*) this serves as an explicit link between the pomp of Gahmuret's entry at Kanvoleis, just described (62,28ff.), and his similar entry at Zazamanc (18,17ff.).[55] If Kaylet acts as a bridge between the two scenes of Gahmuret's exploits and is now in the exceptional position of being able to recognise him, it makes good sense that, when the Anschouwe knights eventually learn of Gahmuret's presence, this news should come to them ultimately from Kaylet (98,29: *'mir sagt der künec Kaylet, / der Anschevîn wær Gahmuret'*).

We are therefore shown how Gahmuret is recognised at the tournament by Kaylet and his immediate circle, but is unknown to all others. This is the factual explanation why the narrator can refer to him throughout by an anonymous circumlocution or epithet, reserving the equally unrevealing title *künec von Zazamanc* for the public setting where he is still unknown and the name Gahmuret for the more private kind of context where he is known to kinsmen and intimates. At what precise point the king of Zazamanc is recognised as Gahmuret even in the public setting is not made clear by the narrator, although Herzeloyde must have learned this by 82,3.[56] It is also fitting that the narrator's alternative references to Gahmuret throughout the episode, by name or by royal function, should be brought together in the context of Kaylet (85,9: ... *daz eine daz was Kaylet. / der sach den künec Gahmuret*...), for Kaylet is the one person who from the beginning is acquainted with these

54. On the background to this tent see Harroff, *Wolfram*, pp. 17f.
55. Cf. Green, *Auszug*, p. 71, and Etzler, *Komposition*, pp. 10ff. If in both these instances it is stressed how much more pomp was displayed at Kanvoleis than at Gahmuret's entry into Zazamanc, this still implies the need to correlate these two passages. Verse 64,23 in MS D has *ê* instead of *ie*, which acts as a more precise pointer to the earlier occasion at Zazamanc, but even *ie* can still serve as a generalising reference to a particular occasion.
56. This presupposes that the poet has chosen not to narrate the actual moment when Herzeloyde learns Gahmuret's identity. This would therefore be another instance of a narrative detail, not previously narrated, being subsequently implied (see above, p. 41). Wolfram's work also contains other examples where the actual moment of recognition is left unclear, e.g. the encounters between Parzival and Condwiramurs (p. 75), Parzival and Jeschute for the second time (p. 122), Parzival and Gawan (p. 131), Parzival and Trevrizent (p. 224, fn. 172), Parzival and Cundrie for the second time (p. 254). Cf. also the encounters between Gawan and Vergulaht (p. 143), Gawan and the four queens (p. 156).

Gahmuret (Books I and II)

two aspects of his kinsman: that the king of Zazamanc[57] is none other than Gahmuret of Anschouwe.

Gahmuret's anonymity for the majority at Kanvoleis stands out even more obviously by contrast with the identifiability of almost all other participants. Despite the poet's touch of realism,[58] a tournament is a stylised and well regulated social pastime and differs from the chaos of a pitched battle in that the individual contestants are generally known to each other beforehand, so that their identity is not normally a problem,[59] as Wolfram makes clear from the spectators' point of view (73,11: *der strît was wol sô nâhen, / daz gar die frouwen sâhen / wer dâ bî prîse solde sîn*). Accordingly, two methods are used to pinpoint the identity of the knights taking part. One is for the narrator to give us explicit details about them (full information consists of social rank + personal name + place of origin, but this is not always given so fully). Such information is given us twice, first in a preview of those taking part (65,26ff.) where seventeen combatants are listed,[60] then in the course of the tournament itself (72,9ff.) where sixteen are named (a few of whom are repeated from the first list).[61] The second method is for the narrator to stress the visibility of the combatant's coat of arms and hence the possibility of recognising him, as is clear from the women spectators. The knights thus singled out are Gahmuret by means of his heraldic *anker*,[62] Kaylet by virtue of his crest in the form of a *strûz*,[63] Hardiz by *daz vorder teil des grîfen* (72,24), his followers by *eins grîfen zagel* (72,21), and the Anschouwe prince by his local coat of arms (80,6ff.). That Kaylet is to be recognised from his *strûz* we know since 39,16; we are told immediately that the griffin device is associated with the *künec von Gascône*, whom we already know from 67,25ff. to be Hardiz; about the Anschouwe prince the only important thing is that he should be recognised as coming from

---

57. By 85,9f., however, Gahmuret's royal status has been enhanced: he is not merely king of Zazamanc, but has also acquired authority over Herzeloyde's territory by marriage (85,14f.) and is soon to acknowledge his obligations as ruler over Anschouwe (99,13ff.).
58. 78,5ff. Cf. Green, *Homicide*, pp. 34f.
59. The kind of situation, as in Chrétien's *Lancelot*, where a knight conceals his identity in a tournament by adopting a disguise, is quite exceptional.
60. 65,30; 66,10; 66,15; 66,23; 66,26; 66,29; 67,1; 67,13; 67,14; 67,15; 67,16f.; 67,18; 67,19; 67,22; 67,23; 68,21; 68,22.
61. 72,10; 72,25; 73,14; 73,18; 73,21; 73,22; 73,29; 73,30f.; 74,5; 74,6; 74,21; 74,29; 78,25; 79,13; 80,7; 82,10.
62. 72,8; 73,1; 79,15; 80,5; 98,26.
63. 72,8; 72,30.

Anschouwe. By contrast, only Kaylet knows that the *anker* stands for Gahmuret; for the others this heraldic sign is a disguise rather than a mark of identity. Between them these two methods highlight the fact that, apart from Kaylet, Gahmuret should not be recognised for what he is at Kanvoleis, even though he is in a position to recognise anyone else there.

If Gahmuret cannot be recognised at the tournament, the narrator has to provide a special motivation for the scene, inserted as a static interlude in the course of the jousting, in which Ampflise's messengers encounter Gahmuret and pass on to him the letter from his mistress. It is later made clear that Ampflise is informed about Gahmuret's victory in the Middle East (97,19: '*man tet mîner frouwen kunt / daz ir vor Pâtelamunt / den hæhsten prîs behieltet / unt dâ zweir krône wieltet*'), but no indication is given that she, let alone her messengers, is also informed about such a detail as the change in Gahmuret's coat of arms. Indeed, given the fact that the narrator provides a special motivation for their recognition of him, this is most unlikely. The poetic problem is to show how they were able to recognise him and also to extract him temporarily from the jousting so that the meeting can take place at all. The solution is to have Gahmuret seek a fresh horse after he has been fighting for some time (75,23: *dô reit der künec von Zazamanc / hin dan dâ in niemen dranc, / nâch eim orse daz geruowet was*) and for him realistically to profit from this interval by taking off his helmet and hood for fresh air (75,26: *man bant von im den adamas, / niwan durch des windes luft, / und anders durch decheinen guft. / man stroufte im ab sîn härsenier*). When this is followed by a brief descriptive touch (75,30: *sîn munt was rôt unde fier*), this serves the particular purpose of indicating that Gahmuret's features are now visible. It is precisely at this moment that the narrator introduces Ampflise's messengers into the narrative (76,1ff.) and he is now able to suggest that the *kappelân* (*wîs* by contrast with the young pages and therefore probably acquainted with Gahmuret from his days in France) was able to recognise the man he was seeking (76,9: *vil schiere bekanter disen man*).

Gahmuret and the Anschouwe knight

This episode is a repetition of the situation when Gahmuret encountered Kaylet at Zazamanc: in both cases a personal encounter between acquaintances fighting on opposite sides is carved out of the general *mêlée*, in both cases Gahmuret recognises what is afoot and is able to avoid a potentially tragic combat.

We are told at the start of the episode that Gahmuret recognised this *fürste ûz Anschouwe* (80,7) from his heraldic device (80,11: *diu wâpen er rekande*) which he sees to be that of Anschouwe, granted by his brother Galoes (80,14ff.). Because of this Gahmuret deliberately avoids fighting this compatriot,[64] just as he had earlier gone out of his way to avoid combat with Kaylet. But this prince of Anschouwe fails to recognise Gahmuret for his part, at least to judge by the impetuousness with which he charges at this adversary of his (80,6), so that his failure in recognition makes him as eager for combat as Kaylet had been in a similar situation (39,15). On this occasion we do not need to be told expressly that the failure in recognition resulted from Gahmuret's changed coat of arms, although this reason certainly lies behind the later insistence of this *Anschevîn* and those with him[65] that Gahmuret cannot be present at Kanvoleis (98,19: '*wer was von Anschouwe dâ? / unser hêrre ist leider anderswâ, / durch rîters prîs zen Sarrazîn*').[66] Such certainty could have been undermined only if Gahmuret had been bearing the coat of arms of his dynasty.

Despite his ability to recognise these compatriots Gahmuret is in another respect the victim of his ignorance. The narrator tells his listeners of the death of Galoes (80,17f.),[67] but also that Gahmuret does not know this for certain (80,28: *daz enwesser leider, wie / er starp vor Muntôrî*), even though, because the *Anschevîn* carries his shield upside down (80,9f.; cf. also 92,1ff.), he suspects the worst (80,19ff.) and curses himself for not having asked Kaylet the obvious question about his brother (80,23ff.).[68] When an oppor-

---

64. It is left uncertain whether this knight from Anschouwe may not be related to Gahmuret. On this episode see also Harroff, *Wolfram*, pp. 25f.
65. In 80,7 Gahmuret's compatriot is mentioned in the singular, but from 98,15 (*Die den schilt verkêrt dâ hânt getragn*) with its plural formulation it is clear that he was accompanied by followers.
66. The failure in recognition described in 98,19ff. is the converse of Gahmuret's recognition of Kaylet at Zazamanc: the knights from Anschouwe believe that their feudal lord is in the Middle East, whereas Gahmuret had been assured that Kaylet was present, and they are also led astray by the change in Gahmuret's coat of arms, whilst he had been helped by recognising his kinsman's crest.
67. On the restriction of this narratorial comment to the listeners see above, p. 39.
68. We are not told why Kaylet failed to mention the death of his brother to Gahmuret, but this is presumably because he assumed that Gahmuret had heard of this already or because of the heat of excitement over the approaching tournament.

tunity later presents itself Gahmuret now asks Kaylet, voicing his suspicion that Galoes must be dead (91,9ff.). Kaylet confirms this assumption, converting it into final certainty by giving circumstantial details (91,16ff.), more than even the listeners were earlier told by the narrator. At this point we are told expressly that Gahmuret now knows the truth for the first time (92,9: *Dô er vernam des bruoder tôt, / daz was sîn ander herzenôt*), whereas before he could only assume it. This is also the occasion for him to realise that his wanderings are over and that he now succeeds his brother as ruler of Anschouwe (92,12ff.).

Gahmuret's tragic enlightenment has one more step to go, however, for he next learns from Kaylet of the quite unsuspected death of his mother (92,23ff.). Here there is no learning by instalments for him and hence no cushioning of the shock (as there had been with the death of his brother), but equally no advance information is conveyed to the listeners by the narrator (as with the death of Galoes). This serves to increase the effect of sudden shock which the listeners are made to experience with Gahmuret and which is heightened by our being told the mother's name (92,24f.) ånd therefore something of her individuality only at the moment when we learn that she is irrevocably lost.

When he encounters the prince from Anschouwe we are left in no doubt about Gahmuret's superior knowledge: he recognises this prince, even though the converse is not true. This inferiority of the would-be opponent is stressed again when an unspecified friend tells this *Anschevîn* and his followers that the victor of the tournament is likewise from Anschouwe (98,15: *Die den schilt verkêrt dâ hânt getragn / den begunde ir friwent ze velde sagn / 'frou Herzeloyd diu künegîn / hât behabt den Anschevîn'*). They claim to know of no other *Anschevîn* present, the only one absent from their horizon is Gahmuret who they are sure is still in the East (98,19ff.). They are corrected on this, and fittingly the facts on which this correction is based come from Kaylet, the bridge between Zazamanc and Kanvoleis. More specifically, they are told that the bearer of the heraldic *anker* and Gahmuret are one and the same (98,23: '*der hie den prîs hât bezalt / unt sô mangen ritter ab gevalt, / unt der sô stach unde sluoc, / unt der den tiwern anker truoc / ûf dem helme lieht gesteinet, / daz ist den ir dâ meinet. / mir sagt der künec Kaylet, / der Anschevîn wær Gahmuret*'). The succession of four descriptive relative clauses, reinforced by the threefold anaphora of the relative

Gahmuret (Books I and II)

der, before the first hint of an equation is given in v. 28 heightens the tension and gives added emphasis to the final revelation.[69]

In these three encounters Gahmuret may not be recognised by others for what he is, but he is always able to recognise them and to act properly in the light of that knowledge by avoiding combat with a kinsman or compatriot. Even when he may not know an aspect of the situation for certain, as with the death of his brother Galoes, he is shown interpreting the sign of the inverted shields correctly and thus arriving at the truth (just as he is also shown to be correct in his intuitive assumption about Killirjacac's *Minnerittertum*).[70] In this ability to read the signs correctly, not to put a foot wrong, Gahmuret is as unproblematic as Gawan, who is also able to read correctly the sign of the three drops of blood in the snow.[71] The problem, the difficulty in acquiring the art of recognition, lies rather with the hero of the romance, Parzival.

---

69. Bartsch–Marti, fn. to 98,24–6, stress rather the impression of breathlessness achieved by the repetition of *unt*. A similar use of anaphora and repeated relative clauses to convey tension (and the nervousness with which the final confession is made) occurs in Parzival's admission to Trevrizent that he failed to ask the question at Munsalvæsche (488,16ff.).
70. In 46,24 the narrator tells his listeners of Killirjacac's motive in joining the expedition to the Middle East (*in wîbes dienster was gevarn*). Gahmuret is not privy to this communication, but he nonetheless guesses correctly in his assumption (47,6: '*ôwê junc süezer man, / waz solte her dîn kranker lîp? / sag an, gebôt dir daz ein wîp?*'). We are enabled to appreciate both Gahmuret's lack of actual knowledge and also the accuracy of his insight.
71. 301,21ff. See below, p. 128.

3
Parzival's youth (Books III and IV)

These two opening Books of the Parzival narrative belong together for a number of reasons: they treat of the period of Parzival's youth,[1] they demonstrate how he attains to knighthood, first in being taught it by Gurnemanz and then in putting it into practice for the first time at Pelrapeire,[2] and they also incorporate the folktale pattern of the hero setting out into the world, gaining an unexpected victory and the hand of a queen in marriage.[3] They constitute a unity which justifies us in taking them together as the first period in the hero's career.

Unlike his father, Parzival proceeds from a non-social context when he sets out from the wilderness of Soltane. Whereas Gahmuret was in a position to encounter people on his travels whom he already knew and could therefore recognise, Parzival knows nobody outside Soltane, so that the possibility of recognising or failing to recognise does not arise with him at the start of his travels. Nonetheless, the theme of recognition is relevant to the hero's early career in another sense, for at this stage we are repeatedly shown how he fails to recognise the relevance of what he has previously learned or experienced to his present situation. Already in his encounter with the knights what Parzival recalls of his mother's instruction on God accounts for his confusion of them with God[4] and he can assess knightly equipment only ludicrously in terms of

---

1. On Parzival's youth as the period in which he enters on his father's inheritance in Books III and IV see Green, *Departure*, pp. 399ff. On the start of the Parzival narrative in Book III see Schirok, *Aufbau*, p. 472.
2. Parzival's acquisition of knighthood is signalled by the use of the term *ritter* from the Gurnemanz episode on (170,6; 176,20; 179,14). The need to include Book IV in this process in which knighthood has to be practised and not merely learned is suggested by the various stages indicated by the narrator (174,14f.; 175,5f. (see below, p. 61); 197,3).
3. On this folktale pattern in Books III and IV see Green, *Departure*, pp. 352ff.
4. See below, pp. 62f.

Parzival's youth (Books III and IV)

the non-chivalric world of his upbringing.[5] This dogmatic clinging to what he already knows is especially true of the way in which Parzival applies his mother's counsel to the situations he encounters after he has set out,[6] but the poet is careful to extend this failure in recognition to other situations as well.[7] In addition, although the recognition of a person's identity may be irrelevant to Parzival's early career, he can be shown failing to recognise an essential truth about him (as with the chivalry of Karnahkarnanz,[8] the unique function of king Arthur,[9] his own kinship with Ither)[10] or as simply ignorant of the truth they have to give him (he might have learned about love from Jeschute, he does learn of chivalry and courtliness from Gurnemanz, just as he is told his own name by Sigune). Finally, since Parzival proceeds from the anonymity of a non-social context, others may fail to recognise who he is (this is true of his distant kinsmen, Arthur and Ither, as opposed to Sigune, who does recognise him) or may recognise him only externally and superficially.[11]

As with Gahmuret, a number of linguistic details alert us to the need to pay close attention to possible hints by the narrator. Something is conveyed to us, but not to Parzival, when his victory in the jousting sports organised by Gurnemanz (175,5) is commented on by the narrator (175,6: *er wart ouch sît an strîte wîs*). Although Parzival has reached a new stage by his jousting victory, we are reminded by the narrator's forecast that another stage still lies ahead, that he will have to demonstrate his knightly skill in

---

5. 123,28ff. and 124,11ff.
6. See Green, *Advice*, pp. 38ff.
7. He thus asks whether Schionatulander was killed with a *gabylôt* (139,3). His demand to Ither for his armour rests on the belief that Arthur has given it him (154,6; cf. 150,4ff.), which in turn derives from the view that the answer of Karnahkarnanz (123,7ff.) confirms Parzival's original question (123,6: *'wer gît ritterschaft?'*). In the scene with Iwanet Parzival insists on wearing the *ribbalîn* given by his mother under his knightly armour (156,25ff.) and still clings to his rustic *gabylôt* (157,17ff.). He sees the castle of Gurnemanz in terms of the agricultural world of Soltane (see below, p. 64) and is hard to budge from the horse which he thinks Arthur gave him (163,22ff.).
8. Parzival is so blinded by external appearances that he takes the resplendent knight to be the God about whom he has learned from Herzeloyde. The hero's career from *tumpheit* to *wîsheit* can be summed up in the need for him to learn how to pierce through the external appearances to which he falls victim in his first encounter.
9. See Bartsch–Marti, fn. to 147,21.
10. See below, p. 83.
11. This point has been well made by Hahn, *Schönheit*, pp. 218f.

serious combat as well as in a mere tournament.[12] Such a comment is anything but straightforward, however, when the narrator adopts what appears to be a conventional courtly stance, regretting the inability of Parzival and Condwiramurs, because of their inexperience, to profit from their nocturnal meeting in his bedroom (193,8: *ober si hin an iht nem? / leider des enkan er niht*). That we should not interpret this stance straightforwardly as regret (*leider*) is made clear only later in the episode of the *trinoctium castitatis* at the start of their married life, where their chastity is now seen entirely positively and indeed as a higher form of sensitive tact (201,21: *mit sölhen fuogen*)[13] than the conventional courtly response shown by the narrator in earlier regretting their wasted opportunity.

Again as with the Books devoted to the hero's father, the narrator can also manipulate his listeners by presenting things from one character's subjective point of view, so that we experience them as he does, but also by allowing us to realise more of the situation than he can possibly know. Yet when this technique is employed in the case of Parzival, we should realise what a contrast this represents to the position with his father. Gahmuret's point of view, when we were allowed to share it, was essentially knowledgeable and well-informed (by recognising others he could avoid combat with a kinsman); it was others whose point of view was no more than partial (the majority at Kanvoleis know him only as *der künec von Zazamanc* and his compatriots are ignorant that he too is an *Anschevîn*). By contrast, Parzival's point of view is incomplete and ill-informed, to the extent that he learns from others it is they who are knowledgeable.

Parzival's subjective thought processes are objectivised for us by the narrator when he confuses the knights with gods. When this confusion is first reported to us (120,27f.), no reason for his belief is given; when it is mentioned on a second occasion, a partial, purely visual reason is given (121,30: *den dûhter als ein got getân: / ern hete sô liehtes niht erkant*); whilst only on the third occasion is an explicit reference given to Herzeloyde's teaching on God (122,21: *der knappe wânde, swaz er sprach, / ez wære got, als im verjach / frou Herzeloyd diu künegîn, / dô sim underschiet den liehten schîn*). By presenting his explanation in several stages the narrator captures

---

12. Cf. Bartsch–Marti, fn. to 175,5.
13. On this scene see Schumacher, *Auffassung*, pp. 37ff.

Parzival's youth (Books III and IV)

something of Parzival's gradual perception of what he regards as the truth, that the resplendence of these knights means that they are the God[14] of whose splendour he has learned from his mother. Such narratorial comments as insights into Parzival's thoughts need not always demonstrate how wrong his opinions are, as is clear from the scene where Parzival sits silent in the company of his hostess Condwiramurs.[15] We are at first given a general assessment by the narrator (188,15: *sîn manlîch zuht was im sô ganz*), but this is then qualified by the considerations which guided Parzival in acting like this (188,16: *sît in der werde Gurnemanz / von sîner tumpheit geschiet / unde im vrâgen widerriet, / ez enwære bescheidenlîche*). Parzival acts correctly by following the advice of his courtly mentor, so that the narrator's comment here objectivises his subjective psychology, it does duty for the thoughts passing through his mind.[16]

For the most part, and certainly before his training is taken in hand by Gurnemanz, this point of view technique is applied to Parzival to bring home to us the extent of his ignorance. The description of the knightly splendour of Karnahkarnanz (121,30ff.) is presented from the boy's point of view, so that we can appreciate the forceful impression it makes on him and why he asks his string of questions. This descriptive passage is therefore introduced in terms of Parzival's mental reaction (121,30: *den dûhter*) and of what he sees (122,1: *ern hete sô liehtes niht erkant*) and the boy's questions show us the knight's armour from his lowly position on foot before the mounted warrior (123,24: '*dort oben unt hie unden*').[17] Even before this visual highlight, when the other three knights are first glimpsed by Parzival, the narrator's focus reflects what the boy can see (120,24: *nu seht, dort kom geschûftet her / drî ritter nâch wunsche var*). By his interjection *nu seht* the narrator invites his audience, as it were, to look over Parzival's shoulder at the approaching knights, whilst the adverbs of place (*dort, her*) force the boy's perspective upon us as much as when he uses them himself in addressing

---

14. By regarding each of the three knights as a god (120,27f.) and then also Karnahkarnanz (121,30) Parzival is shown naïvely taking what amounts to an individualised proper name as an appellative, as is later also the case with Arthur (147,22), Liaze (188,1ff.) and possibly Lähelin (155,25, see below p. 82).
15. On this scene see Green, *Advice*, pp. 55f.
16. This is also suggested by the reference to Parzival's thoughts on other occasions when he acts in accordance with Gurnemanz's advice (203,2; 213,29).
17. A similarly specific point of view is suggested by the use of the word *diz* in 124,2 ('*war zuo ist diz guot*') in talking of the knight's chainmail. A more impersonal attitude would have called forth *daz*.

Karnahkarnanz (123,24). Parzival's perspective is also presented to us in very visual terms as he draws near to the castle of Gurnemanz. As with the description of knightly splendour, we catch our first glimpse of the castle with Parzival himself (161,23: *er dersach*), what we are shown comes to us through the medium of his thoughts as he sees it (161,25: *dûhte*; 161,28: *wânder*). In his inexperience[18] the boy can only take his perspective as the objective truth, so that for him, as he approaches, the towers of the castle appear to be growing visibly, a miraculous fact which he can interpret only from the agricultural preoccupations of his earlier existence at Soltane by imputing such rapid growth of what he takes to be plants to the 'Königsheil'[19] of king Arthur (161,25ff.).[20]

In these examples we have been allotted a viewpoint identical with Parzival's by the narrator presenting things to us in a carefully limited perspective. There are other ways open to him, however, which allow him to equate his audience with his hero, to include us in Parzival's experience. The least important of these, because the most obvious, is the occasional plea of ignorance, as on the occasion of the battle at Pelrapeire, where the narrator leaves it an open question whether the besieged inhabitants will in fact be rescued (185,17: *ir lîp ist nu benennet phant, / sine lœse drûz diu hôhste hant*) or what the outcome of Parzival's single combat with Clamide is to be (210,27: *ûz kom geriten Parzivâl / an daz urteillîche wal, / dâ got erzeigen solde / ober im lâzen wolde / des künec Tampenteires parn*).[21] By a pretence of ignorance the narrator has placed his listeners temporarily within the restricted horizon of those engaged in the narrative action, particularly Parzival as the centre of that action.

This is also done in the narrator's first reference to Parzival's stupidity. The three knights are quick to see this (121,5f.), but the narrator then comments on it himself (121,7: *ein prîs den wir Beier*

---

18. Cf. 161,25 (*den tumben*) and 162,1 (*der tumbe man*).
19. Both Martin (*Kommentar*, under 161,29) and Bartsch–Marti (fn. to 161,29) take *heilikeit* as implying that Parzival regards Arthur as a Christian saint, even though this leads the latter to comment: 'Es ist auffallend, daß der *tumbe* Parzival von Heiligen etwas weiß'. We avoid this discrepancy if we explain Arthur's agricultural success in terms of his 'Königsheil', which also has the advantage of showing Parzival interpreting something new only on the basis of what he already knows (see above, pp. 60f.). On the concept of royal 'Geblütsheiligkeit' in the Middle Ages see Hauck, *Geblütsheiligkeit*, pp. 187ff., and on its agricultural implications see Chaney, *Cult*, pp. 86, 90, 94, and 113. See also the quotation from Alcuin given by Bosl, *Frühformen*, p. 31: *Regis bonitas est ... terrae habundantia*.
20. Another subjective impression is given when Gawan approaches the castle of Logroys (508,2ff.), but this is attributed in a generalisation to any *tumbe* who might see it, whereas in 161,25ff. the *tumbe* is specifically Parzival alone.
21. This is comparable to what we saw above, p. 40.

Parzival's youth (Books III and IV)

tragn, | muoz ich von Wâleisen sagn: | die sint tœrscher denne beiersch her). This has generally been interpreted in terms of the equation between poet and hero,[22] but more important in our context is the fact that *wir Beier* also establishes a possible link between the audience and the hero, so that the listeners are forced to feel uncomfortably close, rather than necessarily superior to *dirre tœrsche Wâleise* (121,5), specifically in terms of the proverbial lack of wisdom common to both.[23] Something similar, but with more obviously positive implications, is suggested when Parzival excuses himself for leaving Gurnemanz with the plea that he needs to put his recently acquired chivalry to good practical use before he can think of love (178,29: *dô sprach er 'hêrre, in bin niht wîs: | bezal abr i'emer ritters prîs, | sô daz ich wol mac minne gern, | ir sult mich Lîâzen wern'*).[24] If it is the beginning of wisdom to realise that one is not wise, then Parzival, referring not just to the practical skills of chivalry but to the purposes which it should serve, has now taken a decisive step in this act of self-recognition, but one which is comparable with what the narrator said of the *wîser man* among his listeners (2,5ff.), that he should acknowledge that he had much to learn from Wolfram's work.[25] If both Parzival and this category of listener are to traverse the same path from *tumpheit* to *wîsheit*, this emphasises how close these listeners are to the hero's predicament, how they are to regard his stumbling progress as their own.

Other links between Parzival's ignorance and the audience are less tangible, but more extensive in their ramifications. If Parzival grows up in childish ignorance of his own name and learns it only when he encounters Sigune for the first time,[26] it is an indication of the narrator's control of his audience that we are told his name at the same point, so that our path to enlightenment is identical with his.[27] A similar parallel between Parzival's experience and how it is presented to us underlies his movement through space, not merely

---

22. Cf. Haas, *Tumpheit*, p. 63.
23. On the Bavarians' reputation in this respect see Martin, *Kommentar*, under 121,7ff., and Meissburger, *Grundlagen*, pp. 30f. On the similar reputation of the Welsh see Hilka's edition of Chrétien's *Perceval*, pp. 620f., note to v. 243f., and Le Rider, *Chevalier*, pp. 143ff. The link between Bavarian audience and hero which I suggest here is true only of those occasions when the poem was recited in this part of Germany. On other occasions the listeners could be made to feel superior.
24. See Haas, *op. cit.*, pp. 91f.
25. See above, p. 24.
26. See below, p. 79.
27. This needs to be qualified in the light of the point made above (pp. 17ff.): the perceptive listeners have already been discreetly given the means of recognising the protagonist's name, so that the synchronising of enlightenment concerns Parzival and the less perceptive members of the audience.

in Books III and IV but up to the moment when he departs from Munsalvæsche in Book V. It has been shown that miraculous, ultimately providential guidance is at work in Parzival's movement through space after setting out from Soltane, taking him unfailingly from station to station and leading him to Munsalvæsche.[28] Parzival is quite unaware of this, however, so that nothing more than good fortune or chance seems to him to be involved. The listeners for their part only begin to appreciate the significance of this guidance at the point where Parzival has forfeited it (249,4: *alrêrst nu âventiurt ez sich*), so that we feel the full magnitude of his loss in learning of this miraculous privilege when it has just been withdrawn from him.[29] Although the listeners now know more than Parzival, they were nowhere before this point provided with narrator's comments unequivocal enough to indicate that supernatural assistance was guiding the hero from Soltane to Munsalvæsche. Instead, the narrator's comments over this early span of Parzival's journey are so ambiguous that, whilst reconcilable with the fact of miraculous guidance, they nowhere afford us certainty or allow us to grasp this fact at the time. By rhetorical means the narrator therefore puts us in the same position as Parzival, who witnesses and experiences events without understanding their significance. Parzival's ignorance of the situation is reflected in the narrator's withholding of information from his listeners.

So far the narrator's technique has been to make us share Parzival's point of view, to place us on the same level of understanding, but it grows more complicated when, by contrast, he also provides the listeners with information withheld from Parzival.[30] If

- 28. Cf. Wynn, *Speculum* 36 (1961), 393ff.
- 29. I have developed this argument in greater detail in two different contexts: *Weg*, pp. 11ff. and *Pathway*, pp. 174ff.
- 30. Although the position of Parzival is what primarily concerns us, this technique can also be used occasionally of other people. When Herzeloyde commands her serfs to keep her son away from knighthood (117,22ff.) we already know (and do not have to wait for the narrator's forecast in 117,29) that this is a vain hope from earlier narratorial forecasts of the hero's warrior career (109,10f. and 112,28ff.). When Orilus voices his suspicion that Jeschute has a lover (133,10) we know that this is not so and that Parzival is comically far from such courtly eroticism, as is explicitly confirmed later (139,15ff.) by the narrator's contrast of him with his father. We are also enabled to see through Clamide's groundless accusation (212,4ff.) that his opponent is scoring an unfair advantage over him by having a sling-machine hurl stones at him. We realise that Parzival has no need to fall back on such unfair means, because we already know from Kingrun's combat with him that Parzival's blows can indeed be compared with the force of a sling-machine hurling stones (197,20ff.).

Parzival's youth (Books III and IV)

we follow through the events centred on the hero, his ignorance is contrasted with the knowledge transmitted to us by the narrator on a number of occasions. We know from his express formulation that when her son leaves her Herzeloyde dies for grief (128,20ff.), whereas Parzival, unlike his French counterpart, does not look back and knows nothing of this until he learns it from Trevrizent (476,12ff.). From Orilus's boasting to his wife we learn of a close connection between himself and Parzival, for he claims it as a sign of his prowess that he killed Galoes, the hero's uncle (134,23ff.). This death had been reported earlier (91,16ff.), but without any mention of Orilus as responsible, so that the truth comes out in instalments[31] – for the audience, but not for Parzival who has passed on out of this scene before Orilus returns to his wife. For the same reason we know, but Parzival is blithely unaware, that Orilus sets out in pursuit of him (138,3: *doch wesse der unverzagte / niht daz man in jagte*), which is accentuated when, wishing to avenge Schionatulander (who was also killed by Orilus), Parzival is deliberately put on the wrong track by Sigune,[32] anxious to avoid further tragedy (141,25ff.). Cunneware's prophetic laughter at Arthur's court also reveals a gulf between our understanding and his. All that is visible to Parzival is the fact of her laughter (151,19), whereas in the preceding lines (151,11ff.) the narrator tells us details unknown to him: her name, the fact that she had never laughed before and the reason why she should do so now. Traces of *tumpheit* still cling to Parzival when, on first catching sight of Condwiramurs, he uses the name Liaze almost as a generic term (188,1ff.), as he had that of Arthur at the Round Table. If he shows thereby that he has no standards by which to judge supreme feminine beauty, this is corrected for us, but not for Parzival, by the narrator's comment (188,6f.) leaving us in no doubt about the superiority of Condwiramurs.[33]

These examples have not touched the episodes of Parzival's encounter with Ither and his activity at Pelrapeire, in both of which the listeners are several times given more information than the protagonist. It is ironic that in impatiently demanding Ither's

---

31. On the effect of these recurrent instalments see Green, *Homicide*, p. 47.
32. Cf. Gibbs, *MLR* 63 (1968), 872.
33. Another interpretation would be to see Parzival not using the name of Liaze as a generic noun, but as struck by the likeness between Liaze and Condwiramurs, since they are after all cousins (cf. 189,27f.). Even so, Parzival's equation of the two still has to be corrected by the narrator.

knightly gear for himself Parzival should say '*ob du bî witzen sîst*' (154,10), thereby using a conditional formulation elsewhere used of himself.[34] Parzival cannot realise, as the listeners can from their repeated observation of his folly, that the boot is on the other foot and that this formula is more justifiably used of himself. The account of the killing of Ither is followed immediately by a narratorial forecast of the grief it will cause (155,12ff.). More important than the Round Table's ignorance of what has happened is Parzival's unawareness of the qualities of his opponent (so far from being another Lähelin, 154,25, Ither was in fact *der valscheit widersatz*, 155,11) and of the fact that Parzival has here proved himself to be much more like Lähelin.[35] In taking up this lament for Ither again (161,1ff.) the narrator anticipates a future when Parzival's greater insight will cause him to repent this youthful folly (161,7f.) – of this future growth in insight, as of his present lack of it, Parzival is unaware. The same is true of the sigh and regret felt by Gurnemanz for Ither's fate (170,4) – this tactfully unvoiced reaction is conveyed to us by the narrator, thereby bypassing the hero.

At Pelrapeire the narrator, contrary to his pretence of ignorance, can forecast Parzival's forthcoming victory (183,2).[36] In describing the starvation of the besieged inhabitants he states that this was the result of their queen turning down Clamide's offer of marriage (184,19: *des twanc si ein werder man, / der stolze künec von Brandigân: / si arnden Clâmidês bete*). We are not told that Parzival knows anything of this, but the retentive listener, recalling what Gurnemanz has said of Clamide's attack on Condwiramurs (177,30ff.), has an advantage over the hero in being able to surmise, if not to know for certain,[37] that Parzival has arrived at the city of Condwiramurs. We are also told expressly that Parzival was initially unaware of the extent of suffering at Pelrapeire (185,26: *ir grôziu nôt was im unkuont*). All he knows so far is the aggressive defensiveness of the inhabitants (181,11ff.)[38] and the fact that an army is campaigning against the city (182,20ff.). Parzival later learns of this suffering from Condwiramurs herself and is thus impressed by it far more,

34. Cf. 123,2 ('*ob du ze rehte kundest spehn*'); 124,20 ('*ob du mit witzen soldest lebn*'); 131,25 ('*wært ir ze frumen wîse*').
35. Green, *Homicide*, pp. 67f.
36. Cf. also 199,18.
37. On the remaining element of uncertainty in this see below, p. 84.
38. We learn more than this, namely that they are so aggressive because they take Parzival for Clamide (181,18). See below, p. 85.

Parzival's youth (Books III and IV)

first by her factual remark (190,7f.) and then much more effectively by what she says in the bedroom scene (194,14ff.). If Parzival by such stages catches up with the knowledge given to the listeners in the beginning, this example is not unique in these two Books and presupposes a narrative period when we know more than he because of what the narrator passes on to us.[39]

The two techniques we have been following complement one another: in one case the narrator conveys facts to his listeners which are concealed from Parzival, whilst in the other such information is withheld and they are forced into the same position of ignorance as he. That these two rhetorical approaches are meant as complementary can be shown from passages where the listeners both enjoy superior knowledge and are still ignorant of its full implications. Even if they may know more than the hero, the fact that they still have more to learn involves them in the same journey towards *wîsheit* as he. When Parzival encounters the knights in the forest he is clearly in the wrong in equating the brilliance of their armour with the resplendence of God and the listeners realise that he is mistaken. However, Parzival remembers more than what his mother had said of God's resplendence (119,19), he also recalls what she said of His willingness to help (119,23f.) and accordingly approaches the knights in this light, too (121,2: '*hilf, got: du maht wol helfe hân*'). Neither the boy nor the listeners can know that in this respect he has hit the nail on the head and that the narrative will confirm for us that knighthood does resemble God in being ready to

---

39. Thus, in 123,11 Parzival hears as a surmise from Karnahkarnanz the fact, known to us from his birth, that he is of knightly descent, and in 128,3ff. he learns from Herzeloyde the details of his royal birth with which we are already acquainted. Although we may apparently learn as much as Parzival when Sigune tells him his name (but see above, pp. 17ff.), he catches up with us when she also gives him details of his family (140,25ff.). From Gurnemanz's humorous comparison of his daughter Liaze with Jeschute (175,29ff.) Parzival also learns belatedly to appreciate the error of his ways in the earlier scene.
   A short-scale example is provided by Parzival's first glimpse of Schionatulander in Sigune's lap. The listeners are told from the start that this knight is dead (138,21: *Schîanatulander / den fürsten tôt dâ vander*), whilst Parzival grasps the truth in stages, assuming first that he is only wounded (138,30: *ritter wunden*), then using an ambiguous word (139,2: '*wer hât in erschozzen?*' – does this mean simply 'wounded with a spear' or 'killed with a spear'?) and finally arriving at the truth (139,4: '*mich dunket, frouwe, er lige tôt*'). This manner of conveying the boy's thought processes when confronted with a novel phenomenon resembles the technique of showing us what he thinks when he takes the knights in the wood to be gods (see above, p. 62).

bring help in an emergency.[40] When Parzival is told enough by Karnahkarnanz to show him that chivalry does incorporate compassion and helpfulness (122,15ff.) this only confirms him in the belief that this knight is God (122,26). Our superiority to Parzival's confusion in this encounter threatens our ability to see that in one sense he is unwittingly correct.

Gurnemanz recognises from Parzival's beauty that his guest must be not just a knight by birth,[41] but a ruler (170,21f.), and accordingly he opens his instruction by giving advice specifically suited to a future ruler (170,23ff.). The knightly mentor therefore imparts his superior wisdom to one in need of it (171,14f.) and the audience is in a position to appreciate both this superior wisdom and its adequacy to Parzival's needs.[42] But neither Gurnemanz nor the listeners can realise at this stage that this advice is even more relevant to one who will later become a particular kind of ruler, the Grail-king, and that it has an unexpected bearing on Parzival before Anfortas on his first visit to Munsalvæsche.[43] Gurnemanz cannot know this (for the further dimension to his words is imparted only by the narrator using him as a mouthpiece), Parzival has no conception at all, whilst the listeners are enlightened only subsequently. A similar undermining of the listeners' position (the superiority of their knowledge to Parzival's ignorance is relativised by their ignorance of a vital fact) is achieved in the scene when Parzival takes what he regards as temporary leave from Condwiramurs after his marriage to her (223,15ff.). He is specific about a short period of absence (223,22: *zeiner kurzen stunt*) and about his wish to see how things are with his mother as well as to seek adventure. Parzival's first motive clearly places the listeners in the superior position of dramatic irony, for they already know of her death when he left Soltane (128,20ff.), whilst Parzival was unaware of this, a fact which is underlined again at the conclusion of Book IV (223,19: '... *wiez umbe mîne muoter stê.*/*ob der wol oder wê*/*sî, daz ist mir harte unkunt*'). But this knowledge of the listeners is combined with an

40. When Karnahkarnanz asserts (122,29) '*Ich pin nicht got,/ich leiste ab gerne sîn gebot*', this is in direct response to Parzival's request (122,26: '*nu hilf mir, hilferîcher got*'). The knight therefore rejects one part of the boy's words, the suggestion that he is God, but claims of the knightly function of bringing assistance that it is a way of serving God.
41. As had first been suggested by Karnahkarnanz (123,11).
42. For they will recall that this is what Parzival has hitherto been deprived of (118,2: *an künecliche fuore betrogn*).
43. See Mohr, *Hilfe*, p. 186 and Green, *Advice*, pp. 67ff.

ignorance which they share with Parzival: neither can realise that the separation from Condwiramurs will not be short, but will last for years, or that the adventure which awaits the hero (at Munsalvæsche) is an unconventional one, testing him in an unexpectedly non-chivalric way,[44] or finally that, in gaining access to Munsalvæsche, he is unwittingly returning, if not to his mother, then to his mother's realm, for it is only through her that he can be considered as a candidate for the Grail at all (333,30).[45]

This double technique of the narrator, supplying privileged information to his readers, but also withholding it from them at times, is reflected, as with the Gahmuret narrative, in the way in which he conveys the names of characters involved in the action of Books III and IV, either naming them immediately they begin to play a part or deferring the revelation of their name for a lengthy period.

The immediate naming of a character presents little difficulty and it is true of almost all the characters in these Books. Sometimes their name is given in the first line in which they are referred to in the narrative action (e.g. 129,27: *duc Orilus de Lalander*), but sometimes the timelag is a few lines only (e.g. 129,28: *wîp*; 129,30: *die herzoginne rîche*; 130,2: *si hiez Jeschute*) or at the most a 'Dreissiger' or two (e.g. 135,22: *eime fürsten*; 138,21: *Schîanatulander*). Such a negligible timelag is incapable of creating the suspense which arises whenever a character remains in baffling anonymity over a longer stretch of narrative action, so that all such cases can be grouped together as unproblematic examples of immediate naming. They comprise the vast majority of characters who first enter the action of Wolfram's work in Book III (in narrative sequence they run from

---

44. See Green, *Aventiure*, pp. 137ff.
45. Green, *Departure*, pp. 405ff. On the implications of this line see below, pp. 215f.
   Other examples of the listeners knowing more than a character in the work, but still having more to learn are connected with the figure of Orilus in particular. We know from the beginning who Jeschute's husband is by name (129,27), but not yet that he is the brother of Lähelin, of whose violence we have just learnt from Herzeloyde (128,3ff.). From Orilus himself we learn that he is the brother of Cunneware (135,14f.), but this means nothing to us until she enters the Parzival action. Similarly, Orilus's boast about having recently killed an unnamed knight (135,21ff.) only begins to assume importance for us when we witness the corpse of Schionatulander in the next episode. When Parzival, eager to gain vengeance on Orilus, is deliberately misdirected by Sigune (141,25ff.), even this concealed assistance leads him into danger of another kind, since the path she points out takes him to the encounter with Ither and the killing of a kinsman (see Gibbs, *MLR* 63 (1968), 872). In all these cases what is ultimately revealed as the partial knowledge of the audience is not shared by Parzival.

Karnahkarnanz to Liaze) and Book IV (from Clamide to Galogandres).[46] The fact that this technique is used of nearly all the characters in these Books inevitably draws our attention to the two exceptions which are, hardly surprisingly, Parzival and Condwiramurs: these are the only characters whose naming does not take place immediately, but is deferred for some time.

Reference had been made at the close of Book II to the hero of the romance (112,5ff.), but since at this point he is a newly born baby he cannot be said to play any part in the action and it is hardly surprising that he should not yet be equipped with a personal name. But when, after the lapse of some years, Herzeloyde's son first enters the narrative action in Book III (from 117,15) he is from our point of view still nameless; the narrator continues to use a variety of circumlocutions of him from the beginning of the Book until 140,16 (*'deiswâr du heizest Parzivâl'*), when we are told his name by Sigune at the same time as he.[47] This point has to be qualified, since this is not the first occasion for the name of Parzival to be mentioned. Before the Sigune episode it occurs once only, in Book I when the beauty of Kaylet is qualified by the observation that it is to be surpassed by two others not yet born, by Beacurs, the brother of Gawan, and by Parzival (39,24: *unz an zwên die nâch im wuohsen sît, / Bêâcurs Lôtes kint / und Parzivâl, die dâ niht sint: / die wâren dennoch ungeborn, / und wurden sît für schœne erkorn*). Yet we cannot

---

46. The evidence for this immediate naming is as follows. In Book III we encounter Karnahkarnanz (he enters the action in 121,15 and is named for us by 121,26f.), Jeschute (the timelag is from 129,28 to 130,2), Orilus (named in 129,27 before he enters the action in 132,28, but this is soon followed by his name again in 133,5), Sigune (from 138,11 to 138,17), Schionatulander (referred to anonymously 135,22, but named in 138,21), Arthur (143,23, but then named again as he enters the action in 148,29), Ither (from 145,7 to 145,15), Keii (150,13), Cunneware (referred to by name in advance in 135,15, but then again when she enters the action in 151,11), Antanor (152,23), Gurnemanz (162,6) and Liaze (from 175,13 to 175,25).

    Book IV brings rather fewer characters under this heading: Clamide (mentioned in advance in 178,3 and 181,18, but again when the action concerns him in 184,21), Kingrun (mentioned in advance in 178,3 and again once the action touches him in 194,15), Kyot (186,21), Manpfilyot (186,22) and Galogandres (from 204,21 to 205,9).

47. I have discussed some of the circumlocutions used for Parzival in *Namedropping*, pp. 127ff. Cf. also Green, *Naming*, pp. 103ff. An important point is that the narrator, once he has chosen to defer naming his hero until 140,16, cannot avoid falling back on anonymous epithets and circumlocutions before this point, but that he may choose for reasons of his own to revert to this anonymous technique even after this point.

argue from this early mention of his name that we have been enabled to pierce Parzival's anonymity and realise who he is from the moment we encounter him in narrative action at the start of Book III.[48] At the time when Parzival's name is first mentioned in Book I we have no idea who this Parzival is, whose *kint* he is (by contrast, we learn something about Beacurs, that he is the son of Lot),[49] what he may have to do with the story, let alone whether he is *dirre âventiur hêrre* (140,13). Before Sigune's revelation we know from 112,5ff. that the son of Gahmuret and Herzeloyde is *dirre âventiur hêrre*, but only from 140,16 do we learn his actual name.

The narrator's technique in naming Condwiramurs is very similar. She first enters the narrative action anonymously in Book IV as the daughter of Tampenteire (180,26f.)[50] and thereafter she is referred to by equally anonymous epithets[51] until 187,12, when we are informed of her name for the first time. As with Parzival, the initial anonymity of Condwiramurs is not abolished for us by the fact that her name has previously been mentioned by Gurnemanz at the close of Book III, when talking of the death of his son while defending her against Clamide (177,29: '*der was geheizen Schenteflûrs. / dâ Cundwîramûrs / lîp unde ir lant niht wolte gebn, / in ir helfer flôs sîn lebn / von Clâmidê und von Kingrûn*'). Again as with Parzival, there is no unequivocal link between this woman's name and the anonymous queen whom we encounter soon afterwards, and even if we may suspect their identity we are not given certainty on this point until 187,12. Before that we know from Gurnemanz that Condwiramurs is queen of an unnamed land[52] and from the narrator at the start of Book IV that an anonymous lady is queen of

---

48. Cf. Cucuel, *Eingangsbücher*, p. 7. See also above, pp. 17ff., for a necessary qualification.
49. Lot is named to us as Gawan's father soon afterwards in *Parzival* (66,9ff.). Quite apart from this, Gawan's father was known to be Loth already in Geoffrey of Monmouth's *Historia Regum Britanniae* and in Chrétien's *Erec* (1737) and *Yvain* (6267).
50. To call Condwiramurs the daughter of Tampenteire on the first occasion when the action concerns her directly is not so informative for the listeners as to refer to Beacurs as the son of Lot, for they will know who *Lôt von Norwæge* is, but will have no prior information about Tampenteire, a figure peculiar to Wolfram's work.
51. Over this stretch of the narrative Condwiramurs is referred to as *kint* (180,27; 186,24), *küneginne* (182,30; 183,20; 186,12 + 19 + 25; 187,4), *frouwe* (186,12; 187,1) and *wirtîn* (187,11).
52. 177,30f.

Brobarz (180,18), so that we are denied the facts we need in order to equate them beyond doubt.[53]

Two effects are achieved by this delayed naming of the hero and the woman destined to be his wife. As far as Parzival is concerned, it is clear that the narrator has chosen for him a technique which is the converse of that used in the case of his father. In the first two Books Gahmuret had stood out by being individually named for us from the beginning (together with Belakane),[54] whilst other characters were introduced anonymously and given a name only later,[55] but in the next two Books the majority of characters are named immediately, whilst only Parzival and Condwiramurs remain nameless for a time. Each technique focuses our attention on the respective hero, Gahmuret and then his son, for each is made to stand out from the crowd in this way, but from Parzival's initial anonymity and ignorance of his own name we may already conclude that the problem of identity and self-recognition will preoccupy him as it did not his father.

The other effect can best be observed if we consider the possibility that, after Parzival is known to us by name, this name is free to be used of him by the narrator in subsequent episodes,[56] but that there may occur the occasional episode where the narrator withholds this name temporarily. We find this, for example, at the start of the Pelrapeire episode. Parzival is not recognised[57] by the inhabitants, who even mistake him for Clamide, so that the narrator last refers to the hero by name (182,7) as he crosses the bridge leading to the battlefield outside the city gate, then uses anonymous epithets and circumlocutions of him until 187,5,[58] when he is next referred to by name again. This short span of anonymity for Parzival reflects the fact that the inhabitants of Pelrapeire do not know who he is, whilst the similar anonymity of Condwiramurs captures the hero's

---

53. Another possibility of assuming a link between what Gurnemanz reports in Book III and the narrator recounts in Book IV is provided by the figure of Clamide, common to both. On the uncertainty of this, however, see below, p. 84.
54. And also the three princes defeated by Gahmuret, who are named as a means of attesting to his renown as victor (see above, p. 43).
55. See above, pp. 43f.
56. See below, p. 80.
57. Indeed, he cannot be recognised at Pelrapeire, since there is no previous link between them.
58. Parzival refers to himself by a courteous circumlocution (182,25: *'ein man | der iu dienet'*), whilst the narrator uses a number of nameless epithets: *helt* (182,18; 186,9 + 13), *gast* (185,22; 186,6) and *degen* (187,2).

Parzival's youth (Books III and IV)

ignorance of her identity. Moreover, the narrator's resumption of Parzival's name (187,5) coincides with his explicit revelation of Condwiramurs's identity (187,12), both names are revealed at the moment when they first meet (186,28ff.) so that the narrator's technique with their names stands in for their formal introduction and exchange of names, which need not be expressly narrated.[59] Both the knight and the lady thus step out of anonymous obscurity (with Parzival this is relative, with Condwiramurs absolute) on the same occasion, our attention is implicitly drawn to them before the narrator makes an explicit commentary on them as an obvious couple (187,24: *ez wâren wol nützia wîp, / die disiu zwei gebâren, / diu dâ bî ein ander wâren. / dô schuof wîp unde man / niht mêr wan daz si sâhen an / diu zwei bî ein ander*). This synchronised naming of Parzival and Condwiramurs at Pelrapeire also duplicates what we saw with Gahmuret and Herzeloyde at Kanvoleis;[60] in each case the

---

59. Other details not expressly narrated include the actual circumstances of the death of Galoes (this was reported to us in Book II (91,16ff.), but only from Orilus in 134,23ff. do we learn that he was responsible) and the boastful, overconfident message of Kingrun to Clamide (implicit in 204,5ff., but not previously narrated, cf. Bartsch–Marti, fn. to 204, 6–12).

Since in the preceding chapter (pp. 40ff.) we looked at this feature together with the narrator's predilection for opening up wider narrative dimensions, it would be as well to include the latter here briefly. He therefore narrates the death of Herzeloyde (128,17ff.) and the Karnahkarnanz episode (121,16ff.; cf. also 125,11ff.) through to its successful conclusion, he includes the quarrel scene between Orilus and Jeschute (132,25ff.) after Parzival has departed from the latter and he gives the lament for Ither's death at the Round Table (159,5ff.). In all these passages the listeners are given information not available to Parzival, but these digressions also serve a further poetic purpose in giving flesh and blood to motifs important to Wolfram. The conclusion of the Karnahkarnanz episode is significant in that it provides the first illustration in the Parzival story of altruistic chivalry in action, the scene of Herzeloyde's death acquires ironic force at the end of Book IV when Parzival hopes to return to her, the quarrel between Orilus and his wife is important for Parzival's second meeting with Jeschute (see below, pp. 118ff.), and the lament for Ither underlines the enormity of Parzival's killing.

Wolfram's widening of narrative horizons can also take in other romances of his day, including them within his narrative world and appropriating them for his own ends. Examples of this are the figure of Meljahkanz (cf. Martin, *Kommentar*, under 125,11, and Zimmermann, *Kommentar*, pp. 263ff., on Wolfram's acquaintance with Chrétien's *Lancelot*), the detail that Jeschute is presented as the sister of Erec and that her punishment at the hands of Orilus parallels that meted out by her brother to his wife, the introduction of king Arthur as a typical Hartmannesque figure (143,21ff.), and the incorporation of two figures from *Erec* amongst those who killed two of Gurnemanz's sons (on this see Rosskopf, *Traum*, pp. 181ff. and Green, *Irony*, pp. 62ff.).

60. See above, p. 46.

narrator carefully chooses the moment when he allows anonymity to be broken.

That this temporary withholding of a person's name for rhetorical purposes is no chance phenomenon can be shown from two related passages in which Kingrun and Clamide, each defeated by Parzival at Pelrapeire, are sent in turn to offer their *sicherheit* at the Round Table. These two figures act as links between the events at Pelrapeire and Arthur's court, so that it is fitting that they should allude to Parzival, their victor, by the type of anonymous reference by which alone he is known at the Round Table. We are not told that Parzival disclosed his name to the Round Table and this is rendered unlikely by the way in which, after Iwanet has reported to them the encounter between Parzival and Ither (including presumably the *rêroup*), they know him simply in terms of the red armour he now wears.[61] When Kingrun comes to the Round Table the narrator employs the distinctive circumlocution *den man dâ hiez den ritter rôt* (206,16) and the equally anonymous *meister* (206,27)[62] as a reflection of the Round Table's terminology. When he switches back to events at Pelrapeire (at 207,4) he reverts to the personal name by which Parzival is now known here (e.g. 207,12 and 23). In short, the narrator's readiness to use his name or to withhold it over an admittedly short span depends on the state of knowledge of the persons involved in each scene.

What is true of Kingrun is true of his lord Clamide. When he comes to the Round Table Parzival's name is avoided by the narrator over a longer span than with Kingrun and he is instead referred to as *der ritter rôt* (or simply as *ritter*, once this point has been made) or by an anonymous circumlocution of the type *der mit mir streit*.[63] Once the narrator again abandons this narrative thread and returns

61. Parzival is first referred to as *der ritter rôt* in the context of the Round Table in 206,16 and can continue to be so termed (see below, p. 104). Before this point he is referred to in this way at the castle of Gurnemanz (170,6; 176,20), by implication at the start of Book IV (179,14, see Hirschberg, *Untersuchungen*, pp. 81f.) and at Pelrapeire (202,21 and by implication in 203,29ff., see below, p. 87).
62. I take 206,10f. (*dô warber als in Parzivâl / gevangen hete dar gesant*), because of its use of the pluperfect, to refer to the preceding scene and not the present one, so that the name of Parzival is still withheld by the narrator from the Round Table.
63. The evidence is as follows: *ritter rôt* (218,4; 221,6) and *ritter* (220,13). The circumlocutions are '*der mit mir streit*' (218,10), '*der âne liegen ist gezelt / mit wârheit für den hôhsten prîs*' (221,24f.) and *den man gein im in kampfe sach* (222,2).

Parzival's youth (Books III and IV)

to Pelrapeire (at 222,10) he refers to Parzival, now in the context of those who know him, by name (222,13). In this case, as with Kingrun, the immediacy with which a change of scene involves a change in naming technique is the real pointer to what the narrator hopes to achieve by this double technique: he refers to the hero by terms which reflect the subjective point of view of others involved, of those who know Parzival and those who cannot recognise him. With this observation we may now approach the various encounter scenes in these two Books in which one type of recognition or another is involved. Not all encounter scenes yield material on this theme and it is for this reason that I pass over the meeting with the knights in the wood and start with Parzival's first encounter once he has actually set out from Soltane.

Parzival and Jeschute

We learn from the beginning who Jeschute is by name (130,2) and also the identity of her husband (129,27). Since this encounter comes at the start of Parzival's movement into the world, there is no possibility of his recognising or failing to recognise Jeschute, so that there is no reason why the narrator should withhold her name (or that of her husband) from the listeners. The audience is therefore in a superior position to Parzival for they are informed of the name of this couple and they also witness the quarrel scene between them, important for its future ramifications,[64] after Parzival has passed on out of this episode. In another sense, however, the listeners are on the same level of ignorance as the hero since, although they learn the identity of Orilus by name and something of his violent character, they are not yet told the vital fact that he is the brother of Lähelin, the equally bloodthirsty knight of whom Parzival has recently learned from his mother (128,3ff.).

If recognition of identity is out of the question as Parzival moves through an initially quite unknown world, recognition of what behaviour is called for is certainly relevant, especially since this is the first encounter where the boy's misapplication of his mother's advice results in dire consequences for another person. Parzival comes to regret his unseemly behaviour towards Jeschute only later, when Gurnemanz brings it home to him (175,29ff.), but at the moment he is conscious only of dutifully following his mother's

---

64. See below, pp. 119ff.

advice[65] about correct behaviour towards a lady (127,25ff.). The audience are certainly in no need of an express narratorial comment to register the full discrepancy between how Herzeloyde meant her advice and how her son carries it out, but nonetheless the narrator's choice of words underlines this. The situation is an eminently courtly one (a luxurious tent, a beautiful woman, the temptation she incorporates), so that the boy's impetuous, self-centred behaviour stands out all the more clearly, especially since the narrator describes this behaviour in terms pointing emphatically in the same direction. His actions are violent ones (*twanc*: 130,27: 131,13; *ranc*: 130,28; *spranc*: 131,1), they offend against the need for tact and moderation (*ze vil*: 131,9; cf. also 132,2f.), pay no regard to the other person's wishes (*ern ruochte*: 131,12; 132,1; *ân urloup*: 132,22; *âne den willen mîn*: 133,20), they amount to robbery (*roubes*: 132,25), discourtesy (*ungefuoge*: 131,18) and dishonour to his victim (*entêret*: 131,8). The narrator's later express comment (139,15ff.) is also meant, on the surface at least,[66] to show how far Parzival's behaviour fell short of the courtly ideal incorporated in his father by stressing how differently Gahmuret would have behaved in such a situation. But of none of these facts, obvious to the audience, does Parzival show any awareness and it is significant that his first assessment of his behaviour should have to be brought home to him by someone else, Gurnemanz.

Parzival and Sigune

In this scene, too, we learn Sigune's name and that of her dead lover from the beginning (138,17 and 21). Although Parzival learns during this meeting of his kinship with Sigune (140,22), we are not shown him also learning her name, but must assume that this happened, even if it is not narrated, because he addresses her by name when they meet on the next occasion (252,28). As with the Jeschute encounter, Parzival is referred to anonymously, at least at the beginning of the scene, since it is only from Sigune that he and we learn his name.

If at this important turning-point the hero's name is at last to be divulged by Sigune, the narrator has to motivate convincingly how this came about. Struck by the boy's beauty and compassionate

---

65. Cf. 130,29f. and 132,23f.
66. This qualification is necessary in view of Wolfram's later positive interpretation of Parzival's *trinoctium castitatis* as true courtesy (cf. Schumacher, *Auffassung*, pp. 37ff.).

Parzival's youth (Books III and IV)

eagerness to help her (139,25ff.), she asks him his name (140,4), to which Parzival replies by giving the pet-names by which he was known at Soltane (140,6: *'bon fîz, scher fîz, bêâ fîz, / alsus hât mich genennet / der mich dâ heime erkennet'*), a detail which had been carefully prepared for soon after the boy's birth (cf. 113,4). To anyone else these childish pet-names would have been as uninformative as in Chrétien's version when Perceval replies in similar terms to the knights in the forest when they ask him who he is (344ff.), but Wolfram is careful to motivate why this should not be so with Sigune and how pet-names of this kind allow her to recognise who this is (140,10: *si erkant in bî dem namen sân*). She can recognise him because of her kinship with his mother (140,22: *'dîn muoter ist mîn muome'*), so close that she owes her upbringing to Herzeloyde (141,13: *'dô zôch mich dîn muoter'*).[67] Their relationship is such that we are allowed to assume, as one of the background details not always directly narrated but partly visible to us,[68] that Sigune knew of the birth of Parzival and of the pet-names used by the doting mother even before she withdrew into the solitary wilderness. In addition, it is permissible to assume, given the way in which Sigune is led to ask Parzival his name after being struck by his beauty and *triuwe*, that these qualities, so characteristic of Parzival's family,[69] confirm his identity for her. She is thus able to tell Parzival his proper name (140,11: *nu hœrt in rehter nennen*), which is just as much news for most listeners, for only now are they told this individual detail of the hero (140,12: *daz ir wol müget erkennen / wer dirre âventiur hêrre sî*). How vital Sigune considers her information to be is shown by her equation of Parzival's name with the truth about himself which she is revealing to him (140,23: *'und sag dir sunder valschen list / die rehten wârheit, wer du bist'*) and by the details of his birth on both sides[70] and kingship over Norgals[71] which she then divulges to him (140,25ff.).

The question with which this scene confronts us is why Parzival

---

67. See Bartsch–Marti, fn. to 140,10. Cf. also *Titurel* 28ff.
68. Mohr has also treated of these in *Hintergründe*, pp. 174ff.
69. On the beauty of those belonging to Parzival's family see Johnson, *Beauty*, pp. 273ff. On Parzival's inherited *triuwe* see especially 451,3ff. and Schmid, *Studien*, pp. 179ff.
70. The importance of these genealogical connections has been discussed by Schultheiss, *Bedeutung*, pp. 1ff. and by Schwietering, *Natur*, pp. 450ff..
71. She thus tells him more about his feudal realms than he had learned from his mother in the different context of Lähelin (128,3ff.), but nothing about the possibility of Grail-kingship inherited from his mother.

should be depicted learning his name at this particular point in the narrative, whereas in Chrétien's version this happens later, on the only occasion when Perceval meets his kinswoman, after his departure from the Grail-castle. That Wolfram wishes to concentrate attention on this episode in particular cannot be doubted, because he not only transfers to it this motif from Chrétien's later scene, he also expunges earlier the question and answer about the hero's name which Chrétien had included in his version of the encounter with the knights in the forest.[72] The answer lies in the placing of the motif in the German work, for Parzival now learns his name not in the shadow of his failure at the Grail-castle, but rather on the brink of a cluster of specifically knightly episodes (Arthur, Ither, Gurnemanz) in all of which Parzival's name is now free to be used by the narrator.[73] This suggests that Parzival establishes his identity as part of the process of becoming a knight, but the predominance of the Ither episode in this cluster also suggests the dubious, sinful nature of that identity. If, as Bezzola has suggested, Chrétien's hero acquires his name in the context of regret for his failure at the Grail-castle,[74] Wolfram's remotivation places greater stress on the specifically knightly guilt incurred by Parzival.[75]

72. On this omission, allowing Wolfram to focus the theme of Parzival's name on this one scene, see Green, *Departure*, pp. 380f.
73. The narrator refers to Parzival by name in the scene with king Arthur in 148,27 and 153,14, in the scene with Ither on many more occasions (155,4 + 19; 156,7 + 10 + 12 + 28; 157,16; 159,30; 161,6), and with Gurnemanz three times (162,27; 165,6; 174,20).
74. Bezzola, *Sens*, p. 56: 'Le jeune homme, consterné de sa faillite au château du graal, se plonge dans l'abîme de sa propre existence et en devine le sens en devinant son nom.'
75. This would agree with the tenor of Mohr's argument, *Schuld*, pp. 196ff. In Chrétien's scene where Parzival guesses his name (3571ff.) his cousin changes his name from *Perceval li Galois* to *Perceval li cheitis* as an expression of the abhorrence she feels for his sin of omission (3578ff.). Wolfram can use nothing of this in his scene where Sigune tells Parzival his name at their first encounter (for he has not yet met Ither or been to Munsalvæsche), but he makes use of the motif elsewhere by transferring it to the Gurnemanz scene at the point where the knight learns how Parzival has acquired his armour by killing Ither (170,5: *sînen gast des namn er niht erliez, / den rôten ritter er in hiez*). To call Parzival *der rôte ritter* is a reminder of his chivalric offence, it is now Parzival's *wâpen*, in negative terms, as much as the *anker* had characterised his father in neutral terms. On Parzival's naming in this scene see also below, pp. 303f.

One other question arises from Wolfram's delayed naming of his hero: how would he have referred to his own work if, in the medieval recital situation, he had been asked in advance what it was about by an importunate member of his audience? What Haidu, *Lion*, pp. 53ff., has to say about Chrétien's 'rhétorique du titre' may help us here. He argues that only with his third romance did

Parzival's youth (Books III and IV)

Sigune passes on to her kinsman more than the immediate facts of his birth, however, for she also tells him about the net of feudal obligations in which he is unwittingly enmeshed (141,2ff.). She first informs him that Schionatulander was killed in the defence of Parzival's own territory (141,2f.) so that, although he may not have realised it, Parzival does have an obligation towards him and was instinctively right in offering vengeance (139,7ff.). But the net of obligations grows tighter when Parzival learns that Lähelin and Orilus are brothers (141,5ff.)[76] and also that Orilus killed not merely Schionatulander, but also Parzival's uncle, Galoes (141,8f.). The kinship of the two killer knights is as new to the listeners as to Parzival, but we at least already know from the boasting of Orilus to Jeschute that he was responsible for the death of Galoes (134,23ff.).[77] We could also suspect, without knowing, that he was guilty of killing Schionatulander, for the close juxtaposition of his claim to have killed an unnamed knight only that morning (135,21ff.) with the scene of the slain Schionatulander in Sigune's lap (138,21ff.) is revealing, if not explicit. Sigune makes it explicit and shows Parzival how the network of feudal obligations has enmeshed him, even without his knowledge.[78]

Chrétien discover the advantages of such a rhetoric and entitle it *Le Chevalier de la Charrette*, rather than use the personal name of his hero as he had in *Erec et Enide* and *Cligès*, for recognisable symbolic reasons and that the same is true of *Le Chevalier au lion* (he does not discuss *Le roman du Graal*). This may be so, but what these three last romances also have in common is the fact that the identity of the hero is deferred in each of them for some considerable time (Green, *Namedropping*, pp. 96ff.). I should therefore argue that the technique of delayed naming used in these works also brought about the 'rhétorique du titre' which they exemplify, that the poet could not afford to jeopardise the effects of the former by continuing to use a title which revealed the name of the hero from the start. As far as Wolfram is concerned, he describes the theme of his work in the prologue in abstract terms (4,10: *daz seit von grôzen triuwen*) and introduces his hero in terms of his qualities rather than by name (4,18: *er küene, træclîche wîs, / (den helt ich alsue grüeze)*). See also above, pp. 15ff.

76. This information expands on earlier points (128,3ff.; 129,27ff., 135,13ff.).
77. This point is withheld from the hero, since it is mentioned by Orilus to Jeschute in the absence of Parzival.
78. Corresponding to the net of Parzival's obligations growing more complex the narrator's technique has to be more complicated at this point. If we distinguish a simultaneous enlightenment of both Parzival and audience from those cases where the audience are enlightened before him, four possibilities exist: (i) Parzival and the listeners already know a particular point (Lähelin's seizure of Parzival's lands); (ii) Parzival and the listeners now learn something at the same time (that Lähelin and Orilus are brothers); (iii) Parzival now learns something which the listeners already know (that Orilus had killed Galoes and, if we can take correct surmise as close to knowledge, that he also recently killed Schiona-

If Parzival apparently catches up with the audience here in knowledge, we are in turn given a further lead on him in the shape of advance information, allowing us to appreciate (potentially or in the near future) that his various obligations are conflicting. If he is to avenge himself on Orilus he will only increase the suffering inflicted on Jeschute. Moreover, if Orilus is the brother of Cunneware (135,14f.), any vengeance on him or Lähelin will bring pain to her, whereas Parzival soon afterwards promises at the Round Table to make good the insult done to her by Keii (158,24ff.). To keep one obligation means breaking another. The listeners already appreciate this in the case of Jeschute and are soon to realise it with Cunneware, whilst Parzival remains in ignorance.

Parzival and Ither

As with Jeschute and Sigune, Ither is introduced to the listeners by name on the first occasion (145,15), whilst Parzival, after his naming by Sigune, is also free to be referred to by name.[79] Only a very little later than the listeners Parzival himself comes to learn of the Red Knight's name from Arthur himself (150,9: *'ez ist Ithêr von Gaheviez'*). Because Parzival knows this aspect of the Red Knight as well as the listeners, it cannot be the case, as has been suggested,[80] that Parzival's impatient, angry words to the knight (154,25: *'du maht wol wesen Lähelîn, / von dem mir klaget diu muoter mîn'*) imply that he is confusing Ither with Lähelin. If he knows full well that this is Ither, not Lähelin, then Parzival must be using a personal name naïvely as an appellative[81] (as he does in the case of Arthur himself) or making an insulting comparison between someone who incurs his annoyance and the first enemy of his family of whom he had learned from Herzeloyde (128,3ff.).[82]

If Parzival rapidly draws level in this detail with the privileged

  tulander); (iv) Parzival remains ignorant of something which the listeners already know or are very soon to know (that vengeance on Orilus would cause grief to Jeschute or to Cunneware). With an amazing narrative economy the poet has succeeded in building all these different levels of recognition into his presentation of this scene, thereby reflecting in the complexity of his technique something of the tragic complications of the feudal world into which Parzival is moving.
79. See above, p. 80, fn. 73.
80. Cf. Harms, *Kampf*, pp. 151f. and Zutt, *Kämpfe*, pp. 185f. Their case has been effectively demolished by Johnson, *Ironie*, p. 137.
81. As is suggested by Bartsch–Marti, fn. to 154,25.
82. Green, *Homicide*, p. 67. Cf. also Boesch, *Lehre*, pp. 35f.

Parzival's youth (Books III and IV)

position of listeners informed by an omniscient narrator, there is another aspect of this encounter where we remain in a superior position. When Ither is first introduced into the narrative action, the narrator tells us not merely his name, but also the fact that he is related to king Arthur and was brought up by Arthur's father (145,11: *... sprach Artûses basen sun. / den zôch Utepandragûn*).[83] To the attentive reader this is more than just a descriptive detail, for he is meant to relate it to what he has already been told of Parzival's forebears on his father's side. He knows from the beginning of the Gahmuret narrative that Parzival's grandfather was Gandin and from the genealogical details in Gahmuret's letter to Belakane he learns that Gandin's father was in turn Addanz, who belonged by birth to the Arthurian dynasty (56,11: *der was von arde ein Bertûn: / er und Utepandragûn / wâren zweier bruoder kint*). Wolfram is therefore not content with simply stating that Parzival is related to Ither on his father's side, he also provides us with the scattered evidence to realise this at the very moment when these two first meet,[84] as long as we have by now learned the necessity to pay attention to apparently disparate details and realise their possible associations.

What is possible for the retentive listener, however, is not possible for Parzival, for although he learns Ither's name from Arthur soon after the audience have been informed of this by the narrator Arthur does not also convey to him the second detail mentioned by the narrator, namely Ither's kinship with Arthur. Nor would this fact have meant anything to Parzival even if Arthur had mentioned it, for neither does Parzival know anything of his relationship with Arthur (as we do from 56,6ff.) nor can Arthur have any grounds for thinking that he, the paragon of chivalry, is related to this uncouth young stranger before him. In other words, the reasons for Parzival's ignorance have been carefully built into the narrative motivation. We know that Parzival is about to fight with a kinsman, we know that he does not appreciate this fact, and we have been given reasons why this should be so.[85]

---

83. We know already from 65,30ff. that Utepandragun is Arthur's father, even if we were unacquainted with this from other Arthurian romances (e.g. Hartmann's *Erec* 1787 or *Iwein* 897).
84. I have argued this in reviewing Harroff, *Wolfram*, in *MLR* 71 (1976), 955.
85. When Gurnemanz sighs in sorrow for the fate of Ither (170,2ff.) this cannot be because he recognises that Parzival and his opponent were kinsmen, but rather because he regrets the loss to chivalry and courtesy which his death represents (cf. 160,11ff.). Parzival is aware of none of this.

Parzival at Pelrapeire

When Parzival first approaches Pelrapeire we are left in no doubt about the hostile reception he is given by knights defending the city (181,11: *dort anderhalben stuonden / mit helmen ûf gebuonden / sehzec ritter oder mêr. / die riefen alle kêrâ kêr: / mit ûf geworfen swerten / die kranken strîtes gerten*). Nor are we left in ignorance of the reason for this behaviour, for the narrator tells us omnisciently that they took Parzival to be Clamide, their lady's enemy (181,18: *si wânden ez wær Clâmidê*).

The recent mention of the city's name Pelrapeire (180,25; 181,6) or of the kingdom Brobarz (180,18) meant nothing to the listeners, since in his recapitulation of events Gurnemanz had mentioned neither place-name (177,27ff.), whereas the name he did mention, that of Condwiramurs, is not released by the narrator until much later in Book IV. But the allusion to Clamide as a possible enemy does provide a hint that this might be the besieged city of Condwiramurs, since the name of Clamide had been mentioned by Gurnemanz (178,3). This hint is available only to the listeners, because although Gurnemanz had referred to Clamide while talking to Parzival the suggestion that the knights of Pelrapeire take Parzival to be Clamide comes to us, but not to the protagonist, from the narrator. Even so, this is no more than a hint; the audience still lack certainty on this point. We have no idea how long the siege of Condwiramurs's city, mentioned by Gurnemanz as the occasion of the death of his son Schenteflurs, may have continued after his death, we cannot know for certain that Clamide may not be active elsewhere, exercising his violence against another victim. The same is true of another reference to Clamide, when the narrator tells us that the damage inflicted on Pelrapeire in the siege was the result of Clamide's request (184,21: *si arnden Clâmidês bete*). It is true that Clamide had requested the hand of Condwiramurs in marriage (Gurnemanz had referred to this in 177,30f.) and that he attacked the city when turned down, but there is no certainty that this must be the actual function of *bete* in 184,21.[86] Again we are given a hint,

---

86. In saying this I do not wish to suggest that Martin, *Kommentar*, under 184,21, is wrong to render *bete* by 'Bewerbung'. But this rendering is an interpretation rather than a straightforward translation, it depends on our later knowledge that this is in fact the Condwiramurs of whom Gurnemanz spoke and on what she later expressly says of her relationship with Clamide (194,14ff.). My point is rather that we cannot know that *bete* has this precise meaning when we first come across it.

Parzival's youth (Books III and IV)

but no real knowledge, whilst even this degree of enlightenment is not available to Parzival. Our uncertainty is finally removed only in 187,12, when the name of Condwiramurs as the queen of this city is mentioned for the first time, for only now is the link between the past situation described by Gurnemanz and the present course of events at Pelrapeire made expressly clear. Although the audience have been given a number of hints in advance of Parzival, they attain to final certainty only at the same time as he.

If the defenders of Pelrapeire at first take Parzival for Clamide we have a right to ask why this should be so, only to find that such a question has been anticipated in the detailed motivation of the scene. As the besieged party, these defenders are naturally quick to regard anyone approaching the city as an enemy (cf. 182,20f.), not as a potential helper (cf. 189,11f.). Although Parzival cannot realise it, his behaviour is all too reminiscent of Clamide's in approaching the city with such imperious confidence (181,18: *si wânden ez wær Clâmidê, / wand er so küneclîchen*[87] *reit / gein der brücke ûf dem velde breit*) that the defenders fully expect his army to be following behind (182,6: *græzer her si vorhten*), as had obviously happened more than once before (181,17: *Durch daz sin dicke sâhen ê*). Yet for Parzival to be taken for Clamide, his distinctive red armour (acquired from Ither, cf. 170,6) must not be clearly visible to the defenders. This had been previously accounted for when the narrator introduces the Pelrapeire episode by describing Parzival's long ride all day from Graharz to Brobarz (180,15ff.), for this means that he arrives as night begins to fall (180,20: *der tac gein dem âbent zôch*) and cannot be distinctly made out in the halflight. We are therefore shown the full extent of the misunderstanding, but also how neither Parzival nor the defenders can be aware of it.[88]

---

87. Martin, *Kommentar*, under 181,19, translates *küneclîchen* 'mit dem Stolze, der Siegeszuversicht eines Königs'. Ironically, although Clamide is the *künec von Brandigân* (184,20), he wants to be king of Pelrapeire, which is what Parzival becomes.
88. Quite apart from the realistic motivation provided by Wolfram, there is a telling symbolism about Parzival being taken for Clamide, even though his considerate behaviour at Pelrapeire stamps him as someone quite different (in 189,15ff., especially when he tells her that he has just come to her from Gurnemanz, Condwiramurs can see in Parzival another Schenteflurs, rather than a Clamide). At the same time, there is some point in this implicit link, since both are killer knights and Wolfram has taken care elsewhere to provide disturbing symbolic links between Parzival and such figures (cf. Green, *Homicide*, pp. 66ff.).

85

Parzival and Condwiramurs

Within the Pelrapeire episode at large I single out this brief, but telling scene as an example of insight and recognition practised by Condwiramurs, even though the impetus comes to her from Parzival. The scene illustrates the extent of Parzival's courtly breeding as a result of Gurnemanz's teaching, specifically with regard to the injunction not to ask too many questions, by his sitting silently in front of his hostess and tactfully allowing her the first word (118,15ff.).[89] Condwiramurs reacts to this by taking his silence at first for tacit mockery (188,25: *Diu küneginne gedâhte sân | 'ich wæn, mich smæhet dirre man | durch daz mîn lîp vertwâlet ist'*), but soon abandons this in favour of a positive explanation (188,28: *'nein, er tuotz durch einen list: | er ist gast, ich pin wirtîn: | diu erste rede wære mîn'*), suggesting her guest's tactful courtesy (189,3: *'er hât sich zuht gein mir enbart'*). That she is correct in this positive explanation is suggested by the narrator's agreement with her on the essential point of Parzival's courtesy at the start of this scene (188,15: *sîn manlîch zuht was im sô ganz*), so that both are at one in seeing the guest tactfully and discreetly urging her to a realisation of her obligations as a hostess to speak first. Although the scene is primarily concerned with illustrating Parzival's *zuht* (his progress since Gurnemanz and the correctness of such conduct at least in the feudal, secular context of Pelrapeire),[90] from our point of view it is also important as an example of the insight shown by Condwiramurs, her ability to read tacit signs correctly and recognise their import.

Parzival and Clamide's men

This and the next example are minor illustrations of the problem of recognition, but precisely their fleeting nature, without further echoes, can be taken as a token of the importance attached by Wolfram to this problem, to which he returns even on minor issues.

One of Clamide's pages reports to his lord the prowess of one knight among the defenders of Pelrapeire (who can only be Par-

---

89. Green, *Advice*, pp. 55f.
90. The implied contrast is of course with Parzival's silence at Munsalvæsche. Cf. Green, *Advice*, pp. 71ff. Of equal importance is the similarity between the scenes: in that Parzival follows Gurnemanz's advice on both occasions, the earlier scene with Condwiramurs prepares the way for the disaster at Munsalvæsche.

Parzival's youth (Books III and IV)

zival) in terms suggesting that all and sundry take this knight to be Ither (203,29: *'iwer soldier jehent besunder, | daz von der tavelrunder | diu küneginne habe besant | Ithêrn von Kukûmerlant'*). Again, it is not enough simply to state this failure in recognition, it also has to be explained, which is done by reference to Ither's armour and trappings, now worn by Parzival (204,3: *des wâpen kom zer tjoste für | und wart getragen nâch prîses kür*), as is made clear a little later when Parzival begins his combat with Clamide (211,6: *von samît ein decke rôt | Lac ûf der îserînen. | an im selben liez er schînen | rôt schilt, rôt kursît*). No further purpose is served by this passing detail, other than to remind us of the dubious beginnings of Parzival's chivalry and to impress upon us that a knight wearing unexpected trappings can be as much a source of confusion as was Parzival's father with his *anker* coat of arms.

Kingrun and Clamide

After Kingrun, Clamide's seneschal, has been defeated by Parzival and sent to Arthur's court to offer his *sicherheit*, the same sequence of events is re-enacted in the case of his lord, Clamide, so that when he in turn arrives before the Round Table his own seneschal is amongst those assembled there. Nonetheless, it is made clear to us that Kingrun recognises his lord only when the latter takes off his helmet and hood. They are removed from him in one line (219,3: *dô manz von im strouft. unde bant*), and in the next line the act of recognition takes place (219,4: *Clâmidê wart schiere erkant*), with specific reference to Kingrun (219,5: *Kingrûn sach dicke | an in kuntlîche blicke*). There can be no doubt that only at this point does Kingrun recognise that this is Clamide: the double mention of recognition (*erkant* and *kuntlîche blicke*) comes only after removal of helmet and hood, and its suddenness is made clear by the use of *wart* and the adverb *schiere*. It is the sudden shock of recognition which also explains Kingrun's grief on learning of Clamide's defeat (219,7ff.) and his later uncontrolled outburst (221,13ff.). But for this shock to be possible, Kingrun must have failed to recognise his lord *before* his helmet was taken off and this has to be motivated by the narrator. He does this in advance, thereby making his preparations for this kind of critical question, by mentioning the detail that Clamide's helmet and shield, the two pieces of equipment which proclaimed the knight's heraldic identity, had been battered unrecognisable in the recent combat with Parzival (217,23: *sîn helm, sîn schilt verhouwen*).

This failure in recognition at the Round Table, specifically on the part of Kingrun, is also conveyed to us by the narrator's technique in abandoning Clamide's name for the short period of his anonymity in this scene. Before this he is regularly referred to by name from the moment when he first takes part in the action, but for the duration of this scene he is last referred to by name in 217,19 as he rides to join Arthur's assembled company (just as Parzival's name had last been mentioned in the Pelrapeire episode as he rode over the bridge to approach the city-gate, 182,7) and his name recurs next only at the moment of recognition (219,4). Nor is it the case that in this admittedly short passage there was no call for the narrator to make any reference to him, for as the newcomer Clamide is the focus of attention and the narrator refers frequently to him, but without using his name.[91] This scene therefore includes two examples of anonymity: Clamide is not referred to by name until he is recognised by Kingrun, and Parzival (here as in the preceding Kingrun scene) is similarly nameless and remains so until the Round Table learn his name in Book VI. Each figure is therefore presented by the narrator from the subjective point of view of those who fail to recognise either Clamide or Parzival. This parallel with Parzival, together with the focus of the Clamide scene on his sudden recognition, suggests that the narrator's temporary withholding of his name, although of only short duration, is not fortuitous and is meant as a rhetorical reflection of the situation presented.

91. In this narrative span Clamide is referred to anonymously as *man* (218,21) and *gevangen* (218,29), but for the rest by a surprisingly large number of pronouns (217,22 + 23 + 25 + 27 + 29; 218,1; 219,1 + 3).

4
Parzival's failure (Books V and VI)

Books V and VI may be taken together because they jointly illustrate Parzival's first testing and failure on a new narrative level. Both he and the audience expect events to continue on the feudal, secular level of Books III and IV in which Parzival, by acquiring and practising knighthood, entered on his father's inheritance.[1] Unexpectedly, however, he is taken into the realm of the Grail, where the knightly and courtly criteria of his recent success at Pelrapeire prove unavailing or irrelevant.[2] His failure is made clear to us early on by the narrator, Parzival is given a number of early indications, but the full catastrophe strikes him only with Cundrie's arrival at the Round Table in Book VI.[3] A clear break is represented by Parzival's departure from the Round Table and by the switch to events centred on Gawan in the subsequent Books.[4]

The episodes which we now have to consider present a double contrast. First, within themselves: at Munsalvæsche Parzival fails to recognise the significance of what he sees, whilst in the remaining episodes the theme is one of recognition between people who have met before. Two types of recognition are present here: failure in intellectual recognition or moral perception at Munsalvæsche and a return to people earlier encountered in the other cases. Secondly, the first of these episodes contrasts with what immediately went

1. Cf. Green, *Departure*, pp. 399ff.
2. I have discussed this in *Aventiure*, pp. 145ff. On the novelty of the narrative beginning at 224,1 see Schirok, *Aufbau*, pp. 490f.
3. These premonitory indications, preparing us for the Cundrie scene, have been discussed by Haug, *DVjs* 45 (1971), 695ff. and in a wider context by Hirschberg, *Untersuchungen*, pp. 99f. and 299ff.
4. This break is also underlined by the new prologue-like beginning of Book VII (338,1ff.) as well as by the epilogue-like conclusion of Book VI (337,1ff.). Bonath, *Untersuchungen* I 111, has established that the large initial at 338,1 belonged to the archetype (cf. Schirok, *Aufbau*, p. 443). On the textual problem of the conclusion of Book VI see Kochendörfer and Schirok, *Textrekonstruktion*, pp. 162ff. (in favour of the 'Vorveröffentlichung' hypothesis).

before. Parzival's failure to recognise what is expected of him at Munsalvæsche differs markedly from his success in this respect at Pelrapeire. Like his father at Zazamanc he unerringly brought help to those who needed it and in his tactful insight he was fully master of the situation in the scene of his silence before his hostess. In both these respects he fails at Munsalvæsche, not because he has unaccountably lost the qualities of helpfulness and insight, but rather because he is now confronted with a novel type of situation in which more than a knight's readiness to help by military means or the tactful self-restraint imposed by courtly breeding is called for.

The technique of providing the audience with information not always available to a character in the story and making them aware of this discrepancy demands perceptive listeners, which in turn presupposes a poet making skilled use of the niceties of language to convey ambiguous hints. In these Books especially, where Parzival realises his error at Munsalvæsche much later than the audience, such a controlled use of language is called for. When the figure of Anfortas is first introduced, for example, his luxurious attire is described (225,9: *der het an im alsolch gewant, / ob im dienden elliu lant, / daz ez niht bezzer möhte sîn*). Here the conditional clause, apparently meant as part of the hyperbole, turns out to be literally true in terms of the supreme power exercised by the Grail-king (cf. 252,5ff.),[5] but at this stage the listeners cannot grasp this implication or realise that it applies more appositely to Parzival as one due to succeed Anfortas in this office.

A comparable irony is at stake when Orilus, defeated in his combat with Parzival, is twice pointedly referred to as *Orilus der fürste erkant* (270,9 and 271,25). In the usual sense of knightly renown this description is perfectly true, but in the alternative sense of 'known, recognised' the audience are in a position to appreciate that this is not the case, for Parzival has failed to recognise that his opponent is Orilus, whilst we can see that such ignorance constitutes good fortune for him.[6] In the scene of the drops of blood in the snow, where Parzival is challenged by knights from the Round Table, the contrast between his own intentions (pacific, because he is lost in rêverie) and Keii's[7] is brought out by alternative readings of the same conjunction. When Parzival's stance is summed up in the words *als er tjostierns wolde pflegn* (284,2) we know

5. Cf. also 254,28f.
6. See below, pp. 123f.
7. On Keii's aggressiveness see below, p. 127.

from his rêverie that appearances speak against the facts and that *als* must mean 'as if' (an unreal hypothesis), whereas Keii's aggressiveness invites us to read the phrase used of him (293,21: *alser strîtes gerte*) as a real comparison ('as one who sought combat'). The use of an identical construction reflects how the Round Table is able to misinterpret Parzival's intentions, whilst the alternative readings of *als* underline the difference between his motives and Keii's. Semantic ambiguity is exploited when the narrator refers to the Arthurian custom of eating on any day only once an adventure has presented itself (309,7: *nehein rîter vor im az / des tages swenn âventiure vergaz / daz si sînen hof vermeit. / im ist âventiure nu bereit*). Arthur assumes that Parzival's arrival and the preceding combats are enough to constitute an adventure and that the meal can begin (by 314,14ff. they are already eating), but the real adventure in this episode is the arrival of Cundrie and then Kingrimursel, with the devastating effects of their accusations. The listeners are lulled into a false belief by the ambiguity of the word *bereit*: does it mean 'ready to hand, already present', as Arthur assumes, or rather 'about to present itself', as is later revealed? When the narrator introduces this passage with the repeated appeal (309,3: *nu râtet, hœret unde jeht*), he is not just addressing his listeners conventionally, but asking them to pay close attention to the implications of what follows.[8]

Not all the above cases, however, are accessible to a listener at a first hearing, no matter what perception he shows, for their implications are made clear only by the subsequent course of the narrative.[9] A narrator who wishes to ensure that his listeners at times enjoy more information than is available to characters will have to fall back on other methods, one of which is the point of view technique which we saw him employing in the first two Books of the Parzival narrative. In this chapter we shall see this technique used

8. One further passage may serve as an example of the attention to linguistic detail demanded by the poet. When Parzival departs from the Round Table at the end of Book VI his armour is described as *lieht wîz îsernharnasch* (333,4). The use of *wîz* is regarded as an error in the commentary on this line in the Bartsch–Marti edition: the adjective could refer to silvery metal, but not to armour coloured red. But we should recall that Parzival's equipment had been so battered by blows (cf. 283,28f.) that the red colouring had been possibly stripped from the metal. At any rate, it is not visible to members of the Round Table (the page, Segramors, Keii and even Gawan), who would otherwise have recognised Parzival as the *rôte ritter*.
9. On the difference between a first and subsequent recitals, especially with regard to dramatic irony, see Green, *Irony*, pp. 259ff.

The Art of Recognition in Wolfram's *Parzival*

above all of the Munsalvæsche episode to cause us to grope in the dark almost as much as the stumbling Parzival, but also to give us the superior knowledge necessary if we are to appreciate how much astray he is.[10]

However much information about the Grail is revealed to the listeners by the narrator while Parzival is at Munsalvæsche, and then to both the listeners and Parzival by Sigune shortly afterwards,[11] they are kept in ignorance of one vital fact about the Grail-family, namely that Parzival belongs to it on his mother's side. At the time when details about the Grail-family are released by Sigune (251,2ff.) we have no means of seeing that a central fact is being withheld from us,[12] for the listeners (as opposed to Parzival) are given a hint of this only later when the narrator describes Parzival's departure from Arthur's company in search of the Grail (333,27: *schildes ambet umben grâl / wirt nu vil güebet sunder twâl / von im den Herzeloyde bar. / er was ouch ganerbe dar*). We know enough of Gahmuret's genealogy to suspect that Parzival's Grail inheritance is unlikely to stem from his father and that accordingly *ganerbe* might be fittingly used here in close conjunction with the mention of the hero as his mother's son.[13] In the crucial scene at Munsalvæsche we are therefore given as little knowledge on this point as Parzival himself, but our provisional enlightenment, how-

10. In her discussion of the narrative perspective used in the Grail episode Hirschberg, *Untersuchungen*, pp. 122ff., stresses that we are not merely shown things from Parzival's point of view, but are also informed by the narrator of things that escape the protagonist.
11. See below, pp. 111f. and 117, fn. 97.
12. To the extent that Sigune fails to mention certain facts to Parzival on this occasion these details are still withheld from the listeners, who learn them only later from the narrator in the Kyot digression (453,11ff.). This does not mean that Sigune practises here the same kind of conscious concealment as the narrator, but rather that he achieves his ultimate ends by using her as a mouthpiece. Sigune does not mention her own membership of the Grail-family, through her mother, because she is talking of the four children of Frimutel who survived him (whereas Schoysiane died before in giving birth to Sigune). Similarly, she does not mention Parzival's membership of the Grail-family, through his mother, because she is dwelling on the present dynastic position at Munsalvæsche, therefore mentions Frimutel's two sons by name (Anfortas, Trevrizent) and has no call to name his daughters (Repanse de schoy, Herzeloyde). Sigune does not deliberately conceal these points from Parzival, but simply has no occasion to refer to them. This situation, well motivated from her point of view, is exploited by the narrator for his own purposes.
13. On the occurrence of circumlocutions like *Herzeloyden kint* in the significant context of the Grail see Green, *Namedropping*, pp. 135f. On the remaining uncertainty of 333,30, however, see below, pp. 215f.

ever belated, still precedes his. Elsewhere, the narrator may go a step further towards informing his listeners by giving them implicit hints which, whilst they may remain obscure or even unrecognisable as hints at the time, are later revealed as built-in anticipations of a subsequent revelation. Under this heading I shall mention, without discussing further, the concealed suggestions made by the narrator about the miraculous nature of Parzival's guidance as he approaches the Grail-castle (224,19ff.) and when this assistance is withdrawn from him as he sets forth again (249,1ff.);[14] the insinuation, confirmed only much later by Trevrizent,[15] that the mantle lent Parzival at Munsalvæsche is not the conventional clothing of a travel-weary guest by considerate hosts, but instead amounts to Parzival's symbolic designation as a potential ruler (228,7ff.),[16] and finally the far-reaching ramifications of the innocuous seeming snowfall (281,12ff.), closely connected with the divine conjunction of apparently unrelated details as a means of prompting Parzival to ask the decisive question.[17]

A further point in the narrator's control of his audience is reached when he clearly differentiates them from Parzival by passing information to them which is not divulged to him, as is specially the case when he comes to Munsalvæsche. Although the narrator largely presents the central scene in the hall from Parzival's point of view,[18] so that we mostly see things as he experiences them, he also makes us privileged bystanders, apprised of vital details which escape the hero or seem insignificant to him. When Parzival and Anfortas first meet at the start of Book V the narrator refers to the sick Grail-king as *der trûric man* (225,18) without giving any indication that this fact, conveyed to us by his omniscient function, is also visible to Parzival.[19] The odds are against this because the hero encounters Anfortas clad in fine courtly attire (225,9ff.), pursuing

---

14. I have discussed this problem in fuller detail in *Weg*, pp. 11ff., and *Pathway*, pp. 174ff.
15. 500,23ff.
16. Cf. Mersmann, *Besitzwechsel*, p. 130 and Gibbs, *GLL* 21 (1968), 302.
17. Cf. Deinert, *Ritter*, pp. 12ff. and especially p. 35, and Weigand, *Parzival*, pp. 49ff.
18. Cf. Wolff, *PBB(T)* 77 (1955), 263.
19. The only previous mention known to me of the discrepancy between what is shown to us and what is realised by Parzival in this scene is by Bauer, *Euphorion* 57 (1963), 77ff., as part of a larger argument which is likely to distract attention from the importance of the point. Bauer sees correctly that for Parzival the signs visible at Munsalvæsche are less clear and meaningful than for the listeners, that he is prompted by factual curiosity and that, if he had asked a

the pastime of fishing (225,3ff.)[20] and playing the rôle of potential host (225,19ff.). Indeed, as far as explicit evidence is concerned, Parzival learns of Anfortas's condition only from what Siguwne later tells him (253,20: '... *ob in sîn töun / læzet, den vil trûrgen man*'), whilst it is not until after her passionate criticism of him that he can be said to have taken this to heart (256,1: *Daz er vrâgens was sô laz, / do'r bî dem trûregen wirte saz, / daz rou dô græzliche / den helt ellens rîche*). What we learn immediately from the narrator is imparted to the hero when it is already too late.

The same technique is employed when Parzival makes his way to the courtyard of the Grail-castle. As we accompany him into it the narrator describes it to us (227,9: *durch schimpf er niht zetretet was / (dâ stuont al kurz grüene gras: / dâ was bûhurdieren vermiten), / mit baniern selten überriten, / alsô der anger z'Abenberc. / selten frœlîchiu werc / was dâ gefrümt ze langer stunt: / in was wol herzen jâmer kunt*). The point of these lines is to bring home to us the full extent of the Grail-community's grief (it even prevents them from following the knightly pastime of jousting for pleasure), but what the narrator makes clear to us is nothing like so obvious to Parzival, deprived of the services of a knowledgeable commentator. All that is visible to him is the fact that the courtyard is covered with a grass lawn: he may (or may not) ask himself why this should be so, but he cannot be certain, as we are, that this is because no jousting has taken place for a long time, let alone that this in turn is because of the grief reigning at the castle. Nor is Parzival even allowed to suspect that anything is wrong (227,17: *wênc er des gein in enkalt*), for he is greeted with full courtly ceremonial (227,18ff.) which apparently confirms his first impression of Anfortas as a courtly host.

The same is true when the guest is offered a drink of welcome (228,25: *man schancte im unde pflac sîn sô, / die trûregen wâren mit im vrô. / man bôt im wirde und êre: / wan dâ was râtes mêre / denne er ze*

> question, it would probably have been one of curiosity, rather than compassion. But it does not follow from this that a question of curiosity is what was expected of him and that this is the kind of question he should have asked. If the question he should have asked on the first occasion is not of the same compassionate nature as the question he asks on the second occasion, we are confronted once more with the spectre of the 'verschobenen Gralsprämissen', a problem which Bauer, perhaps understandably, does not discuss. See also, more briefly, Hirschberg, *Untersuchungen*, pp. 128 and 160.

20. When Trevrizent later makes it clear (491,1ff.) that Anfortas is taken to lake Brumbane only in the hope of distraction from his suffering (cf. 491,18: '*der trûrige, niht der geile*'), Parzival admits that he earlier saw his fishing only in terms of *kurzewîle* (491,23).

Parzival's failure (Books V and VI)

Pelrapeire vant, | die dô von kumber schiet sîn hant), for what we are shown is not identical with what Parzival sees. All he sees is that the company is *vrô*, whilst we learn that they are really *trûrec*,[21] just as in the courtyard he had simply seen a grass lawn, whereas we had been shown the reason for this in *herzen jâmer*. Furthermore, the following comparison between the wealth of Munsalvæsche and the poverty of the besieged Pelrapeire, whilst true, is deceptive because it suggests that the two castles are on the same level and therefore fit to be compared, whereas in the Grail-realm Parzival has gained access to something unique. I do not regard this narrator's comparison as intended to mislead his listeners (because he has already revealed his hand to them in v. 26), but rather as a narrator's remark meant to reflect what is passing through Parzival's mind and showing him to be as blind to the uniqueness of his experience at Munsalvæsche as when he later judges it in terms of another feudal, secular castle, that of Gurnemanz (239,14: *'waz op mîn wesen hie geschiht | die mâze als dort pî im?'*).[22] In all these passages the narrator distinguishes between what we know and what Parzival realises, thereby emphasising how unaware he remained of the grief dominant at Munsalvæsche and of what kind of reaction was expected from him. This helps to account for his ignoring the one explicit, but passing reference conveyed to him in the court-jester scene (229,17: *'swie trûrc wir anders sîn'*), for Parzival has no previous clues, as we have, with which to connect this isolated remark (tucked into a subordinate clause) and is in any case so carried away by violent anger at the insult which he imagines done to him (229,8ff.) that such a brief hint is unlikely to have made any impression on him.[23]

21. The theme of these lines is, in the terminology of Hartmann von Aue, *trügevreude*. On this see Eroms, *Vreude*, pp. 128ff and Ragotzky and Weinmayer, *Identitätsbildung*, p. 231. Wolfram appears to share none of his colleague's critical reservations on this score.
22. Cf. Green, *Advice*, pp. 72f.
23. Parzival's later remark to Trevrizent on his evening at Munsalvæsche (492,14: *'des palas | sach ich des âbents jâmers vol'*) cannot safely be taken as summing up his experience there at the time, for since then he has been informed of the central importance of the grief at the Grail-castle by Sigune, by Cundrie and not least by Trevrizent himself. On this process of Parzival's retrospective concentration on the suffering Anfortas as the true focus of the earlier scene see Hirschberg, *Untersuchungen*, pp. 130ff., especially p. 139. Yet even if we connect this later judgment by Parzival (492,14ff.) with the point in the evening at Munsalvæsche when the lance was brought in and grief was cryingly obvious (231,23ff.), this still suggests that Parzival may have realised the fact of suffering only at this point (but still without acting on it), not before.

The Art of Recognition in Wolfram's *Parzival*

A similar discrepancy between our enlightenment and Parzival's is detectable as he leaves the Grail-castle on the following day. When he wakes up, wonders at the absence of pages to clothe him and drifts to sleep again, we are given an explanation of what briefly puzzles him (245,26: *nieman dâ redete noch enrief: / si wâren gar verborgen*), a fact of which Parzival remains unaware until he wakes up again and finds himself in a deserted castle (247,3ff.). Even now he cannot conceive that they have actually concealed themselves from him, but thinks instead that they have ridden out to combat and expect him to join them.[24] He likewise misinterprets the significance of his knightly gear lying ready for him (246,1ff. and 28ff.), rightly taking this to be a tacit reproach, but seeing in it a reminder to repay his host's hospitality by offering him knightly assistance (246,11ff.) rather than an invitation to take up his things and depart without more ado. The motif of the Grail-community's concealment from him is touched on again when *ein verborgen knappe* (247,21) abruptly pulls up the drawbridge as Parzival leaves the castle – here the timespan between our being told this by the narrator and Parzival learning it for himself is much shorter, for the closing of the bridge is accompanied by a curse on Parzival for not having asked his host the question (247,26ff.). Parzival now knows that his behaviour has been disastrously wrong, but still imagines that he can put things right by knightly means, for he reverts to this comforting thought as he follows the Grail-knights' tracks (248,19ff.). That this consolation is vain is brought home to us by what the narrator says of the grief and suffering now to befall Parzival for the first time (248,14ff.)[25] and of the withdrawal of miraculous guidance at precisely this point (249,1ff.).[26]

---

24. Green, *Aventiure*, p. 151.
25. On the importance of this narratorial comment see Hahn, *Schönheit*, pp. 221f. Parzival's nightmare while he sleeps at Munsalvæsche (245,1ff.) gives him forebodings (246,8ff.), so that he suspects the worst, but the narrator's equation of his nightmare with Herzeloyde's dream presaging Gahmuret's death (245,6ff.) tells us more of the tragic future than he can realise.
26. When Sigune recognises Parzival and reminds him of their kinship (252,14ff.), her use of the present tense (v. 15 and 17: *ist*) indicates her unawareness of Herzeloyde's death (cf. also the present tense in 251,12, where the three members of the Grail-family are also meant to include Herzeloyde, although this is not obvious at the time, since Parzival's maternal descent from the Grail-family is still being withheld from us). Since Sigune knows nothing of Herzeloyde's death, nor can Parzival – this knowledge is deferred until his meeting with Trevrizent (476,12ff.), where its impact is all the greater because Parzival now realises the full extent of his sinfulness (see below, pp. 201f.). Within the shorter narrative span of Books V and VI, however, Parzival catches up

Parzival's failure (Books V and VI)

As in earlier parts of the work, the narrator's rhetorical control of his listeners, now giving them more information than Parzival, but now placing them on the same level of ignorance, also extends to his technique with naming his characters, sometimes informing us of this badge of their identity, but sometimes withholding it for clearly recognisable reasons.

If we start by asking once again what new characters are named immediately they enter the action and what ones have their naming deferred, a difference between these two Books emerges straightaway. In Book V, devoted largely to the events at Munsalvæsche, the only new character to be named without delay is Repanse de schoy (first mentioned in 235,15, then named in 235,25),[27] whereas in Book VI we find Gawan, Segramors, Cundrie, Kingrimursel and Beacurs.[28] The unique position of Repanse de schoy is not because of any paucity of new characters in this Book, but can rather be explained by the fact that the converse technique of delayed naming is clearly focused on events at Munsalvæsche. Anfortas is first brought into the action anonymously (225,8: *einen*) and is named only in 251,16 by Sigune, whilst Titurel, introduced anonymously somewhat later (240,27: *den aller schœnsten alten man*), is also named by her on the same occasion (251,5).[29] That the delayed naming of

with the narrator's audience in knowledge concerning the suffering of Anfortas (see above, pp. 93f.), the nature and extent of Grail-kingship from Sigune (254,20ff.), and the events at Munsalvæsche from Cundrie (315,26ff.).

In these two Books, as elsewhere, a number of details need not be narrated, just as conversely further narrative perspectives can be opened up to us. When Parzival reveals that he knows of Gawan by hearsay (304,4f.) we realise that this has not been presented to us in the narrative, just as the shattering of his spear in combat with Keii has to be read out of what we are told at the close of the preceding combat with Segramors (288,25: *und daz dez sper doch ganz bestuont*) and out of Gawan's words (304,23: '*hie ligent ouch trunzûne ûf dem snê / dîns spers*'). The detail that Parzival removed his helmet after the encounter with Gawan is also passed over in the narrative (see below, p. 131, fn. 128). On Sigune's name see below, p. 116, fn. 94. Further narrative dimensions are hinted at in the case of Cunneware (284,12) and her marriage to Clamide (336,28ff.)

27. The names of Sigune, Jeschute and Orilus are released with only a short-term delay within their respective scenes for the reasons which I discuss below, pp. 113ff. They are in any case not new characters within the work.

28. Gawan is named first in collective action at the end of Book V (277,4) and then when the action first focuses on him individually (299,19). Others are named as soon as they enter the action: Segramors (285,2), Cundrie (with a short timelag from 312,2 to 26), and Beacurs (323,1). Only with Kingrimursel is the delay slightly longer (from 319,21 to 324,21), presumably to heighten the tension of his accusation.

29. It needs to be stressed, however, that the equation of Titurel in 251,5 with the old man glimpsed in 240,27 is by no means explicit at this stage.

The Art of Recognition in Wolfram's *Parzival*

these two Grail-kings is not fortuitous is suggested by the fact that Sigune's passage (in addition to mentioning Frimutel and Trevrizent)[30] also includes the names of two Grail localities (the castle Munsalvæsche, 251,2, and the realm Terre de Salvæsche, 251,4), which had similarly been referred to earlier without a name (225,22: *ein hûs*, whilst the unnamed lake in 225,2 is the first spot on Grail territory to be reached by Parzival). In other words, the names which are divulged to us belatedly in Book V refer to central aspects of the Grail-world (the two Grail-kings still alive, the castle, the realm); they are precisely those details which the narrator, at the beginning of the 'Bogengleichnis', promises to reveal only later (241,1: *Wer der selbe wære, / des freischet her nâch mære. / dar zuo der wirt, sîn burc, sîn lant*).[31] By this technique, to which he here draws attention explicitly, the narrator once again persuades us to witness events from Parzival's point of view. As events unfold at the Grail-castle Parzival is ignorant of the identity of people and place and their names are consequently withheld from us too, but later we learn them from Sigune at the same time as Parzival.[32]

The essential anonymity of events at the Grail-castle, at the time when we experience them with Parzival, is also brought out by the contrast between the two figures most vitally engaged in these events, for throughout Parzival is referred to by name, but Anfortas anonymously. A variety of nameless epithets and circumlocutions is used of Parzival by the narrator in this episode as elsewhere in the work,[33] but alongside these he regularly makes use of Parzival's

---

30. 251,6 and 15.
31. Cf. Hirschberg, *Untersuchungen*, p. 127: 'Der erste Gralkönig wird gerade in dem Moment mit dem Protagonisten in Verbindung gebracht, in dem mit dem Umschwung der Szene alles für immer versäumt zu sein scheint. Ich verstehe diese Zusammenfügung und damit den Sinn der Perspektivstelle als Hinweis darauf, wie nur über die Kenntnis der Geschichte des Gralgeschlechtes, die Parzivals eigene Geschichte ist, eine Wiederholung des Gralbesuches einmal gelingen kann.'
32. One character whose naming is delayed and who clearly falls outside the Grail context is the pagan queen Ekuba at Arthur's court (see Schirok, *Aufbau*, p. 487). The only reason I can think of for the application of this technique to her is that it is through her that we are again reminded of the existence of Parzival's pagan halfbrother Feirefiz (328,2ff.). By means of the tension roused by delaying the naming of the informant the narrator might be stressing the significance of the information itself. Furthermore, by being Feirefiz's cousin once removed (328,22f.) Ekuba can back up Cundrie's information about him (317,3ff.).
33. The epithets include *junger man* (228,1; 242,25; 245,29; 247,13), *minneclîche wîne* (228,6), *der wol gevar* (228,10), *gast* (229,6; 239,24; 242,12; 248,1), *helt* (243,23), *hêrre* (244,24), *der junge wol gevar* (245,6), *wîgant* (245,24; 247,1), *der*

98

Parzival's failure (Books V and VI)

name, from the moment when he leaves the lake to seek the castle of his host (226,10) to the moment when the drawbridge is unceremoniously pulled up behind him (247,24).[34] This readiness to use the hero's name at this point makes good sense within the narrator's terms of reference, for to withhold it would suggest that the Grail-community was ignorant of his identity, whereas it is later made clear that one guided so miraculously to Munsalvæsche as Parzival is equally miraculously announced in advance (470,21: *'die aber zem grâle sint benant, / hœrt wie die werdent bekant. / zende an des steines drum / von karacten ein epitafum / sagt sînen namen und sînen art, / swer dar tuon sol die sælden vart'*).[35] Whether he realises it or not, Parzival's name and identity must be known at Munsalvæsche at the moment when he arrives there.[36] The converse is not the case, however. Parzival knows nothing of the castle into which he has unexpectedly found his way, Anfortas is unknown to him, and accordingly the narrator refers to the Grail-king by anonymous epithets or circumlocutions descriptive of his functions rather than his identity: he is at first the *vischære* because this is how Parzival first comes across him, but more frequently he is the *wirt* because of the importance and prolonged description of the ceremonial meal in his castle.[37]

This contrast between the naming of Parzival and the anonymity of Anfortas is at times stressed by the juxtaposition of these two quite different types of reference. As the hero enters the palace a relative clause circumlocution for him (230,21: *in den palas kom gegangen / der dâ wart wol enpfangen*) quickly gives way to his personal identification (230,23: *Parzivâl der lieht gevar*), while his host remains in the anonymity of a circumlocution (230,24: *von im der in sante dar*). Elsewhere, Parzival can be referred to by name and Anfortas as the *wirt* either both in the same verse (240,18) or separated by no more than a line or two (237,7–9; 242,21f.). Such pointed juxtapositions underline the contrast between these two

---

    küene (245,30), *degen* (246,1 + 27). Circumlocutions are used at 224,2 + 5; 248,8; 249,1.
34. These occasions are: 226,10; 229,9; 230,23; 236,12; 237,9; 239,8; 240,18 + 23; 242,3 + 21; 243,4 + 28; 244,26; 245,1; 247,1 + 24.
35. Cf. also 781,15: '*daz epitafjum ist gelesen: / du solt des grâles hêrre wesen*'.
36. On this see below, pp. 320ff. (Appendix A).
37. *Vischære*: 225,13; 226,1 + 26; 227,3; 229,20; *wirt*: 229,7; 230,15 + 26 + 30; 231,1; 233,7 + 24 + 26; 236,11; 237,7; 239,24; 240,7 + 18; 241,3; 242,12 + 22; 246,3 + 11; 247,29. Other nameless references are *einen* (225,8) and *der trûric man* (225,18). One circumlocution is used (230,24).

naming techniques and suggest that the problem of recognition in the Munsalvæsche episode lies firmly with Parzival: whereas he is already known to his host, he knows nothing of Anfortas and has to learn about him. This cognitive progress of the hero is imposed on the listeners by the narrator's technique of withholding, keeping them in suspense about the host's identity, the nature of his suffering and of the mysterious events at his castle.

Although we shall have to look at Parzival's second encounters with Sigune and Jeschute in further detail below, the naming technique used in them permits the same conclusion as the Munsalvæsche episode. The encounter between Parzival and Sigune begins soon after the former's departure from the Grail-castle (at 249,9). In this scene Parzival is referred to by name, not merely at the point when Sigune recognises who he is (251,29), but also before it, when he first greets her (249,26). If Sigune for her part is at first kept anonymous,[38] this not merely contrasts with the narrator's readiness to refer to Parzival by name, it also differs from his technique in the first Sigune scene, when both she and Schionatulander were identified by name as soon as they were introduced.[39] Parzival can of course be named by the narrator because we have accompanied him on his travels into this scene,[40] so that the task awaiting him in this encounter (to recognise in the greatly changed external appearance of this *frouwe* the Sigune whom he met before) is also imposed upon us by the narrator's method of initially withholding her identity from us.

The same task awaits Parzival in the immediately following episode, when he comes across Jeschute in drastically different circumstances and has to identify her as the first person he met on his travels. Again, the narrator's naming technique reflects the cognitive progress which the hero has to make. He can be referred to by name as he first addresses her (258,1) and subsequently in his conversation with her (259,4; 260,18), whilst she is kept initially anonymous, like Sigune. The narrator begins this encounter with a lengthy description of Jeschute's present sorry state, but puts us in the same position as Parzival, with whom we behold this apparent stranger, by using the anonymous *frouwe*,[41] varying it by *blôze*

38. The anonymous terms used of her are *frouwe* (249,12) and *magt* (249,15; 251,25; 252,11). Similarly, Schionatulander is referred to anonymously as *ein gebalsemt ritter tôt* (249,16).
39. See above, p. 78.
40. The narrator refers to him by name in 248,17, just before the start of the encounter with Sigune.
41. 256,15 + 24 + 29; 257,5; 258,24 + 30; 259,27; 260,7; 268,26.

Parzival's failure (Books V and VI)

frouwe (260,19; 261,22) and *diu frouwe mit ir blôzem vel* (268,19) because of her tattered clothing. This polite form of address can be retained until the end of the episode, because we are nowhere given grounds for thinking that Parzival had learned Jeschute's name at their first meeting, as he had Sigune's. However, the narrator's references to Jeschute in the episode grow more specific when the next epithet to be introduced is *diu blôze herzogîn* (260,3), referring back to his use of her title in the earlier meeting (130,28: *herzoginne*)[42] and soon confirmed by his explicit naming of *der herzoge Orilus* (260,25) as her husband. If this is not enough to enable the listener to identify her, she is later referred to in even more specific terms as *frou Jeschute*,[43] at which point even the least attentive listener must have caught up with the others. The technique of naming therefore gradually becomes more specific and individualising (*frouwe – blôze frouwe – diu blôze herzogîn – frou Jeschute*), thus reflecting by such objective references what there are grounds for taking as a parallel path of subjective recognition of Jeschute by Parzival himself.[44]

In each of the episodes discussed hitherto the task of recognition falls essentially to Parzival, he has to learn the identity of Anfortas, Sigune and Jeschute (if the two women also have to recognise him this is disposed of more quickly: Sigune recognises him before he learns who she is, Jeschute recognises him immediately).[45] In the remaining episode, Parzival's encounter with the Round Table, the cognitive process is reversed, since Parzival is for the most part unconscious and lost in rêverie, so that first Cunneware's page, Segramors and Keii fail to recognise their opponent and then Gawan is enabled to see that this is the *rôte ritter* sought by king Arthur. Accordingly, the narrator now reverses his technique, this

---

42. Cf. also the first reference to Jeschute in the work: *duc Orilus de Lalander, / des wîp* (129,27f.).
43. 262,25; 263,24; 264,22; 268,8 + 12.
44. Corresponding to this technique, Orilus is also referred to anonymously at first: *degen* (259,19), *helt* (259,25), *man* (259,28) and a circumlocution (260,18). If he is also referred to by implication as Jeschute's husband (259,23), this comes before the narrator's naming technique shows us unambiguously that Parzival now confronts Jeschute again. He is named only in 260,25, so that his name is released at the same time as we realise Jeschute's identity beyond any doubt.
    Once the combat between Parzival and Orilus begins the narrator uses both their names freely, often in close juxtaposition (262,1 + 3; 263,14 + 19; 264,20 + 21; 265,4 + 11; 265,25 + 27; 268,3 + 4). This use of names is permissible within the narrator's terms of reference since, if Parzival realises by this stage who Jeschute is, he has no knowledge of Orilus's name and identity, nor has Orilus of Parzival's.
45. See below, pp. 116 and 121.

time naming from the beginning each of the members of the Round Table,[46] but using terms of Parzival which convey nothing to these other characters and thus preserve his identity until the close of the multiple encounter.

The narrator makes his point not merely by naming Segramors, Keii and Gawan in turn,[47] but more specifically by releasing their name at the very beginning of each encounter: when Segramors first challenges his opponent (287,21: *Segramors sprach alsô*), when Keii rides out to deliver combat (293,19: *Keie der ellens rîche | kom gewâpent rîterlîche | ûz, alser strîtes gerte*), and when Gawan approaches with conciliatory intent (300,6: *sus kom Gâwân zuo zim geriten*). On each occasion, therefore, the name of the challenger is expressly mentioned at the beginning and then subsequently, but if we can imagine the narrator in the function of a ringside commentator speaking aloud, the release of such information means nothing to Parzival because, as we are repeatedly told, he is unconscious and therefore unaware of what may be going on.[48]

By contrast with this technique of immediate naming of Arthurian knights Parzival is referred to, if not entirely anonymously, at least by terms which convey nothing to his challengers. This is of course clear when the narrator uses impersonal or passive constructions of actions carried out by Parzival, so that a construction like 284,22 (*'iu ist durch die snüere alhie gerant'*) or 295,17 (*Keie Artûs schenescalt | ze gegentjoste wart gevalt*)[49] avoids specifying who was responsible. The same anonymous effect is achieved when the narrator employs a circumlocution or epithets such as *degen, gast, knabe, man* or *ritter*.[50] However, he apparently comes closer to identifying this opponent of the Round Table on those occasions when he refers to him as *der Wâleis*,[51] and apparently leaves no

---

46. The only exception is Cunneware's page, too junior to merit designation.
47. Segramors after already being named at Arthur's encampment (287,21; 286,6 + 15 + 23; 289,3 + 19); Keii is similarly named in the Arthurian context before the encounter with Parzival (293,19 + 28; 294,10; 295,1 + 10 + 13 + 17 + 24; 296,13); the same is true of Gawan (300,6 + 21; 301,8 + 21).
48. Parzival's unconsciousness is carefully stressed on each separate occasion, with Segramors (287,9; 288,9 + 14; 289,1f.), Keii (293,6f. + 27; 296,4) and Gawan (300,12f. + 20ff.). If on the third occasion Gawan's name is mentioned by the narrator after Parzival has regained consciousness (302,19; 303,1) this happens just on the brink of Parzival learning this name from Gawan himself (303,28).
49. Cf. also 298,9.
50. *Degen* (284,1; 293,6; 302,21), *gast* (290,25; 294,30; 295,28), *knabe* (290,6), *man* (284,26), *ritter* (284,7). Circumlocutions: 287,6; 290,1; 299,1.
51. 293,29; 294,9 + 27; 295,3 + 15; 300,1 + 20; 301,26.

Parzival's failure (Books V and VI)

room for doubt when he describes him as *des künec Gahmuretes kint* (293,23; 301,5), *dem den Herzeloyde bar* (300,15) or even as Parzival.[52] This is the point where we can see most clearly how the narrator's technique is geared to the subjectivity of the people whose point of view it aims to reflect, for if all these last named terms are meaningful to the listeners and can only designate Parzival,[53] they have no such significance for the Round Table. Each of these descriptive details, long since known to us, is communicated to the members of the Round Table only in the subsequent scene when Cundrie, in accusing the knight they have just honoured, tells them these details about Parzival for the first time. Only from Cundrie do Arthur and his followers learn that the young boy who first came to them, killed Ither and has now been accepted into their midst is the son of Gahmuret (317,11: *'nu denke ich ave an Gahmureten, / des herze ie valsches was erjeten. / von Anschouwe iwer vater hiez'*). Only now do they also realise that this same figure is the son of Herzeloyde (318,3: *Herzeloyden barn*), the queen whose tournament at Kanvoleis had been attended by several members of the Round Table[54] to whom it would therefore now be clear that the knight they had been seeking was a *Wâleis* on his mother's side. Only from Cundrie do they finally learn that the name of this knight is in fact Parzival (315,9: *'hêr Parzivâl'*). None of these facts had been communicated to the Round Table when Parzival first came there and we are not told of any subsequent occasion when they could have been apprised of them. Nor can we argue that this might be a case where Wolfram has chosen not to narrate a particular detail which he can later presuppose, for it is independently confirmed by the narrator that the Round Table indeed learned all this only from Cundrie (325,17: *von Cundrîen man och innen wart / Parzivâls namn und sîner art, / daz in gebar ein künegîn, / unt wie die 'rwarp der Anschevîn*). In other words, the Round Table know none of these facts about Parzival, not even his name, before Cundrie's appearance before them, so that the narrator's references to him in apparently individualising terms during the course of his

---

52. 287,9; 288,3 + 8 + 16 + 27; 289,14; 293,6; 296,1; 300,12; 302,2.
53. The term *Gahmuretes kint* can also be used elsewhere to designate Feirefiz, but apart from the later mention of him by Cundrie (317,3ff.) and Ekuba (328,3ff.) he nowhere plays a part in the narrative at this stage.
54. We know from 65,29ff. that many Arthurian knights had attended this tournament, including Utepandragun, Lot and the young Gawan. It would therefore be known that the son of Herzeloyde must himself be a *Wâleis* (cf. 59,23 and 60,9). All this is explicitly taken up again by the Round Table in 325,21ff.

encounter with Segramors, Keii and Gawan mean nothing to them. If these opponents are referred to by name, but Parzival by terms which do not permit immediate recognition by them, this suggests that in this episode at least, because of Parzival's unconscious state, the onus of recognition lies with them. Because *frou Minne* has temporarily rendered Parzival out of action, it is now these others who must progress from ignorance to a realisation of the truth.[55]

The last stage of our argument can be confirmed from another angle if we ask ourselves how Arthur and his knights know Parzival and refer to him over this early stage of the story, if the terms used by the narrator are not available to them. The answer is that they know him as the *ritter rôt* after Iwanet has told them of his defeat of Ither and acquisition of the armour on which he had set his heart. We have seen this in Book IV when both Kingrun and Clamide are sent to offer their *sicherheit* at Arthur's court, for on each occasion Parzival is referred to by anonymous epithets or as the *ritter rôt*, by contrast with the setting at Pelrapeire where his name is free to be used among those who know him personally.[56] A similar situation arises in Book V, when this time it is Orilus who is dispatched to the Round Table under similar auspices. This occurs long before the Round Table learns the facts from Cundrie and in his combat with Parzival Orilus was nowhere shown learning the name of his victor, so that it is unavoidable that a circumlocution referring to Parzival's external appearance should be used by both sides when Orilus arrives at Arthur's court (276,4; 276,21; 278,25).

This continuous usage, arising whenever Parzival sends a defeated foe back to the Round Table, does not dispose of the problem, however, for Book VI is largely concerned with bringing Parzival and Arthur's court together again. When at the start of this Book we are told of Arthur's quest for the victor over Kingrun, Clamide and Orilus, he is referred to by the same term as was used in the Arthurian context on these three earlier occasions (280,8: ... *sô daz er suochens pflac / den der sich der rîter rôt / nante*). The same term recurs next when Parzival has been found and recognised by Gawan[57] and brought back to Arthur's encampment (305,9: *vil volkes zorse unt ze fuoz / dort inne bôt in werden gruoz, / Gâwâne und*

---

55. This is not to deny that a particular problem of recognition faces Parzival (discussed by Dewald, *Minne*, pp. 39ff.), but merely to stress that it does not concern the identity of the persons he encounters in this scene.
56. See above, pp. 76f.
57. On the process of recognition see below, pp. 130f.

Parzival's failure (Books V and VI)

dem rîter rôt), then when the news of this is received by the Round Table (307,17: *die heten alle ê vernomn, / der rôte rîter wære komn / in Gâwânes poulûn*) and when Arthur confers on Parzival the honour of the Round Table (309,15: *der künec Artûs daz gebôt / zêren dem rîter rôt*). Only with the arrival of Cundrie and the named identification of the *ritter rôt* as Parzival which she makes possible for Arthur do we find his name now juxtaposed with this descriptive epithet (315,9: '... *die drüber gap hêr Parzivâl, / der ouch dort treit diu rîters mâl. / ir nennet in den ritter rôt'*), in terms which suggest that Cundrie almost regards this epithet as a specifically Arthurian reference to Parzival.[58]

Throughout the length of Book VI, therefore, from the beginning of Arthur's quest for this victorious knight to the moment when he learns his proper name from Cundrie, the Round Table know the hero only as the *ritter rôt*: this is their way of referring to him, since they do not learn his name earlier. But there is a negative point about this distribution of the evidence which is highly significant,[59] for the term by which Arthurian knights know and recognise the knight they are seeking is not employed by the narrator between 280,9 (the Round Table sets out on its quest) and 305,11 (Gawan has now found Parzival). In other words, this distinctive term for Parzival is used both before and after the episode in which Parzival encounters the Arthurian knights Segramors, Keii and Gawan, but nowhere in this episode in which they fail to recognise him as the one they are seeking. By withholding the term *ritter rôt* over this stretch the narrator indicates the Parzival has not yet been recognised in this episode.[60] As soon as Gawan does recognise him, the term can be used again, at least until Cundrie supplements it with Parzival's actual name. Both this name and the descriptive term which stands in as a possible alternative are therefore used by the narrator to reflect the subjective state of awareness of those whose task it is to recognise his identity.

In exercising his rhetorical control over his listeners the narrator

---

58. After this passage Cundrie twice refers to Parzival by name as *hêr Parzivâl* (315,26 and 316,25) in terms which must be bitterly ironical. On this see Johnson, *MLR* 64 (1969), 69f. and Green, *Irony*, pp. 207f.
 319,13 is therefore the first occasion for the narrator to employ Parzival's name in the context of the Round Table since 148,27 and 153,14 (used at a time when this name meant nothing to them in any case and when Parzival had not yet defeated Ither, so that the term *ritter rôt* was not yet available).
59. I have discussed this from another point of view in *Namedropping*, pp. 141f.
60. On the failure in recognition, and the reasons for it, see below, pp. 126ff.

uses many other means in addition to those we have been considering. To appreciate this we can best discuss his ways of motivating success or failure in recognition in a number of encounters, the first of which is one of the most important encounter episodes in the whole work.

Parzival at Munsalvæsche

As we have already looked at the point of view technique used of Parzival's impressions when he first arrives at the Grail-castle (he is aware of less than is revealed to us) I shall concentrate now on what is in any case the most important part of the episode, the hero's reception in the hall of the castle. Here the point of view technique is taken further in that we are shown things predominantly from what amounts to the hero's standpoint, but are also allowed to question how far this standpoint is adequate to the situation and to glimpse more than he can see or understand.

The marked feature of this reception scene is the overall impression of light, brilliance and resplendence. This is suggested by a number of recurrent details working towards the same end. The hall is bathed in light from a hundred chandeliers and numerous wall-lights (229,24ff.), but this is further enhanced by the fact that some of the damsels taking part in the Grail-procession themselves carry candlesticks (232,21; 233,15; 234,27) or glass vessels in which burning *balsem* produces even more light (236,1ff.). Secondly, the effect of light is made more variegated and lively by the frequency of precious materials (231,14: *ein durchliuhtic rubîn*; 233,17: *einen tiuren stein, / dâ tages de sunne lieht durch schein*; 235,20: *einem grüenen achmardî*; 236,26: *guldîn becken*; 237,23: *manec tiwer goltvaz*).[61] Some of these examples have included the specific effect of colour, but this is carried further by the prevalence of adjectives of colour to describe the total visual scene that presents itself to Parzival as he witnesses this ceremonial.[62] Finally, although this is conventional medieval usage, the beauty of what is seen on this occasion is presented frequently in terms of light or colour (e.g. 232,15: *juncfrouwen clâr*; 233,4: *ir munt nâch fiwers roete schein*; 233,10: *wol gevar*;[63] 235,16: *ir antlütze gap den schîn, / si wânden alle ez wolde tagen*).

---

61. Cf. also 238,25: *kleiniu goltvaz*.
62. 232,20 (*val*) + 26 (*brûn scharlachen*); 233,29 (*wîz als ein snê*); 234,4 (*grüener denn ein gras*) + 21 (*wîz*); 235,13 (*röcke geteilt*) + 20 (*grüenen achmardî*); 236,29 (*wîze*); 237,5 (*var nâch wîze*).
63. Cf. also 236,28.

Parzival's failure (Books V and VI)

All this adds up to an overwhelming impression of unsurpassed wealth, luxury, pomp and ceremony, details which the narrator stresses explicitly. Wealth and luxury are clearly implied by the presence of so many precious materials, but are also specified in several other respects (e.g. 230,14: *jenz wâren kostenlîchiu werc*;[64] 233,24: *dâ obe der wirt durch rîchheit az*; 237,21: *hœrt mêr von rîchheite sagen*; 239,9: *die rîcheit*).[65] Pomp and ceremony, on the other hand, are conveyed by the outstanding frequency with which the various actions constituting Parzival's reception at Munsalvæsche are described as being carried out *mit zuht* or *mit zühten*.[66] This type of phrase is applied in particular to the ceremonial nature of the Grail-procession, in which the narrator emerges almost as a master of ceremonies, anxious that everything should go off in the proper way. He is painstakingly careful to number the damsels in each separate group and to make us aware of the grand total of twenty-five in this procession,[67] he groups the various participants in ascending order of social rank,[68] and makes us mentally aware of the final tableau they represent: queen Repanse de schoy as the senior in rank fittingly carries the Grail herself and takes up a position in which she is flanked by twelve on either side (236,18: *dô liezen si die hêrsten / zwischen sich; man sagte mir, / zwelve iewederthalben ir*).

All the above, especially the effects of light, colour, manifest splendour and the symmetrical grouping of the damsels in the Grail-procession, amounts to a predominantly visual impression. This is conveyed to us by other means as well. Thus, we are told

---

64. Cf. 236,2: *diu wârn von armer koste nieht*.
65. See also 242,10f.
66. The examples are: 227,27; 234,1; 235,4; 236,7 + 16; 238,5 + 30; 240,19 + 22. In 229,18 the same *zuht* can also be demanded of Parzival by those at Munsalvæsche. Cf. Huth, *Wahrheit*, pp.136ff.
67. The narrator's careful counting of the participants is made repeatedly obvious: 232,11; 233,1f. + 5 + 13; 234,16 + 28 + 29; 235,4ff. + 8 + 15; 236,16f. How obvious this is meant to be is suggested by the narrator's comment in 235,6: *ob i'z geprüevet rehte hân*. Cf. Curschmann, *DVjs* 45 (1971), 637: 'Im Gegensatz zu dem Helden der Erzählung wird der Hörer geradezu daran *gehindert*, sich an die Szene zu verlieren, und zur Konzentration auf den Erzählvorgang selbst aufgefordert.'
68. The various participants in the procession are listed in an ascending order of aristocratic rank: the first rank to be specified is that of a *grævîn* (232,25), which is followed in turn by *herzogîn* (233,1), *fürstîn* (234,16) and *künegîn* (235,15). How important this gradation by rank is felt to be can be seen from the central position allotted to queen Repanse de schoy as the senior (236,18: *die hêrsten*). On this gradation see Mergell, *Parzival*, pp. 124f., and Hirschberg, *Untersuchungen*, p.108.

specifically three times that this is what Parzival saw (229,28: *er ... vant*; 236,12: *Parzivâl / ... sach*; 239,8: *gemarcte Parzivâl*), but in five cases the use of the impersonal *man* with a verb of seeing implies that a particular detail was beheld by all those present, including the hero.[69] But apart from Parzival all those present are members of the Grail-community, to whom all this courtly finery and ceremony would presumably be nothing new,[70] so that essentially the narrator's focus is on Parzival, the newcomer who witnesses all this for the first time, so that it is presented to us as he sees it, we watch it with him. This looking over Parzival's shoulder is finally suggested by two narratorial interjections, inviting the listeners to behold things as Parzival does (233,12: *seht*; 235,7: *hie sulen ahzehen frouwen stên. / âvoy nu siht man* ...). This last example is particularly instructive. It combines an interjection to the audience, asking them to pay close attention (*âvoy*), with a verb of seeing governed by a collective subject (*siht man*), so that the narrator's audience are equated with those present at Munsalvæsche; the former's task of listening carefully is transposed to the latter's act of watching. This equation of two separate audiences (the one inside the work, the other listening to it) is further underlined by the narrator's use of the present tense (*siht* in place of *sach*) and of two adverbs which place his listeners firmly in the context of the events he is recounting (*hie* and *nu*).

This presentation of things at Munsalvæsche from the beholder's point of view (which means essentially Parzival's) also underlies the long list of courtly objects (together with one action, the Grail-procession) which are enumerated from the moment Parzival enters the palace (229,23). These include the equipment of the hall itself (lighting, beds, seats, carpets, fireplaces, etc.), but also the various objects used in the ceremonial meal (bowls, towels, trolleys, condiments, etc.) of which the Grail, as a miraculous provider, is the centrepiece. By providing such a long list of details the narrator conveys to us how Parzival is overwhelmed by a mounting visual impression of supreme luxury. Although the Grail itself is men-

69. 232,24; 234,16; 235,8; 235,18; 236,30. By comparison with this overwhelming visual impression an acoustic dimension is brought in only by the narrator asking for attention from his listeners (232,12; 234,30; 237,21; 238,2).
70. Weigand, *Parzival*, p. 100, has suggested, without being able to prove it, that the ceremonial procession with the Grail took place only on the two occasions explicitly described in the work. Yet even if we accept this suggestion about the ceremonial, none of its accompanying luxury would have been at all novel to the members of the Grail-community.

Parzival's failure (Books V and VI)

tioned (235,20ff.) about half-way through this list of approximately two dozen separate objects, I should not wish to suggest a parallel between this symmetrical position and the visual symmetry of Repanse de schoy, the carrier of the Grail, flanked by a dozen damsels on either side, if only because this would involve us in the kind of number-juggling associated with the adherents of number symbolism as an organising feature of medieval literature. It is enough to suggest that the central position of the Grail in the numerous details listed by the narrator corresponds closely to the symmetrical disposition of the Grail-procession.

Although we are thus shown things as Parzival experiences them, the narrator at times takes us beyond his restricted point of view by prompting doubts (whose significance is revealed only later) whether this visual impression goes far enough. Thus, at the close of the Grail-procession we are told that Parzival concentrates his gaze and his thoughts on Repanse de schoy (236,12: *dez mære giht daz Parzivâl / dicke an si sach unt dâhte, / diu den grâl dâ brâhte*),[71] whereas it is later made clear that what was urgently called for was rather for him to concentrate his thoughts on the Grail and its mysteries or, more crucially, on Anfortas himself. A little later we are told that Parzival notices the provision of food by the Grail (239,8: *wol gemarcte Parzivâl / die rîcheit unt daz wunder grôz*), but by the sequence of these two terms the narrator insinuates that the hero's attention may be taken up more by the incredible luxury (*rîcheit*) than by any miraculous qualities of the Grail, whilst even the term *wunder* could be meant only additively, suggesting nothing more than amazement at such luxury. Even the question which we are told Parzival did not ask (239,10) may have turned out to be, if he had brought himself to ask it, little more than a question

71. I wonder whether the syntactical construction used here is meant to reflect Parzival's order of priorities. When the narrator simply describes Repanse de schoy carrying the Grail in an almost liturgical procession he grants priority to the Grail as the centre of the ritual by making it the grammatical subject and by converting the logical subject, the carrier, into a grammatical object (235,25: *Repanse de schoy si hiez, / die sich der grâl tragen liez*). That this is no chance formulation is confirmed by its recurrence in 809,10f. When the retreating procession is seen explicitly from Parzival's point of view, however, and we are shown him paying more attention to the human carrier than to the miraculous stone (as in 236,12ff.) this 'liturgical syntax' is abandoned and the Grail is made the grammatical object. See also below, p. 257, fn. 94. There is of course a non-stylistic reason for the narrator's 'liturgical' formulation (477,13ff.: the Grail miraculously demands complete purity from those who are to carry it), but this reason does not affect the difference between the narrator's point of view and Parzival's.

about such luxury[72] (of which Repanse de schoy, on whom his gaze had recently been fixed, was the focal point), rather than one about Anfortas's suffering.[73] Parzival's concentration on the wrong thing is also suggested at the point when the procession removes the Grail from the hall at the conclusion of the meal (240,21: *si brâhten wider în zer tür | daz si mit zuht ê truogen für. | Parzivâl in blicte nâch*). The hero's impressions are still visual ones, he is still preoccupied with the luxury he can see and his gaze is therefore directed away from Anfortas by whose side he is sitting and whose condition should be uppermost in his mind, his eyes are directed not at the Grail itself, but at the members of the procession (*in*).

These hints, prompting no more than occasional doubts, are reinforced by comments made by the narrator which reveal to us more than can be grasped by Parzival. With the first class of narratorial comments, emphasising the suffering of Anfortas and the grief to which this subjects the Grail-community, we revert to the point of view technique applied before Parzival actually entered the palace of Munsalvæsche.[74] We are now given an early reminder of Anfortas's mortal sickness (230,18: *ez was worden wette | zwischen im und der vröude: | er lebte niht wan töude*),[75] but if this is made unambiguously clear to us, we have to ask how far this may be externally visible and whether Parzival actually sees it. We are given no indication that he does, and it may even be the case that Anfortas's placing on the *spanbette* (230,15ff.) and this accompanying commentary both fall before Parzival has entered the hall itself (he enters the palace building in 229,23, *si giengen ûf ein palas*, but is shown joining his host only in 230,21: *in den palas kom gegangen*).[76] A little later the host's invitation to his guest to sit down next to him

---

72. Cf. above, p. 93, fn. 19. *Wunder* in 239,9 would therefore mean, from Parzival's point of view, the object of his amazement and wonder, the luxury and ceremony which he has witnessed. On this less than metaphysical sense of *wunder*, the measure of Parzival's failure to grasp the metaphysical dimensions of Munsalvæsche, cf. also the more conventional use of *wunder* in 143,13 and, again in the context of Munsalvæsche, in 234,19.
73. 240,3ff.
74. See above, p. 94.
75. Of one effect of this sickness (namely that Anfortas cannot stand up) the listeners are given a slight hint by the narrator in the preceding lines (230,15ff.), but then a retrospective explanation, at the same time as Parzival, by Signue in 251,16ff. Even the slight hint is denied to Parzival.
76. The description of the hall (229,24ff.) is thus given before Parzival actually enters (230,21ff.), but it nonetheless anticipates what Parzival himself sees (229,28: *er . . . vant*).

Parzival's failure (Books V and VI)

by one of the fireplaces (230,25ff.)⁷⁷ is explained by the narrator in these terms (230,30): *sus sprach der wirt jâmers rîch. / Der wirt het durch siechheit / grôziu fiur und an im warmiu kleit.* If we postulate a distinction between what is revealed to us and is visible to Parzival, it is clear that within these three lines he can only be aware that his host has just addressed him, that the fires are lit and that Anfortas is wearing warm clothing. What is not necessarily clear to him, however, is the fact that his host is *jâmers rîch* and seeks warmth *durch siechheit*, and even if he wonders about the need for warmth this could be explained by the cold, snowy weather which comes soon afterwards and which is felt by Anfortas in advance.⁷⁸ When at the end of the evening meal the narrator again takes up the theme of suffering (242,1: *Ich wil iu doch paz bediuten / von disen jâmerbæren liuten. / dar kom geriten Parzivâl, / man sach dâ selten freuden schal, / ez wære buhurt oder tanz: / ir klagendiu stæte was sô ganz, / sine kêrten sich an schimphen niht*), he is directly addressing only his listeners, so that his use of *ich* and *iu* excludes Parzival, just as his generalising *selten* conveys a lasting fact about Munsalvæsche which cannot be accessible to him. The most that Parzival can perhaps now grasp is the fact, made glaringly obvious with the lance (231,15ff.), that grief predominates on this one occasion,⁷⁹ but even here he cannot tell that it has been brought about by Anfortas's sickness (237,8 is thus another narratorial comment which bypasses him) and that this sickness is the focus of all he witnesses in this castle.⁸⁰ Anfortas's suffering is thus not completely invisible to Parzival, but much less easily visible than the narrator has made it to the listeners. Parzival's task is to grasp the significance of what he can see (of what, so he learns much later, was providentially made more apparent for him on this occasion than at any other time)⁸¹ and act accordingly. He fails to show the necessary perception.

Other facts are communicated to the listeners, but withheld from Parzival. We learn of the name of *li roy Frimutel* (230,4f.) at this

---

77. The closeness of the fireplace has been made clear from 230,15ff.
78. Cf. Deinert, *Ritter*, p. 27. On the apparent discrepancy between this snowy weather and the heat of the day pointed out in 256,5 see Weigand, *Parzival*, pp. 48ff.
79. Cf. also 239,26f., but compressed into a subordinate clause and overshadowed by the magnitude of Anfortas's gift of his valuable sword to Parzival.
80. In the couplet 237,7f. (*der wirt dô selbe wazzer nam: / der was an hôhem muote lam*) the first line shows what Parzival himself can see, but the second line what is revealed by the narrator to the listeners alone.
81. See below, p. 209, and Deinert, *Ritter*, p. 14.

castle, even though we do not know who he is and might perhaps assume from this passage that he is still king of the Grail-community, and also of Repanse de schoy (228,13; 235,25). We are also informed of the name of the Grail, its paradisiac and almost metaphysical nature, and the condition of chastity which it imposes (235,20ff.; 238,21ff.). If this is passed on to us by the narrator without Parzival having any means of sharing it, the same is true, I suggest, of the miraculous feeding qualities of the Grail (238,2ff.). If we seek for the common ground between what we are told here and what Parzival can see for himself, it will be found in lines 3–7 (a hundred pages collect bread in front of the Grail), but even here one may ask the realistic question as to how much would have been visible to the guest, with so many waiters crowding together at this spot. For the rest, the lines describing the miraculous properties of the Grail (238,8ff.) are exclusively narrator's commentary, he huddles together with his listeners and by making them partly responsible for his wondrous information he conspiratorially gets them onto his side,[82] thus effectively shutting out Parzival.[83] Exactly the same technique is used with the sword presented to Parzival by his host (239,21: *sîn gehilze was ein rubîn, / ouch möhte wol diu klinge sîn / grôzer wunder urhap*). Parzival is capable of seeing for himself that the hilt is of ruby, but cannot be credited with recognising the miraculous qualities of the blade, of which he in fact learns only later from Sigune (253,24ff.). Finally, it is in connection with this gift of the sword and then as Parzival retires for the night that the narrator bursts out with his remarks on the vital urgency of the question which should have been asked (240,3ff.; 242,16ff.), stressing its close connection with Anfortas's suffering (240,7ff.). Again, Parzival knows nothing of this and has his first intimation on the necessity of asking the question only as he leaves Munsalvæsche (247,28f.).

On a number of points, therefore, the listeners are provided with information superior to Parzival's and at the same time are enabled to recognise this fact. However, this still does not free them entirely from his position of needing to know more, so that they alternate between different degrees of knowledge and ignorance, as is

---

82. Cf. Wolff, *Schriften*, p. 272 and Nellmann, *Erzähltechnik*, pp. 68f.
83. Even if we assume that Parzival could see for himself what is narrated in 239,1–4 (*Môraz, wîn, sinopel rôt, / swâ nâch den napf ieslîcher bôt, / swaz er trinkens kunde nennen, / daz mohter drinne erkennen*), he would certainly have had no access to the narrator's explanation (239,5: *allez von des grâles kraft*).

Parzival's failure (Books V and VI)

brought out in theoretical terms in the 'Bogengleichnis'. They still need to know how all these separate and apparently disparate details fit together and, even if they have as yet no grounds for suspecting this dimension, they are later to learn with Parzival from Trevrizent how providential control is at work in all this, even in the most trivial details.[84] Even though the listeners may be in some respects in advance of Parzival on their path to enlightenment, their journey is on the same route as his from the events at Munsalvæsche in Book V to the explanation provided by the hermit in Book IX. In other words, the tension between experience and comprehension suggested by the 'Bogengleichnis' extends further than the names released by Sigune in her second encounter with Parzival (251,2ff.):[85] the narrator uses *nennen* (241,4) not merely in the sense of naming, but also in the fuller sense of telling us all about, explaining the detailed happenings at Munsalvæsche which we find with Trevrizent.[86] Meanwhile it is to the first stage of this explanation, the partial one given by Sigune, that we must now turn.

Parzival and Sigune

Two processes of recognition are involved in this scene. Each of the participants has to recognise the other and the narrator has to motivate this in detail in order to be realistically convincing, but in addition to this Parzival and in some measure the listeners have to be brought to a first, partial recognition of the significance of events at Munsalvæsche.

As we have accompanied Parzival on his departure from the Grail-castle we come across Sigune and experience the encounter with her from Parzival's point of view: just as he at first fails to recognise her, so are we put in the same position by the narrator referring to her at first only in anonymous terms.[87] As the scene progresses, however, a number of clues, still far from explicit, are provided.[88] One of these we share with Parzival, for with him we see that this woman nurses the corpse of a knight in her arms

---

84. See below, pp. 209ff.
85. As is suggested, in an all too literalist understanding of the text, by Nellmann, *Erzähltechnik*, pp. 89ff.
86. On the possible meaning of *nennen* here and on the fulfilment of the promise of enlightenment given in the 'Bogengleichnis' only in Book IX see Green, *Irony*, pp. 148f., and below, pp. 202ff.
87. See above, p. 100, fn. 38.
88. Cf. Harroff, *Wolfram*, pp. 64f.

(249,16f.) and may recall the similar situation in the first encounter between Parzival and Sigune (138,20ff.).[89] But two further clues are provided to us by the narrator which are not available to Parzival. First, we are told that, even though he does not recognise her, she is in fact his cousin (249,23: *si was doch sîner muomen kint*), a detail which reminds us that at their first meeting Sigune had told Parzival this (140,22: '*dîn muoter ist mîn muome*'). Secondly, there is a tacit parallel between the narrator's comment that this woman grieving for the knight deserved compassion (249,18: *swenz niht wolt erbarmen, / der si sô sitzen sæhe, / untriwen ich im jæhe*) and the phrasing of Sigune's remark to Parzival at their first meeting, when he offers to help (140,1: '*du bist geborn von triuwen, / daz er dich sus kan riuwen*'). Although what was first said by Sigune is later taken up by the narrator and although her particular remark has given way to his general observation, this parallel is still meaningful, since the generalisation has particular force here: it refers to Parzival, as is clear a few lines later (249,26ff.) when he shows *triuwe* by reacting compassionately, as on the first occasion. Since these two clues involve the narrator, it is through him that the listeners are given these extra means of judging the situation, whilst Parzival can go on nothing else but the situation of a woman grieving over a dead knight.

The narrator also demonstrates that each party in this scene fails to recognise the other. With Parzival he tells us this explicitly (249,22: *der wênic si bekante*) and then confirms it by having him address Sigune as a perfect stranger, using *frouwe* and the polite pronoun *ir* (249,27ff.), both of which details contrast with his usage once he recognises her as a kinswoman (252,28: '*bistuz Sigûne*') and with his use of *du* at their last meeting once he had learned of their kinship (141,25f.). No explicit remark is made about Sigune's initial failure to recognise him, but it is implied by her using the formal *hêr* (251,1 and 21) and the pronoun *ir* from the beginning of her dialogue (250,11f.), again in contrast with her usage when she sees who he is (251,29: '*du bist Parzivâl*') and at their earlier meeting (140,16).

---

89. Although in the restricted segment of the world of reality presented by a work of fiction these two similar situations may be felt to belong together by the audience, the fact of knightly homicide plays so large a part in this work (see Green, *Homicide*, *passim*) that women grieving over slain knights may be regarded as commonplace. There is therefore no certainty that this woman encountered by Parzival is the same as the one he met in Book III.

Parzival's failure (Books V and VI)

The position so far is that each party fails to recognise the other (in Parzival's case despite the one uncertain clue he is given) and that the audience are given clues which, if they are receptive enough of past details, enable them to move ahead of the characters involved and to suspect, if not to know, that Parzival and Sigune have come together again. But Wolfram also builds into this scene indications why these two should fail to recognise each other immediately, thereby countering any objections on the grounds of improbability. With Sigune this task was easy. Her inability to recognise Parzival is sufficiently accounted for by the difference in his external appearance (a child in fool's clothing has become a knight in armour), but this implicit point is reinforced by other details. Parzival not merely wears armour, but is hidden in it, since he comes across Sigune while following the Grail-knights and therefore ready for immediate combat on behalf of Anfortas,[90] so that he has taken the precaution of putting his helmet on, which makes his features invisible. This is also suggested by the probability that his voice was muffled within the helmet, since although Sigune eventually recognises Parzival by his voice (251,28: *bî der stimme erkante sie den man*) this happens only after he has already addressed her three times,[91] so that there can be nothing straightforward about it. Moreover, the armour worn by Parzival (stripped from Ither) is misleading in another respect, for Sigune refers to it as a stranger's armour (250,19: '*ir traget doch einen gastes schilt*'). She means by this that he does not bear the Grail coat of arms and therefore cannot come from Munsalvæsche, as he claims, but we can see how she regards him as a stranger in another sense, for if he now wears Ither's red armour she has no means of seeing in him a kinsman, the son of the man who had married her aunt.

Parzival for his part must have found difficulties in recognising Sigune. We learn from his lament once he finds out who she is how drastically changed her appearance is (252,27ff.), how prolonged grieving has ravaged her beauty, since at their first meeting, coming immediately upon her lover's death in combat (cf. 135,21f.), she had

---

90. How completely ready he makes himself for the combat he expects is made clear from 246,24: *von fuoz ûf wâpent er sich wol / durch strîtes antwurte, / zwei swert er umbe gurte*. Hahn, *Schönheit*, p. 230, also reads this scene as implying that Parzival is enclosed within his helmet when he encounters Sigune on this occasion.
91. 249,26ff.; 250,13ff.; 251,25ff. For other literary examples where recognition is made difficult or possible by a person's voice see Peil, *Gebärde*, p. 133, fn. 92, and p. 184.

The Art of Recognition in Wolfram's *Parzival*

only just begun to tear her hair and disfigure herself (138,17ff.) and Parzival's arrival had put a temporary stop to this, so that he still remembers her as red-lipped and long-haired and sees nothing to connect the woman he now comes across with the Sigune he once met.[92]

This three-point relationship, in which the audience are potentially somewhat in advance of the others in recognising what is afoot, does not remain static for long, since Sigune comes to see that the knight before her is Parzival. She recognises him at length not just by his voice (251,28), but also by a type of unconscious association of which Wolfram avails himself elsewhere.[93] By this I mean in this particular case that Sigune is unconsciously led towards recognising him or that her recognition of his muffled voice within his helmet is activated by the fact that she has just been talking (251,2–20) about the various members of the Grail-family to which Parzival belongs, so that her thoughts are already unwittingly focused on the area in which the truth will present itself to her when, in reply, Parzival speaks to her for the third time and she realises whose voice it it. Typically, because the theme of the work is the hero's slow progress to insight and understanding, Parzival takes longer to recognise Sigune than she does him. When she says in recognition that he must be Parzival (251,29), he asks in return how she has recognised him (252,10: *'wâ von habt ir mich erkant?'*), but still uses the formal *ir* in contrast to her recent resumption of *du*. She then has to describe their earlier meeting to him (252,11ff.) and remind him of their kinship, so that her words (252,15: *'daz dîn muoter ist mîn muome'*) enable Parzival at last to draw level with the audience, who had been apprised of this fact early by the narrator (249,23). Only now does Parzival see that this must be Sigune and begin to use the pronoun *du* himself (252,27ff.).[94]

The pattern of recognition in this scene is therefore based on three chronological stages: first the listeners are given clues which

---

92. To this we must add that the two meetings take place in different locations (the first in Brizljan, the second near Munsalvæsche), although Wolfram has done nothing to motivate this change of place on Sigune's part.
93. I have discussed the subconscious movement of Trevrizent's thoughts towards recognition of Parzival in 474,1ff. in *Homicide*, p. 74. See also below, p. 190.
94. Parzival's question *'bistuz Sigûne'* (252,28) shows that he can identify Sigune by name, even though the earlier encounter between them, as narrated to us, nowhere showed us Sigune naming herself to him. This is a clear example of a detail which may not be narrated at the time, but which later events show must have nonetheless taken place. As such it must be included in the examples given above, p. 96, fn. 26.

Parzival's failure (Books V and VI)

allow them potentially to see the truth, then Sigune recognises the situation as it is, and finally Parzival, so that by now, on a new level, all three members of this three-point relationship are abreast of one another again, as they had been at the start. This is the position as regards the simple question of the identity of these two people, but in another respect the same scene shows us, intertwined with the thread we have been following, how Sigune now falls behind both the listeners and Parzival as regards knowledge of the situation.

When Parzival says that he has just come from what can only be Munsalvæsche, she cannot believe this (250,17f.; cf. 251,1) and accuses him of dishonesty, so that both the listeners and Parzival know a truth which Sigune cannot imagine to be such. Along this line of motivation she is now the last to learn the truth. Once she has recognised who Parzival is, Sigune is eventually persuaded that he has been at the Grail-castle (251,29ff.).[95] But the object of her ignorance now changes, switching from an unreadiness to accept that he has been at Munsalvæsche to an inability to conceive that, while there, he failed to ask the redeeming question (251,21ff. and 252,2ff.), so that the dramatic irony of her new ignorance underlines the vital importance of the question which Parzival had neglected to ask, a detail which is painfully accentuated by the dithyrambic praise of Parzival into which she now optimistically launches (252,4ff.) and which we, together with him, know to be quite unjustified.[96] That the Grail-king exercises supreme authority, as this praise makes clear, is something new to us and of course to Parzival,[97] but by releasing his information in controlled instal-

---

95. Neither the listeners nor Parzival can realise at this point that Sigune may be the more ready to believe this of Parzival, now that she grasps his identity, because of her advantage in knowing that he belongs to the Grail-family by birth. Another reason why Sigune should now believe that Parzival has in fact been at the Grail-castle is that she is convinced by noticing that he is girt with Anfortas's sword (253,24: '*du füerst och umbe dich sîn swert*').

96. The irony of Sigune's ignorance at this stage is brought out by the syntax of her words at 253,19ff. (*diu sprach 'sol mich iht gevröun, / daz tuot ein dinc, ob in sîn töun / læzet, den vil trûrgen man. / schiede du helflîche dan, / sô ist dîn lîp wol prîses wert*'). Sigune here uses a polite conditional formulation three times in succession, meant more for reasons of etiquette than because she literally believes it (how convinced she is has already been made clear in 252,4ff.). We know however that this is literally true: Parzival begins to suspect more of the enormity of his omission, whilst Sigune still remains ignorant.

97. This is the point at which to indicate the varying levels on which Sigune provides information about Munsalvæsche. Such information falls into two categories (revealed or still concealed), each of which subdivides into two further classes. (1) Parzival and the listeners simultaneously learn a point (that Grail-territory is defended to the death against intruders, 250,3ff.; that the

ments the narrator achieves incomparably more powerful effects, ensuring that both we and Parzival learn the truth only when the opportunity has already been squandered. When finally Sigune does realise the facts about Parzival and the question (255,1), she reacts in horror by taking up her original distance from him again in reverting to the pronoun *ir* (255,2: '*ôwê daz iuch mîn ouge siht*').

If we take into account these two processes of recognition (one in which Sigune is quick and one in which she is slow to see the truth) we can distinguish in all five levels of failure in recognition in this scene. (1) Parzival fails to recognise Sigune, (2) Sigune fails to recognise Parzival, (3) Sigune does not realise that Parzival has been at Munsalvæsche, but when she does learn this, (4) Sigune does not know that Parzival has failed to ask the question. (5) Underlying all these levels, Parzival fails to grasp what was at stake at the Grail-castle. These five levels are carefully built into the narrative, but in addition the narrator links them up with the information he feeds to his listeners, allowing them sometimes to know more than one or other party involved, but sometimes placing them on the same level of ignorance.[98]

Parzival, Jeschute and Orilus

After Sigune has cursed Parzival for failing to put an end to Anfortas's suffering the knight sets out on his journeying again. There follows as a bridge to the next scene a short passage (256,1ff.) which, combining psychological with realistic details, shows us how the heat of the day, together with the hot emotions of grief and

> Grail-castle cannot be consciously sought,250,26ff.; the names of the castle and its territory, 251,2ff.; the name of the Grail-king, 251,16ff.; the extent of the Grail-king's authority, 252,4ff. and 254,20ff.). (2) The listeners already know, but Parzival now learns (that the Grail is the sum of earthly perfection, 250,25, as the listeners have already learnt from the narrator, 235,24; the name of the Grail, 251,30, cf. the earlier remark to the listeners, 235,23; the fact of Anfortas's suffering, 253,21 and 256,21ff.). (3) Parzival and the listeners still remain in ignorance (that Titurel, named in 251,5, is identical with the old man glimpsed in 241,27 and about whom enlightenment is promised in 241,1f.; that Parzival belongs to the Grail-family on his mother's side, see below, pp. 214ff.). (4) The listeners may suspect, but Parzival still remains ignorant that miraculous guidance and election conducted him to Munsalvæsche (this follows in retrospect from 250,26ff. but the full extent of his providential guidance is revealed only in Book IX, cf. Green, *Weg*, pp. 15ff. and *Pathway*, pp. 177ff.). On the information about Munsalvæsche not provided by Sigune at this point, see above, p. 92, fn. 12.
>
> 98. On another failure in recognition in this scene, shared at this point by Parzival and the listeners, see below, pp. 216f.

Parzival's failure (Books V and VI)

anger with himself, causes Parzival to perspire and take off his helmet to cool himself, and how his beauty still shines through the rust caused by perspiring in his helmet. At the end of these ten lines the next scene is upon us, in which Parzival encounters Jeschute for the second time, riding in tattered clothing and on a broken-down horse some distance behind her husband who is inflicting this punishment on her, as he threatened to in Book III when he returned to her tent after the young Parzival's departure and discovered apparently incontrovertible evidence of her disloyalty.

Like the recent meeting with Sigune, this encounter starts with an anonymous reference to Jeschute by the narrator (256,15: *eine frouwen die er sach*),[99] so that we are once more put into the same position as Parzival, we cannot know at first who this woman is. But again as with the preceding scene the listeners are given clues not available to the knight.[100] One group of clues concerns the description of the lady and her horse, which is exactly what Parzival can also see for himself, but whereas he can see *all* the many physical details, we see only a selection filtered through to us by the narrator, so that we can assume that if these details serve more than merely descriptive ends they will include points which it is important for us to recognise. We are therefore shown the starving condition of her horse (256,17ff.) and are meant to recall the terms of Orilus's earlier threat (137,2: '*iwer phert bejagt wol hungers teil*'); the detail that the reins are of hemp (256,21) refers back to the same context (137,1: '*iwer zoum muoz sîn ein bästîn seil*'); the short description of the battered saddlegear (257,1ff.) is the tangible result of the violence earlier inflicted on it by the husband (137,7: *er zersluoc den satel dâ se inne reit*); the woman's torn clothing (257,8ff.) follows from Orilus's insistence that she will be allowed no change of clothing (136,29f.). Even the first detail in the description of Jeschute (256,11ff.: there are two sets of horse's tracks, those of an *ors* alongside her *barfuoz pfäret*) points back to the conclusion of the earlier scene, when Orilus and his wife set out together on their travels (cf. 137,14 and 138,1). All these details refer to Jeschute's punishment at the hands of her husband and they are available to the perceptive listener who

---

99. See above, p. 100. By adding *die er sach* at the start of this new encounter the narrator once more ensures that his listeners experience it from Parzival's point of view, at least at the beginning.
100. Cf. Harroff, *Wolfram*, pp. 40f., and Hirschberg, *Untersuchungen*, pp. 18f., 23, 151ff. The parallels between Parzival's two encounters with Jeschute listed by Hirschberg, p. 151, are not enough to establish her identity beyond doubt, but they constitute the basis on which the more telling clues rest.

The Art of Recognition in Wolfram's *Parzival*

recalls such points, seemingly unimportant at the time, from two Books earlier. But these points are not available to Parzival as hints, since Orilus had uttered his threats and begun punishing his wife only after Parzival had passed on out of the earlier episode. The listeners therefore potentially know more than Parzival can.

Another group of clues is given to the listeners in narratorial comments, so that again Parzival is deprived of such hints. The woman's lips are mentioned as red (257,18), just as the earlier scene gave the same detail (130,5). This is as visually obvious to Parzival as the narrator has made it clear to us, but what the hero cannot observe is the narrator's comment on these lips on the second occasion (257,20: *man hete fiwer wol drûz geslagen*), a humorous hyperbole harking back to the similar narratorial assessment on the earlier occasion (130,9: *der truoc der minne hitze fiur*). Something similar is true of the narrator's assertion that Jeschute's punishment was unmerited (257,27), which refers back to what was made amply clear in the first encounter, that she was the innocent victim of Parzival's folly.[101] This may now be retrospectively clear even to Parzival (cf. 176,8), but since he knows nothing of Orilus's decision to punish his wife or of the narrator's observation on her unmerited punishment he has no hint, as we have, that these two scenes may be connected. When the narrator mischievously betrays his emotional weakness for the woman on horseback (257,31: *doch næme ich sölhen blôzen lîp / für etslîch wol gekleidet wîp*) and alludes to her noble birth (257,7), these two details mean something to the listeners, but not to Parzival himself, for in the first scene the narrator revealed to us his sympathy with her (137,30) and her aristocratic rank (130,28), unknown to Parzival.

Although we in the audience are given clues (I have listed nine altogether), if not complete certainty, even these hints are withheld from the hero and it is from his point of view that the narrator at first refers to the lady anonymously. But the narrator can dispense with Parzival's consistency in using *frouwe*, because he also, as the clues to his listeners mount to near certainty, gradually closes in on Jeschute's identity by moving from *frouwe* to *blôziu frouwe* to *diu blôze herzogîn* (260,3).[102] This last detail is significant for the listeners, since they learned from the narrator in the earlier scene that Jeschute is the wife of Duke Orilus (129,27f.) and therefore a duchess (130,28), but not for Parzival, who knows nothing of

---

101. This was made clear as early as 131,6ff. Cf. also Jeschute's protestation (133,11ff.) and the narrator's later comment (264,15).
102. See above, pp. 100f.

Parzival's failure (Books V and VI)

Jeschute's status as a duchess (either that the lady in the tent was one or that this lady on horseback is). A little after this point in the later scene the narrator makes it clear that the lady's husband is *der herzoge Orilus* (260,25), whom we know from the start of the first encounter between Parzival and Jeschute as the latter's husband, so that implicitly we now know for certain whom he has encountered here. This is confirmed from 262,25 on, where the narrator starts to use *frou Jeschute* explicitly.[103]

This grouping of hints at the very start of the scene and the distribution of initially anonymous and then gradually more explicit references to Jeschute mean that, as the scene progresses, the listeners come to realise who she is and that Parzival has met her before, in other words, that the danger of a confrontation with Orilus, earlier avoided when Sigune deliberately put him on the wrong track (141,30ff.), has at last caught up with him. Theoretically, the perceptive listeners can grasp the presence of dramatic irony from the clues bunched together at the beginning, but some may have realised it only from the mention of *diu blôze herzogîn*, whilst the more obtuse may have needed to wait for the explicit mention of *frou Jeschute*.

The point at which the perceptive listeners may have already realised Jeschute's identity is simultaneous with the point when Parzival greets her and she recognises him (258,1: *Dô Parzivâl gruoz gein ir sprach, / an in si erkenneclîchen sach*). A poet so concerned with coherent details has to motivate how this is possible. It is accounted for explicitly when the act of recognition is reported (258,3: *er was der schönste übr elliu lant; / dâ von sin schiere het erkant*), for we know how deeply impressed Jeschute was by Parzival's beauty (133,17f.) and at what cost in rousing her husband's jealousy (133,21f.; cf. 271,4f.). But an implicit explanation is also given, since we need to be told how Jeschute can recognise Parzival from his beauty, whereas recently Sigune was unable to recognise him at first. This has already been provided for in the bridge passage between these two scenes (256,1ff.) by the point that Parzival, after leaving Sigune, had to take off his helmet and that his beauty was still visible through the rust.[104]

---

103. See above, p. 101, fn. 43.
104. From this we see that Wolfram accounts for non-recognition and recognition in two adjacent scenes by devising an occasion between the two scenes for the knight to remove his helmet and thus make his features visible. We saw a similar example in Gahmuret's fighting at Kanvoleis (see above, p. 56) and we shall see the technique repeated in the case of Cunneware at the Round Table (see below, p. 131).

By now the listeners (even if only theoretically)[105] and Jeschute (in fact) have reached the same stage of comprehension, whilst Parzival still does not grasp the situation. When she expresses her recognition to him (258,5: *'ich hân iuch ê gesehn'*) she couples this with a reproach to him (258,6ff.) about something quite unknown to him, namely the punishment meted out to her by Orilus as a result of their first meeting. Since Parzival knows nothing of this he rejects her reproach (258,15ff.), arguing from this that he also knows nothing of her, so that her recognition and accusation must be unfounded. But the listeners can appreciate the unwitting irony of his denial (258,17: *'jane wart von mîme lîbe | iu noch decheinem wîbe | laster nie gemêret | ... | sît ich den schilt von êrst gewan | und rîters fuore mich versan'*), for they know that the earlier meeting came before Parzival acquired his knightly equipment from Ither. His generalisation about his chivalry implies that for Parzival the period before Ither is a thing of the past,[106] but here it has caught up with him. His over-confident recommendation to Jeschute (258,15: *'merket baz'*) could more fittingly be directed at himself. Alongside this psychological reason for his failure to recognise Jeschute we are also given a more factual one, since her dishevelled state (257,5ff.) removes her completely from the impression of courtly beauty she earlier conveyed (cf. Orilus's threat in 136,5f.) so that it is difficult to recognise in her the seductive woman she was once, even if Parzival were psychologically disposed to remember details from a past of which he is heartily ashamed.

At the start of this scene, therefore, Parzival clearly does not recognise Jeschute, he denies that he has ever had anything to do with her, but by the time when he swears her innocence to Orilus he must have realised who she is, since he refers to specific details of their earlier meeting (269,22f.; 270,2f.). Somewhere in the course of the encounter Parzival, like those listeners who fail to recognise Jeschute from the beginning, must have come across the truth, but where? Is it perhaps at the point where the narrator gives up referring to Jeschute only by a term like *frouwe* and for the first time uses the specific *diu blôze herzogîn*? Is the narrator's change of

---

105. The listeners now possess a further clue in Jeschute's recognition of Parzival, since they suspect that if she knows him they must know her.
106. Parzival's dismissal of the past before he became a knight, specifically with regard to his meeting with Jeschute, is possibly an example of psychological repression, caused by a sense of shame of which Gurnemanz had first made him aware (176,8).

Parzival's failure (Books V and VI)

reference meant as an objective reflection of a change in Parzival's subjective awareness? If so, this is certainly not in the sense that this new reference would simply objectivise what may now be passing through Parzival's mind, since Parzival does not know that Jeschute is a duchess.[107] But this explanation could be applied in another sense, in that the narrator's change of term indicates the stage when Parzival begins to grasp, not that this woman is a duchess, but that she is a person whom he had met once before (and to whom the narrator had referred by her title of duchess) and that the suffering woman in front of him is one for whose condition he himself is responsible.

The encounter between Parzival and Orilus, the second scene in this episode, is of secondary importance since they have never met in person before, so that there is no possibility of mutual recognition as with Parzival and Jeschute. However, this encounter touches upon recognition of identity in an important negative sense, for it is a benign providence that guards each of the combatants from learning the other's identity. At the close of his setpiece description of Orilus in his armour,[108] just before the combat begins, the narrator reminds us in a minor detail that this knight is the brother of Lähelin (261,27: *sîn ors von Brumbâne / de Salvâsche ah muntâne: / mit einer tjost rois Lähelîn / bejagetez dâ, der bruoder sîn*). Parzival knows too that Orilus and Lähelin are brothers (he learned it at the same time as we from Sigune, 141,5ff.), but he does not know that the knight facing him is none other than Orilus, as we have realised since 260,25 at the latest.[109] The tragic reverberations of knightly homicide,[110] brought nearer by this encounter which Sigune had earlier managed to prevent, are avoided only by mutual ignorance at this stage. On the one hand, Parzival does not know that this is Orilus, the brother of the arch-enemy of his family and himself the enemy of his dynasty (if he were to realise this and kill him, he would only worsen the position of Jeschute and Cunne-

---

107. The references to Jeschute as a duchess in the earlier scene had all been conveyed to the listeners by the narrator, thereby bypassing Parzival (129,27f. + 30; 130,28; 131,15; 132,9 + 21) or had been mentioned expressly in conversation only once Parzival has passed out of the scene (134,2f.).
108. On the implications of this descriptive passage see Johnson, *Ironie*, pp. 138ff., and, as regards the difference between listeners and Parzival, Hirschberg, *Untersuchungen*, p. 20.
109. On the different information available to listeners and to Parzival see Hirschberg, *Untersuchungen*, p. 15.
110. On these see Green, *Homicide, passim*. Wolfram refers to the tragic implications of this combat in 264,25ff.

The Art of Recognition in Wolfram's *Parzival*

ware).[111] On the other hand, Orilus has no means of knowing until Parzival's oath (269,18ff.) that this is Jeschute's '*amîs*' in front of him (by the time he does hear this it is too late, he has already given his *sicherheit*). The dramatic irony of this mutual ignorance skirts the realm of tragedy very closely, however, when the defeated Orilus offers Parzival as ransom one of the two kingdoms held by his brother Lähelin (266,21: '*mîn leben kouf ich schône. / in zwein landen krône / treit gewaldeclîche / mîn bruoder, der ist rîche: / der nim dir swederz du wellest / daz du mich tôt niht vellest*'). Both the listeners and Parzival know that the two kingdoms held by Lähelin have been wrested from Parzival's dynasty and rightly belong to him (128,3ff. and 141,7), but only the listeners can realise that what is here being offered Parzival is a kingdom which is rightly his anyway and that a dangerous turn to the situation is avoided only by Orilus happening to mention the name of neither his brother nor the realm offered. If we can see in this chance the workings of benign providence, keeping Parzival from further tragic involvements, then we must acknowledge that in a situation of this order providence is as much concerned to keep him in ignorance as it is elsewhere to bring him to recognition of the truth.[112]

---

111. I have discussed this danger in *Homicide*, pp. 31f. Cf. also Mohr, *Hintergründe*, pp. 183f.

112. The presence of Jeschute's husband Orilus provides two further clues to her identity. The danger that both she and Parzival might be killed (259,11ff.) by someone who is revealed as her husband only in v. 23 acts as a reminder for the listeners of what they have already learned of Orilus as a killer knight (134,23ff.) and of his threat to fight with Parzival if he were to come across him (137,15ff., cf. also 135,19f.). These two earlier points are meaningful only for the listeners, but even Parzival can appreciate the danger which Jeschute anticipates from her husband if he can recall what she had said of her husband on the first occasion (132,12ff.).

The second clue is that it is specifically from her husband (cf. 259,23) that Jeschute anticipates danger. The listeners know this already from the earlier episode (136,1ff.) and even though Parzival knows nothing of this marital quarrel, he is in a position to realise that he may have created tension between man and wife in the past (cf. 132,12ff. again).

These last two clues show us the two lines of recognition (the listeners' recognition and Parzival's) drawing closer together. Parzival is beginning to suspect what has been made implicitly available to the audience from an earlier point in the encounter. It is meaningful that these two lines should begin to converge just before the narrator's more explicit reference to *diu blôze herzogîn* (260,3) and then to *der herzoge Orilus* (260,25). The narrator's technique of gradually homing in on the truth in his references (259,11ff. and 259,23ff.: the two lines begin to converge; 260,3: *herzogîn*; 260,25: *Orilus*) are meant as an objective reflection of Parzival's gradual realisation of the truth that this is Jeschute.

Parzival's failure (Books V and VI)

Orilus and Cunneware

At the moment when Parzival stipulates the terms of his *sicherheit* to the defeated Orilus (267,12ff.) the listeners have enough information to see that he is being ordered to render tribute, without knowing it, to Cunneware whom we know to be his own sister (135,13ff.). Orilus fails to see this because Parzival refers to Cunneware by means of a circumlocution (267,15: '... *zeiner magt, die blou durch mich / ein man, gein dem ist mîn gerich / âne ir bete niht verkorn*').[113]

The close of the encounter between Parzival and Orilus is marked by a descriptive realistic detail about the battered state of their helmets and shields (271,16f.) and the same point is stressed again as Orilus arrives at Arthur's encampment: his shield and helmet are battered almost to the point of unrecognisability (275,2: *sîn helm sîn schilt was sô versnitn / daz niemen dran kôs keiniu mâl*; 275,10: *Orilus der werde degn / leit schildes schirben ûfez gras*). This makes it difficult, but not quite impossible to recognise him, since his sister Cunneware catches sight of heraldic dragons on his coverlet (275,21: *bî den trachen ûfem kursît / erkande sin wol*),[114] but even so she still cannot tell whether this is Orilus or Lähelin (275,23: *si sprach 'du bist der bruoder mîn, / Orilus, od Lähelin*'). In other words, the dangerous fact that these two are brothers comes out into the open only when Parzival has safely passed out of the episode.

Orilus would be fully able to recognise his sister at the Round Table, especially since he already knows that she is there (135,13ff.), but he is presumably unable to see her at first because of the throng that quickly gathers round him (275,7f.). In any case, Orilus is

---

113. From the fact that Parzival here refers to Cunneware by an anonymous circumlocution (cf. the similar namelessness of his instructions to Kingrun and Clamide, see below, p. 126) it might be possible to conclude that he was driven to such roundabout phrasing by ignorance of her name (see also below, p. 131, fn. 127). Even though Cunneware's name had been mentioned in Parzival's presence at the Round Table (153,2), something of this point could be rescued if we recall Parzival's anger and frustration at this point (153,14ff.) together with his impatience to claim his due from Ither (153,23ff.). On this see Schaefer, *Beobachtungen*, p. 227. In the grip of these more powerful emotions, Parzival may not have registered the less decisive detail of a name, but there is nonetheless a slight gap in Wolfram's motivation at this point.

114. Although we had been told nothing of this when Parzival first saw Cunneware at Arthur's court, she has the same heraldic design as her brothers on her tent, as we are told a little after Cunneware and Orilus recognise each other (278,11ff.). Orilus recognises this detail of her tent once he sees it (278,19: *dâ bî erkandez Orilus: / wan sîniu wâpen wâren sus*) just as readily as Cunneware had recognised it on his coverlet (275,21f.).

unaware that the lady at the Round Table to whom he is to give his *sicherheit* is Cunneware, because Parzival had couched his order in a type of anonymous circumlocution (267,15ff.) which is also adopted by Orilus at Arthur's court (275,12: *nâch ir, durch die er komen was, / begunder vrâgen al zehant*). If these lines capture the terms of his inquiry, the narrator intervenes in the next lines to reveal what Orilus does not know (275,14: *froun Cunnewâren de Lâlant / zeigte man im, wâ diu saz*). How carefully the narrator works here, allowing Orilus to ask after this unnamed woman before his sister's name is mentioned, may be seen by comparing this offer of *sicherheit* to Cunneware with two other cases (Kingrun and Clamide) where no relative of hers is involved. Although Parzival had used the same kind of anonymous reference to Cunneware in addressing Kingrun (198,26ff. and 199,9), this is not repeated by the seneschal when he arrives at the Round Table and Cunneware's name is mentioned without any delay (206,12: *froun Cunnewâren de Lâlant / brâhter sîne sicherheit*). Nor is the woman's name expressly mentioned by Parzival in his instructions to Clamide (215,6ff.), but again the defeated knight is led straight to the named Cunneware (217,28: *vil gedrungen / wart sîn lîp, ê er sitzen vant / froun Cunnewâren de Lâlant*). Only on the third occasion, when brother unexpectedly confronts sister, is Parzival's anonymous reference repeated on arrival as a reflection of Orilus's unawareness of the surprise which awaits him and to which we have been privy since Parzival gave him his order.

Parzival and the Round Table

Parzival, lost in a rêverie as he contemplates the three drops of blood in the snow, is taken by members of the Round Table to be an aggressive lone challenger[115] and is accordingly not at first recognised as the *rôte ritter* whom Arthur is seeking. The narrator motivates this situation in detail from several points of view.

He makes it clear first of all how Parzival's intentions could be so misunderstood. The knight is first sighted by Cunneware's page, who notices signs of extreme use on his knightly gear (283,27ff.) and

---

115. Parzival's unconscious rôle of a lone challenger halted in the vicinity of the Round Table ironically repeats the situation in which he first encountered Ither outside Nantes in Book III. This parallel is strengthened by Parzival now wearing Ither's knightly trappings.

Parzival's failure (Books V and VI)

his stance with upright spear (284,3: *mit ûf gerihtem sper*). From this he deduces that Parzival is seeking a joust (284,2), which is the more credible to him in the light of Arthur's recent warning about attacks to be expected from Grail-knights (280,28ff.), even down to the detail of upright spears (281,1: *'Uf gerihtiu sper wir müezen sehn'*). The page's report to the Round Table confirms this reading of Parzival's intentions as aggressive (284,21f.).[116] But we know that this is incorrect, that Parzival is in fact lost in a lover's rêverie (283,16ff.) which removes him from all thought of knightly adventure. In fact, he is quite unaware that Arthur is nearby and realises this only when he much later comes to his senses (304,8ff.).

This initial misunderstanding is taken further by Segramors. This is subjectively because of his headstrong eagerness for combat (285,2ff.) and wish to be first at all costs (285,28ff.), so that he does not stop to consider the facts of the situation. He is also led to misjudging things because Arthur repeats his warning about combats to be expected (286,10ff.), so that from the Round Table's point of view Parzival is already playing his future rôle as Grail-ruler in 'defending' its territory, although he is certainly unaware of this. Like the page, Segramors interprets Parzival's stance as readiness for combat (287,22f. and 27). But again the listeners have enough knowledge to see that this is incorrect. The two subjective motives of Segramors may characterise *him*, but need not be true of everyone or of Parzival; if Parzival acts as a defender of Grail-territory, he is certainly ignorant of this rôle; and we are again reminded that his stance is not that of a challenger, but of one lost in a trance of inactivity (287,6 and 9ff.).

Keii is responsible for the next stage of misunderstanding. By reporting the defeat of Segramors to Arthur, Keii sides with him, makes his attitude his own and thereby refers to Parzival's wish for combat (290,6f.), which he too sees in his upright spear (290,12f.). This is so obvious for him that Keii equates his wish to find out what Parzival wants (290,11) with a wish for combat (290,19), so that he sets out armed and ready (290,23). To these considerations must be added the motive of the insult which Keii imagines is done to Arthur and his queen by Parzival's challenging behaviour (290,13;

---

116. Ironically, what the page reports of Parzival's supposedly aggressive intentions towards Arthur (284,22: *'iu ist durch die snüere alhie gerant'*) is soon afterwards shown to be more applicable to Segramors (285,14: *Segramors im durch die snüere lief*).

cf. 294,1).¹¹⁷ In all this, too, the listeners can assess how far the seneschal is wrong – from facts already given, but also because the narrator reminds them again. Parzival's supposed combativeness is already undermined for us by 289,13ff., then by the interpolation on *Frou minne* (291,1ff.), telling us about his state of mind, a closed book to his opponents, and especially by the discrepancy between his rêverie and their aggression (294,9ff. and 26ff.). The imagined insult is rendered invalid by Parzival's unconscious state: the Round Table may be able to see him (289,13f.), but there is no indication before 304,8ff., when he comes to himself, that he is aware of them.¹¹⁸

Finally, this repeated misunderstanding is avoided by Gawan's tact and discretion. He pauses to give the matter thought and hence sets out without shield, sword or spurs (299,29f.; 302,22) and true to these pacific intentions does not charge at Parzival (300,6ff.), but asks a polite question instead (300,9f.). When this is met by blank silence (300,12ff.), Gawan's imaginative sympathy allows him to guess the reason (301,8f. and 21ff.), which the listeners can confirm is right, and he discreetly covers the three drops of blood with a cloth, thus allowing Parzival to come to himself.

Because of this well motivated misunderstanding of his intentions Parzival's identity is not recognised either. Things start off on the wrong foot, since he is first noticed not by a mature, experienced knight, but by a young page (283,25: *Cunnewâren garzûn*). The page's ability to recognise who this lone knight may be is hampered by the battered state of Parzival's armour (283,27: *der sach an den stunden / einen helm mit maneger wunden / und einen schilt gar verhouwen*), already explained as a result of his recent encounter with Orilus (271,16f.). The narrator uses irony to stress the discrepancy between the page's behaviour and what it would have been if he had realised the truth known to us (284,5: *het in der knappe erkant enzît, / er wær von im vil unbeschrît, / deiz sîner frouwen ritter wære*):¹¹⁹ this 'opponent' is in fact in the service of Cunneware, the page's own mistress. We are shown the implications of the situation, but the page cannot see them because of his inability to

---

117. The defeat of Segramors must also have confirmed Keii in his belief about Parzival's aggressiveness.
118. We have been shown the element of chance in Parzival's defeat of Segramors (288,5ff.) and are therefore able to assess the lack of intention, and hence lack of aggressiveness, in his victory.
119. Cf. 283,30: *in dienste des knappen frouwen* (with reference to Parzival's defeat of knights whom he has compelled to pay homage to Cunneware).

Parzival's failure (Books V and VI)

recognise Parzival, brought about by his inexperience, the shock of coming across a knight immediately on leaving the Round Table and because, fresh from Arthur's warning (280,28ff.), he naturally assumes that Parzival is one of these opponents.

Segramors also fails to recognise Parzival. The hero's armour is still just as battered as before, but Segramors's greater experience (by comparison with the page) is outbalanced by his headstrong wish for combat at any price (287,5: *der unbescheiden helt*).[120] The situation is again highlighted by irony, for Segramors addresses Parzival as an opponent of the Round Table (287,27), whereas we know that this is the knight sought by Arthur.[121] Furthermore, when he tries to justify himself after his defeat by maintaining that his opponent would never have stayed for combat if he had recognised Segramors's shield (289,27–9) we can see that the shield which *should* have been recognised is not his own, but Parzival's.

Keii's approach is similar: he comes ready for combat (293,19ff.), but motivated more by pride (293,30ff.) than by headstrong aggressiveness, but the result is the same, he pays little attention to the question who this knight might be and what his motives could be. His lack of perception is similarly ironised in his plea to Arthur (290,20: '*wær wir alle blint oder toup, / ir soltz im weren: des wære zît*'), for what is meant as a remote hypothesis we see to be in fact true: they are indeed, except Gawan, all *blint* and *toup*.

The problem is more difficult in the case of Gawan. The poet's effects depend here too on a delayed recognition, but since Gawan is anything but hotheaded or arrogant and takes time to consider things, the narrator must somehow make it more difficult for him to recognise Parzival. Even though Gawan (unlike Keii) was not mentioned as present at Parzival's first visit to the Round Table, he would as an Arthurian knight be aware that Parzival had acquired Ither's trappings and was therefore known as the *rôte ritter*.[122] If despite his greater perceptiveness Gawan is not to recognise Parzival from his equipment, the answer must be to make this armour even less easily recognisable. This is why the narrator

---

120. Segramors's inability to pause and consider is also well known to Arthur (286,4: '*dîn unbescheidenheit*').
121. Cf. 280,8ff.
122. Since Gawan is present at Arthur's court when Orilus arrives there (cf. 277,4) he can be presumed to have been privy to Orilus's statement that *der rîter rôt* (276,21) defeated him, to the general acknowledgment of *des rôten rîtters ellen* (278,25) at the Round Table, and to Arthur's departure in quest of *der rîter rôt* (280,9).

reminds us again that this armour was battered as before (300,3: *er truoc drî tjoste durch den schilt, / mit heldes handen dar gezilt: / ouch het in Orilus versniten*), but also stresses that the shield had been made even less recognisable by the recent jousts with Segramors and Keii.

The corresponding narratorial task, to account for Parzival's failure to recognise his opponents, was simpler to motivate. We know from the hero's first visit to the Round Table only that he had met Keii (neither Segramors nor Gawan is mentioned as involved). Accordingly, when Parzival eventually learns who Gawan is he speaks as if he had known him only by hearsay (304,4: *'ich hôrte von dir sprechen ie'*) and has to ask whether he is in fact Gawan (304,1: *'bistûz Gâwân?'*).[123] Furthermore, in each encounter Parzival is so lost in thought that he has no chance of recognising the other person, as the narrator takes care to specify repeatedly with Segramors, Keii and Gawan.[124] In the first two cases Parzival is conscious only just long enough to dispatch his opponents, but if he converses for longer with Gawan, the latter's identity is concealed by the absence of any shield (302,22).

Even when Parzival does come to himself he still has to learn what happened during his trance, he has to catch up with the listeners in knowledge. He notices the absence of his spear (302,17f.), which must have been shattered in the combat with Keii.[125] Parzival is at first so far from readjusting to reality that he cannot accept Gawan's explanation (302,20: *'hêrre, ez ist mit tjost vertân'*), especially since he sees that Gawan is unarmed (302,22f.) and hence suspects him of ironic mockery (302,24f.). He is next told enough to realise that the Round Table is nearby (303,22ff.) and can now even see their tents (304,8ff.). He also learns that he has defeated Segramors (305,2ff.) as well as Keii, whose behaviour towards Cunneware has now been punished (304,18ff.).

The final act of recognition is necessary on both sides. It is described explicitly on the part of Parzival: Gawan invites him to accompany him to his lord (301,1ff.),[126] Parzival understandably

---

123. Because Parzival and Gawan have never met before and Parzival knows of him only by hearsay I take these words as a genuine question by contrast with the rhetorical question with which Parzival works towards recognition of Sigune when he crossed her path a second time (252,28: *'bistuz Sigûne'*).
124. See above, p. 102, fn. 48.
125. See above, p. 96, fn. 26.
126. This invitation has to be repeated in 303,6ff. after Parzival has regained consciousness.

Parzival's failure (Books V and VI)

asks whom he is to accompany and also to visit (303,11ff.) and Gawan at first circumscribes and then names his lord (303,15ff. and 24) and finally gives his own name (303,25ff.). Parzival now realises that this is Gawan before him (304,1), he realises what is expressly called the truth (304,25: *dô Parzivâl die wârheit sach*). On the other hand, Gawan's act of recognition is referred to only implicitly. In response to Gawan's invitation Parzival is hesitant to join the Round Table because of his shame at Keii's insult (304,10–12), as yet unavenged, as he thinks (304,13ff.).[127] When Parzival refers so circumstantially to this past episode at the Round Table, Gawan must realise, from 304,13ff., that this is the *rôte ritter* in front of him.

As we have seen, it is from this point that the narrator again feels at liberty to use the term *rôte ritter* of the knight sought by the Round Table, known to them only by this circumlocution, and now recognised as such by Gawan. Accordingly, this term is used again as the two knights, after their mutual recognition, ride to the Round Table (305,11: *Gâwâne und dem rîter rôt*). At this point, Cunneware sees them coming and recognises Parzival as the *rôte ritter* (305,16: *diu wart vrô, mit freude enpfienc / diu magt ir rîter, der si rach / daz ir von Keien ê geschach*). If just after this the narrator refers to Parzival by name (305,21: *sus sach si komen Parzivâl*), we must recall that the Round Table are still unaware of this name, but that the circumlocution used of Cunneware's welcome (*ir rîter, der si rach / daz ir von Keien ê geschach*) shows that Cunneware equates the knight accompanying Gawan with the knight sought by Arthur, that she has in fact recognised Parzival. She is in a position to do this because Parzival has by now taken off his armour, or at least his helmet (305,24: *im was sîn harnasch ab gezogen*).[128] Since she has seen him before, she can recognise him again, his beauty still shines through the rust from his armour (305,22: *der was gevar durch îsers mâl / als touwege rôsen dar gevlogen*).

In this episode concerned with Parzival and the Round Table gradually coming together again the poet has illustrated various levels in the process of recognition. Segramors and Keii incorporate a headstrong or arrogant failure in recognition, whilst tact,

---

127. The fact that here too Parzival refers to Cunneware anonymously (304,16: *'ein werdiu magt'*) lends further support to the suggestion that he is ignorant of her name (see above, p. 125, fn. 113).
128. I base my reading that Parzival's helmet was already removed at this point on the pluperfect construction with *was* instead of with *wart*. In other words, this is another detail of the action which was passed over when it actually took place.

patience and insight bring Gawan to the truth. To Cunneware on the other hand the truth is made immediately obvious, as she was able to recognise him as the one destined for a supreme goal at their first meeting (306,1: *'unz iuch mîn herze erkande'*). Greater precision is brought finally by Cundrie, from whom the Round Table learn that the name of this hitherto anonymous knight is Parzival.

5
Gawan
(Books VII–VIII and X–XIII)

In this Chapter we shall have to consider the Gawan narrative with regard to the problem of recognition. The six Books taken up by this narrative form a self-contained whole by being devoted primarily to Gawan, while Parzival steps more into the background, a change of focus justified explicitly by the narrator in the prologue-like introduction to Book VII (in which he defends his turning aside from *des mæres hêrren Parzivâl* (338,7) for a time)[1] and referred to again at the close of Book VIII when we are told that the narrative is returning *an den rehten stam*, 678,30.[2] For these six Books the narrative concentrates on Gawan, he is the main focus of attention and it is, often explicitly, from his point of view that events are presented or assessed, no longer from Parzival's.[3]

Since as many as six Books have to be covered in this one Chapter, it is advisable to abandon the discussion of general points before looking at the separate encounters (the method followed elsewhere with regard to Gahmuret and Parzival). Instead, it will be more manageable to organise the material under three locations where the action takes place (Bearosche, Schanpfanzun, Schastel Marveile), two separate encounters of Gawan (with Urians and

1. Cf. Schirok, *Aufbau*, pp. 463f. On the (temporary) closure of the Parzival narrative at the end of Book VI see Maurer, *DU* 20,2 (1968), 68.
2. Schirok, *Aufbau*, p. 464. Schirok also discusses (*ibid.*, pp. 512f.) whether the narrative switch from Gawan to Parzival comes in 678,16/17 or 678,30/679,1, but the difference is too slight to concern us here. On the self-contained nature of Book IX, hollowed out from the surrounding Gawan narrative, see p. 176.
3. In 380,1ff. (*Dô ersach mîn hêr Gâwân / daz geflohten was der plân, / die friunde in der vînde schar*) the *friunde* are so termed from Gawan's point of view (see the fn. to 380,3 in the Bartsch–Marti edition). The point of view chosen can also be spatial, as with the use of *anderhalp* and *disehalb* (623,3 + 6) or *hie* (676,18) to suggest how things present themselves to Gawan. Cf. Mohr, *Obie*, p. 12: 'Er [der Hörer] sieht nicht so sehr Gawan, er sieht und hört *durch* Gawan, was sich da tun wird.'

Gramoflanz) and one theme which has reverberations throughout all the latter part of the Gawan narrative (Gawan's surprise).[4]

Bearosche

The problem of recognition is posed in Book VII by the fact that, at Bearosche, Gawan has come into territory which he does not know and where he is equally unknown. This is first suggested in 340,18ff., where he fails to recognise the heraldic devices on the banners and shields of the army approaching the city. For Gawan, the paragon of knight-errantry, to be in such a position suggests that his journey from Plimizœl to Bearosche must have been one of considerable length, which the narrator implies by leaving it in deliberate obscurity (339,13: *des enweiz ich niht wie mangen tac*) as a token of the strangeness of the surroundings in which he now finds himself.[5] How strange these surroundings are is revealed by Gawan's correct surmise that, if he fails to recognise the knightly army approaching Bearosche, they cannot know him either (340,22: '*disem her ein gast ich pin*', / *sus sprach der werde Gâwân* / '*sît ich ir keine künde hân*').[6] Such mutual ignorance is emphasised by repeated references to Gawan's ignorance of the people he now encounters[7] and to the fact that he is quite unknown to them.[8] If he is therefore unknown at Bearosche and is nowhere depicted in this episode as being asked who he is and invited to name himself,[9] this means that Parzival, when he appears briefly on the other side at Bearosche without actually meeting his friend, has no means of learning that Gawan is also present. While the narrative is depicted from Gawan's point of view, failure in recognition is not allowed to

---

4. I have taken over this term from S. M. Johnson, *GR* 33 (1958), 285ff. and Poag, *Wolfram-Studien* IV, pp. 71ff.
5. Cf. also 343,4ff. and 393,5f. (despite their widespread fame, Gawan and Parzival are unknown here).
6. Mutual ignorance is also implied by the words of Scherules to Gawan (361,27: *dô sprach er 'hêrre, ir sît ein gast: / guoter witze uns gar gebrast, / sît ir niht herberge hât'*), for the context makes it clear that *gast* means 'stranger' and not 'guest', and that Gawan so far lacks accommodation because he knows nobody at Bearosche.
7. Cf. 343,1ff.; 350,27ff. In 342,18ff. Gawan's ignorance of the knights in the army (coupled with their false assessment of him, 342,3ff.) means that his innocent question is taken by the page as ironic mockery, who cannot imagine that Gawan does not know all these knights (342,27ff.).
8. Cf. 351,13 (*unkünde*); 352,3 (which renders necessary the question in 352,12). Accordingly, Gawan can also be referred to as *fremder ritter* (368,17; 373,19) and as *fremder gast* (374,23).
9. On this topos in the case of Gawan see Ruberg, *Schweigen*, p. 228.

Gawan (Books VII–VIII and X–XIII)

go as far as a potentially disastrous combat, so that the two friends, fighting on opposite sides, do not actually exchange blows. Gawan's position is therefore similar to that with Gahmuret and quite distinct from Parzival's who, when the focus of narrative attention, is dogged by the repeated danger of the Ither situation of combat with a kinsman.[10]

There are several good reasons why Gawan should be presented as a stranger and therefore unrecognised at Bearosche. It allows the poet to illustrate the contrast between Obie and Obilot in their reaction to him: the one, for reasons which are made psychologically clear to us, rejects the truth about Gawan, whereas the other recognises it intuitively. Gawan's anonymity also provides the background to the failure of Gawan and Parzival to learn in time of each other's presence and helps to motivate it. Finally, in contrast with this, Gawan is shown immediately recognising some Arthurian knights on the opposing side and avoiding combat with them. These are the three aspects under which the theme of recognition is treated in this episode.

The first mention of Gawan's name by the narrator while he is at Bearosche occurs in 350,24.[11] Although Gawan is known personally to neither side here, we accompany him in this Book and the narrator is ready to use his name throughout (whereas he later withholds Parzival's name for a clear purpose).[12] By contrast, the people at Bearosche cannot refer to Gawan by name, they have to fall back on descriptive epithets. For Obilot and for those who, like her, immediately accept the obvious truth when confronted with it Gawan is the *ritter* quite simply, or sometimes *der fremde ritter*,[13] whereas for Obie, anxious to deny Gawan the knightly status which, if accepted, might threaten the chivalric standing of her

10. The difference between the Parzival and Gawan narratives can be seen with regard to the theme of a combat between them. When Gawan occupies the foreground, as at Bearosche, the theme is blunted and no combat is allowed, but when the narrative returns to Parzival (at 678,30) his typical danger of a combat with a kinsman becomes reality even in the case of Gawan (see below pp. 240ff.).
11. In 350,16 (*Gâwân gein Beârosche reit*) Gawan it still approaching the city, but by 350,24 he is among the participants in the action at Bearosche.
12. See below, p. 139.
13. Gawan is described as *ritter* by Obilot in 352,24; 372,30; 396,6; by Obie, quoting her, in 353,29; 358,2; by others implicitly in 364,1; 366,15; and by Gawan himself implicitly in 368,28. Obilot also refers to him as *fremder ritter* in 368,17 and 373,19. Other anonymous terms applied to Gawan include *gast* with regard to his relationship with Scherules (362,4; 363,24; 364,28; 372,3), *fremder gast* (374,23; cf. 361,27), *werder man* (374,18) and *mîn hêrre* (392,9).

135

lover Meljanz, Gawan is described by terms demeaning to a knight: as a *koufman, wehselære* or even *valschære* and *trügenære*.[14] When Gawan occupies the narrative foreground the same technique is not applied to him as with Parzival – other characters may not know him by name, but the narrator himself is not thereby driven to make use of anonymous references. The problem of identity does not exist for Gawan, as it does for the hero of the work.

The contrast between these two types of anonymous references, chivalric and non-chivalric, is adequately explained by the characters who make use of them. Without knowing the actual facts Obilot intuitively perceives Gawan's chivalric status (352,20: *'du zîhst in daz doch nie geschach: / swester, des mahtu dich schamen: / er gewan nie koufmannes namen. / er ist so minneclîch getân, / ich wil in zeime ritter hân'*) and thereby arrives at the truth as immediately and surely as did Cunneware when confronted by Parzival at Arthur's court (151,11ff.) or Gawan when he came across Parzival in his love-trance (301,21ff.).[15] Others see the truth about Gawan as readily as Obilot. Her mother is just as quick to reject Obie's suggestion that he is no more than a merchant (353,14: *'tohter, welch koufman / kunde alsus gebâren?'*),[16] and although Scherules is sent by Obie to confiscate the 'merchant's' wares he quickly sees the truth of the situation (361,19ff.), accepts Gawan as his guest and proclaims his knightly status (363,29: *'seht sîn gebâr, hœrt sîniu wort; / in mîme hûs liez ich in dort: / Kunt ir dan ritters fuore spehen, / ir müezt im rehter dinge jehen'*).[17] With Obie the position is more complicated, however. Although the combat at Bearosche

---

14. The evidence is as follows: *koufman* (352,16; 358,13; 361,10; 396,6), *wehselære* (353,26), *valschære* (362,24; 363,16), *trügenære* (363,14). These terms are used by Obie herself or by those who are explicitly quoting her opinion. When he jokingly says of himself *'sol ich kipper wesn'* (351,17), Gawan uses of himself a non-chivalric term such as those which Obie will soon mockingly direct against him. Gawan's humour is justified by the manner in which he is made to feel an outsider by knights who pay no attention to a stranger (351,13 + 15), so that he jokingly sees himself as non-knightly.
15. On these and other examples of the truth being intuitively grasped see below, pp. 284f.
16. When Obilot's mother learns of her younger daughter's decision to accept a knight's service she realises immediately that she must have the stranger Gawan in mind (374,22: *'er süezer man vil guoter! / ich wæne, ir meint den fremden gast'*).
17. Cf. also Lippaut's reaction when he first catches sight of Gawan (364,25: *er reit da er Gâwânen sach. / zwei ougen unde ein herze jach, / diu Lyppaut mit im brâhte dar, / daz der gast wær wol gevar / und rehte manlîche site / sînen gebærden wonten mite*). On the ability of all except Obie to assess Gawan correctly see Zimmermann, *Kommentar*, p. 162.

originated in the quarrel between her and Meljanz, the narrator shows the listeners something of her true feelings, concealed from Meljanz. We are given a glimpse of these as early as 347,18 (*in klagt ouch Obîe*), it is his knightly exploits alone which she follows from the castle (357,27ff.)[18] and in 365,1ff. the narrator confirms for us the strength of their feelings for one another. It is in this last passage, however, that we are shown how the crisis in the relationship between Meljanz and Obie dictates her reaction to Gawan's presence.[19] Up to now the narrator has depicted her behaviour and especially her denigration of Gawan without any indication of her motives, but now he provides an explanation which will allow the listeners to forgive her (366,2: *nune wîzetz Obîen niht*). Her love for Meljanz is such that she sees in him the paragon of chivalry (365,24: *ir herze Meljanze jach, / er müest vor ûz der hôhste sîn*), but her attitude has received a jolt from Gawan's arrival on the scene in that she recognises in him, even if only instinctively, a rival capable of outdoing her lover in chivalry. In other words, Obie's reaction to Gawan is fundamentally as correct as her younger sister's. Although she may have her own reasons for denying her intuitive insight, she sees the truth about Gawan from his appearance and bearing as readily as the others at Bearosche: in his case the pointers are so unmistakable that recognition, in the sense of a correct assessment of his character, is accessible to all concerned.

In the case of the Arthurian knights on the other side at Bearosche the act of immediate recognition proceeds from Gawan. When the listeners first learn that the opposing ranks contain some captured Arthurian knights fighting under Duke Astor (356,17ff.), this fact is revealed out of Gawan's earshot.[20] This apparently trifling detail assumes greater importance when we are given a renewed reference to the presence of Arthurian knights on the opposing side (again in conjunction with Duke Astor),[21] recognisable by their battle-cry (382,12: *dicke Nantes wart geschrît, /*

18. Cf. also her use of *mîn ritter* in 358,2 to refer to Meljanz.
19. On this cf. Zimmermann, *Kommentar*, p. 165.
20. This is made clear by the narrator's comment 354,1ff., switching the narrative from a scene hitherto overheard by Gawan, within sight of the castle wall (352,27ff.), to one within Bearosche itself.
21. 382,9: *dô streit der herzoge Astor*. These repeated references to Astor (356,19; 379,21; 382,9) act as a signal to the perceptive listener that these Arthurian knights cannot be far away, so that we know in advance what awaits Gawan as a possibility. For the same reason we are reminded at this point of Gawan's background (380,11: *der werden tavelrunder bote*).

Artûss herzeichen. / die herten, niht die weichen, / was dâ manc ellender Berteneis).[22] Soon afterwards another reason is given why these Arthurians should be readily recognisable, for their badge is a *gampilûn* on helmet or shield in accordance with the coat of arms of Arthur's son Ilinot (383,1: *Ouch het ieslîch Bertûn / durch bekantnisse ein gampilûn / eintweder ûf helm odr uf den schilt / nâch Ilinôtes wâpne gezilt: / daz was Artûs werder suon*). When Gawan comes across these knights in the course of battle these marks of recognition are accordingly seen by him (383,7: *dô er diu wâpen sach*) and recognised for what they are (383,11: *erekande wol der wâpen schîn*), so that he is in a position to avoid combat with them (383,13: *er liez die von Bertâne / sus tûren ûf dem plâne: / er wolde mit in strîten niht, / als man noch friwentschefte giht*). Gawan's position here, where his superior knowledge enables him to avoid a tragic conflict, resembles that of Gahmuret when he avoided fighting his kinsman Kaylet in the Middle East and his Angevin compatriot at Kanvoleis. Gawan, like Gahmuret, recognises the facts of the situation and can take conscious steps to avoid combat with a kinsman. By contrast with them Parzival fails to recognise the facts and hence incurs guilt (as in his encounter with Ither) or has to be protected from this apparently by chance, but in reality by the operation of beneficent providence, as in the narrow avoidance of a combat between Parzival and Gawan at Bearosche, to which we must now turn.[23]

The fact that these two friends can come close to combat is due above all to Gawan's anonymity at Bearosche: because he is unknown, his name cannot be used there and hence no word of his presence reaches Parzival on the perimeter of the action. Other reasons are provided to render this more credible. We are told for example that Gawan leads a band of knights in battle under the banner of his host Scherules (381,22: *do ergienc sîn poynder mit*

---

22. Cf. also 382,27ff. It is part of Wolfram's realistic range of details that he does not confine himself to mentioning this battle-cry alone. He thus makes a general point (379,27: *vil fremder krîe man dâ rief*) and also illustrates it by particular examples (381,16f.; 385,2f.) in addition to the cry used by the Arthurian knights.
23. As with the use of Astor as a signal to the presence of Arthurian knights, the narrator alerts us to the possibility of this encounter by previous hints of Parzival's presence at Bearosche. Thus 383,23ff. is a general reference to his presence, in 388,6ff. both he and Gawan are singled out anonymously, whilst 388,28ff., although still anonymous, is a much more specific and detailed reference to Parzival. 389,25ff. finally shows how near the danger was, it belatedly clarifies 385,10ff.

Gawan (Books VII–VIII and X–XIII)

kraft, | mit sînes wirts baniere | beschutter harte schiere | von Jâmor den werden)[24] — since these other knights presumably wear the coat of arms of their lord Scherules,[25] this alone must make it difficult to recognise Gawan in their midst by his own coat of arms. In addition, before Gawan and Parzival come close together in the mêlée we learn that Gawan's shield, the most easily recognisable part of his equipment, has been hacked to pieces in his combat with Meljanz (385,16ff.).[26]

The narrator also builds further on the fact of anonymity: if Gawan's presence at Bearosche cannot be divulged to Parzival because no one knows Gawan's name, the converse is also true. Parzival is equally unknown there by name, but this time the narrator reflects this situation by his choice of anonymous circumlocutions for him, of which the reference to his red equipment is the most significant (383,23: *den burgærn manege tjost dâ bôt | ein ritter allenthalben rôt: | der hiez der ungenante, | wande in niemen dâ bekante*).[27] Here it is the *burgære* who know of the presence of a knight in this distinctive equipment, elsewhere it can be other participants or the listeners who learn this fact which eludes Gawan until a certain point. Thus, when the narrator sums up the battle for his listeners in terms of the leading knight on either side (388,6: *inrehalp wart ez dâ guot getân | durch die jungen Obilôt, | und ûzerhalb ein ritter rôt, | die zwêne behielten dâ den pris*) this comment about the *ritter rôt* bypasses Gawan, whilst the reference to Obilot would have conveyed nothing at all to Parzival.[28]

Only when the knights captured by Parzival report to Meljanz in Gawan's presence what has happened to them[29] does Gawan at

---

24. Cf. also the reference in 380,20.
25. As is suggested in another context in 341,10.
26. This is suggested of Gawan's shield, but also of his opponent's, and a little later the same thing is said of Meljahkanz (386,23ff.). In other words, as with the battle-cry of the Arthurian knights the narrator carefully gives more details than are required simply to motivate the point at issue.
27. Parzival is referred to in this episode anonymously in terms of his red equipment in 388,8; 389,4 + 29; 392,20, and retrospectively also in 398,5. He is also termed *der gehiure* (390,7) and referred to be a circumlocution in 392,25 (*der mit in dâ streit*).
28. In addition to the references to his distinctive equipment the presence of Parzival is made amply clear to the listeners by the terms of the *sicherheit* he imposes on defeated opponents (388,28ff.), including a quest for the Grail and, failing that, homage to the queen of Pelrapeire. In all these references the listeners are told the necessary facts, but Parzival's name is still avoided until the moment of Gawan's recognition of what nearly happened.
29. What follows makes it clear that what these knights report (392,23) must have

length recognise that Parzival, although hitherto unnamed, was present at Bearosche (392,24: *dô Gâwân hête vernomn / sîniu wâpen, der mit in dâ streit, / und wem si gâben sicherheit, / und dô sim sagten umben grâl, / dô dâhter des, daz Parzivâl / diss mæres wære ein urhap*). Gawan is here apprised of details which were earlier conveyed to the listeners and like them he can conclude from this information that the victorious knight was none other than Parzival: the reference to his *wâpen* or red equipment and to his search for the Grail is enough to make this quite clear. Now that Gawan realises that Parzival was present, the latter is no longer referred to anonymously as the *ritter rôt*, but by his proper name, so that the use of Parzival's name by the narrator is correlated with Gawan's recognition that this other knight must have been Parzival.[30]

Gawan also thanks God for having kept himself and Parzival apart in combat (392,30ff.), but we have already been allowed to see in retrospect just how imminent the danger had been. This is suggested when we learn that Parzival had acquired Gawan's horse in battle at the moment when Gawan, just unhorsed, was about to defeat and capture Meljanz (389,25ff. thus clarifies 385,10ff. retrospectively), for at this point the two friends must have been perilously close to one another.[31] In Gawan's case the good fortune which protects him here is like that which allowed him to recognise the Arthurian knights in good time, whilst of Parzival one can say that it is the danger in this situation which is more prominent than the happy outcome, the reminder of the Ither situation still dogging him, as is made clear once again in Book VIII in regard to Vergulaht.[32] Whilst it is certainly true that both Gawan and

included both the fact of their defeat and the terms imposed upon them, which agree sufficiently with what was narrated directly in 388,28ff. The reference to the Grail means something for Gawan, for he knows of its importance for Parzival from 329,25ff.

30. How far the narrator's use of a character's name or of an anonymous circumlocution for him is connected with the point of view technique may be seen by comparing this episode with the encounter between Parzival and the Round Table in Book VI. In the present context the references to the red knight give way to Parzival's name at the moment of Gawan's recognition, because Gawan now knows Parzival by name (since 315,9; cf. 325,17ff.), but in the earlier context, while Parzival was still known to the Round Table only as the red knight, it was this type of reference which was avoided in favour of genealogical references to Parzival or even his name, because these details were then unknown to the Round Table (see above, p. 103).

31. This has been persuasively worked out by Zimmermann, *Kommentar*, p. 300.
32. See below, pp. 145f.

Parzival are ignorant of the imminent danger of their fighting one another, the ignorance refers primarily to Parzival. Gawan is after all heavily engaged in combat with Meljanz at this point, it is Parzival who then approaches, bringing with him the danger which is so narrowly avoided. Both may be ignorant, but only Parzival's ignorance is critical. After the danger has passed, Gawan does at least learn something of the facts, whereas by now Parzival has left Bearosche behind and is not even aware that Gawan was also present.

Schanpfanzun

Gawan's rapidly acquired knowledge of the situation in which he finds himself from the beginning of the narrative in Book VIII contrasts significantly with what Mohr has shown to be the case in Chrétien's version, where not merely the listeners but most probably Gauvain himself remain ignorant of the dangerous position in which he finds himself, unaware that he has arrived at the enemy's court where the judicial combat awaits him.[33] Wolfram's Arthurian knight at first shows similar ignorance, but this is rapidly laid aside and henceforth Gawan's knowledge is superior to that of others. In 398,22f. (*mit sehn gewan er küende | erbûwens lands, hiez Ascalûn*) the narrator tells his listeners that Gawan is now in sight of Ascalun, the goal of his journey[34] in enemy territory, but nothing tells us that Gawan is also aware of this. But he soon learns this: knowing that he must be near he asks his way (398,24: *dâ frâgter gegen Schanpfanzûn | swaz im volkes widerfuor*), then sees a castle (398,28) which he correctly assumes must be Schanpfanzun.[35] Since the names of both land and castle had been mentioned to Gawan by Kingrimursel he is unlike Parzival in knowing this much of his goal, in being able to ask his way to it and in coming across people who can direct him to it.[36]

---

33. Cf. Mohr, *Kingrimursel*, p. 24.
34. The listeners know that Ascalun is Gawan's goal since 324,19ff. and 335,1ff.
35. The listeners are able to judge the correctness of this, since they have just received a warning from the narrator (398,9: *nu nâht och sînes kampfes zît*), where *kampf* refers to the single combat arranged at Schanpfanzun (cf. 324,24).
36. The relevance of the last point should still be clear to the listeners from the recently described reaction of the knights defeated by Parzival at Bearosche whom he wished to send on a quest for the Grail (388,29: ... *oder daz si erwurben im den grâl. | sine kunden im ze keinem mâl | Niht gesagen wâ der was, | wan sîn pflæge ein künec hiez Anfortas*).

The Art of Recognition in Wolfram's *Parzival*

When Vergulaht is first introduced he is named almost immediately to the listeners (400,5),[37] but not to Gawan. The listeners are also told that he is a king, and from the way in which, when next mentioned, he invites Gawan to stay at his castle Schanpfanzun, it is clear to us that this must be the *künec von Ascalûn* mentioned by title, but not name, by Kingrimursel in his original challenge (321,19). There is enough about Vergulaht's general air to suggest to Gawan that this must be the ruler of the land he has now entered,[38] but this is confirmed for him when, knowing that he is in sight of Schanpfanzun, Gawan is invited to stay there by one who must be lord of the castle and hence the king who is Gawan's enemy. If any doubt remains for Gawan, this is soon removed by Vergulaht confirming that the castle is Schanpfanzun (402,20). By this point at the latest Gawan learns the facts of the situation, which is confirmed by another point. When Antikonie comments that, for all her guest's sexual eagerness, she does not even know his name (406,9ff.) she thereby tacitly invites him to introduce himself,[39] but Gawan accepts this invitation only playfully and refuses to give anything away (406,14: '*ich sage iu, frouwe, daz ich pin / mîner basen bruoder suon*'). Gawan seeks to remain anonymous at Schanpfanzun (cf. 398,30: *des landes gast*), as he is at Bearosche throughout, but there is now an urgent reason for this: he knows by now, from his recognition that this is Schanpfanzun and that his host is the king of Ascalun, that he is in enemy territory.[40]

---

37. His name is thus given very soon after he has been introduced anonymously into the narrative (399,28: *einer*). After an ensuing episodic interlude (on this see Schnell, *PBB(T)* 96 (1974), 246ff.) and a literary comparison with Hartmann's *Erec* (cf. Schnell, *PBB(T)* 95 (1973), 324f.), the narrative returns to Vergulaht, who is then named again (402,7). Any doubts we may feel about these two knights not introducing themselves by name when they first meet are played down by the narrator's report of their conversation only after it has apparently already begun (cf. Curschmann, *DVjs* 45 (1971), 628).
38. What Gawan can see of the situation is made equally clear to us: Vergulaht has a natural air of authority (399,28: *ob den alln was einer hêr*) and his beauty marks him out as someone distinct (400,6: *sîn blic was tac wol bî der naht*), cf. the reaction of Gurnemanz to the beauty of Vergulaht's kinsman Parzival (170,21: '*ir tragt geschickede unde schîn, / ir mugt wol volkes hêrre sîn*').
39. Although there is a period of time in Book VIII when neither Vergulaht nor Antikonie knows the identity of their guest, Gawan's name is not withheld by the narrator to suggest their failure in recognition. In that the names of these three main characters are freely used throughout, the position here resembles that in the preceding Book, with the exception of Parzival (see above, pp. 135 and 139f.).
40. Cf. Hagen, *Erkennen*, p. 29. Here I disagree with the suggestion that Gawan is unaware of the position in which he finds himself (cf. the fn. to 406,15 in the

Gawan (Books VII–VIII and X–XIII)

Gawan's protective anonymity cannot be maintained, however, for there are some at Schanpfanzun who can recognise him as the enemy of their kingdom: certainly Kingrimursel, for he issued the challenge to Gawan personally,[41] but also the man who enters the room and recognises him at a delicate moment in his relationship with Antikonie (407,11: *dô gienc zer tür în aldâ / ein ritter blanc: wand er was grâ. / in wâfenheiz er nante / Gâwânen, dô ern erkante*).[42] When this intruder shouts out the truth, Antikonie must now also know the answer to her recent inquiry about Gawan's identity – not necessarily because vv.13f. mean that Gawan's name was actually mentioned (for the verbal phrase could simply mean a call to arms against this man, named by the narrator, but not by the intruder), but rather because reference is made to what Gawan is accused of (407,17: *'mîns hêrren den ir sluoget'*, cf. the terms of Kingrimursel's accusation, launched against Gawan by name, in 321,5ff.), which reveals that this guest can only be Gawan. When Vergulaht himself arrives on the scene a little later, he too must learn the truth about the guest to whom he rashly and unwittingly extended an invitation – although his act of recognition is not explicitly narrated it must be presupposed from the way in which he can later address Gawan by name (e.g. 428,13).[43]

When the intruder denounces Gawan as the killer of his lord he is also led, by the circumstances in which he finds him with Antikonie, to accuse him of raping his daughter as well (407,18f.). We know from the narrative scene interrupted by his arrival that there can be no talk of *nôtzogen* in a situation where Antikonie is a

---

Bartsch–Marti edition: 'daß er sich jetzt in Feindesland befindet, scheint er nicht zu wissen'). When Bartsch–Marti say in the same context 'Auch schon in Bearosche blieb Gawan unerkannt (393,4), wo auch kein Grund ersichtlich war', the answer must be that the Bearosche narrative presents no occasion like the encounter between Gawan and Antikonie where the former is directly asked to name himself.

41. Kingrimursel therefore knows Gawan by name (415,11) and as Arthur's nephew (416,6).
42. The faintest of hints as to how this knight could know Gawan is given by the mention of his age (cf. Hagen, *Erkennen*, p. 30). Cf. the use of *wîse* (76,8) on the similar occasion when Ampflise's chaplain recognises Gahmuret (see above, p. 56).
43. Although we are nowhere shown Gawan learning Antikonie's name, he can be seen learning that of Vergulaht: although Antikonie at first refers to him anonymously as her brother (405,10; 406,3), she later addresses him by name (414,14) in what must be assumed to be Gawan's presence, for it is later suggested that he was present during this discussion (cf. 418,9 and 422,9ff.).

perfectly willing partner,[44] and can judge that this accusation is as unfounded as the other (about which the narrator has already given us his opinion that Gawan was unjustly accused in 398,13: *âne schulde er was derzuo erkorn*). We are therefore in a position to discount Vergulaht's grievance against Gawan (412,7: '... *disen man, / der mir den schaden hât getân*') and also that of Liddamus (417,2ff.), the more so since the narrator again explicitly confirms Gawan's innocence (413,13: *unschuldec was hêr Gâwân: / ez hete ein ander man getân*). This point later assumes importance when the narrative returns to Gawan at the beginning of Book X and the narrator fills in a gap for us by saying that the combat arranged between Gawan and Kingrimursel (cf. 418,9ff.) was abandoned once the kinship between Gawan and Vergulaht came to light (503,14: *dô nam diu werlt ir sippe war, / und schiet den kampf ir sippe maht*). This point about their kinship was not stressed before, but was certainly accessible to an attentive listener. From 56,1ff. he knew of the kinship between Gahmuret (and hence Parzival) and Arthur, he also knows of Gawan's closer kinship with Arthur (416,6 is an example from Book VIII itself) and therefore of Parzival's more distant kinship with Gawan. Yet if Parzival is related on his father's side to Vergulaht (we shall see that this plays an important part in Book VIII),[45] then Gawan must also be related to Vergulaht. The material with which to recognise this is available long before the start of Book X, but only now is it utilised to motivate the abandonment of the combat.[46]

This minor piece of motivation involves the poet in a minor inconsistency. If Gawan is known well enough for Kingrimursel to know his exact relationship to Arthur (416,6) and therefore ultimately to Vergulaht himself, why should not the recognition of kinship have been active before and stopped any thought of combat? Certainly this difficulty is blurred over by having the recognition of kinship put into the past, so that it is merely reported, not narrated,[47] and the narrator falls back on a further

---

44. Cf. the references to both Antikonie and Gawan in 407,5f. (*von der liebe alsölhe nôt gewan / beidiu magt und ouch der man*) and 407,9 (*des willn si bêde wârn bereit*).
45. See below, pp. 145f.
46. Cf. also Hagen, *Erkennen*, p. 33.
47. The failure in recognition involved in the arrangements for a combat between Gawan and his opponent at Schanpfanzun does not so much affect Gawan as Vergulaht, on whose behalf the challenge had been issued in the first place (cf. also Gawan's reluctance to be involved at all, 323,27ff.). The position with this

Gawan (Books VII–VIII and X–XIII)

reason to account for the abandonment of the combat. Gawan's innocence, previously made clear to the listeners, is now convincingly enough revealed to Kingrimursel for him to be able to 'pardon' Gawan (503,16: *wand ouch der grâve Ehcunaht / ûf im die grôzen schulde truoc, / der man Gâwân zêch genuoc. / des verkôs Kingrimursel / ûf Gâwân den degen snel*).

The theme of kinship and its recognition plays a rôle, however, not merely in the subsequent relationship between Gawan and Kingrimursel but also, within Book VIII, in the relationship between Vergulaht and Parzival who, as in Book VII, is briefly visible in the narrative background. When Vergulaht is first introduced into the action we are told something of his fairy descent from Mazadan (400,7: *sîn geslähte sante Mazadân / für den berc ze Fâmorgân: / sîn art was von der feien*) which agrees in detail with what we have long since known of Gahmuret's similar descent (56,17ff.).[48] In other words, Vergulaht must be related to Gahmuret and hence to Parzival,[49] and we have been told enough to realise this long before we eventually learn of an encounter between Vergulaht and Parzival, just as at the point when Ither and Parzival met we were given the means to appreciate their kinship.[50]

The relationship between Vergulaht and Parzival's family is then suggested by further references. At one point Antikonie refers in passing to her kinship with Gahmuret (406,3: *'ich erbiutz iu durch mîns bruoder bete, / daz ez Ampflîse Gamurete / mînem œheim nie baz erbôt'*), but Gawan, just introduced to her and struck by her beauty,

frustrated combat resembles that with the combat against Parzival which is avoided at Bearosche (see above, p. 140): although in both cases Gawan may be unaware of the whole situation, this is played down to the extent that the danger does not come from his ignorance, but from the intervention of others (Parzival and Vergulaht).
48. The essential points common to both passages and allowing them to be equated are Mazadan, Famorgan and the fairy descent (*von der feien*).
49. When first introducing Vergulaht the narrator switches from addressing the listeners to showing us Gawan's reaction to his appearance (400,13: *Gâwânen des bedûhte*...): Vergulaht's resplendent beauty is so great that Gawan can only compare it to Parzival's or to Gahmuret's at the moment when he arrived at Kanvoleis (400,14ff.). On this last point the narrator may address the listeners again (400,17: *alsô diz mære weiz*), but what he omnisciently says is not in conflict with what Gawan can know and feel, for he too as a boy had been at Kanvoleis (cf. 66,15ff.) and is therefore in a position to make this kind of comparison. Gawan's thoughts are therefore moving in the right direction here, he shows his usual insight and, without actually knowing of their kinship yet, sees intuitively the similarity between Vergulaht and Parzival. Cf. also Hagen, *Erkennen*, p. 25.
50. See above, p. 83.

is understandably so taken up with other things that he makes no comment on this, even though he knows that Gahmuret was the father of his friend Parzival.[51] When Vergulaht returns to his castle, finds the attack against Gawan in full progress and then joins in against someone who should rather enjoy the privileges of a guest, the narrator can best criticise such behaviour by measuring it against the standards set by Gandin, the grandfather of both Vergulaht and Parzival (410,21: *dô tet der wirt selbe schîn, / daz mich riwet Gandîn / der künec von Anschouwe, / daz ein sô werdiu frouwe / sîn tohter, ie den sun gebar, / der mit ungetriwer schar / sîn volc bat sêre strîten*). Finally, it is from Liddamus that we learn of both aspects of this kinship again, the fact that Gandin was the grandfather of Vergulaht, and that Gahmuret and Galoes were his uncles (420,8: '... *sîn an der künec Gandîn. / ich wil iuch baz bescheiden des, / Gahmuret und Gâlôes / sîn œheime wâren*').[52]

From the moment of his introduction into the narrative and then by means of three further references we have not been allowed to ignore the fact that Vergulaht is closely related to Parzival. This is the more telling in view of the fact that the last of these reminders (the remark made by Liddamus) is soon afterwards followed by a passage (424,15ff.) in which Vergulaht relates how he was recently defeated in an encounter with an opponent whom we at least can recognise as his own kinsman Parzival. Despite their close kinship there is nothing in Vergulaht's account to indicate his awareness of who it is he has fought with – he uses anonymous terms such as *ein ritter* (424,18) and *der helt* (425,2), an impersonal construction in 424,15 (*ez wart mit mir gestriten*), and even the otherwise distinctive reference to red equipment is missing as presumably of no significance to one who is unacquainted with the hero's previous history. Nor does Vergulaht know his opponent's name, since by convention it was not incumbent upon the victor to reveal it. Conversely, there is equally little to show that Parzival grasped that his opponent was a kinsman of his – the hero spent his early years in seclusion from his knightly family, Vergulaht has not crossed his horizon before this, and even if it were argued that he might have heard of Vergulaht (but this had been omitted from the earlier narrative) we are still nowhere led to believe that they had ever met and could therefore recognise each other.

---

51. Gawan must have heard this said by Cundrie before the Round Table (317,11ff.).
52. Cf. Johnson, *Beauty*, p. 286.

Gawan (Books VII–VIII and X–XIII)

The listeners, however, are told enough to see that Vergulaht's unknown opponent must have been Parzival. The *sicherheit* demanded by the victor is that this victim should depart in search of the Grail (424,22: '*er twanc mich des daz ich den grâl / gelobte im zerwerben*'), a detail which tells Vergulaht little, but us everything. Furthermore, the victor demands that if he is unsuccessful in his quest for the Grail he is to render his homage to the queen of Pelrapeire (425,5ff.), referring to his victorious opponent as *der si lôste ê / von dem künige Clâmidê* (425,13f.). The detailed terms of this *sicherheit* mean nothing to Vergulaht, since he knows nothing of his victor's past history, but they would have meant something to Gawan if he had overheard this, since he knows of Parzival's connection with the Grail and defeat of Clamide.[53] These detailed terms also mean something to the listeners, who know what Vergulaht does not know and hear what Gawan does not hear. They realise that Parzival has unwittingly come close to the Ither situation again, a knightly encounter with a kinsman.

These references to the kinship between Vergulaht and Parzival are therefore blind motifs as far as the Gawan narrative is concerned. Vergulaht's genealogy is not utilised to show that Gawan cannot fight against a kinsman of his friend and kinsman Parzival (even though he comes to learn of the kinship between Vergulaht and Parzival),[54] but rather to stress that once again Parzival has unwittingly fought with a kinsman. In this respect, as in the near clash at Bearosche, Parzival remains *des mæres hêrre*.

Gawan and Urians

In Book X Gawan encounters a knight accompanied by a lady, but fails to realise until it is too late that he and Urians have met before. Although the encounter starts with Gawan glimpsing a shield (504,9), this is not as informative as it might be. One reason is that the shield is badly damaged (504,10: *dâ was ein tjoste durch gezilt*; 505,1: *Der schilt was ouch verhouwen*), but Gawan's attention is also occupied by the presence of a horse with a lady's saddle (504,11) and

---

53. Gawan knows of Parzival's involvement with the Grail from Cundrie's words at the Round Table (316,26ff.) and from Parzival's soon afterwards (329,25ff.), but also of his defeat of Clamide from the moment of the latter's arrival at the Round Table (217,19ff. and, with a special connection with Gawan himself, 221,1ff.).
54. He learns this from Antikonie (406,3ff.) and then from Liddamus (420,4ff.). In the latter case the lines 418,23ff. make it likely that Gawan must have been present.

he is puzzled more by the anomalous conjunction of a lady's horse with a shield (504,15: *dô dâhter 'wer mac sîn diz wîp, / diu alsus werlîchen lîp / hât, daz si schildes pfligt?'*) than by the identity of the shield. When we are shown Gawan approaching and looking at the shield more closely (505,2ff.), the damage to the shield is all we are shown of what Gawan actually sees (505,4f.) and even at this point his attention is distracted by the presence of a lamenting woman with a wounded knight in her lap (505,10ff.). All this is meant to explain why Gawan fails to recognise Urians when the latter first speaks to him (506,19), but it is even more remarkable that Gawan still does not recognise him when he says that he set out from Punturtois (506,26), since he knows quite well, once he has recalled Urians, that his full title is *Urjâns der fürste ûz Punturtoys* (526,21). This creates the impression that Gawan's failure in recognition in this scene is only partially motivated, but in insufficient detail to be as convincing as the other scenes we have considered. Questions are raised to which, by contrast with elsewhere, the answers appear not to have been anticipated by the narrator and built into the narrative. Why should Gawan not recognise the knight, even when he says that he comes from Punturtois? Or by his voice?[55] Or by his features (since a wounded knight would have presumably had his helmet removed)? What is the function, in this one instance, of Gawan failing to recognise someone or the facts of a situation? One wonders whether there is any connection between the anomaly of this last point and the presence of such unanswered questions, in other words whether this scene has not yet received its final working.

On the brink of the wounded knight's seizure of Gawan's horse a remark by the narrator alerts us at the last possible moment, only seconds before Gawan is himself aware of it, to the plot between Urians and his lady against Gawan (522,22: *er zôhz ir verr: diu frowe gienc nâch, / sanfte unt doch niht drâte, / al nâch ir mannes râte*). The last line suggests a previous arrangement between the two or a silent nod or gesture which escapes Gawan but, thanks to the narrator, not us.[56] Having appropriated his horse Urians now reveals that he

55. We have seen that Wolfram regards this as a serious possibility, even when a knight's voice may be muffled by his speaking from inside a closed helmet, from Parzival's second encounter with Sigune (see above, p. 115). On the general theme of recognition by voice in the medieval epic and romance see Mölk, *RJb* 15 (1964), 107ff.
56. Cf. the fn. to 522,24 in the Bartsch–Marti edition.

at any rate has recognised Gawan, for v. 524,10 (*unt sprach 'bistuz Gâwân?'*) is phrased as a question only in derision, not because he has to make sure. This is the occasion when Orgeluse, witnessing this, first learns Gawan's name,[57] but Urians also reveals that his present action is to pay back what he regards as Gawan's earlier slight to him (524,11ff.). There is no suggestion here that Urians has suddenly just recognised Gawan, so that he presumably saw who he was from the beginning. Whereas Urians enjoyed this superior knowledge at the outset, we are not allowed to share it with him at Gawan's expense, nor does Gawan grow towards recognition before this point.[58] In other words, although failure in recognition is present as a motif here, even in the case of Gawan, we are not given the means of looking down on Gawan's ignorance, as we can on Parzival's. This need to ensure that the listeners do not receive enlightenment in advance of Gawan is also served by the narrator's technique of naming in this scene. In 524,13ff. Urians has told Gawan enough for the latter to recognise him at last, and we learn the name of Urians at the moment when Gawan recognises him (524,19: *dô sprach er 'bistuz Urjâns?'*). Our recognition therefore keeps pace with Gawan's, and this synchronisation has been made possible by the narrator referring to Urians before this point entirely anonymously.[59]

Not because it forms an integral part of his encounter with Urians, but because it gets under way at the same time in Book X, I add a few words on Gawan's relationship with Orgeluse as part of the theme of recognition. When Orgeluse first enters the narrative,

57. That we have to reckon with this is made explicitly clear later by Gawan's suggestion to Orgeluse in 620,1ff. (see below, pp. 166f.).
58. Hirschberg, *Untersuchungen*, p. 208, has usefully emphasised the parallelism between Gawan's present encounter with Urians and their past encounter, as he recounts it to Orgeluse (525,11ff.), and draws the following conclusion: 'Wenn Gawan so im wiederholten Geschehen der Gegenwart und in der Vergangenheit immer der Gleiche ist, heißt das, daß seine Person in der gegenwärtigen Handlung keines Entwicklungsprozesses bedarf, daß seine Identität der erzählten Geschichte schon vorausliegt, nicht erst im Laufe dieser hergestellt werden muß'. Here too there is a clear distinction to be made between Gawan and Parzival.
59. Urians is thus referred to as a *rîter* (505,15 + 25; 506,5), *man* (505,22) and *helt* (505,24; 506,18), but also in regard to his particular situation as *der wunde man* (507,17; 524,9), a *rîter wunt* (517,4; 521,20; 522,11; cf. also 522,26) and *der wunde* (521,23; 522,20). After we, together with Gawan, learn the identity of Urians in 524,19 his name is now free to be used by Gawan (526,21; 540,18; 545,30), even complete with the addition *ûz Punturtoys* which at first meant nothing to Gawan when he heard it, without his name, from Urians in 506,26.

descriptive circumlocutions are used of her which anticipate Gawan's relationship with her (508,16 + 28ff.), but her name is revealed to the listeners immediately (508,26: *si hiez Orgelûse de Lôgroys*) and a little afterwards it is made clear, to Gawan as well, that she must be ruler over Logroys (cf. 514,6ff.).[60] In the course of his combat with Lischoys Gwelljus in the same Book Gawan learns Orgeluse's name and thus catches up with the listeners with but little delay, for his defeated opponent admits that he has been fighting in Orgeluse's service (543,3: '*durch Orgelûsen minne, / der edelen herzoginne, / muose mir manc werder man / sînen prîs ze mînen handen lân*') and Gawan himself sees both contestants as fighting on behalf of the same woman (543,14ff.). In other words, Gawan by now knows enough of the general situation to realise that the name of the mistress of Logroys must be Orgeluse and that she is a duchess. This is confirmed somewhat later when Gawan himself refers to his mistress as *Orgelûs diu herzoginne* (587,20). When somewhat later Gawan catches sight of Orgeluse by looking in the magic *sûl* at Schastel Marveile, asks who she is and is told by Arnive (593,29: '*sagt mir, wer mac diu frouwe sîn?*' / *si sprach 'daz ist diu herzogîn / Von Lôgroys, diu clâre*'), this is not meant to imply that this is the first occasion when he learns this and that the narrator has forgotten the earlier passages 543,3ff. and 587,20.[61] Gawan could equally well simply be seeking confirmation that he has seen correctly through the magical instrument which, since this is the realm of Clinschor, could be deceiving him (cf. 593,9: *in dûht diu sûl het in*

---

60. The position is as follows regarding the release of information about Orgeluse to Gawan and the listeners. In 506,25 (... *komen dar gein Lôgrois*), before even meeting Orgeluse, Gawan is told by Urians that he has reached the general area of Logroys. Gawan gives voice to this awareness in 507,13, and its correctness is confirmed to us by the narrator 507,28f. (*er sach in kurzen zîten / Lôgroys die gehêrten*). In 508,26 the narrator tells us the name of the newly introduced Orgeluse de Logroys, whilst in 514,6ff. Gawan learns that the lady who for him so far is anonymous is mistress of the land which he knows to be called Logroys. Finally, in 543,3f. he learns from Lischoys Gwelljus that this same lady is in fact called Orgeluse and is a duchess. By this point at the latest Gawan has caught up with the listeners' enlightenment given in 508,26, he knows that this is Orgeluse de Logroys. Confirmation is provided by 587,20, where Gawan himself speaks of her as *Orgelûs diu herzoginne*.
61. See also Hagen, *Erkennen*, pp. 45f., although I find unconvincing his suggestion that Gawan cannot be deliberately concealing his identity here because he conceives the idea of his surprise only later. The fact that we learn of this surprise in the Gramoflanz episode does not necessarily mean that Gawan may not have been playing with the idea earlier.

betrogn) or, alternatively, he could be trying to find out more about her.[62] As long as these alternatives remain open we should hesitate before ascribing a blunder to the narrator on this point.[63]

Schastel Marveile

The theme of recognition at this location is expressed largely in terms of a gap in information between Gawan and the listeners, but it is also visible if we compare Gawan and Parzival as regards the amount of preliminary knowledge each possesses as he enters on his crowning adventure at Schastel Marveile or Munsalvæsche. If we start by discussing the extent to which Gawan's knowledge falls short of the listeners' in this episode, this must be immediately qualified by the observation that his relative ignorance is of very short duration, so that he soon catches up with the listeners and is in any case, very much by contrast with Parzival, equipped with the vital information needed for his exploit before the adventure actually begins.

When Gawan first catches sight of Schastel Marveile we are made aware of a difference between his point of view and what is conveyed to us by the narrator. Emphasis is placed on Gawan's

---

62. The question of how Gawan comes to realise Orgeluse's full title and name illustrates how carefully we must interpret the information provided in instalments by the narrator. In the fn. to 593,29 in the Bartsch–Marti edition we read the following: '29 will sich Gawan nur vergewissern, daß es Orgeluse ist und zugleich Näheres über die von ihm geliebte Dame erfahren, oder hat der Dichter vergessen, daß er ihren Namen schon von Lischoys erfahren hat (543,3)? Allerdings wird dort ihr Land nicht genannt.' Forgetfulness here seems to lie rather with the editors than with the poet, for if they had remembered not just 543,3, but also the just as significant evidence of 587,20, they would surely have hesitated to ascribe carelessness to Wolfram. Even their addition about the name of the land Logroys rests on a shaky basis (cf. fn. 60).

    S. M. Johnson, *GR* 33 (1958), 290, also lays himself open to misunderstanding in saying: 'Meanwhile, Gawan has found out from Arnive that Orgeluse is *diu herzogîn von Lôgroys* (593,30f) and from Gramoflanz that her name is Orgeluse (606,1–16)'. Both these points are factually correct, but hardly in the sense meant by Johnson, since Gawan had already learned of Orgeluse's rank and name by 543,3f. (cf. the confirmation in 587,20) and of the name of her land even earlier (514,6ff.).
63. In 516,3ff. the narrator warns his listeners against jumping to hasty conclusions about Orgeluse. By stressing *ê* and *unz* in the context of *küende gewinnen* (516,6f.) he implies that they at present lack the knowledge which will later be granted them and by saying that he at least refuses to criticise her (516,14) he reveals that he knows more than they and that they will have to wait for enlightenment.

visual impression at this stage[64] and it is made clear that he sees no more than a castle with a large number of ladies[65] at the windows (534,27: *dar zuo muoser schouwen / in den venstern manege frouwen*),[66] whereas we receive not merely this impression, but also more accurate knowledge from the narrator, who omnisciently can tell us that these ladies numbered four hundred or more and that four of them were of high birth (534,29: *der was vier hundert ode mêr, / viere undr in von arde hêr*). This is no trifling detail, since it refers back to Cundrie's announcement of the adventure of Schastel Marveile to the Round Table (318,16: '*ich weiz vier küneginne / unt vier hundert juncfrouwen, / die man gerne möhte schouwen. / ze Schastel marveil die sint*')[67] and therefore tells us that Gawan has at last come within sight of the Round Table's goal.[68] Yet at this point only the really perceptive reader would be able to make use of this potential superior knowledge. A little later (548,3ff.) Gawan learns at the same time as the listeners that he has penetrated into a magical realm (548,10: '*gar aventiure ist al diz lant*') under the spell of Clinschor. The perceptive listener, aware that Gawan has come to Schastel Marveile, would know the first fact already, but Clinschor is here mentioned by name for the first time. There was an earlier anonymous reference to him in connection with the abduction of Arthur's mother as *ein phaffe der wol zouber las* (66,4), but the listener has no possibility yet of equating this *phaffe* with Clinschor since there is as yet no certainty that Arthur's mother, unnamed in this earlier passage, is one of the four named queens held captive at Schastel Marveile (318,16 and, with their names, 334,18ff.). All that we know so far is that Gawan is approaching his crowning adventure, not that he is about to liberate some of his own kinswomen, but our superior knowledge that this is in fact Schastel Marveile is soon lost as Gawan catches up with us

64. This is suggested by the repetitiveness of *mit den ougen vant* (534,20), *diu ougen* (21), *gesâhen* (22) and *schouwen* (27).
65. That Gawan should not stop and pedantically count the number is not merely probable in itself, but is borne out from his own point of view when he later says '*ich hân in disen zwein tagn / vil frouwen obe mir gesehn*' (554,28f.).
66. Gawan's subjective view of things is also borne out on the following morning (553,13: *vil frouwen ûf dem palas*). Again no precise number can be given from his point of view, and again stress is laid on his visual impression: *kôs* (553,11), *sach* (11) and *dûht* (15).
67. Cf. also 334,4ff.
68. Alerted by such connections the listeners may now correlate the narrator's forecast (529,22: *nu næhet och Gâwânes nôt*) with what had been said earlier of the Round Table's departure for this goal (334,2: *gein dem arbeitlîchen zil*).

on the morning of the adventure when his host Plippalinot tells him that this is Schastel Marveile before him (557,6: *'ze Terre marveile ir sît: / Lît marveile ist hie. / hêrre, ez wart versuochet nie / ûf Schastel marveil diu nôt'*).[69] The listeners, or at least the perceptive amongst them, have known this since Gawan first arrived at this location, but their superiority was of short duration, and Gawan is now apprised of the nature of the adventure in advance, rather than retrospectively as with Parzival at Munsalvæsche, who learns the necessary details when it is already too late from Sigune, Cundrie and Trevrizent.[70]

Apart from the recognition that this castle is the one announced by Cundrie (and even here Gawan's belated realisation is not so delayed that it affects the course of the adventure) it is true to say that on essentials Gawan knows more than all the other persons involved (this is the basis of his surprise) and also for a time more than is released to the listeners by the narrator. This is made clear at the moment when Plippalinot tells him the name of the castle, for at this point Gawan not merely catches up with the listeners in knowledge of what is afoot, but even overtakes them.

Gawan, informed by his host that this is Schastel Marveile, recognises that he has reached his goal, since he can now equate the women he sees in the castle with what Cundrie had announced to the Round Table (318,16ff.) and makes this link explicit in his words *'ich hân ouch ê von in vernomen'* (557,19). But these words of Gawan refer back not simply to Cundrie's anonymous mention of four queens to be liberated, they also take up the passage at the close of Book VI where Clias gave names to these queens (334,16: *'doch sagter mir vier vrouwen namn, / die da krônebære sint. / zwuo sint alt, zwuo sint noch kint. / der heizet einiu Itonjê, / diu ander heizet Cundrîê, / diu dritte heizt Arnîve, / diu vierde Sangîve'*). This reference to Clias has been rejected by Bartsch–Marti (with the suggestion that Gawan cannot have been still in the company of Arthur's knights when Clias made his remark),[71] but against this S. M. Johnson has made it likely that Gawan was indeed still

---

69. The fact that Gawan here catches up with the listeners is underlined by one significant detail. Previously mention had been made of only Schastel Marveile (318,19; 334,7), but now information is also given about Terre Marveile and Lit Marveile, to Gawan in direct speech and hence to us as well, for the first time.
70. See below, pp. 210ff.
71. Cf. the fn. to 557,19 in the Bartsch–Marti edition: '19 ê: schon an Artus' Hofe durch Cundrien 318,19–22; bei Clias' Rede 334,12–22 dürfte Gawan nicht mehr dabei gewesen sein'.

present and heard what Clias said.[72] His remarks can be supported by the suggestion that the poet describes the departure of a large body of Arthurian knights with some measure of realism: they therefore set out in stages, not all at once. At first a large contingent, but still only part of the whole, sets out (334,1: *Dô fuor der massnîe vil*), whereas only in 334,23 (*daz wolt ieslîcher dâ besehn*) is reference made to the departure of the whole retinue, so that the difference between *vil* and *ieslîcher* captures something of these stages. It is between these two points that Clias gives his information and only after the second point that Gawan begins to make preparations for his own separate departure for a different goal (335,1ff.), so that this narrative gradation suggests that Gawan was still present when Clias made his announcement to those of the Round Table who had not already set out with the first contingent.[73] If, as this argument suggests, Gawan heard the names of the four queens at Schastel Marveile from Clias he would have recognised three of them (for Arnive is his grandmother, Sangive his own mother, and Cundrie his sister)[74] and hence would have known, when told by Plippalinot that he had come to Schastel Marveile, that he was about to liberate his own kinswomen. Yet the listeners know nothing of this kinship: they have learned the names of the queens, like Gawan, from Clias, but unlike Gawan they know nothing as yet of their relationship to other characters.[75]

72. *GR* 33 (1958), 286f. Bumke, *Forschung*, p. 195, does not follow Johnson at this point, although his appeal to Mohr, *Euphorion* 52 (1958), 21, is not all that decisive, since the latter keeps an open mind on whether Gawan heard what Clias reported or not. Bumke also suggests that Gawan is still in the dark at this stage because Wolfram usually allows his listeners to grasp the implications of the narrative (which they do here only in Book XII) before the character himself. This loses much of its force, however, if we realise that this may well be true in the case of Parzival, but that Gawan is in a different position, grasping the facts of a situation before they are made clear to the audience.
73. Johnson, *ibid.*, p. 286, therefore accurately says that 'the Krieche Clias informs those *still* present' (my italics).
74. Although there is no reason to assume that Gawan would have any previous knowledge of Itonje (see below, p. 157, fn. 86), it would be an easy assumption that, like the other three, she must be closely related to him. From the words of Clias about the four queens (334,18: '*zwuo sint alt, zwuo sint noch kint*') he would realise that Itonje was of about the same age as Cundrie and likely to be her sister.
75. This interpretation of the revelation made by Clias leaves untouched the question why Arthur did not set out to search for the four queens, one of whom is his mother and another his sister, long before this. On this see Martin, *Kommentar*, note on 334,13, but also Johnson, *GR* 33 (1958), 287 and especially Zimmermann, *Euphorion* 66 (1972), 147.

Gawan (Books VII–VIII and X–XIII)

The disquisition on the power of love exercised over all Gawan's kin (585,11ff., inserted after Gawan's adventure at Schastel Marveile) gives the narrator a chance to sketch in something of Gawan's genealogy and remind us of his kinship with other figures in the narrative.[76] Discreetly tucked into this list is a reference to Itonje (586,22: *diu junge werde Itonjê / truoc nâch roys Gramoflanz / mit triwen stæte minne ganz: / daz was Gâwâns swester clâr*). She is in this list, like all the others, because she is a kinswoman of Gawan's and hence subject to the sway of love, but her presence is important in another respect, for the perceptive listener will recall that the name Itonje was also mentioned by Clias as one of the four queens held captive at Schastel Marveile (335,19). In other words, one of the four queens liberated by Gawan's exploit is his own sister and this fact is here disclosed to the listeners for the first time. However, this fact does not need to be disclosed to Gawan. Although after his combat with the lion he has made contact only with Arnive and two handmaidens (cf. 575,1 and 579,11), while the others remain invisible off-stage (573,25), Gawan knows, since the information given by Clias and then by Plippalinot, that his sister Itonje must be one of the four captive queens.[77]

So far the listeners have been allowed to catch up with Gawan in knowledge about two of these queens, but this bridgehead in their cognitive advance cannot be extended without further help, for the earlier references by Cundrie and Clias left the kinship relationships amongst the four queens in obscurity. The listeners are therefore still unable to draw any further conclusions from the fact now released to them, that Itonje is Gawan's sister. It is for this reason that the passage describing the meeting of Gawan with the four queens is so important for the narrator's technique (590,17: *dô kom diu alte Arnîve, / und ir tohter Sangîve, / unde ir tohter tohter zwuo: / die giengen alle viere zuo*).[78] Because the senior, Arnive, is explicitly termed a queen in this context (590,22; cf. also 591,4ff.) these four ladies now tacitly make up the four queens of whom the

---

76. Gawan's kinship with Parzival and his family is stressed again in particular (586,16ff.).
77. When the narrator tells them that Gawan will be healed of his wounds by Arnive (574,3ff.), this also tells the listeners something which escapes Gawan in his unconscious state, for the percipient ones among them will recall that Clias had earlier mentioned her name (334,21).
78. To this passage belong the lines 591,8ff. (*die clâren frouwen kuster dô, / Sangîven und Itonjê / und die süezen Cundrîê*), where the identification of the four queens by name is completed for the listeners.

listeners first heard from Cundrie.[79] Since the listeners already know (from 586,22ff., helpfully placed quite close)[80] that Itonje is a sister of Gawan (591,9 confirms her presence here), they must also realise that the other daughter (at first unnamed, 590,19, then called Cundrie, 591,10) must be a further sister of Gawan's, that their mother Sangive must be Gawan's own mother and Arnive his grandmother.[81] These surprises are sprung on the listeners all together (but are rendered possible only by the seemingly innocuous reference to Itonje in 586,22ff.):[82] the narrator has kept them in reserve so as to achieve this pile-up effect.

If the narrator prepares this surprise for us, it is much less of a surprise for Gawan. This is the first occasion for him to be conscious and alert after his recent ordeal,[83] and also the first occasion for him to be confronted not just with Arnive (whom he has seen already, but only through the dim haze of his exhaustion), but with all four queens together. It is therefore not surprising that Gawan now recognises his four kinswomen (whom he knows already from Clias to be prisoners at Schastel Marveile, which he realises from Plippalinot to be the castle where he now finds himself), but the point of recognition is not made explicit by the narrator. Instead, he changes his technique at this vital point,[84] for this is the first occasion, now that the conscious and alert Gawan directly meets the four queens, for the narrator to abandon his previous anonymous references to Arnive in Gawan's presence and to make direct use of her name (590,17), together with the other names as well so as to drive the point home. The narrator earlier avoided a direct use of Arnive's name in Gawan's presence to convey to us the knight's failure, in his semi-conscious, exhausted state, to recognise her, but

---

79. And also from Clias in 334,11ff., whose grouping of them into two old and two young corresponds tacitly to Arnive and Sangive on the one hand and Cundrie and Itonje on the other. That we are dealing with four queens has been clear since 577,16.
80. The reference to *diu junge werde Itonjê* in 586,22 allows her to be placed in the second of the two groups specified by Clias in 334,18.
81. Cf. Johnson, *GR* 33 (1958), 288.
82. The technique employed here (the narrator places an apparently unimportant comment shortly before a passage in which its significance is unexpectedly revealed) resembles what we saw above (pp. 145f.), where a number of hints of Vergulaht's kinship with Parzival are carefully given before mention is made of their combat.
83. Cf. 590,27ff. (*do sprach er 'frouwe und meisterin, / mir hât kraft unde sin / iwer helfe alsô gegeben'*).
84. On the naming technique employed before this point see below, p. 161.

is ready to use her name, together with the other three, at this point where Gawan confronts the four queens he has liberated and knows to be kinswomen.[85] This is after all the point in the narrative when Gawan first sees all four queens, and he also sees Arnive for the first time after her healing skill has restored him not just to strength, but also to alertness (590,28: *kraft unde sin*).[86]

In subsequent references to Arnive in Book XII the narrator can collude with Gawan in what has by now become a pretence of non-recognition[87] by still using anonymous terms for her.[88] But he can also remind us of what we know with Gawan, of his kinship

85. Cf. also the narrator's readiness to employ the two names Gawan and Arnive in direct conjunction once Gawan has recognised her (590,21: *Gâwân spranc ûf, dô er se sach. / diu küneginne Arnîve sprach* ...) in contrast with his avoidance of such a conjunction before this point (580,6: *dô sprach der ie was valsches vrî / Gâwân, zer küneginne*). For parallels to this naming technique see above, p. 99 (the contrast between the naming of Parzival and the anonymity of Anfortas in the Munsalvæsche episode) and also below, p. 232 (the naming of Bene alongside an anonymous circumlocution for Itonje).
86. At this point we have to ask why it is that, although Gawan can recognise the four queens as kinswomen of his, they still fail to recognise him. Again the narrator has built sufficient material into his account to allow us to answer this question, as has been shown by S. M. Johnson (*GR* 33 (1958), 285ff.), on whose argument I rely here. The inability of each of the four queens to recognise Gawan depends on the carefully constructed prehistory of their abduction. Arnive was abducted three years before the tournament at Kanvoleis, at a time when her grandson Gawan was still a small boy (Johnson, *art. cit.*, p. 288), she has since been held captive for about 26 years (*ibid.*, p. 289) and understandably is not reminded of this boy by the knight she now heals. Sangive must have come to Schastel Marveile about ten or eleven years later (*ibid.*, p. 289), at a time when Gawan was about 14 or 15 years old (now he must be about 30 or 31), so that for half of his present lifespan Sangive has been separated from her son. Cundrie must at present be 15 or 16 years old (*ibid.*, p. 290) and probably came to the castle with her mother Sangive, in other words at a time when she was too young to remember anything of her brother Gawan. Itonje finally can be presumed to be 14 or 15 years old (*ibid.*, p. 289), was possibly born at Schastel Marveile itself (as is suggested by 632,1ff.) and has therefore never seen Gawan before.
  By contrast, Gawan's position is essentially different as regards the task of recognition. However long the period of captivity of his mother and grandmother, Gawan at least has foreknowledge of their presence here, which enables him to recognise who they must be. Even though Cundrie must have been abducted when only a young child and even though Gawan has never seen Itonje before, his foreknowledge helps him here too. It is for this reason that Gawan has to ask which of the four queens is Itonje (631,6f.), for he has never seen her before and was possibly even ignorant of her existence. At any rate, Johnson's controlled speculation shows up the comment made in the Bartsch-Marti edition (note to 631,6: 'Gawan kennt weder seine Schwestern noch seine Mutter und Großmutter') as too undifferentiated.
87. On this pretence and its origins see below, pp. 165ff.
88. Arnive is thus called *künegin* (591,1) and *meisterinne* (591,27; 593,21).

The Art of Recognition in Wolfram's *Parzival*

with these four queens, in two ways. He can bring the reminder explicitly in an episode in which the queens play no direct part, as in the encounter between Gawan and Gramoflanz (605,6: *Itonjê het in im gesant, / Gâwâns süeziu swester*),[89] but he can also refer to both Gawan and Arnive by name as a sign that Gawan knows who he is dealing with (625,1: *ZArnîven sprach Gâwân*).[90] The narrator's concern in such passages is to show us both that Gawan has now recognised his kinswomen and that he successfully conceals this from them.[91]

Gawan's foreknowledge of what awaits him at Schastel Marveile has so far shown him considerably in advance of the listeners in recognising the facts of the situation, but it is also possible to contrast him with Parzival at Munsalvæsche and to register that Gawan is equipped with the kind of information before he embarks on his adventure which would have stood the hero in good stead in his comparable situation. Whereas Parzival acquires this knowledge only after the event (from Sigune, Cundrie and Trevrizent), at a time therefore when it cannot apparently help him towards success, Gawan is apprised of the essential facts, even down to a detailed forecast of what will happen where and in what sequence, by the ferryman Plippalinot before he undertakes the adventure. Gawan insistently asks his host for information about the castle before them, but involved in this is an enlightenment about what awaits the knight who undertakes the adventure there, as is brought out by Gawan's words (558,3: '*nu gebt mir strîtes rât*'). What his host now tells him amounts to advice as to how he may best comport himself in the course of his adventure, what he is to expect at each stage and what finally is at stake. From him Gawan therefore receives the gift of a shield[92] in a better state than his own,[93] hacked

---

89. For a parallel with this technique cf. below (p. 235), where Gawan's name is withheld in the description of his combat with Parzival, but is used in the simultaneous episode of Arthur's messengers parleying with Gramoflanz. We saw also from an earlier example (pp. 76f.) how Parzival could be named in the context of Pelrapeire, but kept anonymous in the Round Table episodes of Kingrun and Clamide.
90. Cf. also the different use of names in 624,28f. (*dô fuort in an sîn gemach / Arnîve*), where the use of the pronoun *in* reflects her ignorance of his identity, and in 625,1 (*ZArnîven sprach Gâwân*), where Arnive's name is used because Gawan now recognises her.
91. Gawan's realisation of the identity of his sisters among the four queens is later confirmed (607,10ff.; 634,28ff.), but I see no reason to date his comprehension of the full position as late as either of these points.
92. 557,4.
93. 560,29: '*mînen schilt sult ir tragn. / dern ist durchstochen noch zerslagn*'.

Gawan (Books VII–VIII and X–XIII)

to pieces in the encounter with Lischoys Gwelljus,[94] but also advice on how essential it will be to keep this shield and his sword with him, even inside the castle.[95] Apart from these general points Gawan also learns of detailed aspects of the forthcoming adventure: he is to leave his horse behind at the entrance to the castle (561,3ff.), once inside the castle he is to expect to find the palace deserted (561,14ff.) but is to penetrate inside the *kemenâte* where he will find *Lît marveile* (561,20ff.), an obvious focal point of what awaits Gawan because of its parallel with Terre Marveile and Schastel Marveile and because Plippalinot had regarded it as sufficiently important for specific mention in his first explanatory words to his guest (557,6ff.).

How helpful this detailed forecast is and therefore how justified the ferryman is in what he says about his instructions (560,26: '*hêrre, ich tuon iu kuont / wie ir sult gebâren / gein iwers verhes vâren*') can be measured by the extent of agreement between what he says awaits Gawan and what Gawan encounters in the course of his adventure.[96] Plippalinot first mentions that Gawan will find a *krâmer* (561,5) at the gateway of the castle with whom he is to leave his horse, and this is in fact what happens to Gawan first of all (562,22ff.). The ferryman next mentions the deserted palace (561,14ff.), which is the next stage to be described once Gawan has entered the castle (565,6ff. + 21ff.). The informant's focus had next concentrated on the *kemenâte* and *Lît marveile* (561,20ff.), which is also true of Gawan's path once inside the palace (566,11ff.). The particular warning about the shield (560,29; 562,2f.) then proves its indispensable value in what ensues after Gawan has flung himself on the revolving bed (568,26ff.; 571,22ff.; 579,8ff.). Less precise, but still recognisable as advice, is the ferryman's warning that Gawan is to be prepared for the worst just when he thinks it is already behind him (562,4: '*so ir wænt daz ende habe genomn / iwer kumber grœzlîch, / alrêrst strîte ist er gelîch*'), for this again forecasts accurately what happens: after Gawan has survived the furious on-

---

94. Cf. 537,17ff. and 541,15f.
95. 562,2: '*disen schilt unt iwer swert / lâzet ninder von iu komn*'. The gift of the shield symbolises how well equipped (with knightly gear, but also with the necessary information) Gawan goes to his adventure.
96. Cf. Hirschberg, *Untersuchungen*, p. 196: 'Das bleibt eben der scharfe Kontrast zu Parzivals Aufgabe, daß Gawan mit dem rettenden Schild und einiger Information ausgerüstet auf seine Wunderburg kommt und dann wirklich eintritt, was in den Dialogen mit dem Fährmann und dem 'krâmære' vorentworfen wurde.'

slaught of stones and arrows he understandably hopes that this will be all (569,24: *dô het er gedinge, / sîns kumbers wære ein ende: / dannoch mit sîner hende / muoser prîs erstrîten*), only to find that he still has to fight with the lion.

Gawan is also assisted at Schastel Marveile, as Parzival is not at Munsalvæsche, by having been told what is at stake here[97] (he knows that he has an opportunity to rescue kinswomen) and what kind of reward awaits him if successful, for he is left in no doubt that he will then become ruler, as he learns in advance from the ferryman (558,15: '*op daz got erzeige / daz ir niht sît veige, / sô wert ir hêr diss landes*'; cf. 560,5f.). In both these details Gawan's foreknowledge is in striking contrast with Parzival's ignorance of the situation, for while at Munsalvæsche the hero has no idea that the members of the Grail-family are his kindred[98] or that the reward of Grail-kingship is being tacitly extended to him.[99] This is indeed the major difference between Gawan and Parzival in their respective crowning adventures: Gawan knows the essential facts in advance and is therefore successful, whilst Parzival's path to recognition is longer and more painful (he learns the necessary facts only in Book IX) and hence involves initial failure.[100]

One final point about the problem of recognition at Schastel Marveile concerns the narrator's naming technique, more precisely the fact that he refers to Arnive anonymously in Gawan's presence before he meets her and the other queens in full possession of his strength and wits, but is prepared to use named references after this point.[101] If Arnive is referred to in basically anonymous terms during the course of Book XI,[102] there is little difficulty in accept-

---

97. *Ibid.*, p. 197, fn. 18.
98. See below, pp. 199ff.
99. See below, pp. 214ff.
100. From what his host tells him in 557,10ff. Gawan is made aware that a supreme testing awaits him in the castle before him, whilst Parzival is given no such advance warning when he comes to Munsalvæsche.
101. See above, pp. 156f.
102. Arnive is included in the references to *manege frouwen* or *vil frouwen* at Schastel Marveile (534,27; 553,13; 554,29; cf. also *die frowen* in 565,21), which are doubly impersonal, since no name is given and the one person is subsumed under a large number. A term such as *diu küneginne* (578,10; 580,7) specifies Arnive a little further, since she must now be one of only four (cf. 577,16), not four hundred. A further degree of definition is reached by *diu alte künegîn* (579,11; 582,20), since this indicates which of the two pairs specified by Clias (334,18) Arnive must belong to, whilst *diu alte küniginne wîs* (578,4) goes even further in using *wîs* because it is Arnive who heals Gawan (cf. the use of *diu wîse* in conjunction with her name in 574,5). For the same reason, constructions

Gawan (Books VII–VIII and X–XIII)

ing the same kind of explanation as with Parzival's second meeting with Jeschute:[103] Gawan fails to recognise Arnive at first, and consequently the narrator avoids using her name in this episode. But this must be immediately qualified. If Gawan fails to recognise Arnive when she begins to play an active part in the narrative, this is at first because he still lies unconscious after the combat (573,23: *daz er lac unversunnen*), then because he is given a sedative to induce sleep (580,27: *eine wurz si leite in sînen munt: / dô slief er an der selben stunt*), whilst between these two points we have to imagine Gawan, even when he does come to himself (from 576,19), as still weak, exhausted and only semi-conscious. At this point in the narrative Gawan and the listeners share the same ignorance, but only because of Gawan's critical condition. Once he is fully restored, however, he regains his position of superiority to the listeners, for he knows who Arnive and the other queens must be.[104]

An apparent difficulty for this explanation is caused by the fact that the narrator does abandon his anonymous references to Arnive on two occasions in Book XI: once in 574,4f. (... *daz ez diu alte klagete, / Arnîve diu wîse*), where she is also described by two epithets otherwise applied to her as an anonymous queen (*diu alte, diu wîse*), and then in 581,9 (*Arnîve diu alte*), with only one such epithet. Yet these exceptions are more apparent than real. The point of the narrator's technique in the Jeschute episode was that the narrator acts as a commentator on events unfolding in the present and involving the hero, so that he must avoid being 'overheard' as to the identity of an unrecognised person until the protagonist has achieved recognition for himself. But 'overhearing' of this kind is impossible for Gawan on the two occasions when the narrator names Arnive in Book XI, since he has been expressly removed from the narrative action: in the first passage, because the narrator uses the name of Arnive at a time when Gawan is *unversunnen* (573,23) and even apparently dead (573,28f.), and in the second passage, because Gawan has now been deliberately put to sleep (580,27f.) to assist the process of healing. In this second passage the position is remarkably clear. While Gawan is still vaguely aware of what is going on, the narrator refers to the queen anonymously (579,11: *diu alte künegîn*; 580,7: *küneginne*), while he is asleep he can

like *diu wîse* (581,23) and *meisterinne* (582,9) are used with regard to her medical skill.
103. See above, pp. 100f.
104. See above, p. 156.

afford to use the name Arnive (581,9), but reverts to anonymous references (581,23: *diu wîse*; 582,9: *sîner meisterinne,/der alten küneginne*) once Gawan has woken up (from 581,22: *er rewachte*).[105]

With a pattern as clear as this we can therefore argue that the narrator's technique conveys the name of this queen to the listeners, while also showing them that the unconscious Gawan does not yet know this fact. But the listeners still have no idea at this point who this Arnive may be, so that once Gawan comes fully to himself he knows both her name and her kinship relationship with himself and is therefore once more ahead of the listeners in comprehension, which is the normal situation in which Gawan is depicted as regards the theme of recognition.[106]

Gawan and Gramoflanz

In this encounter the narrator freely uses the names of both persons involved, without any technique of withholding.[107] When Orgeluse first gives her instructions to Gawan which are to lead him into conflict with Gramoflanz, neither Gawan nor the listeners learn this opponent's name (601,25: *dô sprach si 'hêrre, jenen stam/den heiet der mir freude nam'*), but by 603,29 this is revealed to

---

105. There are parallels to this elsewhere in the work. Thus, a person's name can be given or withheld in adjacent scenes to reflect the awareness or ignorance of those involved, as with Parzival at Pelrapeire or at the Round Table (see above, p. 76). Equally, the names of members of the Round Table can be released by the narrator in the scene of the drops of blood in the snow, without this conveying anything to Parzival because of his love trance (see above, p. 102).

    The narrator is significantly ready to change his technique when the listeners have caught up with Gawan in knowledge of his relationship with the four queens. He is now prepared to reveal his hand by referring to Sangive explicitly as Gawan's mother (636,24f.) and by calling Cundrie and Itonje *sîn swester bêde* (636,28). He can also use the names of Gawan, Arnive and Sangive together in the same context now that we know of their kinship (640,1ff.) or those of all four queens in the company of Gawan (641,29ff.).

106. Gawan's superiority in recognition is also brought out with regard to the captives of Schastel Marveile, deliberately segregated by Clinschor, for their liberation by Gawan means that men and women previously kept apart can now come together and know each other socially (637,20: *si wârn ein ander unbekant,/unt beslôz se doch ein porte,/daz si ze gegenworte/nie kômen, frouwen noch die man./dô schuof mîn hêr Gâwân/daz diz volc ein ander sach*). *Unbekant* may be used in a special social sense here, but it is still Gawan who puts an end to this state of affairs.

107. This is true of the Gawan narrative throughout, with regard both to the naming of Gawan himself (for the reason given by Ruberg, *Schweigen*, p. 228, with the exception of Schanpfanzun, for which a special reason exists, see above, p. 142) and to the naming of those whom he encounters (because of his superior knowledge of the situation, with the exception of Urians).

the listeners (603,29: *des pflac der künec Gramoflanz*). As is usual where Gawan is involved, this superiority of the listeners is short-lived for already by 608,13 Gramoflanz names himself in dialogue to Gawan (608,13: *'ich pinz der künec Gramoflanz'*) and shortly afterwards Gawan comes out with his own name (609,21). What Gawan really has to learn in this encounter (and the listeners simultaneously with him) is the full extent of the ramifications of his relationship with this knight,[108] to which his name is a key and which Gawan grasps immediately once he has been told the other knight's identity (609,1ff.). This same passage makes it clear that the task of recognition means nothing to Gramoflanz – he already knows that his beloved Itonje is the daughter of Lot (cf. 606,9), and yet he wishes to kill Gawan, her brother, in vengeance, as the son of Lot (608,25ff.).

Over this short span, until the moment when Gawan names himself to the man who has sworn to exact vengeance from him, this encounter is rich in the possibilities of dramatic irony.[109] For example, when he first informs the listeners of Gramoflanz's name the narrator makes a point whose true relevance cannot yet be appreciated by an audience at a first hearing, but only subsequently, for he says that even if Gawan had been two men, they would have endangered their lives in this adventure (603,27: *wærn Gâwâns zwên, die müesen ir lebn / umb den karnz hân gegebn*). At first this looks like a conventional heroic hyperbole, but it acquires real pungency when we learn of Gramoflanz's oath to fight only with two opponents at a time (604,25; 607,18f.). This apparently releases Gawan from any danger, but the trap closes when we learn that Gramoflanz is prepared to make an exception only if he should happen to meet Gawan himself (608,18: *'wan einer, heizet Gâwân'*). Nor are the listeners at a first hearing able to appreciate the irony in 604,19ff. of Gramoflanz now meeting Gawan of all people and not yet realising it. But the net is drawn more closely around Gawan when the narrator tells us that Gramoflanz's sparrowhawk was a gift from Itonje (605,3: *doch fuort der degen mære / einen mûzersperwære: / der stuont ûf sîner clâren hant*)[110] and reminds us

---

108. The complexity of this situation and the stages in which the facts about it are gradually revealed have been demonstrated graphically by Schirok, *Aufbau*, p. 519.
109. This is already true of the corresponding scene with Chrétien, which has been well analysed by Kellermann, *Aufbaustil*, pp. 76ff.
110. This gift must be connected with 586,22ff. and seen as a love-gift.

of her kinship with Gawan (605,7, *Gâwâns süeziu swester*). The listeners are thus made aware of a detail (the lover's gift) withheld from Gawan, and of a relationship (Gawan as the brother of Itonje) not yet grasped by Gramoflanz. Only when Gawan frankly asks Gramoflanz who he is (608,6ff.) and learns of his need for vengeance against Gawan in particular is the dramatic irony of this situation made retrospectively clear.[111]

Yet the ramifications of this encounter extend beyond the relationship between Gawan, Itonje and Gramoflanz. At one stage in his monologue Gramoflanz confesses to having killed Cidegast, Orgeluse's husband (606,6f.), and shows that he is quite aware that behind Gawan's willingness to undertake this adventure lies Orgeluse's wish to be avenged of Gramoflanz (606,15f.). Once Gawan has returned to Orgeluse this hint of the enmity between her and Gramoflanz is complemented from Orgeluse's point of view (612,28ff.; 613,28ff.), she now confesses how much her need for vengeance dominated her past behaviour towards Gawan (614,1ff.), so that from her lips, if not from the narrator himself, we learn what the narrator's excuse for her earlier behaviour (516,3ff.)[112] really was. Since the listeners now understand her position they should be as ready to forgive her as the victim (612,26: '*gein swem sich krenket mîn sin, / der solz durch zuht verkiesen*').[113] At this stage rather more of Orgeluse's past comes to light, since the same wish for vengeance which informs her relationship with Gawan once led her into an affair with Anfortas with the same end in view (616,11ff.), so that with this glimpse into the past the Gawan narrative unexpectedly opens out into the world of the Grail. It does this also in terms of the more immediate past, since soon afterwards (618,19ff.) we learn of Orgeluse's recent unsuccessful attempt to recruit a lover in the person of Parzival whom she might also expect to serve her by fighting Gramoflanz. Orgeluse's failure here is a token of Parzival's ultimate success, since he avoids the temptation to which Anfortas succumbed[114] and which occasioned the crisis at Munsalvæsche,[115] and also demonstrates that his career has little to do with

111. On the operation of dramatic irony at a subsequent recital, when the listeners are more fully informed than is possible on a first occasion, see Green, *Irony*, pp. 259ff.
112. See above, p. 151, fn. 63.
113. Orgeluse's use of the word *verkiesen* thus agrees with the narrator's words in 516,14 (*die râche ich alle von ir nim*).
114. See above, p. 10.
115. On the crisis at Munsalvæsche see below, pp. 216ff.

Gawan (Books VII–VIII and X–XIII)

Gawan's supreme goals in that he passes by Orgeluse as unconcernedly as he fails to show interest in Schastel Marveile.[116]

Gawan's surprise

Under this last heading we touch upon a theme which illustrates Gawan's knowledge of the situation and control of events over several Books and in which, in order to achieve his surprise as a master of ceremonies, he has to manipulate others by deliberately keeping them in ignorance of what he is arranging. With this final effect in mind Gawan is prepared to act secretively towards a number of people, keeping hidden from them, even those closest to him, the facts which he has learned. Even after he has recognised the identity of the four queens he keeps silent about his own identity, he ensures that Arthur shall not be told in advance of his success at Schastel Marveile and he conceals the identity of the approaching retinue of Arthurian knights from both Arnive and even Orgeluse.[117] In view of these long-term concealments we can apply to Gawan in a much wider sense than she has in mind Itonje's recommendation for him to show discretion and tact about her relationship with Gramoflanz (634,5: *'ob ir der zuht ir reht nu tuot, / hêr, diu lêrt iuch helenden muot'*). What follows is a discussion of Gawan's *helender muot* in a much wider context.

We have seen that in 590,17ff. Gawan for the first time meets the four queens whom he knows to be close kinswomen of his. On this occasion he manages to exercise a considerable degree of courteous self-restraint, above all because he has known for some time from the combined information of Clias and Plippalinot that this is the situation which he would confront here. In 590,21 (*Gâwân spranc ûf, dô er se sach*) the verb of movement indicates the shock Gawan receives on seeing these kinswomen in the flesh, as opposed to knowing in theory that they would be here, but he manages to play this down by implying that his movement was one of politeness, getting to his feet as ladies enter (which it no doubt *also* was, but not entirely), so that he now places himself gallantly at their service (590,30). This gesture of courtesy enables him to conceal his shock of recognition, so that he is able to address Arnive as before, as if there were no change in their relationship (590,27: *frouwe und meisterin*). From the fact that Gawan here conceals his recognition

---

116. On Parzival's lack of concern with Schastel Marveile cf. 559, 19ff.
117. Cf. Hirschberg, *Untersuchungen*, p. 236.

of his kinswomen,[118] seeing that they have failed to recognise him,[119] we have to date the germ of the idea of his ultimate surprise.

In view of this it is necessary to qualify Poag's suggestion[120] that Gawan's secrecy is forced upon him by his realisation that combat with Gramoflanz is his only way to Orgeluse's favours, coupled with his knowledge that if Arthur were to learn the true facts of this combat (a brother is to fight against his sister's lover) the king's peaceable nature would surely contrive a diplomatic solution[121] which would block Gawan's chances of winning Orgeluse. I do not deny that such considerations play an important part in explaining Gawan's positive thirst for secrecy at this stage, but they cannot account for the genesis of his idea when he first meets the four queens personally, if only because the possibility of gaining Orgeluse by defeating Gramoflanz is presented to him only later than this encounter.[122] In other words, we still have to attribute the actual start of Gawan's intrigue, his failure to disclose his identity to his kinswomen, to a general wish to spring a surprise on all concerned, to present himself not merely as the victor at Schastel Marveile, but also as a supreme master of events to as large a public as possible. Very soon afterwards, once the possibility of Gramoflanz has been dangled before Gawan, these original motives may well have been reinforced, or even largely ousted, by the more urgent need to prevent any frustration of the planned combat, but this still does not mean, as Poag implies, that Gawan's plot can be explained in its entirety by this motive alone.

Gawan's surprise is so many-sided and involves the movement of such large bodies of people that he cannot possibly stage-manage it alone and he has therefore to take a restricted number of people into his confidence as accomplices. As he rides back to Schastel Marveile in the company of Orgeluse Gawan realises that he will need her cooperation if the four queens, to whom he was careful not to disclose his name earlier, are not to learn it from her. That this danger is a real one does not escape Gawan, for he knows that Orgeluse must have learned his name in the Urians episode[123]

118. Cf. Johnson, *GR* 33 (1958), 288.
119. On the reasons for this see above, p. 157, fn. 86.
120. In *Wolfram-Studien* IV, pp. 72f.
121. Which is precisely what later happens (726,8ff.).
122. In 600,8ff. Arnive foresees what is about to happen, whilst in 600,20ff. Gawan learns from Orgeluse what the conditions are under which he may hope to win her love.
123. See above, p. 149.

Gawan (Books VII–VIII and X–XIII)

(620,1: *Dô sprach er 'frouwe, tuot sô wol, / ob ich iuch des biten sol, / lât mînen namen unrekant, / als mich der rîter hât genant, / der mir entreit Gringuljeten'*). Accordingly, he asks her not to mention his name at the castle, even suggesting an excuse which she can use for this purpose (620,6ff.). Although Orgeluse is the first accomplice to be recruited by Gawan (for a reason which is undisclosed and into which she does not inquire), she cannot realise that Gawan plans to keep her in ignorance in another respect as well.[124]

In order to get Arthur's retinue under way, however, Gawan needs a messenger to go on his behalf to the Round Table. He asks Arnive for one (625,1f.), and swears him to secrecy, so that nobody at Schastel Marveile shall learn what is afoot (625,7: *der knappe swuor des einen eit, / er wurbe lieb oder leit, / daz er des niemen dâ / gewüege noch anderswâ, / wan dâ erz werben solte*),[125] but adds a rider to the effect that a vital fact should also be concealed from the Round Table, namely that Gawan is now lord of Schastel Marveile and the messenger a member of the retinue there (626,19: *'und lâz dir eine witze bî, / verswîc daz ich hie hêrre sî. / daz du hie massenîe sîs, / daz ensage in niht decheinen wîs'*). We see both these precautions being tested in practice in the following narrative. Alerted by Gawan's request for a messenger and driven by natural curiosity, Arnive makes various unsuccessful attempts to find out what is going on: first, as the messenger departs (626,24: *Arnîve sleich im sanfte nâch: / diu vrâgte in war er wolde / und waz er werben solde. / dô sprach er 'frouwe, in sags iu niht, / ob mir mîn eit rehte giht'*), then in annoyance at this rebuff[126] she makes arrangements to interview the messenger herself as soon as he returns (627,5ff.)[127] and finally, exactly as Gawan has foreseen, she tries to learn more about Gawan from Orgeluse (627,12: *wider în durch vrâgen baz / gienc si zer herzoginne. / diu pflac ouch der sinne, / daz ir munt des niht gewuoc, / welhen namen Gâwân truoc. / sîn bete hete an ir bewart, / si versweic sîn namen unt sînen art*). At Arthur's court it is another woman who attempts to find out what is going on, for Guinevere asks where

---

124. See below, p. 172 (Arthur's knights have to pass through Logroys on their way to Joflanze, but because Orgeluse has not been told this by Gawan and has therefore had no opportunity to warn her followers a sharp conflict ensues).
125. Following the Bartsch–Marti edition (fn. to 625,9) I take the *dâ* in 625,9 as referring to where Gawan is at the moment (Schastel Marveile) and the *dâ* in v. 11 to where the message is intended to go (Arthur's court).
126. 627,1ff.
127. The messenger's return, Arnive's renewed attempt and its failure are described in 652,26ff.

Gawan's message has come from, but to no effect (647,23: *'und sage mir, wâ ist Gâwân?' | der knappe sprach 'daz wirt verlân: | ich sage niht wâ mîn hêrre sî. | welt ir, er blîbet freuden bî'*). Why both these feminine inquirers must be frustrated is clear: with Arnive, so that no one at Schastel Marveile should suspect that they are about to be reunited with their Arthurian kindred, and with Guinevere, because the Round Table knows from Clias that the four queens are captive at Schastel Marveile, so that Gawan must at all costs prevent this name leaking out if he is to preserve his surprise for Arthur.

Not content with this, Gawan takes a further precaution with the letter he despatches with the messenger, ensuring that it carries no (external) seal which would have revealed its sender to a third party and making do instead with other tokens of his identity (626,9: *der brief niht insigels truoc: | er schreib in sus erkant genuoc | mit wârzeichen ungelogen*). Accordingly, when Guinevere sees this letter she can recognise infallibly who it must come from (644,27: *einen brief si nam ûz sîner hant, | dar an si geschriben vant | schrift, die si bekante | ê sînen hêrren nante | Der knappe den si knien dâ sach*) and can herself tell the messenger that he must come from Gawan (645,9: *'du bist Gâwânes kneht'*).

Further moves (either pretences by Gawan or reactions by others) are described as Arthur's retinue comes within sight of Schastel Marveile on the way to the appointed place Joflanze. On seeing Arthur's approach Gawan is careful enough to attempt to conceal his tears of joy (661,21ff.), but although the sharp-eyed Arnive notices this (662,3) she misinterprets the cause and attempts to console him with the observation that these must after all be the knights of Orgeluse (622,4ff.), an assumption forced on her by the fact that Arthur's retinue approaches from the direction of Logroys (661,13).[128] Arnive first sees this retinue approaching in general terms (662,8: *'hie kumt der herzoginne her'*), then her focus narrows down to their uniform shields and heraldic devices (662,13: *bî den allen niht wan einen schilt: | des wâpen wâren sus gezilt ...*). We are told that Arnive recognised the coat of arms, which must mean its

128. In 661,6–9 we are told by the narrator that Arthur, following Gawan's request, was due to arrive on that day, but then we are shown how Gawan witnesses this approach (661,10: *manege banier niuwe | sach Gâwân gein im trecken*) from the direction of Logroys. At v. 10, in other words, the emphasis switches from what the narrator tells his listeners to the impression given the participants. What is visible to Gawan can also be seen by Arnive, but her ignorance of what he has arranged leads her to misinterpret what she sees.

bearer, because she involuntarily jumps back a period of time and thinks immediately of Isajes, the marshal of Utepandragun at the time when Arnive was still among the *Bertûne* (662,15: ... *daz in Arnîve erkande, / Isâjesen si nande; / des marschalc, Utepandragûn*). The narrator adds that Arnive is unaware that Isajes and Utepandragun are both long since dead (662,21ff.), implying that time has not stood still in the world outside, as it has in the enchanted Schastel Marveile, for Arnive has no means of telling that the coat of arms of Isajes has been passed on to his son Maurin (662,18ff. + 24f.). Because of the exceptional situation at Schastel Marveile this is an example of a coat of arms leading to a false recognition.

As Arthur's retinue draws nearer, Gawan keeps up pretences and acts as if he feared an attack by them on Schastel Marveile by ordering all boats to be chained fast to the bank (663,9ff.) and the outer gates of the castle to be closed (663,20ff.).[129] He repeats this pretence when a little later he apparently makes preparations for a military foray against the Arthurian knights (666,3: ... *unde schuof ouch sîne reise / gein Artûse dem Berteneise / mit tiuren gezelten*).[130] When just before this point Orgeluse is asked whether the other knights are hers (664,2f.), she can only assume that, because they come from the direction of Logroys but are recognisably not her followers, these must be the knights of her enemy Gramoflanz (664,4ff.). If so (or indeed if they are anyone else, 664,15: *oder swer si sint*), they must have passed through Logroys, where her own knights must have challenged them (664,9ff.). Unwittingly, Orgeluse has indeed hit upon the truth (664,17: *ir munt in louc dâ wênec an*), for Arthur's knights ran into opposition in Logroys and suffered losses (664,18ff.).[131]

129. The narrator stresses at this point how Gawan took care to stage his pretence in public (663,22: *alt und junge hôrten / wes er si zühteclichen bat*), which contrasts markedly with the privacy of his secret preparations when he has to take others into his confidence (cf. below, fn. 130 and 132).
130. The descriptive phrase *mit tiuren gezelten* underlines the public pomp and splendour of Gawan's pretence (*reise* in the sense of a military foray), again in contrast with what he is secretly planning (cf. below, fn. 132).
131. The contrast, made fully clear to us, between Gawan's public pretence and the surprise he is actually preparing, has all the makings of dramatic irony. Thus in 659,17ff. Arnive pleads for the captives at Schastel Marveile to be allowed to return to their kinsfolk, unaware that these kinsfolk are in fact coming to them and that one of them is already standing in front of her (cf. Ortmann, *Selbstaussagen*, p. 51). In 660,12ff. Arnive tells Gawan of her own royal birth and that of her daughter, but is clearly ignorant that Gawan has every reason to know this already. Likewise, her complaint in 660,29ff. ('*hêr, ich hân lange hie gebitn: / nie*

One last arrangement has to be made by Gawan. In order to retain control over the vast numbers he has set in motion on either side, all converging on Joflanze, he has to let some people, in addition to the solitary messenger so far used, into his secret in advance. To this end he appoints four knights to four court offices (666,23ff.), takes them aside[132] and reveals to them the identity of the other retinue (667,15: *'du sihst daz grôze her dâ ligen: | ez ist et nu alsô gedigen, | ir hêrren muoz i'u nennen, | daz ir den müget erkennen. | ez ist mîn œheim Artûs, | in des hove und in des hûs | ich von kinde bin erzogn'*), warning them finally to keep this secret from those in the castle (667,25: *'und lât hie ûffe unvernomn | daz Artûs her durch mich sî komn'*).

All this leads up to a carefully contrived scene of all-round recognition (670,23ff.) which starts with the narrator's mention of the senior queen, Arnive, by name (together with a reference to the other three in terms of kinship 670,23: *Arnîve, ir tohter unde ir kint*), in the company of Gawan, Orgeluse, and her two followers, Lischoys Gwelljus and Florant. When this company is greeted by Arthur and Guinevere, it is clear that the ladies kiss without being formally introduced (671,5: *da wart manec kus getân | von maneger frouwen wol getân*),[133] whereas the two male followers of Orgeluse are kissed by Guinevere only after Gawan has introduced them (671,7ff.). In other words, the names of the ladies in Gawan's company have not yet been released to Arthur and they have not yet been recognised by him, as is clear later from his question to Gawan (672,3: *den bestuont er sus mit mæren, | wer die fünf frouwen wæren*).[134] The lapse in time since Arnive and the others disap-

> *geloufen noch geritn | kom her der mich erkande, | der mir sorgen wande'*) is undermined for the listeners at the moment when she makes it, for they know that Gawan has recognised her and is busily engaged on removing the cause of her complaint. Gawan's reply (661,3: *Dô sprach mîn hêr Gâwân | 'frowe, muoz ich mîn leben hân, | sô wirt noch freude an iu vernomn'*) appears to her to be merely a politely optimistic formulation, but we know that it conceals an imminent truth, invisible to her.

132. Gawan's appointment of these four knights to their special offices is done privately (666,23: *dô nam mîn hêr Gâwân | vier werde rîter sunder dan*), as is also his revelation to them of what he is planning (667,9: *dô nam mîn hêr Gâwân | sîn ambetliute sunder dan*). A similar phrase is used to describe Gawan's reaction to seeing the return of his messenger from Arthur (653,21: *ûf stuont mîn hêr Gâwân: | er nam den knappen sunder dan*).
133. Cf. the similar suggestion made in the Bartsch–Marti edition (fn. to 671,5f.).
134. The phrase 672,15 (*ein ander küssen dâ geschach*) suggests personal rejoicing after the mutual recognition, as distinct from the more impersonal courtly greeting of 671,5f.

peared from the world at large adequately explains Arthur's failure to recognise them immediately, just as this also lay behind the inability of Arnive and Sangive to recognise Gawan. In this respect Gawan is in a superior position, since he was informed in advance of the identity of the four queens and of the castle where they are to be found. In the message he sends Arthur from Schastel Marveile (626,13ff.) Gawan makes no mention of Schastel Marveile by name, for this would have revealed to Arthur what he could expect, and in any case it has been agreed that the combat between Gawan and Gramoflanz should take place at Joflanze (610,21ff.; 611,1ff.). This is where Arthur has been requested to come by Gawan (625,23: ... *daz si beide an triwe dæhten | unt ze Jôflanze bræhten | die massenî mit frouwen schar: | und er kœme ouch selbe gein in dar | durch kampf ûf al sîn êre*; 667,4: *des morgens fruo mit krache reit | gein Jôflanze Artûses her*), for Gawan realises that to get there Arthur must pass by Logroys and then Schastel Marveile, from where he can spring his surprise by following to Joflanze, but only as long as Arthur is kept in ignorance of the fact that Schastel Marveile is now Gawan's base. Once he has been directly asked by Arthur about the identity of the ladies present, Gawan replies in order of seniority by revealing first the identity of Arnive (Arthur's mother), then Sangive (Gawan's mother and Arthur's sister), and finally Itonje and Cundrie (672,5ff.). This revelation to Arthur about them is also a revelation to them about Arthur and about Gawan's identity.[135]

135. My suggestion that Gawan's words 672,8ff. are a bombshell not merely for Arthur, but also for the four queens rests on the assumption that the latter were also present in Arthur's tent at the time. This is implied by Gawan's use of the demonstrative *diz* (672,9 + 11) and *dise* (672,13) in introducing them to Arthur and also by the 'stage-direction' 671,17 (*si giengen wider inz gezelt*), which I take to refer to those in the company of Gawan as well as to Arthur and Guinevere, even though *wider* makes sense only from the point of view of Arthur and his wife, who had come out of their tent in 670,28ff. (cf. the fn. to 671,17 in the Bartsch–Marti edition).

One could also argue that in this short scene of recognition on both sides the narrator makes use of the same kind of naming technique we have seen him employ in a larger context. He is therefore prepared to refer to the senior queen by name and to the others in terms of their kinship relationship before Arthur actually joins the company (670,23: *Arnîve, ir tohter unde ir kint | mit Gâwâne erbeizet sint*). However, once Arthur is present himself (from 670,28f.) the four queens are referred to only anonymously: *ander sîne geselleschaft* (671,3), *maneger frouwen wol getân* (671,6), *al dise frouwen wol getân* (671,22) and *die fünf frouwen* (672,4), until the moment when Arthur learns the truth, for now Gawan mentions the name Arnive (672,9) and refers to the others once more in terms of kinship relationship (672,11ff.). That the narrator is quite prepared to use this naming technique in short scenes as well as longer ones we shall see in

In judging the motivation behind Gawan's surprise we must not ignore the fact than on two occasions the narrator expresses his criticism of his behaviour quite explicitly.[136] Just after Itonje has requested him to show a *helender muot* (634,6) as regards her secret love for Gramoflanz the narrator faults him openly for carrying such secretiveness much further than she has in mind, to the inhuman length of still concealing from her the fact that they are brother and sister (636,6: *ouch het er sich gesündet baz | gein der einvaltigen magt | diu im ir kumber hât geklagt; | wander ir niht zuo gewuoc | daz in unt si ein muoter truoc: | ouch was ir bêder vater Lôt*). But Gawan is not only criticised for exploiting his younger sister in this way, for using her as a puppet and as a means to building up his surprise effect, he is also taken to task by the narrator for not having taken his own beloved into his confidence by warning Orgeluse in advance that Arthur's retinue would be passing through her territory on their way to Joflanze (665,25: *och solte mîn hêr Gâwân | der herzogîn gekündet hân | daz ein sîn helfære | in ir lande wære: | sô wære des strîtes niht geschehn. | done wolters ir noch niemen jehn | E siz selbe sehen mohte*). What is implied here is that Orgeluse, if warned of the facts, could have sent word to her followers in Logroys, thereby ensuring that the harsh fighting which ensued should not have come about, so that the blame falls on Gawan of being responsible for unnecessary bloodshed for such a trivial reason. As when Wolfram elsewhere expresses his doubts about the pursuit of adventure merely for its own sake,[137] the lack of necessity in these combats to which Gawan could so easily have put a stop heightens his irresponsibility.

Direct comments like these are the justification for Poag's interpretation of Gawan's surprise as resting on the selfish wish to subordinate others to his plan for a surprise effect and an indefensible readiness to engage in combat with his sister's lover if this is the only way, as he thinks, to gain the hand of Orgeluse.[138] Of particular relevance to our argument is Poag's demonstration of the

---

    the case of the Loherangrin episode at the conclusion of the narrative (see below, p. 262).
136. Gawan's *helender muot* in preparing his surprise is reminiscent of Gahmuret's in concealing his departure from Zazamanc (cf. 54,16: *mit der rede er si betrouc*; 55,4: *ir sultz helen lîse*; 55,12: *daz wart verholne getan*). Both these characters differ from Parzival in using their superior knowledge to deceive those close to them and both are subject to criticism for this.
137. See Green, *Aventiure*, pp. 137ff.
138. *Wolfram-Studien* IV, pp. 72f.

way in which Gawan, hitherto master of the situation because of his superior knowledge, begins to lose control and faces more and more difficulties which eventually frustrate his wish to fight Gramoflanz, by now the chief *raison d'être* for his surprise. The hand of God, through Parzival, now begins to work against Gawan,[139] for when the combat between these two begins in Book XIV[140] this shows us not merely, from Parzival's point of view, a recurrrence of the Ither situation after Vergulaht, but also, from Gawan's, that he has at length disastrously failed to recognise the truth and has lost control of the situation. This is not without a critical effect on Gawan's plans, for Bene now learns the identity of Gawan[141] and therewith the nature of the combat agreed upon with Gramoflanz. Gawan attempts to keep all the threads in his hand by persuading Bene to keep silent, but this attempt breaks down when Itonje learns the truth and also Arnive, from whose curiosity Gawan had attempted to conceal it all along and who drastically resolves the situation by calling upon Arthur's diplomatic skill to effect a reconciliation. It is part of the happy ending characteristic of the Arthurian world in which the Gawan narrative is set that, although his combat with Gramoflanz is ultimately abandoned, Gawan should not be deprived of the reward of Orgeluse, or, for that matter, of the harmless surprise scene in which various members of the Arthurian family are reunited. What he is deprived of, however, is his selfish, even ruthless wish for combat with Gramoflanz as a means to his end. If at this point Gawan's knowledge and control of the situation reach their limits it is thanks to Parzival's intervention in events, who acts by now as an instrument of grace and 'prevents a selfish intrigue from being carried to its desperate conclusion'.[142] With this reversal of the usual rôles (hitherto Gawan had been the agent for resolving the crisis in which others were enmeshed,[143] but now it is Parzival who starts the movement towards extricating Gawan from his own difficulties)[144] the narrative has returned on a higher level to the Parzival action.

139. *Ibid.*, p. 74.
140. See below, pp. 240ff. on this combat.
141. See below, p. 231.
142. *Wolfram-Studien* IV, p. 75.
143. Cf. Mohr, *Euphorion* 52 (1958), 13f.
144. It may be the diplomacy of Arthur which eventually rescues Gawan from the complexities of his own plan, but Arthur can only play a part at this stage because Parzival's intervention in the Gawan narrative has already acted as the necessary catalyst.

The Art of Recognition in Wolfram's *Parzival*

Our discussion of the recognition theme in the Gawan narrative has had to take account of Parzival at several points and in the last stages has had to judge Gawan's situation from the point of view of *des mæres hêrre*. Similarly, in attempting a summing-up of the Gawan narrative in this respect a comparison with Parzival is called for, although this will presuppose a number of points, especially in connection with Munsalvæsche, which will be discussed in the following Chapter.

If we disregard the point where Gawan's path crosses Parzival's again and he begins to lose control of his intrigue, it is clear that before this Gawan is knowingly in control of the situation throughout (he resolves other people's difficulties at Bearosche and is able to avoid combat with Arthurian knights there, he is aware of his situation at Schanpfanzun, he manages to stage a complicated all-round surprise at Joflanze, and above all he is given the requisite information about Schastel Marveile in advance of his adventure there).[145] He accordingly undertakes his crowning adventure knowingly and successfully. By contrast, Parzival receives his enlightenment only retrospectively, he arrives at Munsalvæsche in complete ignorance of what is expected of him and therefore fails. Gawan's knowledge is even superior to that of his listeners in one vital respect, since he knows from the beginning that the four queens to be set free at Schastel Marveile are his own kinswomen, whilst the listeners have to learn of this kinship gradually.[146] In the case of Parzival, however, the listeners' enlightenment takes place in stages in advance of the hero, who therefore has to catch up with them in knowledge of his relationship with the Grail-family.[147] This distinction can be put in another way – Gawan knows that the queens at Schastel Marveile are his kinswomen, but they are ignorant of him, whilst Parzival is known by name to the inhabitants of Munsalvæsche, but is ignorant of his kinship with them.[148] In both cases, the protagonist's success is linked with his position within his

---

145. The striking exception to this generalisation about Gawan is his encounter with Urians, but we have seen that there are reasons for regarding this anomaly with suspicion (see above, pp. 147ff.).
146. Cf. Johnson, *GR* 33 (1958), 285: 'The concealment of identities forms the basis for the surprise and involves not only the persons in the poem, but the reader as well.'
147. On this see below, pp. 197ff. and 214ff.
148. On the knowledge of Parzival at Munsalvæsche see below, pp. 320ff. (Appendix A), and on Parzival's ignorance of Anfortas cf. Johnson, *GR* 33 (1958), p. 288, fn. 6: 'Here Gawan knows that his relatives are in the castle, while Parzival does not at that time know who Anfortas is.'

Gawan (Books VII–VIII and X–XIII)

family (Gawan restores unity to his family,[149] and Parzival is revealed as the only possible successor as Grail-king within his dynasty),[150] but whereas Gawan learns (from Clias) what his rôle is to be even before he sets out, Parzival learns what his should have been only many years later. Finally, despite the fairytale realm in which Gawan's adventure at Schastel Marveile is set, the course of the adventure shows that this realm is amenable to rational control and that Gawan's knowledge concerns a courtly world of which he shows himself the master, whilst Parzival's ignorance is demonstrated ultimately with reference to a metaphysical world with its own mysteries which set limits to knowledge.[151] The world in which Parzival's ignorance is finally tested is therefore incommensurable with that in which Gawan's superior knowledge is displayed from the beginning, the hero's perpetual struggle with ignorance and recognition brings him an ultimate success which is not catered for in the courtly world in which Gawan is at home and master.

---

149. Cf. Ortmann, *Selbstaussagen*, p. 53: 'Er kann *vreude* bringen, denn – nicht zuletzt ist auch das von Bedeutung – er ist der Enkel, der die Einheit der Sippe wiederherstellen wird und dem *ellende* ein Ende durch *vreude* macht.'
150. See below, pp. 220ff.
151. Cf. Schaefer, *Beobachtungen*, p. 224.

6
Parzival and Trevrizent (Book IX)

Book IX forms a more obviously self-contained narrative unit than any of the groups of Books dealt with in other chapters. Coming after two Books and before another four Books with Gawan as their primary hero, Book IX stands out as being concerned exclusively with *des mæres hêrre*. This is made expressly clear at the start of the Book (433,1ff.) with its prologue-like dialogue with *frou Âventiure*, necessary after Parzival has for so long been lost to view while Gawan dominated the narrative foreground, and at the start of the following Book, when the return of the narrative action to Gawan is likewise pointed out (503,1: *Ez næht nu wilden mæren*).[1] The isolated independence of Book IX is also brought out by the link between the close of Book VIII (432,29f.), where Gawan sets out on his vain quest for the Grail, and the opening of Book X (503,21ff.), where the same quest is reported of him again, a link which contrasts ironically with Parzival's penetration of Grail-territory and instruction in its mysteries in the intervening Book devoted to him alone.[2]

As in other Books, but especially because instruction in the mysteries of the Grail brings to the fore the theme of a cognitive progress,[3] great store is set on the listeners' ignorance or knowledge by comparison with a character in the story. Their superior knowledge, contrived for them by information fed to them by the narrator, is combined with ignorance in two examples early in this Book.

1. Cf. Maurer, *DU* 20,2 (1968), 80. On the break at the start of Book X see also Schirok, *Aufbau*, p. 464.
2. On the irony of these two references to Gawan's quest for the Grail, bypassing the crucial action of Book IX which is actually set in Grail territory, see Green, *Irony*, p. 137.
3. Cf. Horacek, *Sprachkunst* 3 (1972), 220: 'Im neunten Buch des "Parzival" erfolgt ihre [i.e. der Themenkreise] Ausgestaltung und Reihung im Hinblick auf die Erkenntnisentfaltung und seelische Reifung des Haupthandlungsträgers.'

Parzival and Trevrizent (Book IX)

As Parzival's knightly journeying is described to us, the narrator pleads ignorance about when this happened (435,5: *ine weiz ze welhen stunden*), thereby forcing equal ignorance on his listeners, who are therefore ultimately put in the same position of chronological disorientation as the hero himself.[4] If the listeners share Parzival's restricted horizon over this point, this need not stop them being equipped with superior knowledge in another respect, as when a few lines later they are informed of the providential help about to be granted him (435,12: *sîn wolte got dô ruochen*), a vital detail which cannot be known to Parzival. How necessary it is to distinguish between what is seen (and reported) by the narrator and what is visible to a character can be illustrated from Parzival's approach to Sigune in her retreat. When the narrator says (435,13) *er vant ein klôsnærinne*, he is reporting what Parzival can see and judge to be the case himself (even though the following lines pass over to a narratorial comment, meant for the listeners alone).[5] But when this is repeated in different terms (435,19: *Schîanatulander / unt Sigûnen vander*), the position is now radically different: *vander* may again describe Parzival's act of seeing, but what he sees (summed up in the two names) is reported by the omniscient narrator, for it is afterwards made quite clear that Parzival has not yet recognised this anchorite as Sigune (437,22f.).[6]

In the earlier part of Book IX examples of the listeners' ignorance exceed those illustrating their superior knowledge. Their ignorance is stressed already in the opening passage (433,1ff.), for the narrator's dialogue with *frou Âventiure* allows him to plead ignorance about Parzival's exploits and therefore to pass this ignorance

---

4. On Parzival's ignorance of time at this point see below, p. 178.
5. And even though Parzival soon comes to suspect (wrongly) how genuine an anchorite this actually is.
6. On Parzival's process of recognition see below, pp. 180ff. Another example of the listeners' knowledge and ignorance is provided by 442,9ff., where Sigune attempts to help Parzival to Munsalvæsche by putting him on the path recently taken by Cundrie, but where the hero, despite the fresh track, soon loses his way. We are shown this failure immediately (in 442,26 the knight sets out, but only two lines later he has already lost his way), we are told what is happening more quickly than it can have impressed itself upon Parzival riding along the track before eventually losing it. If the listeners learn of this failure from the narrator before Parzival learns it for himself, one may wonder whether even the more perceptive ones among them can have grasped the workings of providential guidance (even though they have been alerted to its presence, 435,12) on a new and far less obvious level, rendered visible only once Parzival's encounter with Trevrizent has brought about his reconciliation with God (on this see Green, *Weg*, pp. 16ff. and *Pathway*, pp. 178ff.).

on to his audience.[7] More restricted in scope is the information withheld from us about the time and place in which the hero's adventures are again narrated at first hand. Thus the narrator's question (443,5: *nu lât in rîten: war sol er?*) is no mere rhetorical question, for such a pretence is meant to involve the audience in ignorance as to Parzival's geographical whereabouts, an ignorance which they are shown to share with the hero when soon afterwards a similar observation is made of him (445,27: *dô reit er, ern wiste war*). A similar technique is used of the time dimension at this same point. The narrator denies pointblank any knowledge on this score (446,3: *desn prüeve ich niht der wochen zal, / über wie lanc sider Parzivâl / reit durch âventiure als ê*),[8] so that the ignorance forced upon his audience in this manner reflects the ignorance soon afterwards confessed by Parzival to the pilgrim-knight (447,20: '*hêr, ich erkenne sus noch sô / wie des jârs urhap gestêt / ode wie der wochen zal gêt. / swie die tage sint genant, / daz ist mir allez unbekant*'). When Parzival learns from this knight that it is Good Friday (448,5ff.) and then from Trevrizent exactly how long he has been unreconciled with God and therefore disoriented in time (460,22ff.), his enlightenment is paralleled by the listeners': the fact that they learn this with him underlines the previous agreement between their ignorance and his. The same point can be made concerning the Grail itself, for although the narrator intervenes to tell us what Parzival cannot know yet, namely that Trevrizent is about to tell him of the mysteries of the Grail (452,29: *an dem ervert nu Parzivâl / diu verholnen mære umben grâl*), this information given us only slightly in advance of the hero is tied up with the narrator's theoretical justification of his technique of *heln* (453,1ff.), a concealment of vital information which has lasted since 241,1ff., when he first promised to reveal all at the proper time only.[9] Our being told what is about to happen just before Parzival actually experiences it

7. The narrator's ignorance is expressed in two ways: by his asking direct questions of *frou Âventiure* (433,8 + 15 + 17f. + 19–21 + 24–6; 434,4–9) and by his requesting her for information in more general terms (433,22f. + 27f. + 29f.; 434,2 + 10).
8. A lapse of time is necessary at this point, so that the Grail-knight just encountered by Parzival should not be exposed to the reproach levelled against the hero (447,13ff.; 448,1ff.; 456,5ff.) of bearing arms on what turns out to be Good Friday. However, this does not alter the fact that the length of time which lapses is left in deliberate obscurity.
9. See above, pp. 29 and 113. On my disagreement with Nellmann, *Erzähltechnik*, pp. 89ff., see above, pp. 28f. Also relevant is the decisively fuller explanation given only by Trevrizent (see below, pp. 207ff.).

Parzival and Trevrizent (Book IX)

is therefore less important than the fact that during the period of his wanderings we have been essentially as uninformed as he.[10]

This repeated emphasis on the parallel between our uninformed state and his means that little room is found to indicate our superior knowledge. In one important respect, however, we certainly know more than Parzival. The narrator may say that on his travels he avoided mortal combat with kinsmen and was content with a victory by simply unhorsing them (434,14: *ez wære lantman oder mâc, / der tjoste poinder gein im maz, / daz der decheiner nie gesaz*), but we know that he was not always master enough of the situation to realise when this was the case. We have already been shown this in the nearness of combat between Parzival and Gawan at Bearosche and in his actual combat with Vergulaht[11] – in neither case is there any suggestion that Parzival realised the fact that he was in danger of fighting with his friend or that Vergulaht was a kinsman of his, in other words, that the Ither situation is still relevant to him. Our superior knowledge is also brought into play at the moment when it is said that Parzival, approaching an anchorite's cell, intends to ask after his way through the forest (436,29f.), for although our disorientation in time and space may match his we at least know two vital truths which escape him: that God is about to show mercy to him (435,12: *sîn wolte got dô ruochen*) and that, in coming across this anchorite, he has encountered his kinswoman Sigune once again.[12] Thanks to the narrator we are told more than is available to Parzival.

Why the listeners' ignorance should be more obviously stressed in these examples can be adequately explained. Because of the dominant rôle granted to Gawan in the two preceding Books little is known to us of Parzival's exploits over this period of time, and it is the function of the dialogue with *frou Âventiure* to bring this home to us. Despite what has been released to us as well as Parzival in his second encounter with Sigune and when Cundrie appears before the Round Table we still need enlightenment about the mysteries

---

10. Our ignorance is also stressed when reference is made, however much in passing, to events which lie outside what is actually narrated. These are hinted at, in the case of Parzival's adventures, by the use of *manec* in the dialogue with *frou Âventiure* (434,12: *er habe erstrichen manec lant*; 434,20: *in mangen herten wîgen*), but also by an uninformative reference to the subsequent breaking of the sword given to Parzival by Anfortas (434,25ff. – on this see Schröder, *ZfdA* 100 (1971), 120ff.).
11. See above, pp. 140f. and 145ff.
12. On this superior information conveyed to the listeners see below, pp. 180f.

of the Grail,[13] and it is the function of the passage 453,1ff. to reduce the tension first created by the 'Bogengleichnis' in Book V.[14] Finally, to force Parzival's ignorance and loss of bearings on the listeners is an obvious means of creating their engagement and sympathy for the hero in his predicament. Even so, superior knowledge is not denied the listeners entirely in this Book. In addition to the two examples quoted from the opening situation, the narrator later makes it possible for them to realise progressively more of Parzival's relationship with Munsalvæsche before this is clear to him and even, to the extent that Trevrizent's knowledge is incomplete or actually mistaken, to know more than Parzival's instructor himself.

Of Parzival's encounters in this Book (with Sigune, a Grail-knight, the pilgrim-knight, Trevrizent) only his meetings with two kinsmen yield anything for our theme. In what follows I shall therefore concentrate on Parzival's third encounter with Sigune and then his first with Trevrizent, this latter being the longest, most complex and most important scene in the whole work.[15]

Parzival and Sigune

This actual encounter begins, in verbal and visual terms, at 436,26, but the narrator gives his listeners advance information already from 435,13ff. He refers to the person whom Parzival is now to meet anonymously at first (435,13: *ein klôsnærinne*), but then soon afterwards by name (435,19f. + 23; 436,24), so that unlike the characters involved the listeners know from the start who meets whom. Although we know about Sigune's character from Parzival's two earlier encounters with her,[16] her position has changed by now and the narrator accordingly gives us omniscient information about her manner of life as an anchorite. We are therefore assured of her love of God (435,14), her religious disposition (435,23–5), her asceticism (435,26ff.), her life in solitude (435,30), and the strength of her love and loyalty beyond the grave (436,1ff.). These observations by the narrator give the listeners more information than is available to Parzival – for them alone the force of the literary comparison with Laudine (436,5ff.) is proof enough of her loyalty, just as the narratorial comment that she wears a hairshirt beneath the grey attire

---

13. On the gradual process of enlightenment about the Grail see below, pp. 207ff.
14. See above, pp. 28f.
15. For this reason I have allowed myself the liberty of referring to this encounter alone in the title of the present chapter.
16. See above, pp. 78ff. and 113ff.

of a recluse (437,24f.) is a detail available to them, but invisible to Parzival. The audience are therefore given the means to judge the position correctly when Parzival wrongly suspects the genuineness of her ascetic vocation.

After this introduction, meant to equip the listeners with superior information, Parzival rides up to the anchorite's cell and the encounter starts (436,26ff.).[17] Since we know that he is one partner in the encounter, Parzival is referred to explicitly by name throughout,[18] but since he is at first unaware that this anchorite is Sigune she is referred to anonymously[19] until the moment when Parzival recognises her and her name is free to be used again (440,20: *Parzivâl verstuont dô sich / daz ez Sigûne wære*).[20] Such a situation, known to us from other encounters, where two characters initially fail to recognise one another demands a double motivation on both sides: how does the failure in recognition come about and how is it eventually resolved?

Various details are built into the scene to account for Parzival's failure to recognise the cousin he has twice met before. He first exchanges words with her without even seeing Sigune in her cell (437,1: *Er gerte der gegenrede aldâ: / 'ist iemen dinne?' si sprach 'jâ' / do er hôrt deiz frouwen stimme was* ...) and even afterwards only speaks to her through the window of her cell (437,14). Moreover, Sigune must have been hardly visible at first within her cell because of her position, for the narrator is not content with a general remark about her mode of life (435,25: *ir leben was doch ein venje gar*), but makes it clear that she was in this prostrate position when Parzival first addressed her (437,21: ... *mit zuht ûf von ir venje stuont*).[21] Once their dialogue gets under way Parzival is invited to sit down

---

17. Peil, *Gebärde*, p. 61, fn. 100, comments that precisely a recognition scene might have been expected here.
18. He is therefore named before the encounter starts (435,3; 436,27 – at the start of the encounter, but before any visual or verbal contact has been made) and also during the course of the dialogue before any recognition takes place (438,2; 439,9; 440,20).
19. The terms used are *frouwe* (437,3), *juncfrouwe* (437,20) and *magt* (437,29). Apart from this the pronoun *si* is used with striking frequency of the anchorite at this point.
20. Cf. also 441,15 (*niftel Sigûn*) and even 442,2 (*liebiu niftel*). When the listeners are informed of the anchorite's identity by the narrator (435,19f. + 23; 436,24), this is significantly before the start of the actual encounter.
21. Gnädinger, *Trevrizent*, p. 142 (especially fn. 1) has suggested persuasively that *venje* here has to be read in the sense of 'prostration on the ground'. Even if we accept the less drastic sense of 'Kniefall' or 'fußfälliges Gebet', suggested in the Bartsch-Marti edition (fn. to 435,25), this would still imply that no very clear view of her could be obtained from outside her cell.

outside the cell on a bench by the wall (438,10ff.), whilst he requests her to be seated within (438,19), so that neither party can see the other as they talk. For the brief part of their conversation before this, when they can still see each other, the narrator avails himself of motivation used before, stressing the effects of grief and asceticism on Sigune's external appearance again,[22] but also suggesting that while he can still see her Parzival's attention is attracted by the glittering jewel in a ring she wears (438,2ff.). It is also because his suspicions are roused by this ring, taking his thoughts in what we know is a false direction, that Parzival is subjectively unprepared to recognise Sigune. He may be perceptive in noticing her ring, but he misunderstands its import since he does not know what the narrator tells us, that Sigune wears it *durch rehter minne rât* (438,5). Suspiciously alerted to the possibility of a love-affair forbidden to an anchorite (439,11ff.), he questions her about her solitary abode (438,22ff.), seeing it as suitable for a secret love-affair, whereas we have already been told that her solitude is genuine (435,30: *durch klage si muoz al eine sîn*). Sigune's reference to other men (438,20f.) and her indifference to food (439,7f.) only confirm his suspicion that she is lying (439,9: *dô wânde Parzivâl, si lüge, / unt daz sin anders gerne trüge*), so that he must also suspect that her cell has a concealed entrance,[23] that she eats well elsewhere and conducts her affair discreetly, using the role of anchorite as a disguise. For various reasons, therefore, Parzival fails to recognise her, as is made expressly clear (437,22: *dennoch was im hart unkuont / wer si wære od möhte sîn*).

For her part, too, Sigune fails to recognise Parzival and sees who he is only once he has recognised her. Wolfram's problem in motivating this was a tricky one: he cannot disguise Parzival to Sigune by concealing him in his armour, since she knows from their last encounter that he wears Ither's distinctive armour and trappings,[24] and cannot effectively conceal this armour by again suggesting that it was smashed and dented, since he has already exploited this possibility.[25] The armour which would normally

---

22. 435,26ff.; 437,20 + 26ff.
23. Cf. the fn. to 439,12 in the Bartsch–Marti edition.
24. In 250,19 Sigune had made a specific reference to this in their last encounter (see above, p. 115).
25. E.g. 385,14ff. and 386,23ff. It is true that the change in Sigune's external appearance (see above, fn. 22) had been used in motivation before, but this time it is employed as only one motif among several, so that less weight falls on it.

conceal Parzival's features would here reveal his identity to Sigune. The narrator solves his problem by indicating Parzival's extreme courtesy when he realises that he is in the presence of a lady inside the cell.[26] He at first approaches and asks his question (436,26ff.), then realises too late that there is a lady inside (437,3: *frouwen stimme*) and that he has impolitely approached her in full knightly gear, on horseback and bearing sword and shield (even so, Sigune cannot have glimpsed his approach since she is still at her devotions inside the cell, 437,20f.).[27] Accordingly, Parzival retires from the cell in haste, regretting his lack of politeness (437,4ff.),[28] dismounts and ties his horse to a tree trunk,[29] but also lays aside his shield and sword *durch zuht* (437,9ff.). Although his helmet is not also explicitly mentioned, it is later made clear that he must have removed this as well. From Sigune's point of view, when she briefly sees him through the window (437,29f.), Parzival is now free of those trappings of Ither's armour which, had she but seen them, would have revealed his identity to her. If she still fails to recognise him, this is because it is made clear that, after removing his helmet, Parzival kept on his hood,[30] which still partly concealed his features as much as the rust on them (cf. 440,26f.). Such details, together with the narrow angle of vision presumably afforded by the cell window and the conversation conducted with both partners seated and out of sight of each other, mean that Sigune, too, initially fails to see who Parzival is, as is implied by her act of recognition being mentioned only later (440,28f.).

Parzival comes to recognise Sigune as she defends herself against his accusation of hypocrisy. She explains that her ring is a token of engagement (439,22: *mähelschaz*),[31] hints that the engagement is in the past and the man possibly dead (439,24f.), then expressly con-

---

26. Sigune's aristocratic rank is clearly recalled to us by the narrator (435,25; 441,3), but what Wynn, *Poetry*, has established about the attractions of the anchorite's way of life for German noblewomen in Wolfram's day explains why Parzival should be quick to assume that this cell contains a lady to whom due respect should be paid.
27. This is true whether *venje* implies prostration or merely kneeling.
28. His impoliteness is stressed by *alze spâte* (437,6; cf. the narrator's short-term anticipation in 436,28: *alze nâhn*).
29. We have to assume at this point that this presumably happened outside the narrow angle of vision through the cell window, so that Sigune was unable to recognise Parzival from the distant horse and trappings.
30. Cf. 440,23ff. – only later, therefore, does he remove the *hersenier*.
31. On Sigune's relationship to her dead lover at this point see Schumacher, *Auffassung*, pp. 49ff.

firms this and adds that he was killed by Orilus (439,30). She describes their relationship, not as the *âmûrschaft* imputed to her by Parzival (439,15), but as *rehtiu minne* (440,3), so that he now knows as much from her as the listeners earlier did from the narrator's use of this term (438,5). When Sigune stresses her virginity (440,7) and says that she regards herself as married to her dead lover in the eyes of God (440,8ff.), Parzival also implicitly learns what we have been told already, that this is no Laudine. Beyond this he cannot go at the moment, since there is no compelling necessity to link the anchorite's lover, killed by Orilus, with his previous knowledge that Schionatulander was also killed by Orilus (cf. 141,8f.): it is after all possible that Orilus killed others (we know, for example, that he also killed Galoes),[32] so that this particular knight mourned by the anchorite need not be Schionatulander. This doubt is removed, however, when the anchorite finally refers to her dead lover by name (440,17: '*ich pin hinne selbe ander: / Schîânatulander / ist daz eine, dez ander ich*'). Even though she humbly puts herself into second place and refrains from mentioning her own name (*ich ... selbe ander;*[33] *dez ander ich*), Parzival now knows for certain from the mention of the one name that this can only be Sigune (440,20: *Parzivâl verstuont dô sich / daz ez Sigûne wære*).

Now that he has recognised her, Parzival reveals himself by taking off his hood (440,23: *den helt dô wênec des verdrôz, / vonme hersenier dez houbet blôz / er macht ê daz er gein ir sprach*). Sigune grasps the implication of this gesture, looks more closely at what is now more visible, recognises his beauty through the streaks of rust (440,26: *diu juncfrouwe an im ersach / durch îsers râm vil liehtez vel*)[34] and expresses her recognition that this must be Parzival (440,28: *do erkande si den degen snel. / si sprach 'ir sîtz hêr Parzivâl*'). Her following questions about his wanderings and quest for the Grail since their last meeting (440,30ff.) take up the narrator's own questions to *frou Âventiure*, thereby once more reminding the

32. Cf. 134,23ff. (see above, p. 67).
33. This phrase conveys its own irony, for Sigune is in effect replying here to Parzival's accusation of *âmûrschaft* by admitting that, as he suspected, she shares her cell with her lover, but that he happens to be dead. This underlines just how correct, and how false, Parzival's judgment of the situation has been which we are given the means of assessing correctly from the beginning.
34. The reference to Parzival's beauty here is no mere topos, for his kind of beauty is characteristic of the Grail-family in particular (cf. Johnson, *Beauty*, pp. 286f.) and, by recalling the impression which it earlier made on Sigune (139,27; 141,5), is revealed as a means of her recognising him again.

Parzival and Trevrizent (Book IX)

listeners of their ignorance at an apposite point when Parzival has once more caught up with them in the process of recognition and they have lost their short-lived lead.

Parzival and Trevrizent

This all-important encounter starts with an act of recognition, but of a different kind from those which have occupied us so far, for in coming to Trevrizent's remote hermitage Parzival recognises that he has been here before.[35] This is made clear to us immediately he approaches the setting of the hermitage, for he is accurately reminded of the place where in Book V he had solemnly sworn Jeschute's innocence to Orilus (455,25: *er erkande ein stat, swie læge der snê / dâ liehte bluomen stuonden ê. / daz was vor eins gebirges want, / aldâ sîn manlîchiu hant / froun Jeschûten die hulde erwarp, / unt dâ Orilus zorn verdarp*). This recognition is taken a step further when Parzival actually penetrates the hermitage, for he now recognises the reliquary on which he swore his oath to Orilus[36] and recalls the spear which he took from there on the earlier occasion. Parzival betrays a memory for details here to which his author is gradually training his audience, but if the act of recognition (stressed by the threefold use of *erkennen* over a short span) here concerns a place and its attributes, this is by contrast with the failure, over a long stretch of Book IX, of Parzival and Trevrizent to recognise each other as persons, as nephew and uncle.

The initial failure of these two to recognise each other is well motivated by the facts of the narrative and also reflected in the technique employed. They may be closely related, but neither knows the other previously, since Parzival's childhood in Soltane has removed him from all contact with the outside world. Something of this initial failure is captured by the narrator's technique of giving or withholding names: although Parzival's name is used regularly by the narrator throughout this encounter (starting at 456,4),[37] the name of the hermit is given us by the narrator in

---

35. Harroff, *Wolfram*, p. 68.
36. This process is described twice, once by the narrator (459,24ff.) and once in Parzival's own words to the hermit (460,1ff.). On both occasions the verb *erkennen* is used (459,24: *dar ûf erschein / ein kefse: diu wart schier erkant*; 460,2: '*dirre kefsen schîn / erkenne ich*'). On the links between this act of recognition and the earlier occasion when Parzival was here, together with Orilus and Jeschute, see Hirschberg, *Untersuchungen*, p. 35.
37. The occasions when Parzival's name is used by the narrator in this encounter can be recovered from Hartl, *Verzeichnis*, p. 448, under *Parzivâl*.

anticipation before the actual encounter (452,15),[38] whilst during the actual scene he is referred to only by a variety of anonymous references[39] and is named again only in 493,9 and 502,24, after nephew and uncle have recognised each other. In other words, between the start of the meeting and their mutual recognition as kinsmen the narrator avoids using the hermit's name; we see him therefore anonymously from Parzival's point of view.[40]

Each therefore starts in ignorance of the other,[41] but each attains to recognition by stages in the course of their encounter. Parzival may have more to learn and more difficult truths to digest about his relationship with other people and hence about himself, but Trevrizent, too, has to undergo a cognitive progress which is made difficult for him in that he does not simply commence with no idea, but with a false idea about Parzival, which has to be demolished before he can start the positive process. I propose to consider Trevrizent's growth in insight first, dividing it into three acts of recognition: (1) the knight who is his guest is not Lähelin, but the son of Gahmuret, (2) this knight is not just the son of Gahmuret, but the killer of Ither, (3) this knight is also the unnamed knight who failed at Munsalvæsche.

38. The hermit's name is released to the listeners by the narrator before the encounter, by contrast with the manner in which, equally in anticipation, the reference to the hermit by the pilgrim-knight, speaking directly to Parzival, is pointedly anonymous (448,23: *ein heilec man*). Such anonymity is necessary for the poet's purposes when Parzival is addressed, for he has earlier been told by Sigune that Trevrizent, embracing poverty for religious purposes (251,13ff.), is a member of the Grail-dynasty. As it is, Parzival has no means at the start of this encounter of realising that this hermit is in fact Trevrizent. The named reference to the hermit when Parzival swears his oath to Orilus (268,30) is made by the narrator to his listeners, once more leaving Parzival in ignorance.
39. The evidence is as follows: *einsidel* (456,5); *guoter man* (457,2; 458,25; 460,19; 476,23; 487,24); *der kiusche* (459,22); *ein kiuscher wirt* (472,12); *wirt* (456,4; 457,11 + 21; 458,26; 459,5 + 9 + 18 + 20; 460,1; 461,27; 464,7; 467,19; 468,1 + 18 + 23; 472,18; 474,26; 475,14; 485,3 + 21 + 23; 486,15 + 21; 487,27; 488,3 + 21; 492,23; 493,15; 500,1 + 11; 501,12 + 17). In addition to the pilgrim-knight's anonymous reference to the hermit before the start of the scene (448,23) the narrator also once refers to him as *hêrre* (452,25).
40. Something similar is true of the narrator's references to the pilgrim-knight. As long as Parzival has no idea of his name he is presented to us anonymously (*ein rîter alt* 446,10; *grâwer rîter* 446,23; 447,13; *grâwer man* 447,7; 449,12; 457,6; *rîter grâ gevar* 448,1; *rîter grâ* 455,24), but the narrator releases his name to us at the moment when Parzival learns it from the hermit (457,11: *der wirt sprach 'daz was Kahenîs'*). See Green, *Namedropping*, p. 124.
41. Schirok, *ABÄG* 10 (1976), 43ff., argues that, from the beginning, Trevrizent must realise that the knight in front of him is either Lähelin or Parzival. On my reasons for disagreeing with him on this see below, Appendix A, pp. 320ff.

Parzival and Trevrizent (Book IX)

The hermit is led by a number of pointers to take Parzival for Lähelin when he asks him this pointblank (471,1: *'Hêrre, sît irz Lähelîn?'*). Our problem is to determine whether he chances upon this possibility suddenly at this point or whether he has been convinced of it all along and has gradually prepared the way for this question. The latter is rendered likely by the skill of Trevrizent's argument (which is a reflection of the poet's skill at this all-important point) and confirmed by the fruitful way in which Tax has asked himself how Trevrizent conceives and reacts to the knight who rides up to his hermitage.[42]

Parzival approaches him wearing his red armour, which, although it may not be explicitly mentioned in this scene, must be presupposed for it from the continuity between preceding and subsequent references to his wearing this same distinctive equipment.[43] In addition, Parzival rides up on a Grail-horse which he won by recently defeating a Grail-knight (445,14ff.). Grail-horses are clearly recognisable, both from the insignia on their saddle (474,5) and from their branding marks (540,26f.), and Trevrizent has every opportunity to observe such details, since he takes personal care of his guest's horse (458,13ff.) and later makes it clear that he has seen these markings (474,2ff.). In the hermit's eyes, therefore, his guest wears red armour and rides a Grail-horse. Trevrizent's knowledge of the Grail-realm tells him that this cannot be a Grail-knight, since he would not be wearing such armour. But he also knows a knight who did wear such armour, since he later reveals that Gahmuret earlier gave him Ither as a page (498,13ff.), to whom he refers as *mîn knappe rôt* (499,11). Yet Ither, related to Gahmuret and not to the Grail-dynasty, could not normally come into possession of a Grail-horse, and in any case Trevrizent can very soon tell that this is not Ither, first by Parzival's voice (456,26ff.) and then when he removes his armour (459,10).

If his guest is neither a Grail-knight nor Ither, how must

---

42. In this I largely follow the argument of Tax, *Trevrizent*, pp. 119ff. My disagreements with him are mainly confined to his interpretation of the second encounter between Parzival and Trevrizent (see below, pp. 257ff.).
43. Examples of preceding references are Parzival at Bearosche (392,20ff.) and, implicitly, the motivation of Sigune's failure to recognise him by removing from her sight Parzival's distinctive armour (see above, p. 183). Subsequent references include 618,21 (Orgeluse's encounter with Parzival) and 679,10 (the encounter between Parzival and Gawan). There is nothing to suggest that Parzival laid aside this hallmark only for the duration of his encounter with Trevrizent.

Trevrizent regard him? He knows nothing about Ither's death,[44] nor that Parzival killed him, so that he can only judge this stranger to be one person, knowing that he wears Ither's armour, rides a Grail-horse, and confesses to being a sinner (456,30). In the whole work, a Grail-horse is captured by an outsider only twice: once by Parzival himself (recently recounted to us, 445,14ff., but with no indication that Trevrizent knows anything of this)[45] and once by Lähelin in his combat with a Grail-knight,[46] an encounter known to the listeners from earlier references (261,27ff.; 339,26ff.),[47] but also to the hermit, since he later talks of it (473,22ff.).[48] The facts available to Trevrizent urge him to one conclusion, which we know to be false: that this knight on a Grail-horse must be Lähelin and that if he wears red armour he must also have killed and robbed Ither (he can be expected to commit *rêroup*, since Trevrizent knows that he has already done it once, 473,30). The hermit knows enough about Lähelin to be acquainted with his general reputation, also known to us: that he is prone to anger (79,13), proud (128,4), a killer of his opponents (Turkentals, 128,8f., or Lybbeals, 473,25f.) and capable of *rêroup*, the robbing of an opponent's corpse (473,28ff.). This is the hardened sinner[49] whom Trevrizent thinks he now faces, whereas we know that in fact he confronts his unknown nephew, Parzival. This discrepancy in point of view opens up the possibility of a double perspective in the first part of this encounter: how far are Trevrizent's words before the mutual recognition, addressed to one whom he takes to be Lähelin, also applicable to Parzival?[50] The spread of examples is a rich one and the point of

---

44. Although Schirok, *ABÄG* 10 (1976), 50, assumes that Ither's death was already known to Trevrizent, I conclude otherwise from his shock on learning of this from Parzival, 475,13ff., so great that it takes precedence over his regret that Parzival has killed a kinsman.
45. The reason for assuming Trevrizent's ignorance would *not* be, as Tax suggests (*Trevrizent*, p. 120), because Parzival has ridden directly from his combat with a Grail-knight to the hermitage, since this takes no account of the jump in time at 446,3ff. (Tax's words 'ohne Umwege' would therefore apply only to the narrative itself, not to the events narrated.) The hermit's ignorance is however suggested by his need to ask Parzival for details of the outcome of this combat (500,3f. + 11f.).
46. Cf. Johnson, *MLR* 63 (1968), 612ff.
47. Cf. Schirok, *ABÄG* 10 (1976), 49, fn. 23.
48. Already hinted at in advance by the narrator in 340,6.
49. He belongs to a generation earlier than Parzival and lacks the latter's excuse of youthful inexperience (*tumpheit*).
50. The possibility of a double reading (what Trevrizent means and what the narrator, speaking through him, means) was first suggested by Tax, *Trevrizent*,

Parzival and Trevrizent (Book IX)

this technique is to give depth to the hermit's question in 474,1, to show how disturbingly close Parzival is to Lähelin. This question therefore has a bearing on his guest which Trevrizent cannot grasp, but which we understand: Parzival's killing of Ither has placed him in the company of killer-knights such as Lähelin.[51]

Yet, however disturbingly close to the mark, Trevrizent's question is unfounded and we know it. In other words, what Trevrizent says to 'Lähelin' and understands him to mean does not always truly apply to Parzival. Whereas Lähelin committed his sins knowingly and intentionally, Parzival acted out of ignorance, so that his *tumpheit* has a positive function here, rescuing him from Lähelin's extremism. Whereas Lähelin was in fact guilty of *hôchvart*, Parzival is no more than warned of this danger,[52] and whereas Lähelin

> p. 122, and yields the following for our question. When the hermit blames the knight before him for seeking combat on a holy day and accuses him of *hôchvart* (456,6ff.), we know that Lähelin can be accused of pride (128,4) and violence almost for its own sake, but also that the same can be said of Parzival (cf. 472,5 and the hermit's warning against *hôchvart*, 472,13ff.). As regards Trevrizent's recommendation in 456,16ff., we do not know whether Lähelin serves a lady, but certainly the hermit feels justified in assuming this of chivalry at large (cf. his own case 458,6f.), so that what he assumes about 'Lähelin' is also true of Parzival. In hearing the words 456,29f. Trevrizent knows enough to realise that Lähelin is sinful and in need of spiritual advice, but we know that this is also true of Parzival (cf. also 467,20ff.). The reference to animals and savage violence in 457,25ff. has an obvious bearing on Lähelin's character, summed up by his heraldic device of the dragon, but it can also be turned against Parzival, the dragon in his mother's dream (cf. 476,27f. and Bumke, *Forschung*, p. 288, fn. 337a). In 461,4ff. Trevrizent learns from Parzival about his fighting for its own sake, his hatred of God and neglect of divine worship. All this, as we know, has a particular explanation in Parzival's case, but Trevrizent knows nothing of this yet and takes these remarks in general terms as a reflection of 'Lähelin's' sinfulness. The hermit's words on Lucifer's fall (463,4ff.) have a particular bearing on 'Lähelin', summing up the theological origins of his *hôchvart* and hatred of God, but Parzival too needs to be warned against *hôchvart* (472,13ff.) and has confessed his hatred for God (461,9). Trevrizent also places great emphasis on Cain's murder (464,16ff.), relevant to any professional knight, but to 'Lähelin' in particular in his rôle as killer *umb krankez guot* (on this see Schirok, *ABÄG* 10 (1976), 53) and also to Parzival's killing and *rêroup* of Ither (not yet known to the hermit).
> 51. On the wider implications of this see Green, *Homicide*, pp. 66ff.
> 52. See below, pp. 200f. and 205. Another vital difference between Parzival and Lähelin comes to the surface when the former states the two goals of his quest (467,25ff.) in what is for him the correct order of priorities (the *grâl* comes before his *wîp*, on this see Dewald, *Minne*, pp. 141ff.). Out of pastoral tact Trevrizent reverses this order in his reply (468,1ff.) because he thinks he is addressing Lähelin and seizes on one point where he can praise him (loyalty in marriage, the nucleus of possible redemption) before criticising him for his folly about the Grail. What is the correct order of priorities for the hero is here reversed because Trevrizent thinks he is dealing with Lähelin.

actually killed a Grail-knight, Parzival avoided this offence to the Grail-community. The point of this double perspective is now to register the difference between Parzival and Lähelin, to show up the hero's offences in a much less harsh light and thereby to console the listeners as to his eventual fate.[53]

Trevrizent has therefore adjusted his words to the particular position and needs of the knight he thinks he faces (and the narrator has further adjusted these words to the particular position and needs of Parzival as well), so that it is unlikely that the hermit's question 474,1 bursts out suddenly and without premeditation. Even so, he must have his unconscious doubts about this question, since the passage it introduces shows him musing aloud, following the course of his free associations and unwittingly getting near the truth.[54] His assumption that this knight is Lähelin because of his Grail-horse leads him to mention the Grail-kings Anfortas, Titurel and Frimutel (474,7ff.). Of the last he says that he loyally loved his wife, is reminded of what Parzival has already told him of his love for his own wife (467,27ff.)[55] and is finally alerted by this tacit parallel between Frimutel and Parzival to their similarity in appearance (474,21). Trevrizent's concluding statement (474,22: *'der was ouch hêrre übern grâl'*) is ambiguous in its use of *ouch*: does it link Frimutel with Titurel and Anfortas (he, like them, was Grail-king) or does it link Parzival with Frimutel (he too is to be Grail-king)? Such ambiguity cannot be intended by Trevrizent, any more than can the double perspective of his remarks applicable to Lähelin and Parzival, but rather by the narrator speaking through him and showing him unconsciously stumbling upon the truth.

These unconscious associations have made Trevrizent doubt his earlier assumption that this is Lähelin and in some confusion he now asks his guest who he is (474,23f.). Parzival replies straightforwardly with pride in his father's end (474,27ff.), mentioning Gahmuret's name and dynasty (475,2f.). Trevrizent now knows that this is not Lähelin, but the son of Gahmuret, and that, as far as he can judge, his previous remarks addressed to 'Lähelin' have been quite irrelevant.

53. Cf. Bumke, *Wolfram*, p. 58.
54. I have discussed the implications of this passage in *Homicide*, p. 74.
55. In 474,18f. (*'sîne site sult ir niuwen,/ und minnt von herzen iwer konen'*) the narrator speaks through Trevrizent to suggest to the listeners more than the hermit can be aware of – Parzival is to follow the model of Frimutel (*sîne site niuwen*) not merely in love of his wife, but also in Grail-kingship. In view of what we are later told about Anfortas (478,17ff.) it makes good sense that Frimutel, and not his successor, should be set up as a model for Parzival.

Parzival and Trevrizent (Book IX)

The next revelation to Trevrizent follows on quickly and naturally from this first one. In saying who he is (the son of Gahmuret) Parzival also says who he is not (475,4): he makes it quite clear that he is not the Lähelin the hermit took him to be, but he has now learned enough about Lähelin to see what they have in common and hence the justification of Trevrizent's mistake. He too has committed *rêroup* (475,5: *'genam ich ie den rêroup'*),[56] he too has killed a knight (475,10: *'den sluoc mîn sündebæriu hant'*),[57] but to make it clear that his victim was not the Grail-knight Lybbeals, as the hermit thought, he has to name him (475,9: *'Ithêrn von Cucûmerlant'*). The hermit has thus been relieved of one worry (the pastoral difficulty of winning over so stubbornly sinful a knight as Lähelin), only to be immediately burdened with another, since now that he knows who Parzival is, he also knows of his kinship with Ither and what this killing really means.

The second revelation proceeds much more speedily than the first, presumably because the narrator seeks a variation in technique by having a slow revelation followed by a quick one (especially since the third revelation will again be a lengthy one, above all because of Parzival's mounting embarrassment and hence difficulty in making his admission). Another result is that Trevrizent is now dealt two hammer-blows in quick succession: after all his earlier assumptions about Lähelin have been shown to be wrong he learns that his nephew has killed a kinsman, moreover a knight who, as his own former page, was close to the hermit himself. One pastoral task has been replaced by another.

Unlike Parzival's recent encounter with a Grail-knight, the event on which the third revelation to Trevrizent is based (the hero's failure to ask the question at Munsalvæsche) lies far enough in the past for the hermit to have heard something of it independently. References to this event in the dialogue arise from Parzival's statement that his primary goal is the Grail (467,26: *'mîn hôhstiu nôt ist umben grâl'*). The hermit tries to divert 'Lähelin' from this goal by stressing its inaccessibility, confirming the truth of this from his own experience, for he too has been at Munsalvæsche (468,12ff.).[58]

---

56. The same has recently been said of Lähelin (473,30).
57. For Lähelin cf. 473,26.
58. Behind 468,16 (*'ich weizz und hânz für wâr gesehn'*) there lurks the truth that Trevrizent is a member of the Grail-dynasty. The attentive listener who can recall what Sigune said in 251,12ff. (Trevrizent is one of the children of Frimutel) will be able to appreciate this point, but it means nothing to Parzival since, unlike the listeners, he does not know yet that this is indeed Trevrizent.

The Art of Recognition in Wolfram's *Parzival*

When the narrator tells us of Parzival's reaction, that he kept silent about having been at Munsalvæsche himself (468,19f.), we are being told more than Trevrizent knows and are alerted to his ignorance of a vital fact.[59]

The difference between Parzival's and Trevrizent's point of view is made clear when Parzival responds to Trevrizent's information about the Grail (concluded at 471,29) by still regarding it as his urgent desire and expecting God to acknowledge this (472,8ff.). He has just learned from the hermit of the necessity of a miraculous calling to the Grail (470,21ff.), so that when he hopes for a *benennen* for himself (472,9: '*der sol mich dar benennen*') we know that this has come his way once before, so that this hope for the future is a hope for a second chance.[60] But Trevrizent knows nothing of this, concludes that 'Lähelin' is hoping for a first chance, and knows that this is out of the question.[61] Our knowledge that if Parzival got to Munsalvæsche once he must have been divinely intended to do so means that we cannot say that God might not have it in mind for him a second time, we need not share the hermit's pessimism on this score.[62]

   Like the less perceptive listener Parzival has to wait until the explicit revelation of 477,19ff.
59. Something similar is conveyed by the wording of 469,5f. ('*hât ir des niht erkennet,/ der wirt iu hie genennet*'). Unaware that his guest has been at Munsalvæsche, the hermit regards it as justified to express this as a mere hypothesis, whilst we know that it is not, for Parzival has indeed seen the Grail. In another sense, however, the tentative hypothesis is fully justified, for if we take *erkennen* in the sense of 'understand, grasp the essence of something', then Parzival is indeed in need of enlightenment at this stage.
60. Schirok, *ABÄG* 10 (1976), 68, stresses the irony of Parzival demanding from God that he be *benennet* to the Grail (472,9) when he has in fact already been indirectly *benennet* there. That this knight was *benennet* to Munsalvæsche is indicated by the nature of his miraculous guidance there (cf. Wynn, *Speculum* 36 (1961), 399ff. and Green, *Weg*, pp. 14ff.).
61. Lähelin is not even a member of the Grail-dynasty, as we gradually learn that Parzival is, whilst his extreme sinfulness and killing of a Grail-knight exclude him on ethical grounds. The question asked of Parzival in 500,11ff. is thus equally applicable to Lähelin.
62. The narrator carefully gives his listeners grounds for hope for the future. In asking his questions of *frou Âventiure* he reckons with the theoretical possibility that Parzival may have been to Munsalvæsche a second time (433,24ff.) and thereby implants this possibility in the listeners' minds as a hope for the future. A similar question is asked Parzival by Sigune (440,30f.), although this could be meant ironically, since she still employs the distant *ir* and her use of *hêr Parzivâl* could be as ironic as it is with Cundrie (cf. Green, *Irony*, pp. 207f.). Certainly, Parzival recognises her aloofness (cf. 441,17), but at this point Sigune relents, resumes *du*, and after this reconciliation still hopes that he may

Parzival and Trevrizent (Book IX)

Later, when talking of the Grail being defended by *templeisen* (473,5ff.) so that it is inaccessible to all except those called there (473,9ff.), the hermit makes an exception of an unnamed knight (473,12: *einr*) who, so it is claimed, got there *unbenennet* and whom he accuses of being *tump* and sinful in not having asked the question (473,12ff.), without realising that he is talking to that very knight. But the force of Trevrizent's grief over this sin of omission, coupled with the fact that he thinks he is talking to someone else ('Lähelin'), leads him to an imprecision in referring to this episode. The hermit wrongly assumes from the knight's failure on this earlier occasion (473,15f. + 19) that he cannot have been called to Munsalvæsche (473,12: *unbenennet*), whereas we have been shown enough of Parzival's guidance to realise that he must have been.[63] We know already from the narrator that Parzival may have been destined for Munsalvæsche (333,30: *er was ouch ganerbe dar*), but not necessarily to ask the question,[64] and a little later the hermit, talking primarily of the Grail and not the nameless knight, expresses himself more accurately (483,21: *'dar solde ein rîter komn: / wurd des frâge aldâ vernomn ...'*): here too the knight is destined (*solde*) only to come there,[65] whilst his asking the question is seen as no more than a possibility, demanding a conditional clause.[66]

---

get to Munsalvæsche a second time (442,9ff.). However desperately, Anfortas's followers at Munsalvæsche also reckon with the possibility that Parzival might come there a second time (788,17ff.). Only later in their dialogue (492,1ff.) can Trevrizent suspect the presence of supernatural guidance in Parzival coming to Munsalvæsche, past all opposition from the Grail-knights (something unheard of, 492,6f.) and without any combat taking place (492,11ff.). The listeners know already that such guidance is still operative (435,12), for in his combat with the Grail-knight Parzival, unlike Lähelin, avoids killing him and is also providentially guided past any further such encounters (445,27ff.). Hope for the future is also provided by the implications of the contrast between Parzival and Anfortas (see below, pp. 200f. and 205), by the hero being unconsciously informed of the formulation of the question and thus equipped for a second, successful visit to Munsalvæsche (see below, p. 194) and by the difficulty for any audience listening to a Grail-romance in regarding narratorial forecasts like 435,12 (*sîn wolte got dô ruochen*) and 487,22 (*got was und wart in bêden holt*) as *not* involving the eventual attainment of Grail-kingship by the hero.

63. To the points made by Wynn and Green (as in fn. 60, above) must be added the implications behind Parzival meeting no opposition from the Grail-knights (492,1ff.).
64. *Ganerbe* need only imply that Parzival was destined to become a member of the Grail-community, not necessarily its king. On further questions left unanswered by this term see below, pp. 215f.
65. *Solde* occurs again in 483,23, but this is dependent on the conditional clause of the preceding verse.
66. On this see Deinert, *Ritter*, pp. 141f., especially p. 141, fn. 2.

Making this exception allows Trevrizent to refer to the only other exceptional case (473,22ff.: Lähelin) of someone penetrating Grail-territory (if not as far as Munsalvæsche itself, as with Parzival), which then allows him to ask Parzival the crucial question about his identity (474,1). This rapidly leads to the hermit's enlightenment on the first two acts of recognition he has to perform, leaving the third recognition still to be clarified. This theme next comes up in 483,20ff. Trevrizent has been talking of vain attempts to find a medical cure for Anfortas's poisoned wound, then briefly mentions the prayers before the Grail (beseeching an end to his suffering) before giving the message of the divine inscription, apparently promising final relief.[67] This promise seems to be fulfilled with the arrival of a knight in 484,21, but the hermit then refers to his earlier remarks about this knight (473,12ff.) and shows how hopes were dashed, accusing this knight of *unprîs, tumpheit* and especially loss of *sælde* (484,24ff.). Because of his incomplete knowledge of Parzival's identity Trevrizent's advice goes wrong: by so roundly condemning the unknown knight as if he were not there he makes it much more difficult for Parzival to broach his admission.[68] The hermit's ignorance about Parzival thus renders his pastoral task even more difficult.

Unwittingly, however, Trevrizent has eased the position for Parzival in another way: not realising that Parzival is the anonymous culprit, he tells him the wording of the question which should have been asked (484,27: '*hêrre, wie stêt iwer nôt?*'). Although the questioner is not to be intentionally told the formulation of the question (483,24ff.),[69] this prohibition is not disregarded here since Trevrizent, not seeing in Parzival the questioner, cannot be said to be telling him intentionally. Those listeners who perceive this may also see in it a promise for the future, the possibility that Parzival may be given a second chance, as he hopes for himself (472,8ff.). Unlike the hermit, we see that these hopes might conceivably be justified.

The difference in attitude between Parzival and Trevrizent is

---

67. 484,9ff. Again, the asking of the question is expressed in a conditional clause (484,12: *swenne im diu frâge quæme*).
68. This repeats what is present on the small scale in Parzival's second meeting with Sigune, where her dithyrambic praise makes it more than ever difficult for him to confess the truth (252,4ff. – see above, p. 117).
69. I take the verb *warnen* here to involve conscious intention.

Parzival and Trevrizent (Book IX)

made clear at this point by a narratorial comment to the listeners (485,1: *Si bêde wârn mit herzen klage*). Both may feel grief, but for different reasons.[70] Trevrizent feels it for Anfortas, and so does Parzival, but he also feels a painful sense of shame and regret for a missed opportunity. This extra dimension of Parzival's grief is known to us, but not to Trevrizent, it further emphasises his difficulty in making his admission, which is indicated objectively to us by Parzival not making this admission now, at the obvious point where he has been brought unwittingly to the brink of it by Trevrizent. Instead, there follows the interlude of a sparse meal, suggested by the hermit, unconscious of his guest's struggle with his embarrassment.

This interlude of the meal is used to underline the difference in point of view between Parzival and Trevrizent still further. The host comments apologetically on the poor fodder available for Parzival's Grail-horse, clearly worse than what it is accustomed to at Munsalvæsche (485,14: '*ich wæn dîn ors dicke gaz / ze Munsalvæsche baz dan hie*'). The next two lines continue the apology in terms of the host's good intentions, but refer not just to the horse, but also to Parzival (485,16: '*du noch ez ze wirte nie / kômt, der iwer gerner pflæge*'). The lack of symmetry between these two pairs of lines calls out for completion by the listeners, who can supply what is missing: not only did the horse eat better at Munsalvæsche, but Parzival as well; both were fed, not merely here, but there as well. That this extra dimension is intended is clear from 486,10ff. – the sparseness of the meal is stressed again, yet Parzival feels gratitude and affection for his host, and can therefore regard this meal as better than what was provided by Gurnemanz *or* at Munsalvæsche. Of this comparison, reported to us by the narrator, Trevrizent has no suspicion.[71]

The theme of hunger, shared by Grail-horse and rider, finally opens the way to Parzival's admission. Host and guest approach the horse after their meal, Trevrizent feels sorrow with it for its hunger and the wretched contrast with Munsalvæsche (487,27ff.). This opens up the theme of the Grail-castle again, and Parzival, linking regrets for the horse with regrets for himself, accuses himself of

---

70. Cf. Harroff, *Wolfram*, p. 73.
71. As part of his thesis Schirok, *ABÄG* 10 (1976), 61, suggests that Trevrizent speaks quite consciously here.

tumpheit (488,15) and then, painfully and indirectly, works up to the admission that he is the knight who failed at Munsalvæsche.[72] Trevrizent now realises the full extent of the truth known to us all along. In his reaction he comes close to despair and to losing pastoral control of the situation (488,21ff.), but he saves the situation by a masterly ironic understatement (488,25: *'sît dîn kunst sich sælden sus verzêch'*), quickly recovers and, by similarly playing down the need for grief (489,1ff.), pulls Parzival back from despair, too.[73] By comforting Parzival now that he knows the full truth Trevrizent tries to undo the damage of his sharp criticism of the unknown knight before he realised that this was Parzival (484,21ff.). What the hermit does here in dealing with Parzival corresponds to what the narrator does with his listeners in a positive anticipation of Parzival's future (487,20: *von der hôhsten hende / empfiengens umb ir kumber solt: / got was und wart in bêden holt*):[74] the narrator consoles the listeners about the future, just as Trevrizent has to keep Parzival tactfully from despair.[75]

The hermit needs enlightenment on one final point, the detail of the Grail-horse over which he went wrong in mistaking Parzival for Lähelin. He asks his guest about this (500,3f.) and Parzival tells him about his victory over a knight and how he gained his horse, adding that his opponent came from Munsalvæsche (500,5ff.).[76] Trevrizent is quick to ask whether this Grail-knight was killed or not (in other words, whether Parzival is really like Lähelin), is reassured by Parzival and can afford to reprimand him gently for taking his horse. For its part, the enlightenment which Trevrizent can give his guest reaches its final limit when he explains the gift of the mantle to him by Repanse de schoy (500,28: *'sine lêch dirs niht ze ruome: / si wând du soltst dâ hêrre sîn / des grâls unt ir, dar zuo mîn'*). He sees that her hopes on that occasion were soon dashed,[77] but cannot know that they will be ultimately realised when Parzival comes to Munsalvæsche a second time, although the listeners may

---

72. 488,16ff. On the syntactical parallel between this passage and 98,23ff. see above, pp. 58f.
73. On the function of this irony see Green, *Irony*, p. 205, fn. 2.
74. In 487,22 I take the verb *was* to refer to Trevrizent, who by withdrawal from the world into a hermitage has already made his peace with God, and *wart* to Parzival, whose reconciliation with God is not yet complete (cf. 501,17f.).
75. 489,13ff.
76. Parzival knows this detail because the Grail-knight had mentioned Munsalvæsche in the terms of his challenge to him (443,16ff.).
77. As is implied by the use of *wænen* in v. 29. On the two levels of irony in this remark by Trevrizent see Green, *Recognising*, p. 53.

Parzival and Trevrizent (Book IX)

have their hopes roused by the consoling hints given them by the narrator.

Parzival's process of recognition, to which I now turn, is much more difficult psychologically, for *tumpheit*, guilt and shame lie with him, and the process also involves a wider spread of themes: (1) his kinship with Ither, (2) with Trevrizent, (3) with Anfortas, (4) his responsibility for the death of his mother, (5) the mysteries of the Grail. Details about the Grail are scattered over the whole length of the encounter between nephew and uncle, whilst enlightenment on the other points is grouped close to the crucial turning-point where the hermit's guest is recognised as Parzival, not Lähelin.

No explicit reference to his guest's kinship with the knight he killed can be made by Trevrizent before he knows that this guest is Parzival, since it is Parzival, not Lähelin, who is related to Ither. Nonetheless, the narrator can employ a double perspective here too to suggest this kinship, already known to his perceptive listeners.[78] As addressed to 'Lähelin', Trevrizent's words about Cain's killing of Abel (464,16ff.) possess the symbolic import which Mohr has seen in them (all men are the sons of God, so that any knightly killing involves fratricide in this religious sense)[79] because, as far as we are allowed to see, Lähelin was not related to either of his named victims, Lybbeals or Turkentals. But if we take these words as the narrator means them, addressed to Parzival, they retain this symbolic import, but also acquire a literal significance, since we know that Parzival and his victim, Ither, are blood-relations. The hermit does not know this,[80] but the narrator speaking through him can hope that some of his listeners are perceptive enough to see it, since he had given them a clue in the earlier episode enabling them to grasp this kinship between Parzival and Ither.

This is all until the moment when Parzival says that he is the son of Gahmuret and that he killed Ither, robbing his corpse (475,2ff.). The hermit knows enough of Parzival's descent on his father's side as well as his mother's to see that he has killed a kinsman, that his own words to 'Lähelin' have a closer bearing on Parzival. He therefore breaks out into a lament on the ways of the world (475,13ff.),

---

78. On the way in which the narrator provides the facts necessary for the audience to grasp this truth see above, p. 83.
79. See Mohr, *Schuld*, pp. 202ff.
80. Trevrizent knows of course of the blood-kinship between Parzival and Ither, as is clear from his immediate reaction in 475,19ff., but when he makes his point about Cain and Abel he does not know that this is Parzival before him.

hesitates over what advice he can really give and accuses Parzival of killing his own flesh and blood (475,21: *dîn eigen verch*; 23: *ein bluot*). In his admission Parzival has shown that he has progressed enough since Gurnemanz to realise that his behaviour was wrong (in 475,2ff. he refers to *rêroup*, *sünde* and *sündebæriu hant*), but he still judges his behaviour by the chivalric code: he describes his offence as *rêroup*. By contrast, Trevrizent refers to guilt in a fully religious sense (475,22: '*wiltu für got die schulde tragn*'), what he castigates is not so much the *rêroup* as the preceding killing (475,21: *erslagn*).[81] The hermit has thus shifted the level of judgment from the chivalric code to Christian ethics, where what is wrong is the act of killing itself.[82] This offence may be heightened by the fact of kinship, but this kinship is a remote one in order to bring it home that Trevrizent's symbolic point about Cain and Abel is still valid.

The other reference to Ither in Book IX comes when Trevrizent, talking about his earlier journeying as a knight, mentions his encounter with Parzival's father and the page Ither granted by him (498,13ff.). This detail explains how Trevrizent knew immediately of Parzival's kinship with Ither, but it also clarifies this kinship. Ither is here referred to as the *neve* of Gahmuret (498,13) and is in fact a cousin twice removed of Parzival's grandfather, Gandin.[83] Whereas Parzival had earlier been told of the fact of kinship with his victim (475,21ff.), now he learns the details of their relationship and thus comes to know as much as had been made available to us when Ither was first introduced by the narrator. Parzival is now apprised of all the levels of this particular guilt (its uncourtly, unchivalric nature; his killing of a kinsman; its symbolic or religious dimension), whereas the listeners were aware of all these points in the

---

81. This order of ethical priorities is not disturbed by what Trevrizent has recently said of Lähelin's killing of Lybbeals (473,22ff.), where more weight seems to fall on the offence of *rêroup*. If this is so, it is because the Grail-horse which Parzival rides has suggested the possibility that this might be Lähelin because of *his* sin of *rêroup*. This is why, after asking his pointblank question (474,1), Trevrizent still cannot tear himself away from the subject of the Grail-horse (474,2ff.). See also Schirok, *ABÄG* 10 (1976), 58.
82. Something similar is expressed in Parzival's words to Gawan on the magnanimity shown by Feirefiz in dispensing with his sword in their combat (759,15: '*er vorhte et an mir sünde,/ê wir gerechenten ze künde*'), where the primary offence avoided is the act of killing, to which the fact of kinship would have been added as a heightening of the original sin. Cf. Green, *Homicide*, p. 18.
83. See the fn. to 475,21 in the Bartsch–Marti edition.

Parzival and Trevrizent (Book IX)

original encounter with Ither,[84] even if the last one has been explicitly stressed only by Trevrizent's words on Cain and Abel.

As in the case of Ither, Parzival's kinship with Trevrizent (the second theme in his cognitive progress) can only come to the surface at the point when Trevrizent realises who this knight is, but it comes close to the surface and is visible to the listeners, if not to the hermit, in his unconscious associations as he begins to wonder about his guest's identity. He has been struck by Parzival's similarity in appearance to Frimutel (474,21), which of course implies his blood-kinship with the Grail-dynasty at large and with Trevrizent in particular.

When Parzival says that he is Gahmuret's son (475,2f.) Trevrizent knows that he has his nephew before him and accordingly addresses him with *du* for the first time (475,20) as he clarifies their relationship for him as uncle and nephew on the maternal side, since Herzeloyde was his sister (475,19: *'lieber swester suon'*). Parzival therefore learns this kinship on his mother's side (with Trevrizent) just two lines before he learns a devastating kinship on his father's side (with Ither).[85] Losing his bearings as the blows fall on him (his kinship with the knight he killed and then his responsibility for the death of his mother), Parzival is quick to cling to this one positive point and acknowledge this relationship with his host (476,19: *'bin ich iwer swester kint'*). He quickly redefines himself in the light of this new knowledge precisely because it does seem to offer him a positive chance of some kind.[86] Trevrizent sees this himself and encourages it by conversely addressing Parzival frequently as his nephew.[87]

The possibility of a blood-relationship expressing itself in external appearances which lay behind the hermit's musings about his guest's identity and Frimutel also comes up briefly in his descrip-

---

84. In this encounter (discussed above, pp. 82f.) the offence against chivalric standards is made clear by the use of a *gabylôt* against a knight (155,9; 157,19 and especially 159,9ff.) and by the victor robbing the corpse of its accoutrements (only named for what it is in 475,5), whilst the killing of a kinsman was made clear, at least to the perceptive listener, at the start of the encounter (cf. 145,11ff.). No medieval listener could presumably fail to realise the religious offence of a knight killing a Christian opponent *umb krankez guot* (464,17), even if it is not pointed out to him in this scene in so many words.
85. 475,21: *'du hâst dîn eigen verch erslagn'*.
86. Parzival also clings to this relationship for support as he gropes towards his most difficult act of confession (488,4: *'lieber œheim mîn'*).
87. Cf. 477,28; 480,20; 486,22; 488,21; 492,23; 494,1; 497,21; 500,3 + 26.

tion of his early meeting with Gahmuret (497,21ff.). Gahmuret, encountering Trevrizent at Seville, knew by his similarity to his wife Herzeloyde that this must be his brother-in-law (497,24: *'balde er mîn ze bruoder jach / Herzeloyden sînem wîbe, / doch wart von sîme lîbe / mîn antlütze nie mêr gesehn'*), where the use of *antlütze* suggests that it is similarity of features which led Gahmuret to his correct assumption. Trevrizent then adds an explanatory rider for Parzival's benefit: he was himself supremely beautiful at that time (497,28ff., such beauty being the hallmark of the Grail-dynasty) and therefore resembled Herzeloyde, and therefore, as Gahmuret is quick to see, must be related to her. Such supreme beauty as a characteristic of his family is what led Trevrizent's earlier musings unconsciously in the direction of his guest's kinship with the Grail-dynasty.[88]

Parzival's kinship with Trevrizent, although a positive point to which he can cling, is also the occasion for further blows to fall on him, since through Trevrizent's own kinship with two other people Parzival now learns how he is himself tied in a web of complex relationships and how his past behaviour has brought suffering to close kindred. In other words, the tragedy of his kinship with Ither on his father's side is enhanced by his kinship on his mother's side. Just as Parzival earlier learned from Sigune of the network of feudal obligations tied around him, even without his knowledge,[89] so now does he learn of his unwitting offence against obligations to his kindred on the Grail side of his family.

The first such offence concerns his kinship with Anfortas, his realisation that in failing to bring help to him he was failing someone who is his own uncle. On the first occasion when Anfortas's name is mentioned by Trevrizent (472,21ff.) he is still unaware of Parzival's identity, but nonetheless the narrator suggests a telling conjunction of Parzival with Anfortas within the context of the Grail, since this passage on Anfortas follows immediately on the hermit's advice to his guest to guard himself against *hôchvart* (472,13ff.). This advice makes good sense when given to 'Lähelin', but its import changes radically if we take it as coming from the narrator, addressing us through the hermit. In this light such advice to one who we know is Parzival immediately precedes the passage in

---

88. Trevrizent is reminded of Frimutel by Parzival's external appearance (474,21: *'iwer varwe im treit gelîchiu mâl'*) and has had ample opportunity to appreciate his guest's beauty once he has laid aside his armour (459,13: *sô daz sîn vel gap liehten schîn*).
89. See above, p. 81.

Parzival and Trevrizent (Book IX)

which Trevrizent talks about Anfortas for the first time, describes his illicit love-affair and sees this essentially in terms of his *hôchvart* (472,26; 473,4). If we relate Trevrizent's advice not to Lähelin, but to Parzival, its implication is to preserve him from the danger of *hôchvart*, so that by avoiding Anfortas's offence he may prove a worthy successor.[90] By implying this the narrator provides another tacit consolation for the future to his listeners.[91]

The next mention of Anfortas shows us Trevrizent unconsciously near to grasping the connection between his guest and the Grail-king, since it occurs in the passage (474,1ff.) where the hermit muses aloud about his guest's identity. In listing the various Grail-kings he naturally includes Anfortas (474,7), but if Parzival reminds Trevrizent of Frimutel and may therefore be related to Frimutel, then he may consequently be related to Anfortas.

Once Trevrizent knows Parzival's identity he realises his Grail-kinship on his mother's side, knows that he is the nephew of Anfortas and reveals this to him after referring to his own sister Repanse de schoy (477,19: *'ir bruodr und mîn ist Anfortas'*). Parzival now knows that he is related to Anfortas, but this realisation reveals that his offence at Munsalvæsche was one against a close kinsman of his,[92] but also against the brother of his present host.[93] When Trevrizent says that Parzival, if he has any *triuwe*, must feel compassion with Anfortas (477,29: *'pfligstu denne triuwe, / so erbarmet dich sîn riuwe'*), this is especially true of one who has seen this suffering in the flesh at Munsalvæsche, as we (but not the hermit) know to be the case with Parzival. This realisation of an offence against a kinsman (Anfortas, but also Trevrizent) makes it even more difficult for Parzival to admit that he was the anonymous knight at Munsalvæsche – again, Trevrizent's advice runs into difficulties created by his ignorance of all the ramifications.

The other offence, the death of his mother and his responsibility for it, is brought home to Parzival at the same critical juncture, in Trevrizent's response to his admission of identity (476,12: *'mîn*

90. Parzival's *triuwe* to his wife (cf. 467,27ff.) and what we know of his *kiusche* from the beginning of their relationship (201,21ff.) are already sufficient for us to see that he is not threatened by this kind of *hôchvart* as was Anfortas. This realisation is quite independent of the later confirmation of the difference between Parzival and Anfortas in connection with Orgeluse (on this see above, p. 10).
91. See above, p. 192, fn. 62.
92. Cf. the use of *œheim* in 479,11 + 25; 491,30.
93. Cf. 478,5 (*'mîn bruoder Anfortas'*) and 478,17 (*'mîn hêrre und der bruoder mîn'*).

swester lac ouch nâch dir tôt, / Herzeloyd dîn muoter'). We have known of this death, thanks to the narrator, since the time when it occurred (128,20ff.) and Trevrizent, as Herzeloyde's brother, must have heard of it in the meantime. Parzival at last catches up in his knowledge of this first result of his decision to seek chivalry.

The hermit's mention of Herzeloyde's death is well motivated psychologically. In his admission Parzival has just made two points: as a knight, he states his descent on his father's side and therefore mentions Gahmuret (475,2: *'mîn vater der hiez Gahmuret, / er was von arde ein Anschevîn'*), but he also confesses that he killed Ither (475,5ff.). The hermit reacts to the first point by understandably seeing it from his own point of view – if Parzival is related to him it is through his sister, so that he sees Parzival instead as his mother's son (475,19: *'lieber swester suon'*). It is this which has brought Herzeloyde to the surface of Trevrizent's mind. But he reacts verbally first of all to Parzival's second point concerning Ither, because this is news to him and staggers him. Having been reminded of Herzeloyde and informed of one death caused by his nephew, Trevrizent naturally continues his remarks on Ither by telling Parzival of another death he has caused (476,12: *'mîn swester lac ouch nâch dir tôt, / Herzeloyd dîn muoter'*),[94] which he again sees at first from his own point of view, passing from *mîn swester* to *dîn muoter*.

Trevrizent then gives a brief account of how and when Herzeloyde died (476,25f.), adding a comment on Parzival's rôle as the dragon in her prophetic dream (476,27ff.), so that his departure for king Arthur represented the fulfilment of this prophecy. Later, in the context of information about the Grail and as a personal illustration, the hermit tells Parzival (and the listeners) about Herzeloyde's first marriage with Castis and the origin of the feudal lands which are now her son's (494,15ff.). The death of Herzeloyde is brought up again in the context of Ither's death, for these two deaths are Parzival's *zwuo grôze sünde* (499,20). When it is revealed that Titurel, the old man glimpsed by Parzival at Munsalvæsche (240,27), is Herzeloyde's grandfather (501,23: *'dîner muoter an'*) a further gap in Parzival's knowledge of the Grail-dynasty is filled in.

Unlike these acts of personal recognition, the impersonal recognition theme (Parzival learns about the Grail) extends before and

---

94. In 476,12 the word *ouch* suggests the continuity in Trevrizent's thoughts between Ither and Herzeloyde.

Parzival and Trevrizent (Book IX)

after the turning-point of Parzival's admission of his identity and informs the whole of his encounter with Trevrizent. The information provided by the hermit on this subject takes further what had previously been released in instalments when Parzival first came to Munsalvæsche itself, then in his second (and third) encounter with Sigune, and finally in Cundrie's accusation of him before the Round Table.[95] Trevrizent's information in Book IX agrees with that provided by Sigune and Cundrie in that it is conveyed to Parzival and the listeners equally, whilst at Munsalvæsche a distinction had to be made between Parzival's point of view and what the listeners were sometimes given as superior knowledge by the narrator.[96] Furthermore, in Book IX the information given by Trevrizent before the recognition-scene when Parzival admits his identity is not given to Parzival as such, but to one whom the hermit takes to be Lähelin.[97] The themes covered by Trevrizent's information about the Grail are as follows:[98]

(1)	468,12–14	The Grail is attainable only to those called
(2)	468,23–469,1	*Templeisen* defend Munsalvæsche as a penance for sins
(3)	469,2–28	The Grail-stone provides sustenance and keeps alive
(4)	469,29–470,20	The Good Friday dove, miraculous food provided by the Grail
(5)	470,21–471,14	The call to the Grail, the miraculous inscription
(6)	471,15–29	Neutral angels as the original guardians of the Grail
(7)	472,21–473,4	Anfortas and his *hôchvart*
(8)	473,5–30	*Templeisen* defend Munsalvæsche, the two exceptions (Parzival, Lähelin)
(9)	474,2–22	Grail-horses, the Grail-dynasty
(10)	477,13–18	Repanse de schoy and the Grail
(11)	477,19–479,30	Anfortas, his kinship, love-affair and wounding

95. The material is to be found in the following passages: at Munsalvæsche (227,7ff.), in the second encounter with Sigune (250,3ff.; 250,25ff.; 251,2ff. + 30; 254,20ff.; 255,5ff.), in the course of Cundrie's accusation (315,26ff.) and in the third encounter with Sigune (441,20ff.).
96. See above, pp. 91ff.
97. Dewald, *Minne*, p. 270, makes the valid point that the listeners learn by stages about the Grail and Parzival's destiny, just as he himself only gradually recognises the nature of his task. Dewald goes too far, however, in claiming that the listeners' perspective is the same as Parzival's in this respect, for the narrator gives them the potential means of arriving at the truth somewhat earlier than Parzival. Audience and hero are engaged on the same journey of recognition, but at different rates.
98. The dividing line between themes (9) and (10) is drawn at the point of Parzival's admission that he is the son of Gahmuret.

(12)	480,25–481,4	The Grail keeps Anfortas alive
(13)	481,5–483,18	Vain attempts to heal Anfortas
(14)	483,19–484,30	The conditions of the question
(15)	489,22–490,30	Disparate phenomena (spear, wound, snow, knives)
(16)	491,1–18	Anfortas as fisher king
(17)	492,1–10	*Templeisen* defend Munsalvæsche
(18)	492,23–493,14	Disparate phenomena (Saturn, wound, snow)
(19)	493,19–494,14	Recruitment of the guardians of the Grail
(20)	495,1–12	The guardians of the Grail and chastity
(21)	500,23–501,4	The mantle and the sword
(22)	501,19–502,3	Titurel

We can best assess the technique used in this Book by considering how this information is released, and then how it relates to information given earlier.

Considerable emphasis is placed on the inaccessibility of Munsalvæsche: in theme (1) as a simple statement of fact, in (2) and (8) as a concrete illustration in terms of the danger to those who try to penetrate there, and in (5) as a miraculous inscription, the condition of being called to the Grail. All this forms part of Trevrizent's *ableitens list* (798,6),[99] his argument that the quest for the Grail by someone not called is futile. All these examples come before the recognition-scene[100] and are therefore addressed by the hermit with an eye to convincing the knight whom he takes to be Lähelin. By contrast, Trevrizent only once alludes to the same theme after the recognition-scene (in (17) he repeats that Munsalvæsche is defended by *templeisen*), but the force of this is blunted for someone whom Trevrizent now knows to be Parzival by the fact that (dangerous or not, cf. 492,1) Parzival did accomplish this journey, as the hermit now knows and as Parzival emphasises again (492,11ff.).

This point ties up with the earlier reference to *templeisen* defending Munsalvæsche (theme 8), where Trevrizent signals the exceptions who got through (Parzival and Lähelin), for there are essential differences between these two. As far as we are told, Lähelin only got through to the outer precincts of Terre de Salvæsche where his combat with Lybbeals took place, whereas Parzival penetrated to the heart of the castle and saw the Grail-procession. Lähelin was involved in combat on his journey, whereas Parzival was miracul-

---

99. On this see below, pp. 257ff.
100. Cf. Hirschberg, *Untersuchungen*, p. 337: 'Es gibt zwar die Aussage, die Parzivals Gralsuche als sinnlos hinstellt (468,10ff.), doch erfolgt sie am Anfang des Gesprächs, als die Identität des Gastes noch nicht feststeht'.

Parzival and Trevrizent (Book IX)

ously steered past it (492,11ff.). Whereas Parzival, when later engaged in combat, avoided killing his Grail opponent (445,8ff.),[101] Lähelin killed the Grail-knight Lybbeals in his encounter.

The mysterious inaccessibility of Munsalvæsche also contributes to its religious atmosphere which is stressed in many other respects. This dimension is brought out by the phrase *ze himel* (468,13; 471,12), the reference to *wunsch von pardîse* (470,14), the conception of the *templeisen* as a quasi-religious community (473,5: *werdiu bruoderschaft* and 470,19: *rîterlîchen bruoderschaft*)[102] acting for religious reasons (468,30: *für ir sünde*) and bearing the heraldic emblem of the dove (474,5), the token of the Holy Ghost also present in the image of the Good Friday dove. Other religious references include the neutral angels as the original guardians of the Grail and the urgent need for the Grail-king to avoid *hôchvart*, the spiritual sin *par excellence*. Such a markedly spiritual atmosphere at Munsalvæsche makes it, in Trevrizent's eyes, more than ever unlikely that a knight like Lähelin, consciously and intentionally robbing and killing, will ever be able to force his way into membership of the Grail.

Here again, the nature of such religious allusions changes once we apply them, not to Lähelin, but to Parzival who was after all once miraculously guided to Munsalvæsche. Parzival may come close to the danger of *hôchvart*, illustrated in the case of Anfortas in theme (7), only once, at the moment of his deepest disgrace before Cundrie, but for the rest he avoids the temptation to which even Anfortas succumbed.[103] Accordingly, such allusions coming *after* the recognition-scene mean something very different in the case of Parzival than with others. Themes (10) and (20) both stress the need for *kiusche* in the context of the Grail and for marital loyalty in the case of the Grail-king, and we know that this is eminently true of Parzival from his *trinoctium castitatis* on marriage to Condwiramurs

---

101. Cf. also 445,28ff.
102. These two examples from Book IX, both used by Trevrizent, are the only ones in the whole work. Cf. Kolb, *Munsalvæsche*, p. 105.
103. Although Parzival's rejection of Orgeluse's offer (618,19ff.) guards him against the danger to which Anfortas succumbed, nonetheless his order of priorities at the start of his quest, as Gawan recalls them (370,18: *nu dâhter des, wie Parzivâl / wîben baz getrûwt dan gote*), exposes him to this danger in another way. This is revealed retrospectively, however, as Parzival's flash-in-the-pan reaction to Cundrie's accusation, since otherwise he regularly places his quest for the Grail before his longing for Condwiramurs (cf. Dewald, *Minne*, pp. 141ff.), which shows up the tragic irony of Trevrizent advising 'Lähelin' to reverse what is for Parzival precisely the saving order of priorities (468,1ff.).

and from the constancy of his thinking about her. Theme (11) makes a similar point by contrasting the relationship between Anfortas and Orgeluse with that between Parzival and Condwiramurs, even though the narrator, speaking through Trevrizent, makes an allusion which the listeners can grasp only later (478,20).[104] There is thus little danger of Anfortas's sin, the occasion of the whole Grail story, being repeated by Parzival.

The conditions of the question, discussed in (14), only apparently tell against Parzival. The first point made by Trevrizent is that the questioner must not be consciously 'warned' about the question (483,24), presumably either the need for it or its actual formulation. But Parzival has already been adequately informed of the vital necessity of the question by those who criticise him for his omission,[105] obviously thinking that he will never be given a second chance. Trevrizent, too, 'warns' him about the form of the question (484,27), this time because he does not even suspect that Parzival was at Munsalvæsche and failed to ask the question. The hermit makes a second point, however, saying that the question must be put on the first night of the questioner's visit at Munsalvæsche (484,1: *'Frâgt er niht bî der êrsten naht, / sô zergêt sîner frâge maht'*), but this negative formulation is then complemented by its positive counterpart (484,3: *'wirt sîn frâge an rehter zît getân, / sô sol erz künecrîche hân'*), where there is an obvious correspondence between *bî der êrsten naht* and *an rehter zît*. This is undoubtedly correct, as we recall from the desolate scene at Munsalvæsche when Parzival awakes on the morning after his failure, but strictly speaking it tells us nothing about the future,[106] about Parzival possibly coming to Munsalvæsche a second time and correctly asking the question then on the first night.[107] Only if we read *an rehter zît* as

104. See above, p. 10.
105. This is already made clear at the moment when Parzival leaves Munsalvæsche and the drawbridge is pulled up behind him (247,26ff.), then soon afterwards by Sigune (254,28ff.; 255,17ff.), but then by Cundrie (316,21ff.) and once more by Sigune at their third meeting (441,25ff.).
106. 247,1ff.
107. This is made emphatically clear when Parzival comes to Munsalvæsche for the second time. He arrives in 794,1ff., is conducted immediately into the castle hall, is greeted by Anfortas and by 795,21ff. begins to ask the question. My interpretation of *an rehter zît* places the emphasis differently, but is certainly reconcilable with the suggestion made by Wapnewski, *Parzival*, p. 102: 'Der Erlöser muß ein ganz bestimmtes Stadium erreicht haben, er vermag nicht vorzeitig zu fragen, zu erlösen, zu herrschen. Die *rehtiu zît* meint nicht den Gral, sie meint den Frager, dessen zeitliche Entwicklung. Er kann erst fragen, wenn er "so weit ist".' Cf. also Weigand, *Parzival*, p. 15.

Parzival and Trevrizent (Book IX)

meaning the occasion of a first (and unique) visit, not the correct time on this or any subsequent visit,[108] do Trevrizent's words mean that Parzival will never be given another chance. As it is, the ambiguity of this formulation is linked with Trevrizent unwittingly telling Parzival the correct terms of the question, thereby equipping him for a second visit, this time successful.[109] Once again, the narrator is able to console the listeners through the words of Trevrizent.

Further light can be shed on Parzival's path to recognition of the Grail if we compare the information released by Trevrizent in Book IX with what has been divulged about the Grail on earlier occasions, the most important of which is Parzival's actual visit to Munsalvæsche in Book V. We saw that the description of the earlier episode proceeded from Parzival's point of view, dwelling on the visual impression he received and listing a whole range of objects, in all about two dozen, seen by him in the castle.[110] These are what his gaze fastens upon, but not necessarily what is really important, as is brought out by the extreme reduction in the number of objects which Trevrizent feels it necessary to mention:[111] the Grail-stone (469,3), the spear (489,22), two knives (490,21) and the sword (501,1). In addition, replying to a question by his guest, he also talks about the mantle (500,25ff.). Instead of all the pomp and splendour that caught Parzival's attention, Trevrizent concentrates on essentials: the Grail-stone as the centrepiece of the ritual, the spear and knives because of their function in the attempts to heal Anfortas's wound, the sword and mantle as insignia of Parzival's potential rôle as successor to Anfortas.

Even apart from this concentration on essentials Parzival also learns new, vital facts about these objects. He learns of the miraculous property of the Grail-stone of providing food and sustaining

---

108. These lines were written before the publication of Tax, *Kingdom*, where on p. 33, quite independently, the same point is made.
109. Wapnewski, *Parzival*, p. 102, introduces his remark quoted in the last but one footnote with the observation that verse 484,3 can only be read correctly if we deprive it of any function as a magical formula. How little depends on the literal wording of the question (which is what would be called for if it were no more than a magical formula) has been well brought out by Johnson, *Beauty*, pp. 288f., in his comparison of the formulation of the question revealed by Trevrizent (484,27) with the actual wording later employed by Parzival (795,29).
110. See above, pp. 106ff.
111. This technique of showing Parzival so much that it is difficult for him to recognise and concentrate on what is really vital is a large-scale example of what we saw illustrated on the small scale in Parzival's second encounter with Jeschute (see above, p. 119).

life (470,11ff.; 469,2ff.), whereas in Book V the listeners had been told of the first property (238,4ff.),[112] but not of the second, whilst both these details remained concealed from Parzival at the time. The spear had earlier been seen by Parzival in the hall of Munsalvæsche, accompanied by obvious signs of grief, but in Book IX we are taken behind these appearances and shown the reason for this (489,24ff.). The same is true of the knives, for earlier they were simply seen and mentioned, but are now expressly related to the wish to remove the frost from the spear (490,11ff.) as part of the attempt to relieve Anfortas's suffering (neither Parzival nor the listeners had been shown anything of this earlier). The sword is now revealed to Parzival as a tacit stimulus to asking the question (501,1ff.), whereas earlier only the listeners had been told this by the narrator.[113] Finally, the mantle is now seen explicitly in the context of royal accession (500,28ff.), whereas Parzival was told nothing of this earlier and only the percipient listener would have grasped this implication.[114] Behind all these objects, thanks to Trevrizent, Parzival can now see the miraculous rite of the Grail-community, the central importance of Anfortas's wound and suffering, the need to ask the question, and the hint of royal succession. What the hermit tells him leads to the heart of the matter at Munsalvæsche.[115]

112. See above, p. 112.
113. 240,3ff.; 242,16ff. (see above, p. 112).
114. Cf. Schröder, *ZfdA* 100 (1971), 127: 'Der Mantel, den Repanse de schoye abgelegt hatte, als die Weissagung sich mit dem Erscheinen Parzivals zu erfüllen schien, und das diesem von Anfortas abgetretene Schwert werden von dem Eremiten, der sie in einem Atem nennt, als Herrschaftszeichen verstanden. Parzivals Ausstattung mit ihnen erweist sich somit als die vertrauensvoll vorsorgliche Investitur eines designierten Thronfolgers.' On the handing over of the sword of Anfortas to Parzival Mersmann, *Besitzwechsel*, p. 136, writes: 'Der Vorgang ähnelt also einer Abdankung, während Parzivals Beschenkung Züge einer Designation trägt!' Mersmann, *ibid*, pp. 127ff., has further underlined the apparent innocuousness of the gift of the mantle (as experienced by Parzival (cf. the fn. to 228,17 in the Bartsch–Marti edition) and expected by the narrator's listeners) by pointing to the conventional literary motif of a knightly guest being clad by his host after he has laid aside his armour and washed himself. Earlier examples in this work concerning the hero himself include Parzival's stay with Gurnemanz (168,1ff.) and his arrival at Pelrapeire (185,30ff.). What is at first presented in conventional terms is later shown by Trevrizent to possess important implications.
115. Other details of Parzival's visit in Book V are likewise only explained to him by the hermit. Whilst at Munsalvæsche Parzival knows nothing of the fact that it can be reached only by those who are called there, and even the listeners learn something explicit about providential guidance only after he leaves the castle (249,4ff.; cf. Green, *Weg*, pp. 14ff.). Parzival learns the name of Repanse de

Parzival and Trevrizent (Book IX)

In the case of two of these objects we can go a step further, for the spear and knives are not merely connected as part of the same healing process, they also tie up with other details and show that what Parzival (and we) regarded as disparate chance phenomena were in fact miraculously brought into harmony with one another and meant by God's grace to give Parzival a tacit prompting to ask the question,[116] so that once more we are taken behind appearances and shown their causal relationship and meaning. With theme (15), therefore, a connection is established between the spear, Anfortas's wound, the snow in summer, and the knives, and all this is placed under the astronomical auspices of Saturn, whilst in theme (18) the spear, the wound, and the snow are again linked together under the auspices of Saturn. This not merely shows us retrospectively that the snowfall scene in Book VI was connected with the events at Munsalvæsche in Book V,[117] it also places the earlier narrative in a wider metaphysical setting, indicating that apparently unconnected phenomena are in fact divinely geared to one another for Parzival's benefit, to entice him to ask the question.[118] Parzival is now shown the working of God's grace in these details, where he had not seen it before, and we realise with him that it was God who made him an offer at Munsalvæsche and he who was blind to it, so that there can be no talk of God's *untriuwe*.

A concentration on essentials is shown in one other respect in Book IX. The description of the Grail-castle in Book V had laid great stress on courtly ceremonial and *zuht*,[119] because it was shown from Parzival's point of view and this is clearly what im-

---

schoy at Munsalvæsche (228,14), only the listeners are told of the need for *kiusche* in her office (235,25ff.), whilst the question of her kinship with Parzival is brought up only by Trevrizent (477,13ff.). The same is true with Titurel. Parzival and the listeners catch sight of him at Munsalvæsche (240,24ff.) and although Sigune mentions his name soon afterwards (251,5), there is no indication that this is the name of this particular person, who is identified for Parzival by the hermit only in 501,22f.

116. Cf. Deinert, *Ritter*, pp. 12ff.
117. Cf. Dewald, *Minne*, pp. 208f.
118. Deinert, *Ritter*, p. 14: 'Für Parzivals Probe sind also die Umstände günstig wie an keinem anderen Tag; die blutende Lanze nämlich, die Wehklage der Bewohner und das Übermaß der Schmerzen des Anfortas müssen ihn weit stärker zur Frage drängen, als wenn er an einem gewöhnlichen Krankheitstag gekommen wäre', and p. 35: 'Zwischen entferntesten Dingen, die ihm begegnet sind – der blutigen Lanze und den Blutstropfen im Schnee –, gibt es eine Verknüpfung, durch die sein ganzes Leben mit der übrigen Welt verflochten und einer höheren Lenkung unterworfen zu sein scheint.'
119. See above, p. 107.

pressed him most. The inadequacy of this point of view is revealed implicitly in Book IX by the fact that *zuht* is now used only once (493,18) to describe Munsalvæsche, and this by Parzival himself as he recalls what he had earlier seen there. By contrast, Trevrizent himself ignores this aspect, not because Munsalvæsche does not display *zuht*,[120] but because this aspect is not important for the problem facing Parzival and his spiritual counsellor.

This sustained discrepancy in information between Books V and IX makes it clear that essential details about the Grail are released only in instalments. While he was actually at Munsalvæsche Parzival saw much, but could not tell what was really important, whilst in a number of cases the listeners were told more than was apparent to him. In this respect the narrative function of Book IX is not merely to tell the listeners more, and Parzival much more (so that he eventually catches up with them), but also to transpose the understanding of past events onto the metaphysical level,[121] explaining them as controlled by divine providence for the sole benefit of Parzival, revealing the operation of grace even though he was earlier quite unaware of this and even, after his accusation by Cundrie, expressly denied it.

Although Parzival's enlightenment about the Grail (as distinct from his own impressions at Munsalvæsche) begins long before he encounters Trevrizent, the narrator's technique of gradual instalments ensures that he still has vital facts to learn only from his hermit uncle, as can be seen if we compare the nature of the information he receives from Sigune (on two occasions, in Book V immediately after his departure from the castle and then in Book IX before he comes to Trevrizent) and from Cundrie (during the course of her tirade against him in Book VI) with what he learns from Trevrizent.

In his encounter with Sigune after his departure from Munsalvæsche[122] Parzival, together with the listeners, is given a provisional, but still incomplete view of what has just happened. He

120. See below, p. 256, fn. 89.
121. On the transition to a metaphysical level between Books V and IX see also Velten, *Plan*, pp. 29f., 39f. and 43f., as part of a general thesis, however, which I find unacceptable (see above, p. 12, fn. 46).
122. 249,11ff. In following through the process of recognition in the two Sigune scenes (see above, pp. 113ff. and 180ff.) I have restricted myself to the theme of personal recognition. The more impersonal process of Parzival coming to a recognition of the nature of the Grail-realm is best dealt with in the present context, since it is so obviously focused on Trevrizent as the highlight.

Parzival and Trevrizent (Book IX)

learns first of all that Munsalvæsche is defended against strangers by knights who give no quarter (250,3ff.), but nothing of what is later stressed by the hermit: that these *templeisen*[123] do this as a penance for sin (468,30; 492,10), that they constitute a quasi-monastic *bruoderschaft*, and that the military obstacle they represent is one aspect of the truth that only someone divinely called may reach Munsalvæsche (473,5ff.). This metaphysical dimension is not denied by Sigune, but simply not mentioned by her. She also tells her kinsman that the Grail-castle is *erden wunsches rîche* (250,25), which may well be true, but still leaves out of account the metaphysical dimension referred to by Trevrizent (470,14: *als den wunsch von pardîse*).[124] Sigune's following point that the Grail can only be attained *unwizzende* (250,26ff.) is later complemented by Trevrizent's observation that the Grail is only attainable to those who are called there. There is no necessary contradiction between these two aspects, but again it is the expressly metaphysical dimension which is supplied by the hermit. Shortly after this Sigune names the castle Munsalvæsche and the realm Terre de Salvæsche (251,1ff.), details new both to Parzival and the listeners, but also something of the genealogy of various members of the Grail-dynasty, although, as we shall see, vital information is still withheld which is to be supplied only in Book IX.[125] The climax of Sigune's eulogy of one who she optimistically thinks cannot have failed to ask the question (254,20ff.) brings more information: the importance of the question (254,30)[126] and the fact that it would have brought Parzival a position of authority (254,21f.), the gift of *sælden krône* (254,24) and of earthly perfection (254,26: *den wunsch ûf der erden*).

123. This revealing term (on it see Kolb, *Munsalvæsche*, pp. 64ff.) occurs for the first time in Book IX, first in narrative action (444,23) and then used by Trevrizent (468,28).
124. In the Munsalvæsche scene itself the narrator had told the listeners that the Grail is *erden wunsches überwal* (235,24), thus making use of the same dimension as Sigune shortly afterwards, but the narrator also opens up the metaphysical dimension in the same context when he says of Repanse de schoy (235,21: 'truoc si den wunsch von pardîs'). Cf. also 238,21ff. From the beginning, therefore, the listeners are acquainted with both the dimensions of which Parzival learns only subsequently and separately, first from Sigune and then from Trevrizent. It is also of a piece with what is revealed only by Trevrizent that the knowledge of the Grail conveyed to the pagan queen Secundille should see it in terms of secular perfection (519,10f.).
125. See below, pp. 216f.
126. The listeners were made aware of its importance by the narrator when Parzival failed to speak (240,3ff.), but so far Parzival has only heard the incomprehensible insult as he left Munsalvæsche (247,26ff.).

The parallel between this last phrase and *erden wunsches rîche* suggests that her explanation still remains on the non-metaphysical level,[127] and although she refers to Parzival's potential authority, only Trevrizent later makes this clear, providing the background and the reason for the possibility of his succeeding Anfortas.[128] In what she passionately says after Parzival's confession that he did not ask the question (255,5ff.) Signe concentrates on much the same central points that are singled out for explanation in Book IX (spear, knives, Anfortas's suffering and the need for showing compassion by asking the question),[129] but again it is Trevrizent who relates these unconnected points to one another. Although Signe takes Parzival's enlightenment about the opportunity he has just squandered an important step forward, the process still has to be continued on vital points by Trevrizent.

From the detailed way in which Cundrie substantiates her criticism of him (315,26ff.) Parzival again learns more about Munsalvæsche and his failure there. He is told that he could have freed Anfortas from his suffering (315,30), is reminded of the necessity for compassion (316,3)[130] and of the (negative) metaphysical consequences of his behaviour (316,7ff.). Although this opens up the metaphysical dimension absent from Signe's information in Book V, it remains for Trevrizent to give a fuller description of the religious implications of the Grail-realm. Like Trevrizent, Cundrie also narrows down for Parzival the range of what was significant at Munsalvæsche by restricting her comments essentially to the sword (316,21), which she sees in conjunction with the necessity to speak (316,23), the Grail (316,26), the spear and knives (316,27). Here too, however, these points remain unconnected, until they are correlated, for Parzival as for the listeners, by Trevrizent.[131]

127. Signe's use of *sælde* in 254,24 is not expressly metaphysical, as can be seen by its contrast with Cundrie's usage in 316,11 (*'ir heiles pan, ir sælden fluoch'*), which follows on a remark in which the transcendental background is made quite apparent (316,7: *'gein der helle ir sît benant / ze himele vor der hôhsten hant: / als sît ir ûf der erden, / versinnent sich die werden'*).
128. See below, pp. 221f.
129. She also mentions by name (255,9f.) Garschiloye and Repanse de schoy, the latter known to Parzival by name since 228,14.
130. This links up with Signe's accusation in 255,17.
131. Parzival also learns other vital facts from Cundrie which are not connected with the Grail-kingdom: the name and distinctive appearance of his halfbrother Feirefiz (317,4 + 9), as well as the name and something of the character of his father (317,11ff.). The bridge between this information and that dealing with the Grail is provided by the mention of Herzeloyde (318,3), whose name had not been divulged to Parzival by Signe in either of their preceding meetings.

Parzival and Trevrizent (Book IX)

The time-gap between Parzival's previous enlightenment about the Grail and what he learns from Trevrizent is shortest in the case of his third encounter with Sigune, placed near the start of Book IX. After what she said on the last occasion she can afford to be brief, but to bridge the remaining gap between what she says and Trevrizent's further revelations soon afterwards the narrator falls back on a technique of deliberate ambiguity in her words. Whereas at their last meeting Sigune had described the Grail as *erden wunsches rîche* (250,25) and *den wunsch ûf der erden* (254,26), now she refers to what Parzival has forfeited by his omission simply as *wunsch* (441,25: '*dâ hete dir vrâgen wunsch bejagt*'), which serves as a transition to Trevrizent's more explicit reference to *den wunsch von pardîse* (470,14). If this metaphysical dimension was not meant to be denied by her earlier remarks, the omission of the epithet 'earthly' more obviously prepares the way for Trevrizent's truth. Sigune's references to what Parzival has lost are also strictly neutral at the start of Book IX (441,20: *freude*; 441,24: *gelücke*), as is her description of his failure (441,28: *sorge*). We learn in retrospect that such terms are meant to embrace both success in this world and salvation in the next, but this is made clear only by the explicitly metaphysical dimension emphasised by Anfortas, for whom the neutral *sorge* is replaced by the religious concept of sin (473,14 + 18). Whereas Sigune remains content with emphasising again the importance of the question (441,25 + 30), it is from Trevrizent that we learn the full context of the question, an explanation of what was to follow from it (483,20ff.) and of the conditions for asking it (483,24ff.).

By following through these instalments in which information about the Grail is gradually released at different rates to Parzival and the listeners we have been able to see the implications of this carefully controlled narrative technique. Parzival acquires his insight gradually: he experiences the world of the Grail with a disastrous lack of comprehension at Munsalvæsche itself, then learns progressively more about it from his two meetings with Sigune, from Cundrie and finally from Trevrizent. Parallel with this the listeners learn a number of details at the same time as Parzival, so that the hero's protracted movement from *tumpheit* to *wîsheit* is made part of their experience, too. Finally, cutting across this parallelism, it is often the case that the listeners learn important facts about the Grail from the narrator and therefore sometimes in advance of Parzival, which enables them to realise his relative *tumpheit* and where he stands on his path to ultimate enlightenment.

Yet it is not simply the case that throughout the course of the narrative and then especially within Book IX Parzival and the listeners learn progressively more about the Grail, for we also have to ask why all this information should be conveyed to Parzival in particular, why it is, as we learn at the latest by this Book, that he has been the beneficiary of providential guidance in first coming to Munsalvæsche and even subsequently,[132] in short, what it is that qualifies him to be *des mæres hêrre* at all. In other words, this information about the Grail is not conveyed to just anyone, but is rather imparted to someone who stands in a very particular relationship to the Grail-dynasty, the nature of which becomes gradually clearer only as the work progresses. Here again, we have to distinguish between what information may be conveyed to us alone by the narrator and what is also imparted to Parzival himself. In this respect, too, we shall find that the narrator works in instalments, releasing his facts only gradually, first to his listeners (and even then only to the most percipient among them who have been trained to have an eye for detail and to correlate the seemingly unconnected), then ultimately to Parzival.

In a work which sets such store by *art* and genealogical kinship[133] it is not surprising that the hero's relationship to the Grail-dynasty should be expressed in terms of blood-relationship, of his being born into membership of that family as the son of Herzeloyde. If we now follow through this aspect of the hero and its implications for Book IX, we must start with a negative fact, but one of decisive importance in Wolfram's narrative technique, for neither the hero nor the listeners are given any hint of Parzival's maternal descent at the point where we might expect it, during the course of the childhood which he spends with his mother.[134] By the time we come to Book III we know enough about Parzival's descent on his father's side, but of his mother we know only that she had been queen of Kanvoleis, and when Herezeloyde withdraws into the wilderness after the death of her husband she is keeping her son away from

---

132. On the necessity to distinguish between the periods before and after Munsalvæsche, but also to see the operation of providential guidance in both, even if working in different ways, see Green, *Weg*, pp. 11ff.
133. On this see Schwietering, *ZfdA* 91 (1961/62), 108ff. and Schultheiss, *Bedeutung*, *passim*.
134. Harroff, *Wolfram*, p. 62.

Parzival and Trevrizent (Book IX)

Gahmuret's knightly world, but also away from what is, for a male member, the equally knightly world of the Grail. After her son has encountered the knights in the wood his thoughts are concentrated on gaining access to the knightly, Arthurian world (126,11ff.) to which his father had also belonged,[135] so that it is fully apt that when Herzeloyde follows her general advice to her son with some concrete information about the world which he is about to enter (128,3ff.) this information should concern the knightly world of his father and the feudal obligations he has inherited from him.[136] By contrast, she makes no mention at all of his maternal inheritance, so that at this stage neither hero nor listeners can have any knowledge of the Grail-world, let alone Parzival's relationship to it.[137]

The first indication of such a relationship is provided by the narrator for his listeners, and thus bypasses the hero, at the point when after Cundrie's accusation Parzival sets out on his quest for the Grail (333,27: *schildes ambet umben grâl | wirt nu vil güebet sunder twâl | von im den Herzeloyde bar. | er was ouch ganerbe dar*).[138] This is the first time that we learn of any relationship between Parzival and the Grail, but even so the passage invites more questions from the perceptive listeners than it answers. From it we learn strictly only that it is Parzival's inherited right to come to Munsalvæsche, which may involve only membership of the Grail-community, not necessarily kingship.[139] Nor do we know whether any particular importance attaches to Parzival's position as heir, for it is pointed out to us that he is only one of several (*ganerbe*, instead of *anerbe*,

---

135. On Gahmuret's links with the Arthurian world, factually and symbolically, see Green, *Homicide*, pp. 27f.
136. The mother's information includes a reference to her two lands of Waleis and Norgals (128,7) which fell to Gahmuret on his marriage to Herzeloyde. This does not mean that they are in any way connected (through Herzeloyde) with the Grail-kingdom, for they had come to her on the death of her first husband, Castis (494,22ff.). Furthermore, since these feudal lands passed to Gahmuret by marriage, they now form part of the father's inheritance to his son when, in his turn, Gahmuret dies. Herzeloyde's information to Parzival thus remains confined to the world of his father.
137. I have argued in *Departure*, pp. 399ff., along very different lines, that the narrative of Books III and IV is concerned with Parzival finding his way into the feudal, knightly world of his father and that it is only from Book V, and quite unexpectedly, that events take him into the Grail-world from which his mother comes.
138. See also above, p. 92.
139. The distinction involved here, where the listener may be tempted to see more than is necessarily present, is similar to the distinction at issue in 483,21f. (see above, p. 193).

reinforced by *ouch*),[140] so that even if the particular privilege of kingship is involved there is still no certainty that it must fall to Parzival and we are given no indication of who these possible rivals might be. Similarly, we are not told whether Parzival's line of inheritance to the Grail runs through his father or his mother. It is true that we have been given information about his paternal line of descent, but even so the vital fact about the Grail could just as easily have been excluded from this information about Gahmuret as later turns out to have been the case with Herzeloyde. Even the significant fact that Parzival is described as *ganerbe dar* in the same context as he is called the son of Herzeloyde (rather than of Gahmuret)[141] acquires its significance only retrospectively, for it is only in 455,19f. that we learn that Herzeloyde is related to Anfortas and therefore a member of the Grail-family. This narratorial comment thus gives us our first hint, but still leaves much unsaid.

This prolongation of our uncertainty has been made possible, as Harroff has shown,[142] by the withholding of information by Signune in her second meeting with Parzival in the very act of communicating other facts to him. In 251,1ff. she provides information for the first time about the names Munsalvæsche and Terre de Salvæsche, adding to this a short genealogy of the Grail-dynasty (Titurel, Frimutel, Anfortas),[143] all of which provides an immediate, but only factual and superficial answer to the questions deferred by the 'Bogengleichnis' (241,1ff.). In the course of providing this information, new to the listeners as well as Parzival, Signune says that Frimutel met his end in a joust and left behind four children (251,11: *'der selbe liez vier werdiu kint'*), which is factually correct, but which we cannot yet realise is not the whole truth, since it is only made clear in what Trevrizent later says[144] that Frimutel in fact

---

140. According to the *Deutsches Rechtswörterbuch* (III, col. 1150f.) *ganerbe* means 'Miterbe (zur gesamten Hand)' (cf. *ganerbet*, col. 1151, meaning 'zu gemeinsamen Erben gemacht'). By contrast (*ibid.*, I, col. 615) *anerbe*, which could have been used if it had met Wolfram's purposes, means 'Erbanwärter' (cf. *anerben* = 'als Erbe jem. zufallen, vererbt werden'). Cf. also Becker, *Recht*, p. 47.
141. On the aesthetic significance of these two types of circumlocution for the hero see Green, *Namedropping*, pp. 133ff. What I have said there takes no account of the sequence and rate at which information is released in instalments by the narrator, which is my present concern.
142. Harroff, *Wolfram*, pp. 63f.
143. She also mentions the name of Trevrizent (251,15), as a member of the Grail-dynasty who is not destined to the office of kingship.
144. 476,12ff. See also below, pp. 220f.

Parzival and Trevrizent (Book IX)

had five children, one of whom died before him. What Sigune does *not* say, however, is even more important, for this fifth child of Frimutel was Schoysiane, her own mother. Had she mentioned this fact she would have therefore revealed her own membership of the Grail-family, which would have been tantamount to Parzival's membership of this family, since she has already revealed that Parzival is related to her by his mother.[145] That this vital information is for the moment being consciously withheld is suggested by another detail on which she keeps silent in this same passage. Of the four children of Frimutel to whom she refers Sigune says (251,12f.): '*bî rîchheit driu in jâmer sint: / der vierde hât armuot*', and then names this fourth one as the hermit Trevrizent (251,15), adding that his brother is the wounded Grail-king, Anfortas (251,16ff.). Two of these four children are therefore unnamed by Sigune in this passage (in addition to the fifth one, Schoysiane), and we learn who they are from Trevrizent in Book IX:[146] Repanse de schoy and Herzeloyde.[147] If Herzeloyde's name had been mentioned Parzival would have known immediately that through her he had been born into the Grail-family, even more directly and strikingly than if the name of Sigune's mother had been voiced.[148] Both directly and indirectly, therefore, the fact of his membership of the Grail-family is withheld from Parzival at this stage by Sigune (and from us by the narrator). Although we saw that this second encounter between Parzival and Sigune was informed by a complex pattern of mutual recognition,[149] we can now place this pattern within a wider context and register its limits on one side: although Parzival comes to recognise her and we are once more reminded of their kinship, this relationship is still established without reference to the most important fact of all, which he and we have still to

---

145. In their first two meetings: 140,22 and 252,15.
146. 477,13ff. and 476,12f. (cf. already 475,19).
147. When Sigune says in 251,12 that *bî rîcheit driu in jâmer sint* she expressly mentions Anfortas and clearly refers to what he suffers from his wound. By the other two (feminine, thus justifying the use of the neuter *driu*) she means Repanse de schoy (suffering with Anfortas, like all those at Munsalvæsche) and Herzeloyde (suffering at Soltane after the death of her husband). Her use of the present tense (*sint*) to cover all three cases, however, implies that she has as yet heard nothing of Herzeloyde's death.
148. The same point would have been made, but less strikingly, if the name of Repanse de schoy had been pronounced, for Parzival would have learned that the person who had equipped him with a mantle at Munsalvæsche was his own aunt.
149. See above, pp. 113ff.

recognise, that he has been born into the Grail-family as the son of Herzeloyde.

The next indication, like the comment that Parzival was *ganerbe dar*, comes to the listeners from the narrator, this time at a point in Book IX just before the encounter between hero and hermit begins. The narrator creates an interval in which to say something about Kyot and the sources of his story, indicating that Kyot came across an account of various members of the Grail-family (455,17: ... *unt anderhalp wie Tyturel | unt des sun Frimutel | den grâl bræht ûf Amfortas, | des swester Herzeloyde was, | bî der Gahmuret ein kint | gewan, des disiu mære sint*). We have learned of the first three names already from Sigune (251,5ff.) and therefore know that Kyot's account is here listing the line of succession in the Grail-dynasty, where the three lines 17–19 name the three Grail-kings in succession down to the present one, Anfortas. This vertical line of dynastic succession, where son twice follows father in his regal office,[150] then gives way to a horizontal movement in line 20, when Herzeloyde is named as the sister of the present Grail-king and we learn, for the first time in the work, of her membership of this family. From Herzeloyde we move, still horizontally, to her husband Gahmuret and then resume the vertical descent with the mention of *ein kint . . . des disiu mære sint* (455,21f.), whom we know by now to be Parzival. These lines are important, but not because 'they are the first indication to the audience that Parzival stands in a *direct* line of ascendancy to the Grail kingship'[151] – for the hero is *not* placed here in any direct line of accession (as is made clear by the sudden side-step, interrupting the direct vertical line). Instead he is significantly placed within this list of male members of the Grail-family as if he might be regarded as next in the line of succession.

Yet this is no more than a possibility suggested to the listeners. To be quite sure, we should need to know more than we have yet been told of the position with Anfortas – what is it that causes the narrator, following Kyot's account, to abandon his direct vertical line at this point? All we have heard of so far is the crisis and illness afflicting Anfortas and through him the whole of his dynasty,[152] but

150. In this passage the narrator expressly reminds the listeners that Frimutel is the son of Titurel (*des sun*) and they already know from Sigune's remarks (251,11ff.) about Frimutel that Anfortas was a son of his.
151. Harroff, *Wolfram*, pp. 66f.
152. From earlier references we have therefore learned that Anfortas is sick (231,1: *Der wirt het durch siechheit | grôziu fiur und an im warmiu kleit*), even quite incapacitated (251,16: '*Anfortas sîn bruoder lent: | der mac gerîten noch*

Parzival and Trevrizent (Book IX)

none of these earlier indications has been explicit enough to tell us that the line of succession in the Grail-dynasty cannot now pass directly through Anfortas. For this clarification we shall have to wait until Parzival's encounter with Trevrizent.[153] Moreover, we do not even know at this stage that the possible honours awaiting Parzival at Munsalvæsche and forfeited there by him actually consisted in accession to the office of Grail-kingship at present inadequately filled by the ailing Anfortas. These preceding references have all been too general to convey this specific possibility: they include general terms like *sælde* and *wunsch*[154] and refer to an Adam-like authority over creation,[155] none of which need suggest Grail-kingship in particular. If we read these general references in this way it is (improperly at this point) in the light of what we learn to be the case only later, for it is only during the course of his dialogue with Trevrizent that we learn with Parzival that what awaited him at Munsalvæsche was the very specific honour of kingship, in succession to Anfortas.[156] None of this is clear to us at

---

    gegên | noch geligen noch gestên') and mortally wounded (230,20: *er lebte niht wan töude*), so that he regards his affliction as a divinely imposed punishment (239,26: '... *ê daz mich got | ame lîbe hât geletzet'*). These references leave us in no doubt at all about the seriousness of Anfortas's sickness, but tell us nothing of what it involves for the future of the office of Grail-kingship. Even when these references acquaint Parzival with the facts as well as the listeners (as is the case with the two latest of the above passages, 239,26f. and 251,16ff.), such information is confined to the present situation experienced by the hero, they afford no glimpse into the future.
153. See below, pp. 221f.
154. For *sælde* cf. 252,4 ('*wol dich der sælden reise!*') and 254,24 (*sælden krône*), for *wunsch* 252,8 ('*ze rîcheit ist dir wunsch gezilt*'), 254,26f. ('*den wunsch ûf der erden | hâstû vollecliche*'), 317,1f. ('*Diu stat hât erden wunsches solt: | hie het iu vrâgen mêr erholt*') and 441,25 ('*dâ hete dir vrâgen wunsch bejagt*'). I call such terms general because they can designate both a worldly and an otherworldly dimension and because (as is clear especially with 254,26 and the terms of the comparison in 317,1f.) they do not suggest the specifically metaphysical context which Trevrizent later reveals (see also above, p. 213).
155. Cf. 252,5ff. ('*wan swaz die lüfte hânt beslagen, | dar ob muostu hœhe tragen: | dir dienet zam unde wilt*') and 254,21f. ('*sô muoz gar dienen dîner hant | swaz dîn lîp dâ wunders vant*'). On Parzival as a new Adam see Deinert, *Ritter*, pp. 51ff. In 254,22 only the word *dâ* suggests that the authority extended to Parzival might have involved kingship over the realm of Munsalvæsche, but even this hint is in danger of being swallowed up in the truly cosmocratic dimensions recently opened up in 252,5ff. and still present in the minds of Parzival and the listeners.
156. Only from Trevrizent, once he has explained that the Grail-dynasty cannot be prolonged through Anfortas (see below, p. 221) or through himself now that he has become a hermit (480,10ff.), do we learn that Munsalvæsche regards its crisis as one of dynastic succession and that a vacancy now exists (480,22: *si sprâchen 'wer sol schirmer sîn | über des grâles tougen?*'; cf. also Anfortas's later

the moment of the narrator's digression on Kyot – from the way in which he mentions Titurel, Frimutel, Anfortas and then passes on to Parzival we may indeed reckon with this possibility, but cannot yet claim certainty on this vital point.[157]

The theme of Parzival's relationship with the Grail-dynasty, like that of the Grail itself, reaches its climax in the explanation given by Trevrizent. After telling Parzival that his mother Herzeloyde was his sister (476,12f.) the hermit proceeds naturally enough to mention his two other sisters (477,1: *'Mînre geswistrede zwei noch sint'*), mentioning by name Schoysiane as the mother of Sigune (477,2ff.) and Repanse de schoy as the carrier of the Grail in the procession at Munsalvæsche (477,13ff.), thereby apprising his nephew of what had not been revealed by Sigune, namely her own kinship with the Grail-dynasty, and informing him that Repanse de schoy is his aunt. The importance of this has been rightly underlined by Harroff, who points out the tacit implication of the hermit's explanation.[158] We know that Herzeloyde's first marriage (to Castis) was unconsummated[159] and that Parzival is the only offspring of her union with Gahmuret. We know furthermore that Repanse de schoy, as yet unmarried, is explicitly described as a virgin by Trevrizent (477,13: *ein magt*) and it is made extremely likely that

> words to his followers at Munsalvæsche, 788,9: *'waz toug ich iu ze hêrren nuo?'*). While still unaware that it was Parzival who omitted to ask the question at Munsalvæsche, Trevrizent refers to what this offender has lost as a successor in impersonal terms, in the third person (484,3: *'wirt sîn frâge an rehter zît getân, / sô sol erz künecrîche hân'*). When he says of this forfeiture (484,30: *'grôzer sælde in dô betrâgte'*), the word *sælde* is now much more specific than in 252,4 and the reference to *künecrîche* shows that *sælden krône* in 254,24 was no mere metaphor. Once he knows the full truth about Parzival, Trevrizent can afford to be equally specific in the second person (500,29: *'si wând du soltst dâ hêrre sîn / des grâls unt ir / dar zuo mîn'*). These explicit references to Parzival's authority as Grail-kingship are then continued when he comes to Munsalvæsche a second time (e.g. 781,16; 793,10; 796,17ff.), but what is significant is that they are first made by Trevrizent in Book IX.
> 157. Harroff, *Wolfram*, pp. 67f., has also pointed out that no explicit reference is made by the narrator in 455,17ff. to Trevrizent's membership of the Grail-family and hence his kinship with Herzeloyde, but that nonetheless the really perceptive listener has already been given sufficient clues to suggest that this is an encounter between uncle and nephew. Cf. the similar technique in the case of Parzival and Ither (see above, p. 83).
> 158. Harroff, *Wolfram*, p. 71. Already, in abbreviated form, in Wapnewski, *Parzival*, p. 105, fn. 126.
> 159. At this point we do not yet know how and why this earlier marriage remained unconsummated, since Trevrizent goes into the reasons only later (494,15ff.). However, the fact that the marriage was unconsummated is clear to the listener who has paid attention to 60,15 (*si was ein maget, niht ein wîp*). See above, p. 38.

Parzival and Trevrizent (Book IX)

Sigune was the only child of Schoysiane and Kyot von Katelangen, the mother dying in childbirth.[160] In other words, only one of the three daughters of Frimutel has given birth to a male child who could be considered as a possible candidate for Grail-kingship: Herzeloyde.

Having significantly narrowed down Parzival's relationship to the Grail-dynasty in this manner (thereby going much further than any of the earlier references by the narrator or by Sigune), the hermit next proceeds to specify Parzival's position with regard to male members of the family. He says that, on the death of Frimutel, his eldest son Anfortas was chosen to succeed him as Grail-king,[161] while still in his youth (478,7ff.), hence before marriage and while still exposed to the dangerous assaults of love (478,10: *'mit selher jugent hât minne ir strît'*). This is indeed what happened (478,17ff. – we learn only later that it was Orgeluse who was responsible for tempting Anfortas away from the strait and narrow path mapped out for a Grail-king),[162] for it is in such forbidden love-service that the poisoned wound is inflicted on Anfortas from which he still suffers (479,3ff.). When it is explicitly made clear that he was wounded in the testicles (479,12: *durch die heidruose sîn*), this is not merely an example of the *lex talionis* (he is punished in that part of the body with which he had sinned),[163] but a clear indication that Anfortas, wounded before marriage, can never be expected to produce an heir to the office of Grail-kingship. This is the particular nature of the crisis which Parzival confronts at Munsalvæsche, the reason why the line of dynastic succession, traced by the narrator in his Kyot digression, could proceed directly from Titurel down to Anfortas, but then had to be taken sideways at this point. The crisis at Munsalvæsche has been rendered even more problematic, however, by the fact that the obvious answer to such difficulties (to make Anfortas's brother Grail-king in place of him) has been excluded by Trevrizent's decision, on learning of Anfortas's wounding, to abandon chivalry and live as a hermit (480,10ff.) in the hope of gaining God's mercy on his brother. Whatever his religious motives,

---

160. Harroff, *Wolfram*, p. 71. Certainly no other offspring of this marriage is mentioned anywhere in the work.
161. Harroff, *Wolfram*, p. 72, points out that this fact, together with the indication that Anfortas is *von art des grâles hêrre* (477,21), underlines the importance of kinship in the dynastic line of succession at Munsalvæsche, a fact already sufficiently stressed to the audience in the case of Parzival.
162. See above, p. 10.
163. As is suggested in the fn. to 479,12 in the Bartsch–Marti edition.

The Art of Recognition in Wolfram's *Parzival*

Trevrizent's decision certainly accentuates the crisis at Munsalvæsche, where the question (480,22: *'wer sol schirmer sîn / über des grâles tougen?'*) still remains unanswered.

This was the position when Parzival came to Munsalvæsche in Book V, but its ramifications have been made implicitly clear only by what Trevrizent has said in Book IX, after learning that the knight before him is his own nephew.[164] From all that the hermit has now said of Frimutel's daughters and sons it emerges that, if the office of Grail-kingship is to be passed down in the same family as hitherto,[165] Parzival is the only member of that family who can qualify.[166] This is the reason why the hero was originally *benennet* there and was the recipient of what is later shown to be divine guidance on his way there. It is also the reason why the narrator, in an earlier commentary, referred to Parzival as *ouch ganerbe dar* (333,30). Parzival is not the only one who could be considered as a possible candidate,[167] but it is only after Trevrizent's explanation about the nature of his brother's wound and his own withdrawal into a hermitage that we are able to grasp, without being told anywhere explicitly, that the hero occupies a unique position in the line of succession to Grail-kingship.

It is in this most crucial aspect of the cognitive progress on which both his listeners and Parzival are engaged that the narrator makes most demands of his audience for, although he carefully makes it possible for them to reach the truth by instalments, he nowhere states it to them explicitly.[168] However, as in other respects, the

---

164. The information released by Trevrizent at this point has to be coupled with the fact that he is still unaware that his nephew is the man who failed to ask the question (cf. Harroff, *Wolfram*, p. 72).
165. On the predominance of this principle of 'Geblütsrecht' within the Grail-dynasty see Becker, *Recht*, pp. 43ff.
166. Tax, *Kingdom*, p. 27, makes the same point ('The reader knows that Parzival is the only possible candidate'), but by saying this in the context of Book V wrongly implies that we know this already when Parzival comes to the Grail-castle for the first time. On the contrary, we are provided with this information only in Book IX.
167. The obvious choice as a successor to Frimutel was his eldest son Anfortas (as in fact happens, 478,1ff.), whilst the obvious choice to succeed Anfortas is his brother Trevrizent, as is clear from the despair at Munsalvæsche when it is learned that this opportunity is not open to them (480,19ff.). If one looks at the situation at the moment of Frimutel's death it is far from obvious that Herzeloyde's son will ever have to be considered as a possible Grail-king, only the events concerning Anfortas's illicit service of Orgeluse (478,17ff.) open up this unexpected possibility for Parzival and show that he is much more than just *ouch ganerbe dar*.
168. Cf. Hirschberg, *Untersuchungen*, p. 142: 'Sooft das Gespräch allerdings an

Parzival and Trevrizent (Book IX)

listeners are given information in advance of Parzival. We thus learn, with him, from Sigune's explanation at their second meeting (251,1ff.) of the line of succession in the Grail-dynasty down to the present (Titurel – Frimutel – Anfortas), but are told nothing of Parzival's place in this dynasty, because there is no mention of Herzeloyde's connection with it. This deficiency is made good for the listeners, but not of course for Parzival, by the narrator's commentary in his Kyot digression (455,17ff.), where the same line of succession is repeated, but this time with the vital addition that Herzeloyde is the sister of Anfortas.

This last vital piece of information has been withheld from Parzival himself, and his enlightenment is not taken further when Trevrizent in his long drawn-out question as to his identity (474,1ff.) mentions the three Grail-kings, but leaves unspecified the position of Anfortas, so that his remark is not even as informative for Parzival as Sigune's had been. It is only after his admission of identity that the position changes for Parzival. After this point Trevrizent now clarifies what had not been obvious in his last remark on this subject, saying that, on his death, Frimutel was succeeded by his eldest son Anfortas (478,1ff.). Parzival already knows that Anfortas is the brother of Trevrizent (477,19) and therefore of his own mother (cf. 476,12). By now Parzival therefore knows of his position within the Grail-dynasty, he is aware that he is the nephew of the Grail-king, so that he has at last caught up with the listeners in this knowledge about himself. He is enabled to catch up with them only because the confession of his identity constitutes the vital turning-point in his encounter with Trevrizent, and the same is true, for him as for the listeners, of the possibility of his succeeding Anfortas: for both this truth emerges implicitly only from what Trevrizent says of his sisters and brothers once he has learned that his guest is after all a kinsman of his.

> einen Punkt gelangt, an dem diese Schlußfolgerung [i.e. that Parzival is the only possible successor to Anfortas] das Naheliegende wäre, wird sie ausgespart. Die Vorinformiertheit des Publikums, der hier die Details dessen, was "ganerbenschaft" heißt, zugeliefert werden, bleibt in Spannung zur Offenheit des Gesprächs, das, sobald die Identität des "gastes" feststeht, alle genauen Angaben hinsichtlich Parzivals Verhältnis zum Gral und auch – allgemeiner – zum Ziel seiner Queste vermeidet.' Cf. also p. 337: 'Seitdem diese [i.e. the identity of Trevrizent's guest] und die Geschichte des Gralgeschlechts, seiner Berufung und seiner Königsfolge offenliegt, wird gerade der Konvergenzpunkt dieser Eröffnungen: Parzival ist der einzige mögliche Nachfolger der Gralkönige, mit keinem Wort berührt und kann allenfalls aus Hörersicht ermittelt werden'.

The Art of Recognition in Wolfram's *Parzival*

The double process of recognition plotted in this encounter (by Trevrizent and Parzival) thus largely hinges on Parzival's admission of his identity to the hermit; this is the point at which blow upon blow falls on each of them.[169] Trevrizent now realises that his guest is not Lähelin, so that much of his advice is now revealed as not relevant in the sense in which it was meant, but also that Parzival has killed Ither, a kinsman of his. For his part, Parzival learns that past victims of his behaviour have been kinsmen (Ither, his own mother, Anfortas) and that the same is true of his host, which makes it more difficult and embarrassing to admit that he failed at Munsalvæsche. Although this last confession is therefore deferred to a later stage,[170] it is the earlier admission of identity which releases all the information given above and leads to all the recognitions in which it is a person who has to be recognised. The same is true of Trevrizent's more objective information, concerning the Grail. Before the crucial hinge of the recognition of Parzival's identity Trevrizent's information serves the end of putting off someone whom he takes to be Lähelin from any vain search for the Grail, but after this point the hermit's remarks, even though he may not realise it, keep it open whether Parzival may not after all be able to put this information to good use on a second occasion.[171] Decisive information can therefore be imparted to Parzival without Trevrizent offending against the rules of the Grail only because of his failure to recognise that Parzival has already been at Munsalvæsche.

The theme of recognition and ignorance thus plays a crucial rôle in motivating Parzival's two appearances at Munsalvæsche – it is no peripheral theme, but rather one with a central function. As far as Parzival himself is concerned, his learning of Trevrizent's identity[172] is tantamount to recognition of his kinship with him, which

---

169. From quite a different point of view (the theme of recognition, rather than the possibility of a symmetrical structure) I therefore place emphasis on Parzival's admission of identity, without following Mergell (*Parzival*, pp. 165ff. and 240f.) in his suggestion that the mutual recognition of Parzival and Trevrizent is the fulcrum around which the rest is symmetrically grouped.
170. It is this which has led Henzen, *Überlegungen*, p. 196, to see the structural fulcrum of Book IX, not in any symmetry as suggested by Mergell, but in Parzival's long deferred confession that it was he who failed at Munsalvæsche.
171. See above, p. 192, fn. 62.
172. Parzival's learning of his host's identity would thus be the same as his learning of Trevrizent's name, as reflected in the narrator's use of circumlocutions for the hermit before the point of recognition and his readiness to use his name afterwards (see above, pp. 185f.). As on other occasions the narrator does not

Parzival and Trevrizent (Book IX)

leads into the heart of Book IX for him. It is only from the man whom Parzival now knows to be his uncle that he learns of his past offences against kinsmen from this family, comes to recognise his own kinship with the Grail-family and realises at length his position as the only possible successor to Anfortas within that dynasty.

> feel it necessary to indicate the point at which Parzival must have grasped that this hermit is the same as the one referred to by name as Trevrizent (251,15) by Sigune in their second encounter. It is enough for him to imply this by the contrast between the consistent withholding of Trevrizent's name throughout most of Book IX and his use of it again towards the end.

7
Parzival's success (Books XIV–XVI)

With the start of Book XIV the narrative reverts to Parzival, so that we are justified in treating the concluding Books under the heading of narrative action concerned with the hero. Although Gawan may still be involved in this action (this is particularly true of the first encounter in this chapter), the narrator makes it clear at the close of Book XIII that in returning to the as yet unnamed Parzival he is once more taking up the proper theme of his work (678,30: *an den rehten stam diz mære ist komn*).[1] Similarly, when at the close of the work the narrator sums up the course of action which reaches its climax in these three closing Books he sees it naturally in terms of Parzival (827,6f. and 17f.), by contrast with which Gawan fades from view without any express mention (cf. 822,2ff.).[2] The first encounter (between Parzival and Gawan) thus acts as a bridge, taking the action back from Gawan to the world of Parzival, so that it is expressly in the hero's world that we now have to consider the problem of recognition.

As on earlier occasions, the narrator makes use of linguistic ambiguity to signal the implications of the action. When Parzival and Gawan engage in single combat without recognising each other, the situation is summed up: *erkantiu sippe unt hôch geselleschaft / was dâ mit hazlîcher kraft / durch scharpfen strît zein ander komen* (680,13ff.). The two abstracts of the first line stand for such personal terms as *die mâge* and *die gesellen* used in 680,19 and indicate that two kinsmen and companions have now clashed, whilst the surface meaning of *erkant* ('well-known') stresses the renown of these two contestants. Behind this lurks another implication, however, for if we take this word not adjectivally, but as the

---

1. Cf. Schirok, *Aufbau*, p. 464.
2. Through the answer to Feirefiz's question we learn briefly and uninformatively what has happened to king Arthur and have to assume that Gawan has returned to Schastel Marveile.

Parzival's success (Books XIV–XVI)

past participle of a verb, the ironic suggestion is now made that these two, together perhaps with the slower members of the audience, have failed to recognise each other for what they are. Narratorial irony is also involved in the unconscious implications of Gawan's wish that the best man may win in the forthcoming combat with Gramoflanz (707,26: *'got ez ze rehte erscheine'*), for the formulation of this wish ('May God support the just cause') also includes the possibility, without this being clear at the moment to Gawan or to the listeners, that God will indeed support the just cause by preventing the combat from taking place at all (by means of Arthur's diplomatic intervention).[3] In imputing these words to Gawan the narrator reveals the future in ambiguous terms; he means more than Gawan can actually have in mind, but in this case his listeners cannot be expected to see the force of his words at the time.

The narrator's technique of revealing and concealing narrative details means, in this segment of the narrative as elsewhere, that not all details need actually be narrated and that on occasions further perspectives can be opened up than are called for by the needs of the immediate foreground action. Details not expressly given include the names of the many people present at Arthur's assembly at Joflanze (699,26ff.), where the rhetorical device of *praeteritio*, a summary listing of details which are to be passed over, is enough to persuade us of the numbers and variety of those present. After the conclusion of Parzival's combat with Gramoflanz, undertaken on behalf of Gawan, Arthur remarks that Parzival has been granted the combat which he earlier sought permission to undertake from Gawan (708,1ff.). When Arthur adds that Gawan refused to allow his friend to fight in his stead and that Parzival bitterly lamented this (708,5: *'unt Gâwân dirz versagte,/daz dîn munt dô sêre klagete'*), we realise that these regrets of Parzival were not expressly mentioned in the earlier narrative (cf. 700,25ff.) and that this is a case where a later passage presupposes a narrative detail passed over at the time.[4]

---

3. See also Green, *Homicide*, p. 32.
4. On the extreme compression of the narrative evident in 711,4, where not all the details have been expressly narrated, see the fn. to this line in the Bartsch–Marti edition. Details of the action are also seen to be passed over in silence when we are told retrospectively that Condwiramurs had received instructions to rejoin her husband at Munsalvæsche (797,1ff.) or when the conclusion of the Arthurian action is simply dismissed as relatively insignificant (see above, p. 226, fn. 2).

Greater weight attaches to the remark with which Parzival concludes the list of his knightly victories which Arthur requests of him (772,24: '*diz ergienc dâ turnieren was, / die wîle ich nâch dem grâle reit*'). If Parzival specifies that all these combats took place while he was questing for the Grail, the narrative itself has referred indirectly to only one of them (without describing it), namely with *von Ascalûn den künec Vergulaht* (772,17).[5] By now the listeners must realise how much they do not know about Parzival's knightly career, how much took place offstage while they were following Gawan's adventures. This impression of ignorance is then reinforced by Parzival's statement that even this list of knights defeated by him is incomplete (772,26: '*solt ich gar nennen dâ ich streit, / daz wæren unkundiu zil: / durch nôt ichs muoz verswîgen vil*'), since it takes no account of his victories in real combat (*streit* by contrast with *turnieren*), where he simply does not know whom he may have defeated in massed encounters.[6] An example of what is meant by this is the battle at Bearosche, where Parzival is unaware how narrowly he avoided a clash with Gawan[7] and where the narrator also confesses ignorance of all those who took part (388,1ff.). The narrator's pretended ignorance at this stage parallels Parzival's actual ignorance, confessed by him to Arthur at this later point. By his guise of ignorance the narrator keeps his listeners in (partial) unawareness, as a reflection of Parzival's own ignorance.

The alternative technique of opening up further narrative perspectives by pointing to what lies beyond the immediate action is mainly used, not unexpectedly, in connection with the winding-up of the story in Book XVI. When Parzival invests his son Kardeiz with his secular kingdoms (803,4ff.) his reference to Waleis and Norgals implies the wish that his subjects will one day help Kardeiz in the reconquest of feudal territories seized by Lähelin (cf.128, 4ff.), but this subjective wish is then confirmed by the narrator's anticipation of this distant future (803,22: *der betwang och sider Kanvoleiz / und vil des Gahmuretes was*), thereby concluding the Lähelin story with this omniscient glimpse into the future. Somewhat later the narrator gives us another glimpse into a future lying outside the chronological framework of his story by telling us of the future of Feirefiz and Repanse de schoy and of the birth of their son,

---

5. See above, p. 147.
6. 772,27: *unkundiu zil*.
7. See above, pp. 140f.

Parzival's success (Books XIV–XVI)

Presterjohn (822,21ff.).[8] Soon after this he describes his task as an account of the history of Frimutel's five children (823,11f.), adding a brief résumé of what we have been told about each of them (823, 13ff.). With 823,27ff., however, the narrator gives us another glimpse of the future lying beyond Parzival's call to the Grail. He does not feel it necessary to dwell on Parzival as the immediately following generation, since we have followed his history in detail and have learned by now enough of his chastity and humility to realise that he will not succumb to the temptations to which Anfortas fell victim. Instead, the narrator goes one step further into the future, recounting in a brief, self-contained episode the coming story of Parzival's son and successor as Grail-king, Loherangrin (823,27ff.).[9] It is with this view beyond its own confines that Wolfram's narrative of events comes to its conclusion.

To withhold some information from his listeners, but also to provide them with more than is immediately available to characters in the narrative means that in this stretch of the story, too, the narrator operates with a point of view technique which sometimes deliberately restricts what the audience is allowed to see and sometimes grants them the privilege of greater insight. Since the narrative is now approaching its end and since those listeners at all amenable to the narrator's technique must also be drawing near to the ultimate insights to be learned from his work, it is hardly surprising that in these three final Books the technique of giving privileged understanding to the listeners should far outweigh that of withholding it.

Indeed, the narrator temporarily withholds knowledge or certainty from the audience above all in the climax of Parzival's knightly career, in his combat with Feirefiz, primarily as a means of informing it with the tension necessary for a climactic scene of this order. At the start of Book XV he anticipates the immediate future, telling us of the unique danger of the combat awaiting Parzival (734,17ff.), but then heightens the tension implicit in this by pretending ignorance as to the ultimate outcome (734,23: *nu bevilh ich sîn gelücke / sîm herze, der sælden stücke, / dâ diu vrävel bî der kiusche lac, / wand ez nie zageheit gepflac. / daz müeze im vestenunge gebn, / daz er behalde nu sîn lebn*). By placing himself in the same

---

8. On the wider significance of Presterjohn and his connection with the story of Parzival see Kolb, *Munsalvaesche*, pp. 73ff.
9. See below, pp. 261ff.

narrative present as the events he is describing[10] and by having to commend his hero's fate to a higher authority the narrator can adopt the guise of uncertainty and pass on this same ignorance to his listeners. The same restricted vision is manufactured when the narrator wishes for a fortunate outcome (738,18: *gelücke scheidez âne tôt*), for here too by placing himself in the narrative present he deprives his listeners of the consolation of a possible glimpse into the future by an omniscient narrator, standing above the course of events. The frequency with which the narrator uses this technique (by voicing an urgent wish he puts himself forward as a spectator commenting on a combat whose outcome is still unknown to him) heightens the tension of this final knightly combat of Parzival's[11] by forcing ignorance and therefore an anxious involvement in Parzival's fate on his listeners.[12]

For the rest, however, the narrator makes it possible for his audience to understand a situation better than those actually involved. This is particularly the case with Bene, sent as a messenger by Itonje to her lover Gramoflanz, for what is first presented is her confidence and lack of concern about his forthcoming combat (686,1: *Bêne unders küneges armen saz: | diu liez den kampf gar âne haz. | si het des künges manheit | sô vil gesehen dâ er streit, | daz siz wolt ûzen sorgen lân*). The narrator stresses this by depicting things from her subjective point of view (cf. 2 *liez*, 3f. *het ... gesehen*, 5 *wolt ûzen sorgen lân*), but the point of view is then changed when he comments omnisciently, underlining her ignorance of the facts of the situation (686,6: *wiste ab si daz Gâwân | ir frouwen bruoder*

---

10. This deliberate restriction of his vision to the present, for rhetorical purposes, is quite different from the narrator's use of the present in a forecast of the future such as 734,15 (*Parzivâl daz wirbet*), where the present indicates certainty about the known future.
11. From the same encounter cf. also the narrator's urgent appeal to the Grail and Condwiramurs (740,19: *daz wende, tugenthafter grâl: | Condwîr âmûrs diu lieht gemâl: | hie stêt iur beider dienstman | in der græsten nôt dier ie gewan*), his prayer to God (742,14: *got ner dâ Gahmuretes kint*), his pressing reminder to Parzival himself (742,27: *wes sûmestu dich, Parzivâl, | daz du an die kiuschen lieht gemâl | niht denkest (ich mein dîn wîp), | wiltu behalten hie den lîp?*), the anxiety he voices on behalf of Parzival (743,9: *mich müet daz der getoufte | an strîte und an loufte | sus müedet unde an starken slegen*) and his appeal to God just as the combat is broken off (744,21: *ez ist noch ungescheiden, | zurteile stêtz in beiden | vor der hôhsten hende: | daz diu ir sterben wende!*).
12. Two other cases where the narrator pleads ignorance and can therefore withhold a detail from the audience concern the precise location of Munsalvæsche (792,14f.; 796,28ff.) and thus help to preserve the mystery of its whereabouts. On this see Wynn, *MLR* 56 (1961), 33.

wære | unt daz disiu strengen mære | ûf ir hêrren wærn gezogn, | si wære an freuden dâ betrogn). Bene knows quite well that Gramoflanz is to fight Gawan,[13] but she does not know that Gawan is the brother of her mistress Itonje – in other words, she has heard Gawan's name mentioned, but cannot equate the name with the person. By 693,21ff. a new stage in Bene's knowledge of the situation is reached. At first, she recognises only that Gramoflanz is the enemy of Gawan[14] and she therefore curses him roundly, but even this stage represents a shift from the bland confidence of 686,1ff. However, Bene still sees Gawan exclusively as the lord of Schastel Marveile and hence as patron of the four queens there, including Itonje,[15] she has no idea yet that Itonje is also Gawan's sister. When this knowledge is at length conveyed to her (694,6: *Itonjê der swester sîn*), the full measure of grief assails her as she realises the close kinship between Gawan and Itonje (694,9ff.) and hence the tragedy of Itonje's quandary (697,1ff.). By now Bene realises what the listeners had been reminded of as early as 686,6f.

However, Gawan now arranges with Bene to conceal the facts of the combat from Itonje (696,21ff.), so that Bene's enlightenment coincides with a situation in which it is now Itonje whose ignorance is stressed. We are then shown Itonje's uncertainty in narrative action (697,28ff.) as she notices the signs of Bene's grief: things are presented from her point of view (cf. 29 *warte*, 3 *dâhte*, 7 *an mir gerochen*), but even so she quickly suspects that something is wrong, if not what. When Itonje eventually learns that her lover and her brother are to fight (710,9ff.), her knowledge is soon revealed to Arnive (710,22ff.), who passes on responsibility to her son Arthur (711,1ff.) to effect a diplomatic reconciliation. With that this particular motif is concluded, but for its brief duration it operated with the contrast between the facts conveyed to us and the restricted point of view first of Bene, then of Itonje.

A similar discrepancy concerns Gramoflanz in this comedy of errors which so dangerously skirts the realm of tragedy. When the mistaken combat[16] between Parzival and Gawan has been broken off, we are shown Gramoflanz arriving on the scene, ready for the

---

13. Gramoflanz's insistence on fighting Gawan, whom he expressly names (684,11ff.; 685,4ff.), is quite well known to Bene, for she is present on this occasion (cf. 686,1).
14. Cf. 693,13ff.
15. 693,26: '*diu muoz doch sînre genâden lebn*'.
16. It is therefore referred to as *dem ungelobten strîte* (691,5), as opposed to that which was agreed upon (684,11: *den gelobten strît*).

appointed combat (691,18: *der wolde ouch rechen sînen kranz*). The narrator's judgment of this detail is conveyed by the word *ouch*, which can only mean that Gramoflanz, for his part too, now wished to fight Gawan. This use of *ouch* makes no sense from Gramoflanz's point of view: he has just arrived on the scene (691,17) and the next thing he learns is what has just happened (691,19: *der vriesch wol daz dâ was geschehn / ein kampf* ...), so that he cannot already know of this in v.18. But the narrator responsible for this phrasing (and we with him) knows that Parzival has anticipated Gramoflanz in this encounter,[17] so that the use of *ouch* underlines the full difference between what we know and what Gramoflanz expects. As such, *ouch* cannot come from Gramoflanz, but only from the narrator.

In the depiction of the combat between Parzival and Gramoflanz an ironic contrast is worked out between Gramoflanz's custom of spurning combat with only one opponent (705,19: *der künec Gramoflanz pflac site, / im versmâhte sêre daz er strite / mit einem man*) and what he thinks is happening to him on this occasion (705,21: *dô dûhte in nuo / daz hie sehse griffen strîtes zuo*). This irony is highlighted by the change in point of view between what Gramoflanz thinks (cf. 20 *versmâhte*, 21 *dûhte*, together with the adverbs *nuo* and *hie*) and what we learn from the narrator (705,23: *ez was doch Parzivâl al ein, / der gein im werlîche schein*). This point of view technique is combined with the use of an anonymous circumlocution when Gramoflanz sends his messengers to Arthur's encampment, for the two women they catch sight of are referred to in different ways (711,15: *einer Bênen sitzen sach / bî der diu zArtûse sprach*). The reason for this difference is clear: the narrator uses a circumlocution to refer to Itonje, because these messengers, like their master, do not know her by sight and therefore cannot recognise her, but only Bene.[18] They see the situation in terms only of what they know (Bene is mentioned by name) and the narrator reflects their partial point of view in his phrasing.[19]

17. In 703,1ff. Gramoflanz regards Parzival as having taken over his combat from him.
18. In this episode the narrator makes it clear that Gramoflanz and Itonje have never met personally (cf. 712,18ff.), but that Bene is quite well acquainted with his messengers (713,1ff.), so that they accordingly know her. This explains why Gramoflanz, in giving instructions to his messengers, tells them to observe the woman with whom Bene is sitting (709,26: '*ir sult ouch sunder schouwen, / bî welher Bêne sitze*'). Like his messengers, Gramoflanz has to proceed from the known to the unknown.
19. Another example of the point of view technique is provided by the narrator's indirect question, meant to reflect the Round Table's opinion when they notice

Parzival's success (Books XIV–XVI)

As a last example of the point of view technique I take the critical scene of Parzival's return to Munsalvæsche in Book XVI. Anfortas, unable to bear his suffering, has requested his followers to allow him to die, but their refusal is expressed in a line which combines two points of view (787,3: *ir triwe liez in in der nôt*), where the use of *triwe* expresses the followers' motives and the narrator's approval, whilst *liez* conveys Anfortas's view that he has been deserted in his suffering. These two points of view derive from the essential reciprocity of feudal *triwe*.[20] Anfortas expects *triwe* from his followers, a willingness to put an end to his pain by allowing him to die, so that when they do not do this he questions their *triwe* (787,9f. + 19; 787, 30ff.). For their part they do not act as he wants them to in the hope that he might yet be saved (788,13ff.) and also (implicitly) out of a reluctance to allow their lord to compound his sins by suicide. A similar conjunction of differing points of view is presented when Parzival draws near to Munsalvæsche and Anfortas's pain reaches its climax (789,16ff.). The opening two lines of this passage convey the judgment of the situation by Anfortas's followers (789,16: *er was unhelfeclîche wunt: / si mohten im gehelfen niht*) and are complemented by their emotional reaction in v. 20 (*si griffen herzen jâmers zuo*), which follows on quite logically. Together these three lines represent the Grail-knights' subjective point of view, but inserted in them are two lines which correct this mistaken assess-

Parzival's absence, that he may be attempting to negotiate a reconciliation between Gawan and Gramoflanz (704,26: *ob erz welle süenen?*) and what he then tells us in his own capacity as the truth (704,27: *dem gebârt er ungelîche: / er streit sô manlîche / mit dem der ouch strîtes pflac*).

When Gawan later notices the external signs of recent combat with both Parzival and his halfbrother Feirefiz (759,1ff.), he is unable to grasp that they have been fighting one another and assumes that they must have fought jointly against a common foe (cf. his question in v. 6, *'gein wem erholt ir disen pîn?'*, with its use of the plural pronoun *ir*, as opposed to his use of *du* when addressing Parzival alone in v. 1). Parzival then tells Gawan the facts about their encounter (759,7ff.), summing up the situation in the oxymoron *disen heinlîchen gast* (759,11), where *gast* reflects the stranger each saw initially in the other and *heinlîch* what was eventually revealed as the truth.

That the narrator, rather like Gawan, is fond of preparing a surprise and makes sure that we enjoy it with him is also revealed by his description of Parzival on the brink of his reunion with his still unsuspecting wife (800,18: *dez harnasch man gar von im dâ nam. / diu küngîn des noch niht enweiz. / Loherangrîn unt Kardeiz / vant Parzivâl bî ir ligen*), where the contrast between what is happening and the reported ignorance of Condwiramurs is further stressed by the difference between the preterite tense of the narrative account (*nam, vant*) and the present of the narrator's comment (*enweiz*).

20. Cf. Schmid, *Studien*, pp. 156ff.

ment when the narrator, appealing to his source for confirmation, tells us what is really happening, unsuspected by those involved (789,18: *iedoch diu âventiure giht, / im kom diu wâre helfe nuo*). A third conjunction of points of view is given as Parzival reaches the borders of Terre de Salvæsche itself. Of the Grail-king's suffering and his followers' grief the narrator says (792,8f.): *sîme volke er jâmers gap genuoc. / doch wirt nu freude an im vernomn*. Here the first line represents the Grail-knights' reaction to events, the way in which they exclusively judge them (the use of the preterite *gap* embeds this line within their narrative world), whilst the following line is a statement of what is actually taking place from the narrator's vantage-point (the use of the present *wirt* now opens up the immediate future, visible only to him). This narratorial statement is then continued in the following lines, for Parzival has now reached Grail-territory (792,10), if not Munsalvæsche itself, so that the *volc* of 792,8 have no means of knowing this yet. The position is different with the *templeisen* guarding the borders, for they see Parzival's approach and know what it portends for them (792,22ff.). They recognise what is afoot after the listeners, but before the other Grail-knights at Munsalvæsche.

We have seen, when Gramoflanz's messengers catch sight of Bene and Itonje, how the narrator can make use of his naming technique (giving or withholding a name) in connection with his point of view technique. He uses the same method with names elsewhere in these concluding Books, especially in the first four of the encounters which we shall be considering, where in every case one or each party in the encounter fails at first to recognise the other.

We approach the combat between Parzival and Gawan in the latter's company, whom we have followed from Book X to XIII until at the close of this Book he catches sight of a knight (678,18: *ein rîter*) with whom he engages in combat at the start of the following Book. This situation means that we know full well who Gawan is, so that the narrator can refer to him by name in the preliminaries to the encounter (679,1 and 17), but that, like Gawan, we can have no certainty as to the identity of his opponent, who is accordingly referred to anonymously (679,5 *sandern* and 12 *der helt*). We witness things from Gawan's point of view, therefore, and this is reflected in the contrast between his naming and the other knight's anonymity just as much as when Gramoflanz's messengers catch sight of the named Bene and the unnamed Itonje (711,15f.). When the combat begins (in 679,23) it is made clear to us that neither recog-

Parzival's success (Books XIV–XVI)

nises the other,[21] so that the narrator puts his listeners in the position of the two contestants by no longer referring to either by name during their combat until they recognise each other. He avoids their names by using an abstraction in place of a personal reference (680,13: *erkantiu sippe unt hôch geselleschaft*) or an impersonal verbal construction where the subject need not be expressed (680,23: *ez wart aldâ verzwicket, / mit swerten verbicket*),[22] but above all by refusing to describe the encounter as one between one knight and another, but rather as one in which both are equally engaged, so that he can fall back on nameless terms such as *beide*, *swer*, *ein ander* or *weder*.[23]

That this avoidance of Gawan's name during the combat is purposeful can be shown by the narrator's technique in the episode, inserted into the course of the combat, in which Arthur's messengers parley with Gramoflanz. In this context, where no failure in recognising Gawan is at stake as with Parzival's fight with his kinsman, narratorial reticence is not called for and Gawan's name can be freely mentioned (684,5 + 13; 685,6; 686,6 + 28). These two narrative strands (the combat, where Parzival's failure to recognise Gawan is reflected in the narrator's avoidance of the latter's name, and the parleying, where no such anonymity is called for) then converge when Arthur's messengers, returning from Gramoflanz, come across the two knights fighting, recognise one of them as Gawan and call out his name in alarm (688,17: *wan daz in klagende nanten / kint diu in bekanten*).[24] This is accordingly the point where the narrator first feels free to refer to Gawan by name in the combat scene (688,6: ... *dâ Gâwân / ûf ir widerreise streit*) and he continues to use it again from this point on (688,13 + 15; 689,9 + 25, etc.), just as Parzival can now use it (689,3). But Parzival himself has not yet been recognised, so that in his case the narrator still uses nameless references (688,13: *Gâwânes kampfgenôz*; 19: *der ê des was sîns strîtes wer*; 23: *gast*; 689,10: *sîme kampfgenôze*).[25] Once Parzival has been asked for his name and reveals it (689,24), the narrator is

21. Cf. below, pp. 240ff.
22. Cf. also the use of a passive construction, where the horses rather than their riders are the grammatical subject, in 679,27 (*mit sporn si wurden des ermant*).
23. Cf. *beide* (679,30; 680,3 (together with *samt*); 680,12); *swer* (680,5 + 16); *ein ander* (680,7 + 20); *enweder* (680,8); *ieweder* (680,18).
24. Cf. also 688,9.
25. In three of these cases, as with Gramoflanz's messengers before Bene and Itonje, the narrator proceeds from the known to the unknown, referring to Parzival only in terms of Gawan, whose name has been released and is therefore the focal point of reference (*Gâwânes, sîns, sîme*).

free to refer to him by name, if not at once (because he first talks of Gawan's exhaustion, 690,3ff.), then at least when he next turns to Parzival's rôle in the narrative (693,1; 694,23 + 26, etc.).[26]

The position changes in Parzival's combat with Gramoflanz, since the hero has undertaken this task on behalf of Gawan and knows who his opponent is, whilst Gramoflanz is unaware of Parzival's identity and thinks that this is Gawan. This situation is captured in the narrator's use of names. Before the combat he uses the name of each participant (703,1 + 22), but once it is joined (from 703,30) he reverts to anonymity by using an impersonal circumlocution (704,29: *mit dem der ouch strîtes pflac*), anonymous epithets (704,16: *die helde*; 707,7: *den kampfmüeden zwein*), and terms such as *weder* and *bêde*.[27] The exception in 704,25, where Parzival's name is mentioned, is more apparent than real, since it comes in a short narrative switch back to Arthur's court, where meanwhile Parzival's absence has been noticed – his name is therefore mentioned in the context of the Round Table, not of the combat.

Despite this, the narrator's technique is not fully adequate to the problem he faces on this occasion,[28] for strictly speaking there is no call for anonymous references to Gramoflanz anyhow, since Parzival is aware of his identity all along. When we are taken back to the combat scene (705,15ff.) after an interlude for Gawan's preparations, the narrator can still refer to the combatants anonymously (706,5: *den küenen wîganden*; 7: *die werden*; 11: *die recken*; 21: *nâch prîs die vil gevarnen*), but he also makes use of their names (Gramoflanz: 705,19 and 706,13; Parzival: 705,23 and 706,17). This can only be because Parzival knows the facts and because the narrator's technique is meant on this occasion[29] primarily to reflect the hero's recognition of the situation. As it is, Gramoflanz remains ignorant of the identity of his opponent, as is brought out by his circumlocutory reference to him (707,13: *den man gein im dâ het ersehn*), by Gawan's similar allusion in talking to him (707,20: '*swer iu disen strît gebôt*'), and by the narrator's express comment, after Gramoflanz has left the scene of combat (707,27), that no one

26. In 694,23 the two names of Parzival and Gawan can now be used weightly in the one line.
27. Cf. *deweder* (703,30); *iewederr* (704,2); *si bêde* (704,6 + 12).
28. This has already been implicitly suggested by Harms, cf. below, pp. 245f.
29. As opposed to the scene of the drops of blood in the snow where, for particular reasons, the onus of recognition falls upon the Round Table or more specifically on Gawan. See above, p. 101.

Parzival's success (Books XIV–XVI)

among his followers knew Parzival (709,11: *dennoch si sîn erkanten niht*).[30]

Parzival's next opponent is introduced to us anonymously at the start of Book XV (734,30: *ob allem strîte ein vogt*; 735,2: *der selbe kurteise*; 3: *ein heidenischer man*). The last reference suggests that this opponent is unknown to us (for when have we seen Parzival encounter a pagan before?), which is confirmed by further anonymous references just before the start of the combat where, in addition to *gast, helt, gehiure* and *werlîche knabe*, this new opponent is also termed *heiden* and *ungetouft*.[31] As we draw closer to the start of the combat, these anonymous references include both contestants (737,11: *die künge*; 19 + 23: *ein ander*; 20: *die mit kiusche lember wâren / und lewen an der vrechheit*) and the same technique is continued into the description of the combat itself (beginning in 738,1 and ending in 744,24).[32] During the combat anonymity is maintained by circumlocutions, impersonal passive constructions, nameless epithets and the liberal employment of terms such as *weder, dise zwêne, ein ander* and *bêde*.[33] These references serve the double purpose of showing how closely involved both combatants are in this encounter and also of keeping Feirefiz in anonymity.

Feirefiz must be singled out in this respect since, by contrast, Parzival is still referred to by name by the narrator. We have after

30. The contrast between Parzival, who knows all along who his opponent is, and Gramoflanz's ignorance on this score is also brought out by the narrator's reference to the conclusion of their combat in such a way that the one combatant is named and the other alluded to by an anonymous circumlocution (707,10: *scheidens dûhte rehtiu zît / Gramoflanzen, der sô sprach / daz er dem siges jach, / den man gein im dâ het ersehn*).
   The more symbolic reading of 709,11 suggested by Harms, *Kampf*, p. 163, is reconcilable with and indeed is based upon the literal fact of non-recognition. See also below, p. 310, fn. 239.
31. Cf. *gast* (735,8); *helt* (735,19); *gehiure* (736,20); *werlîche knabe* (736,25), *heiden* (735,11; 736,4); *ungetouft* (736,20).
32. Although the combat ends in 744,24, the actual process of recognition begins only in 745,25.
33. Circumlocutions are 741,21f. and 742,6f., whilst impersonal passive constructions are employed in 738,30ff. and 739,13ff. As regards nameless epithets, Parzival is once termed *man* (739,8) and Feirefiz *gast* (744,12), but the predominant method is to refer to them respectively as *getoufter* (738,12; 739,23 + 27; 740,14; 741,1 + 26; 742,16; 743,9 + 23; 745,13) and *heiden* (738,11; 739,7 + 23; 740,7 + 13 + 18 + 23; 741,1; 742,1 + 16; 743,1; 744,8 + 11 + 20 + 25; 745,13 + 25). Feirefiz can also be referred to namelessly by an allusion to his headdress (739,16, cf. 736,10) or simply to the helmet he wears (739,18). The remaining terms used in this episode are *ieweder* (738,4 + 9 + 16; 741,25); *sweder* (738,6); *dise zwêne* (738,21); *ein ander* (739,12 + 29; 740,4); *bêde* (739,21; 740,5 + 27 + 28; 741,24; 742,15; 744,22; 745,10ff.).

all accompanied him through Book XIV up to this point, so that the narrator can freely use his name before the combat starts and also during its actual course.[34] This discrepancy between an anonymous Feirefiz and a named Parzival is justified, even though neither combatant immediately recognises his opponent, according to the narrator's technique of acting as if he were a commentator present at the encounter on which he is reporting. If the name of Feirefiz were mentioned by the narrator, this would amount to Parzival's recognition of his opponent's identity, since he already knows that he has a pagan halfbrother named Feirefiz (cf. 317,3ff. and 328,3ff.). Yet the converse is not also true: Feirefiz knows nothing about what happened to his father after he left Belakane,[35] not even that he died, far less that he married again, had another son, and that this son's name is Parzival. The narrator's technique therefore reflects the objective situation of ignorance in which both combatants find themselves, but it also demonstrates the vital point of the encounter: that it is Parzival who must come to recognise the man he now confronts. The process of recognition may be initiated by Feirefiz's chivalric magnanimity,[36] but its goal is Parzival's new insight into his ramified kinship.

That this technique of withholding the name of Feirefiz is consciously employed by the narrator can be shown by the circumstance in which he judges it fit to refer to him by name again. His name is used for the first time in this encounter in 747,19 (*dô sprach der rîche Feirefîz*), precisely at the point when Parzival, invited by Feirefiz to describe his appearance as a touchstone of his identity, is about to learn the truth from his halfbrother (747,29: *der heiden sprach 'der bin ich'*). The narrator has deferred his use of Feirefiz's name until the point when Parzival himself learns the truth, so that our certainty coincides with his. Now that each brother knows the truth about the other, the narrator uses both their names weightily in one verse (748,8).[37] If *bêde* and *ein ander* also occur in this same

---

34. Before the combat: 734,1; 735,5; 737,13. During the combat: 740,25; 742,27; 743,14; 744,2; 744,5. I fail to see the justification for the observation by Harms, *Kampf*, p. 164, that Parzival's name is mentioned in the combat scene only three times.
35. His ignorance is made clear in 750,22ff.
36. See below, p. 249.
37. This is in marked contrast to the earlier occasions where a named combatant (Parzival) is correlated with his nameless opponent: 735,1–5; 740,23: 25; 742,27: 743,1; 744,2: 8; 744,15: 20; 746,2 (in one line, like its converse example 748,8). The regularity of this pattern suggests emphatically that the goal of the cognitive process in this scene is Parzival's recognition of his opponent's identity.

Parzival's success (Books XIV–XVI)

context, this is no longer to convey a reciprocal engagement in combat, but to underline the ties of acknowledged kinship (748,10: *in zam ouch bêden friuntschaft baz / dan gein ein ander herzen nît*). In contrast with his reticence during the combat itself the narrator is quite ready to use the name of Feirefiz after the recognition scene, from now on it becomes the most common form of narrator's reference to him and is used, in close conjunction with Parzival's name,[38] to underline their close kinship.[39]

The last scene I wish to consider in the light of the narrator's naming technique is no longer a knightly combat, but concerns the reappearance of Cundrie at Arthur's court and their initial failure to recognise her. This failure is motivated separately,[40] but its presentation is also assisted by the narrator at first withholding her name from his audience. He refers to this newcomer anonymously, as if from the point of view of the Round Table, by unrevealing terms such as *juncfrouwe* (778,16), *diu wîse, niht diu tumbe* (779,7), *diu werde, niht diu clâre* (780,2), by sketching her arrival as Arthur's company behold it (778,16: *man sach*) and by putting his listeners in the same position as the spectators in the narrative (778,26: *nu lât si heistieren her*).[41] Even more telling is the astonishing frequency with which the narrator refers to this figure by the bald third person pronoun, fully 37 times in a span of no more than 58 lines.[42] This may seem a short span of narrative on which to base a suggestion that the narrator consciously withholds a character's name, but confirmation may be found in the detail that, as with Parzival's recognition of Feirefiz, Cundrie's name is released by the narrator in this scene only at the point where the Round Table recognise

---

38. Both names are now correlated in the same passage: 748,8; 762,18; 763,12f.; 764,16–19; 778,5; 784,24: 26; 786,13.
39. The stylistic device of indicating close kinship which has been recognised on both sides by correlating two names in the same context goes beyond the case of these two halfbrothers. Because Feirefiz, through his father, is related to the Arthurian world (cf. 753,28: *iwerm werden künne*; 754,10: *unser mâge*; 754,18: *unsern rehten art, / liut von den wir sîn erborn*), the same device can now also be used of Feirefiz and Arthur (766,19; 767,1; 779,27) and also of Feirefiz and Gawan (760,7: 9).
40. See below, pp. 250ff.
41. The use of the adverb *her* puts the listeners as firmly in the place of the Round Table as they were earlier put in Parzival's position by the narrator's use of *her* in 120,24 (see above, p. 63). On this technique in the Cundrie scene see also Peil, *Gebärde*, p. 297.
42. In calculating 58 lines for this narrative span I start with the narrator's reference to Cundrie's arrival on the scene (778,13) and go as far as 780,10, the line before that in which he mentions her name as she reveals herself.

who she is (780,11: *Cundrîe la surziere / wart dô bekennet schiere*). This newcomer's identity is withheld from his listeners by the narrator for as long as it escapes the spectators at Arthur's court.

In the next two encounters (Parzival at Munsalvæsche, Parzival and Trevrizent) the hero immediately recognises and is recognised,[43] so that the technique of naming constitutes no problem. It recurs, however, in the final episode of Loherangrin at Brabant, which represents a special case and is so short that the question of naming may best be considered when we analyse this episode. With that we may now turn to the various encounters in which success or failure in recognition plays a part, and register how this is motivated.

Parzival and Gawan

This encounter begins at the close of Book XIII, while we still accompany Gawan on his travels, with a narratorial wish on Gawan's behalf (678,17: *gelücke müezes walden!*). Corresponding to this pretence of ignorance on the part of the narrator, we see things from Gawan's restricted point of view (678,18: *er sah ein rîter halden / bî dem wazzer Sabîns*): we see what he sees and for us, as for him, this other knight is anonymous. But then the narrator and his listeners draw closer together (cf. his use of *wir* in 678,20) as he takes them into his confidence and draws them away from Gawan's point of view by means of a long anonymous circumlocution for this other knight (678,20ff.) which finishes with the narrator telling us that we have returned *an den rehten stam* (678,30).[44] This knight is Parzival, but this has not been made clear beyond doubt, since the narrator has also put the listeners on the wrong track, just as events have misled Gawan. For some time the narrative has been moving towards Gawan's combat with Gramoflanz,[45] so that both Gawan and the listeners expect a meeting with Gramoflanz, and indeed Gawan has ridden out to await this combat (678,15f.). Moreover, the direction from which this unknown knight approaches Gawan is deceptive, since his halting by the *wazzer Sabîns* (678,19) is

---

43. On this see below, pp. 254ff.
44. Cf. the narrator's reference to Parzival as *des mæres hêrren* (338,7) at the moment when he takes leave of him for a time at the start of Book VII.
45. See Harms, *Kampf*, p. 155. Cf. also Hagen, *Erkennen*, pp. 3f.: 'Verunsichert Wolfram Hörer, die aus der roten Rüstung die Existenz Parzivâls erschließen könnten, durch den bisher noch unbekannten Herkunftshinweis der Ithêr-rüstung ("ûz heidenschaft..." XIV, 679,8)?'

Parzival's success (Books XIV–XVI)

reminiscent of Gramoflanz's abode (his tree grows by this stream, 603,29ff. and his castle is likewise called *Rosche Sabîns*, cf. 610,26 and, much more recently, so that it is still in the listener's ears, 677,3).[46] Not merely does Gawan not know who this knight is, he also has every reason to think that it is Gramoflanz himself. The listeners are invited to share this ignorance, but are also given a suggestion that this obvious assumption is incorrect.[47]

With the start of Book XIV Gawan is taken further on the wrong track. The other knight's damaged shield (679,13) accounts further for the difficulty in identifying him, but Gawan is positively misled when he recognises the wreath worn by the knight as coming from the tree of Gramoflanz (679,14: *er hêt ouch gebrochen / von dem boum, des Gramoflanz / huote, ein sô liehten kranz / daz Gâwânz rîs erkande*). Gawan is correct in this, but goes too far in assuming that this must therefore be Gramoflanz with the symbol of the tree he guards, impatiently waiting for combat and thereby putting the laggard Gawan to shame (679,18), even if the combat is now to be a private one, not in full view of courtly society, as agreed (679,20ff.).[48] These external details have all been given from Gawan's point of view (678,18: *er sah*; 679,17: *erkande*; 679,18: *vorht*), but narratorial information has also been conveyed to us – the praise of the other knight (678,20ff.), knowledge of what faces Gawan and confidence in the other knight's ability (679,3ff.), omniscience about the origins of the unknown knight's equipment (679,8f.) and confirmation that his wreath does in fact come from the tree of Gramoflanz (679,14ff.). Gawan knows nothing of this for certain (even though he has guessed correctly about the origins of the wreath), whilst we are given these facts by the narrator.[49]

If we can see that the other knight is not Gramoflanz, we can also recognise who it must be. He was first introduced simply as *ein rîter*

---

46. See also Hirschberg, *Untersuchungen*, p. 255.
47. Cf. also Schirok, *Aufbau*, pp. 512f.
48. Cf. 610,6ff. The narrator briefly reminds us later (681,1) that this condition was not met. How far Gawan is wrong in this assumption about the audience is made clear when the narrative reverts to the Gramoflanz strand (681,30f. and 683,3ff.).
49. The narrator also tells us something more about this unknown opponent of Gawan's in 679,14ff. (*er hêt ouch gebrochen / von dem boum, des Gramoflanz / huote, ein sô liehten kranz*), for if this knight really were Gramoflanz, as Gawan thinks, the words *er* and *Gramoflanz* would have to be transposed in this passage. As it is, we are shown enough to realise that *er* is distinct from *Gramoflanz*, so that we can perceive Gawan's error at the moment when he makes it.

(678,18), but only in the description of his armour is this narrowed down sufficiently, even if only in a poetic comparison (679,10: *noch rœter denn ein rubbîn*), for us to perceive the *rôte ritter*. This is as visible to Gawan as it has been made accessible to the listeners, but he misses its significance because he has been led astray by other pointers. When the combat begins the listeners are given further confirmation in the narrator's comment that both these knights are mounted on Grail-horses (679,23ff.), for outside Munsalvæsche the only horses which we know to come from that realm are those of Gawan and Parzival.[50]

When these two come together we are given reasons to see why Gawan fails to recognise Parzival, but the latter's failure is accounted for only retrospectively. In 701,2ff. Parzival explains how his mistake came about – for the same reason as Gawan, since he mistook the knight facing him for Gramoflanz. In his case this is because Parzival, deliberately seeking adventure, only that morning broke a wreath from Gramoflanz's tree (701,2f.) as a challenge (701,5f.). Understandably, when he came across Gawan he took him to be Gramoflanz (701,9), accepting the challenge, especially since he had no idea that Gawan was in that same area (701,7). The timing is important here: since Parzival took his wreath that very morning, the immediacy with which Gawan then crosses his horizon convinces him that this must be Gramoflanz in answer to the challenge.[51]

The narrator heightens the dramatic irony of the combat by switching midway (681,2ff.) to a simultaneous action in a parallel narrative strand, thereby showing his listeners what is hidden from Gawan and Parzival.[52] Arthur's messengers now find Gramoflanz by the river Sabins (681,7) and the castle Rosche Sabins (681,11), manifestly not engaged in the combat which we have just temporarily abandoned. In this parallel strand further ironic differences are highlighted. Gramoflanz has surrounded himself with

50. We have already been informed that Gawan's steed is a Grail-horse (597,21: *von Munsalvæsche Gringuljete*) and in Book IX we witnessed how Parzival won his horse from the defeated Grail-knight (445,13ff.; cf. 500,5f.).
51. This motivation by timing is similar to what we saw with Parzival's encounter with the Round Table in the scene of the drops of blood in the snow (see above, pp. 126f.): because Arthur has recently warned his knights to expect military opposition from the realm of the Grail, they are ready to believe that the first knight they encounter is offering them a challenge. Cf. also Hagen, *Erkennen*, p. 10.
52. This is an example of what I have called the irony of narrative interlace in *Irony*, pp. 134ff.

Parzival's success (Books XIV–XVI)

people and society (681,30.; 683,3ff.)[53] because he wants them as spectators at his combat, but this retrospectively undermines Gawan's assumption about his opponent (679,20ff.). He is also depicted in a pointedly idyllic and even luxurious setting,[54] in contrast to the severity of the combat which he is missing; he is not even yet armed, we witness the gradual process of his arming while the real combat is being fought out;[55] his intentions (683,3: *Sus wolte der künec Gramoflanz / mit kampfe rechen sînen kranz*) are undermined by what we know is already happening. There is therefore a reciprocal irony at work in these two simultaneous strands: the actual combat underlines the futility of Gramoflanz's preparations (which is further stressed by the excessive pomp displayed), whilst the lengthy preparations of the real challenger bring out the futility of a combat between two friends who have failed to recognise each other.

Unlike Parzival, Arthur's messengers grasp the situation immediately when they come across Parzival and Gawan in combat (688, 5ff.). They are able to do this because they have just left Gramoflanz (688,4f.) and therefore know that he cannot be Parzival's opponent, as the latter thinks (701,9f.), but also because, as members of Arthur's society, they have recently seen Gawan, know the appearance of his present equipment, and, again unlike Parzival,[56] know that he is in the vicinity. Parzival reacts to their naming of Gawan by casting aside his sword and cursing himself (688,19ff.) and from this Gawan, although still ignorant of his opponent's identity, recognises that they must be acquainted and that their combat rests on a misunderstanding (689,12ff.), so that he now asks his question pointblank (689,11 + 17), to which Parzival replies, giving first their kinship and then his name (689,22ff.).[57]

Parzival's recognition of Gawan takes the form of his realising

---

53. The original condition agreed upon (610,6ff.) stipulated that the combat should be observed by *werde frouwen*. Accordingly, it is the presence of women at Gramoflanz's court that the narrator particularly stresses (681,29; 682,1 + 11 + 22 + 25ff.; 683,9 + 16).
54. Cf. the luxurious mattress (683,13ff.), the presence of a pavilion to provide shade (683,19ff.) and the picture of Gramoflanz almost as an Oriental pasha (686,1; 688,1ff. – cf. the fn. to 686,1 in the Bartsch–Marti edition).
55. 683,16ff.; 687,1f. The process is completed only by 687,21.
56. Cf. Parzival's later confession, 701,7.
57. Gawan's path to recognition can be traced in the use of pronouns: *ir* when he first asks his question (689,11: *'ôwî hêrre, wer sît ir?'*), *du* in Parzival's reply as he tells him his name (689,22: *'neve, ich tuon mich dir bekant'*), and *du* once Gawan has acknowledged this (689,29: *'dîn hant uns bêde überstreit'*).

that once again he has unwittingly fought a kinsman (689,1: *'Sus sint diu alten wâpen mîn | ê dicke und aber worden schîn. | daz ich gein dem werden Gâwân | alhie mîn strîten hân getân!'*). Although he knows this to have been the case only with Ither, the enormity of this near repetition justifies his emotional exaggeration in *ê dicke*, whereas we know that his words are fully justified, and no mere exaggeration, if we recall the equally near misses of Parzival and Gawan at Bearosche and Parzival's encounter with Vergulaht.[58] Parzival's words (689,5: *'ich hân mich selben überstriten'*) take up and vary Trevrizent's words to him about the killing of Ither (475,21: *'du hâst dîn eigen verch erslagn'*) and show that he realises the continuity of this danger of killing a kinsman in his knightly career.

Parzival and Gramoflanz

In 702,12ff. the listeners are shown Parzival's preparations for combat (*Parzivâl was sô bedâht, | al sîn harnasch er besach*) and can draw their own conclusions from this after he has just offered to fight Gramoflanz in place of Gawan (701,18ff.) and has had this offer turned down (701,21ff.).[59] His preparations include obtaining a new shield (702,17ff.), because his old one has been damaged in the recent combat with Gawan (cf. 680,25f.), but all this is done secretly. He starts his preparations only once Arthur's society have gone to bed (702,10f.), he is assisted by *sarjande* whom he does not know and who therefore presumably do not know him (702,21f.).

At 703,1 the narrative now switches to Gramoflanz, to his regret that yesterday someone else had fought instead of himself and that he had turned up too late to prevent this (703,6f.). This explains why he should be astir so early today, equipped and ready by daybreak (703,10: *reht indes dô ez tagte | was sîn ors gewâpent und sîn lîp*). Eager because of yesterday's disappointment, he rides out alone (703,17), impatiently awaiting Gawan's arrival (703,18: *den künec daz müete harte, | daz der werde Gâwân | niht schiere kom ûf den plân*). The scene is now set for another combat under false pretences, only this time one of the contestants, Parzival, is aware of the facts and in control of the situation, while we share complete knowledge with him.[60]

The narrative now reverts to Parzival in 703,21: he too is ready,

---

58. See above, pp. 140 and 146f.
59. Hagen, *Erkennen*, p. 6.
60. This is the first time that we can say of Parzival what could repeatedly be said of Gawan, namely that his knowledge of the facts gives him mastery of the

leaves the camp secretly (703,21f.) and, like his opponent, alone (703,26). He soon catches sight of Gramoflanz (703,29) and they begin their combat without exchanging a word (703,30ff.). Parzival has every reason for speed (he wishes to fight before Gawan and the Round Table arrive), whilst Gramoflanz's disappointment yesterday and impatience today account for his haste. At any rate, the combat is begun immediately and without a verbal exchange, so that Gramoflanz has no means of recognising Parzival by his voice and hearing that this is not Gawan. This failure in recognition is motivated by further considerations. We have already been told that Parzival has acquired a new shield for this combat (702,17: ... *unt ein niwen schilt gewinnen*) – since, unlike Gawan, he does not travel around with a retinue and a baggage-train of spare equipment this new shield is unlikely to bear the heraldic markings characteristic of Parzival. Furthermore, the narrator has already carefully made it clear to us that Gramoflanz has never seen Parzival in full knightly panoply, complete with headdress (cf. 693,3: *er het an den stunden / sînen helm ab gebunden, / dâ in der werde künec sach*),[61] so that Gramoflanz lacks this further means of identifying his opponent. Lastly, Gramoflanz's earlier express refusal of this combat to Parzival (693,7ff. + 13ff.), coupled with his own impatience, makes him psychologically unready to entertain any possibility that this might *not* be Gawan. He wants this knight to be Gawan, and therefore he must be.

Nonetheless, as Harms has pointed out,[62] there is a limit set to Wolfram's gift for motivation in this scene, since the fact of Parzival's red armour must have been strikingly obvious. It is significant that in the episode of Parzival arming himself, where the situation could have called for it, his red armour is not specifically mentioned (702,12ff.). From the fact that the narrator keeps silent on this detail we might draw the tentative conclusion that it is not visible to Gramoflanz, who overlooks it in his impatience for combat,[63] just as conversely, when a combatant is unaware of

situation. Although the nearly disastrous misunderstanding with Feirefiz still awaits him, Parzival now begins to take over Gawan's previous rôle in this respect (see also above, pp. 172f.).

61. Cf. Harms, *Kampf*, p. 162.
62. *Ibid.*, p. 162, fn. 134. Cf. also Hagen, *Erkennen*, p. 7, who interprets *man giht* (704,2) as a token of the narrator's embarrassment in escaping from his difficulties by an appeal to a source.
63. Harms, *Kampf*, p. 162, follows W. J. Schröder, *PBB* 74 (1952), 187, at this point.

another's identity, this is reflected in the narrator's withholding of the name in question until recognition is achieved. This remains unsatisfactory, however, since although these two combatants can be referred to anonymously in their encounter, the narrator is also ready to refer to Parzival by name, even though Gramoflanz nowhere learns who his actual opponent is.[64] It looks as if in this scene, although its motivation is less complex than the encounter between Parzival and Gawan (where *each* participant fails to recognise the other and actually takes him for someone else), the narrator has not fully mastered his difficulties.

Parzival and Feirefiz

We saw above that the narrator's anonymous references to Parzival's opponent in the encounter at the start of Book XV put his listeners in the same position as Parzival, forcing on them ignorance as to who this final opponent might be. At the same time, the narrator also conducts them to a vantage-point of superior knowledge by progressively hinting at the truth, first with ambiguous references, then with allusions which must convey the truth to them. I shall take these hints in the order in which they are given.

One of the narrator's circumlocutions for the two combatants (737,20: *die mit kiusche lember wâren / und lewen an der vrechheit*) is not so completely anonymous as it looks. Although something very similar has recently been said of Parzival (734,25: *dâ diu vrävel bî der kiusche lac*), this is not really helpful since we already know that Parzival is involved in this encounter, but rather need enlightenment about his opponent. This is indeed provided, but only if we can make the mental leap back to the point where Gahmuret was first introduced into the narrative (5,22: *der kiusche und der vreche / Gahmuret der wîgant*). If we make this leap, it will be to establish that Gahmuret has passed on these two qualities to his son Parzival, as we have just been reminded, but also to suspect that he may well have passed them on to his other son and that these half-brothers have come face to face.[65]

Ambiguity of another kind informs the narrator's regret that these two knights should have met in combat (737,22ff.), for although this regret is certainly reconcilable with a tragic encounter

---

64. This is said not just of Gramoflanz, but of the whole of his retinue (709,5ff., especially 11), although two of his pages later learn the truth (717,21ff.).
65. Cf. Etzler, *Komposition*, p. 83.

Parzival's success (Books XIV–XVI)

between two close kinsmen, we know nothing of this as yet and are led by the narrator's concern on behalf of Parzival (737,25: *ich sorge des den ich hân brâht*) to concentrate on this narrower possibility and only gradually to recognise that the narrator's lament concerns not just Parzival, but both the sons of Gahmuret. The phrasing of 738,6ff. (especially v. 9: *ieweder des andern herze truoc*) could likewise apply to two kinsmen (like *heinlîch* in the following line), but also to two people who love each other, although this must prompt the question how these two strangers (cf. 738,10: *vremde*) could love each other.

A little later another image is employed to convey a subtle hint (738,19: *den lewen sîn muoter tôt gebirt: / von sîns vater galme er lebendic wirt. / dise zwêne wârn ûz krache erborn, / von maneger tjost ûz prîse erkorn*). The genealogical remark in v. 21 sounds like a metaphor, suggesting that both combatants were 'born' of the clash of spears in jousting, as has recently been said of Parzival and Gawan (680,2: *ûz der tjoste geslehte / wârn si bêde samt erborn*). But this remark is introduced with a truth from the *Physiologus* tradition: the lion-cub is still-born by its mother, but is brought to life by the father's roar (*galm*).[66] What is important about this truth is the function of the father (his roar brings the cub to life, his *galm* is then taken up by *krach* in the genealogical remark), so that the implication is that these two combatants may be linked by birth through their father. But no explicit statement has yet been made.

The listeners are given a further clue in the battle-cries used by Parzival's pagan opponent (739,24: *des krîe was Thasmê: / und swenn er schrîte Thabronit, / sô trat er fürbaz einen trit*). The cry *Thabronit* is conveyed to us and is of course audible to Parzival, so that both parties can relate it to Cundrie's earlier information about this capital city of the realm of Feirefiz's mistress (316,30ff.). But this is not specific enough to tell Parzival that this must be Feirefiz before him, whilst, in addition to other pointers, it conveys further confirmation to the listeners. This is true of the other cry *Thasmê*, for this too links up with Feirefiz's mistress Secundille (cf. 629,20: *in Secundillen lande / stêt ein stat heizet Thasmê*), but this link exists only for the listeners to whom the narrator had earlier passed this detail, not for Parzival. This is confirmed by 740,9ff. (*gein prîse truoger willen / durch die künegîn Secundillen, / diu daz lant ze Tribalibôt / im gap*), where the narrator tells his listeners that the

---

66. On this cf. the note on 738,9 in Martin's *Kommentar*, p. 488.

The Art of Recognition in Wolfram's *Parzival*

pagan knight serves queen Secundille. The listeners know already from 519,2ff. that Feirefiz serves this queen and rules over her land, but this information has come to them from the narrator, bypassing Parzival who is not even involved in the action at this point in Book X. Parzival had admittedly learned from Cundrie (316,30ff.) that his halfbrother Feirefiz served a pagan queen in Thabronit, but her name had not been released to him on that occasion, and in fact he learns of it only from Feirefiz himself at a later stage (768,10ff. and 771,18). The extra information conveyed to the listeners, provided that they can recall it from earlier points in the work, thus allows them to take up hints which are not available to Parzival.[67]

The earlier hints are confirmed, without the narrator having to mention any name, when he admits that both these knights are the sons of the same man (740,2: *ich muoz ir strît mit triwen klagen, / sît ein verch und ein bluot / solch ungenâde ein ander tuot. / si wârn doch bêde eins mannes kint*). We know enough to see that this unnamed knight can only be Feirefiz, as also when the narrator again confirms, through a general observation, that these two are brothers (740,28: *si wârn doch bêde niht wan ein. / mîn bruodr und ich daz ist ein lîp*). Finally, the narrator apparently goes against his own technique of withholding from Parzival any clue to his opponent's identity until the moment of recognition in making use of a genealogical circumlocution in 742,14 (*got ner dâ Gahmuretes kint*).[68] The full force of this wish (the circumlocution is true of *both* contestants, as is confirmed by the narrator in the following two lines) can only be appreciated by the listeners, who by now must realise the facts. If either combatant were to 'overhear' the narrator passing this comment on their fight, each would see less in it than is meant, for each would automatically take it as referring only to himself. We see more than they can grasp and our superior knowledge is then expressly confirmed by the narrator's observation that these two knights would have agreed with him if they had only recognised the truth of their position (742,18: *sus begunden siz ouch meinen, / wærn se ein ander baz bekant: / sine satzten niht sô hôhiu pfant*).

---

67. Another clue to the identity of Parzival's opponent is provided by the narrator's close conjunction of *Thabronit* (739,25) with *Tribalibôt* (740,11). Although there is nothing to link these two names at this point, this has already been done for the retentive listener by the narrator in 374,28f. (*pfelle von Tabronite / ûzem lande ze Trîbalibôt*).
68. On the ambiguity of this phrase see Green, *Homicide*, pp. 32f.

Parzival's success (Books XIV–XVI)

In the dialogue between these knights which replaces their combat, once this has been broken off, each contestant necessarily uses anonymous references like the narrator. Feirefiz addresses Parzival as *werlîcher man* (744,29), *werlîcher helt* (745,3) or simply *helt* (745,14 + 18). This anonymity is forced on Feirefiz by his ignorance of his opponent's identity, but the pause in their combat and the opportunity for dialogue which this creates now allow him to ask Parzival his name (745,2f. + 18f.). This still brings difficulties and risks, however. Parzival equates giving his name with an acknowledgment of defeat and refuses (745,21ff.), but his testiness is apparently overcome when Feirefiz magnanimously gives his name first, accepting any possible *laster* for himself (745,25ff.). But his answer (745,28: *'ich pin Feirefîz Anschevîn'*) creates a new danger when he identifies himself by the name given him by his mother (57,21f.) and communicated to Parzival by Cundrie (317,4).[69] Parzival is given the means of recognising his brother, but is slow to grasp the opportunity, since his touchiness[70] is raised to suspiciousness when Feirefiz adds to his name a description of his status (745,29: *'sô rîche wol daz mîner hant / mit zinse dienet manec lant'*). Parzival sees in this a claim threatening his own regal status and lands (746,8ff.) and he therefore concentrates on the pagan's title *Anschevîn* instead of on the name Feirefiz, which for the moment he ignores in his angry rebuttal, contesting it (746,3: *'wâ von sît ir ein Anschevîn?'*) and claiming this title for himself alone (746,11f.).

Only after this does Parzival belatedly remember what Cundrie had told him (328,3ff.) and recall the existence of a halfbrother (746,13ff.). He must therefore recall Cundrie's use of *Feirefîz Anschevîn* (317,4), but on this earlier occasion he had been told more about this brother by Cundrie and Ekuba, namely his distinctive external appearance (317,9f.; 328,15ff.), so that he now proposes putting things to the test (746,22ff.) by inviting Feirefiz to remove his helmet, promising not to attack him. This is now the turn for Feirefiz to react touchily (747,1ff.): since his sword is intact he has little to fear from Parzival and needs no promise from him, but this

69. At the moment when Cundrie used the title *Anschevîn* of Feirefiz, other things preoccupy Parzival and the shattering blow of disgrace before the Round Table stops him from reacting to the use of this title.
70. Psychologically this is understandable because of the extreme difficulty of Parzival's combat with Feirefiz, a point which is repeatedly stressed by the narrator to underline its function as the hero's climactic knightly encounter (734,17ff.; 739,23; 740,13 + 25; 741,1; 742,5ff. + 27; 743,9ff.).

last obstacle is overcome when Feirefiz generously throws away his sword (747,12ff.).

The narrator has therefore allowed his listeners first to suspect, then to learn the truth about Feirefiz in instalments which keep ahead of Parzival's enlightenment, but he defers his use of Feirefiz's name until the point when Parzival himself learns the truth. His technique is therefore quite different from what is forced on modern readers when they are confronted, at the start of Book XV, with the title given to it in the Bartsch–Marti edition: 'Parzival und Feirefiz'.[71].

Cundrie at the Round Table

We have seen that the anonymous references to Cundrie at her second appearance at Arthur's court are the narrator's way of indicating that she is not immediately recognised. This failure he in turn motivates by having the Grail-messenger wear a long capacious cloak (778,19: *kappe*), whose hood envelops her head and features, showing the bystanders nothing (778,27: *ir gebende was hôh unde blanc: / mit manegem dicken umbevanc / was ir antlütze verdecket / und niht ze sehen enblecket*).[72] Moreover, Cundrie now rides a horse of good quality (779,3f.), whereas before it was a run-down mule (312,6ff.). Once we establish a connection between these two scenes, the symbolism of these mounts becomes clear (the *mûl* shows her lack of respect for one she came to disgrace, the *runzît* her wish to honour the future Grail-king), but before this connection is perceived the difference between her mounts makes it difficult to realise that Cundrie has once again entered the action. As on other occasions, however, the listeners occupy a privileged position in contrast to the spectators at the Round Table, they can be given clues on which to work by the omniscient narrator, allowing them to suspect the truth in advance.

The first type of clue, coming long before Cundrie's arrival, suggests precisely the connection between these two scenes which allow us to suspect that here again Cundrie is to play a part. In 761,5ff. the narrator establishes such a link over a point of detail by reminding us that on this present occasion the pagan Feirefiz is

---

71. *Ed. cit.*, volume III, p. 108.
72. Cundrie was also described as wearing a *kappe* at her first appearance before the Round Table (313,7f.), but on that occasion no hint was given that her features were concealed, and indeed the narrator's description of their ugliness (313,1ff. + 21ff.) implies that they were visible to the bystanders, as is suggested by Cundrie's own words to Parzival (315,24f.).

Parzival's success (Books XIV–XVI)

present whose praise had been voiced *in absentia* at the Plimizœl by Ekuba.[73] Somewhat later the narrator describes how Arthur has the Round Table prepared for festivities, but then reminds us of an earlier occasion when he had it got ready in the open, too (775,6: *ir habet wol gehœret ê, / wie ûf dem Plimizœles plân / einer tavelrunder wart getân: / nâch der disiu wart gesniten*).[74] This double correspondence between the two scenes on trivial details conceals a correspondence on an important point of the narrative, for what is to come will resume the action of the earlier scene: Cundrie is about to come before the Round Table again, but under vastly different auspices. That such innocuous references to the Plimizœl are meant as an indirect allusion to, and anticipation of Cundrie is made clear in retrospect, once we know that Cundrie has rejoined the action, for now the narrator can afford to make an explicit connection between both scenes (780,15: *si fuorte och noch den selben lîp, / den sô manc man unde wîp / sach zuo dem Plimizœle komn*). Even so, there is no necessary reason to assume that Parzival's descent, begun in all public clarity when Cundrie first came to the Round Table, should change into an ascent under the same auspices when she appears there a second time, however satisfying such symmetry may be in retrospect. This is after all Wolfram's innovation, with no precedent in other romances, so that the listeners can receive no assistance from recalling a similar structure in other works.[75]

---

73. Cf. 328,1ff. The link between these two scenes is further strengthened by the fact that in each of them *Plimizœl* rhymes with *Jofreit fiz Ydœl* (761,7f. and 311,5f.). Within the rhyming possibilities exploited in this work, this may be an obvious rhyme, but nonetheless the recurrence of the same person in connection with the same locality in both scenes acts as another pointer.

   The narrator gives an innocuous forecast of the future in 774,28ff. (*manges freude aldâ geschach / smorgens, ob ich sô sprechen mac, / do erschein der süeze mære tac*). The phrasing is conventional (*der süeze mære tac*) and takes the form of an apologetic understatement (*ob ich sô sprechen mac* and *manges*), but this conceals the fact that what is hinted at here is a radical change in Parzival's fortunes, his call to the Grail. The narrator thus 'warns' his listeners, but in such a way that, rather like Parzival and the events he confronts, they can hardly be expected to grasp what is at stake.

74. Cf. 309,18ff. This clue, strengthened by that in 761,5ff., gives further point to the faint hint in 774,28ff., warns the perceptive listener that a change in Parzival's fortunes is about to come and takes up the promise made at the beginning of Book XV (734,1ff.). Each of these hints may be slight in itself, but in conjunction one confirms another.

75. Emmel, *Formprobleme*, pp. 144f., has suggested that Wolfram modelled his conclusion on that of Chrétien's *Yvain*, combined with that of Hartmann's *Erec*. From her point of view she correctly observes that Wolfram remains true to the traditional Arthurian romance, but I should rather stress that he relies on

The remaining clues are given in the description of Cundrie's appearance at Arthur's court. In 778,22f. reference is made to the heraldic device of doves, peculiar to the Grail-kingdom, suggesting that this must be a messenger from that realm. Yet we are not told whether the Round Table sees or recognises this detail (*wunder* in v. 25 suggests wondering, not realisation), the floating syntax of these two lines leaves it unclear which part of her clothing has the doves depicted on it (they may have been concealed by her cloak), and the recurrence of the doves when the Round Table eventually recognise Cundrie (780,11ff.) suggests that this heraldic device becomes visible only now. In any case, even if it had been visible earlier, would it have meant anything to Arthur's knights? This detail was not mentioned when Cundrie first came to the Round Table and Parzival later talks of it as proof of Cundrie's qualifications, saying that he saw this device at Munsalvæsche (783,18ff.). If it is a token of recognition to Parzival, we are not told that it is to the Round Table.

Other clues, like those when Parzival comes across Sigune and Jeschute for the second time,[76] take the form of detailed links between the two Cundrie scenes which are made visible to the perceptive listener by the narrator,[77] but bypass the members of the Round Table who are therefore prevented from perceiving the structural parallel they build up and the reappearance of Cundrie they imply. When the narrator refers to Cundrie as *diu wîse, niht diu tumbe* (779,7), a detail not visible to the Round Table, this takes up an earlier reference in the first scene, likewise a narrator's comment (313,1: *Diu maget witze rîche*). The comment on her courtly breeding (779,22: *mit zuht, diu an ir was*) is a similar echo (312,22: *si was der witze kurtoys*), both points again being narrator's comments. When it is reported that she obtains Parzival's forgiveness without a kiss (779,25: *sô daz er zorn gein ir verlür / und âne kus ûf si verkür*), it is uncertain whether the words *âne kus* represent a narrator's addition, his comment on the speech implicit in *verkür*. In any case, it refers back humorously to what the narrator had said of Cundrie on the first occasion (313,30: *niht nâch friundes minne ger*), but if

---

      his audience's inability to grasp that the conclusion of *Parzival* is a conflation of these two earlier models. Neither *Yvain* nor *Erec* shows them in advance what is at stake in this second Cundrie scene.

76. See above, pp. 113ff. and 118ff.
77. On this technique of implicit links between the two Cundrie scenes see Harroff, *Wolfram*, p. 76.

Parzival's success (Books XIV–XVI)

humour is present it is more likely to be true of the narrator than of Cundrie on this solemn occasion. When the narrator describes the messenger as *diu werde, niht diu clâre* (780,2), this takes up Cundrie's own earlier assessment (315,24: *'ich dunke iuch ungehiure, / und bin gehiurer doch dann ir'*). These words, spoken to Parzival in Arthur's company, were therefore accessible to the Round Table, but this is not so of the narrator's description in 780,2, so that the link between these two scenes which is established for the audience does not exist for the spectators within the narrative.[78]

In 779,29 (*Parzivâl truoc ûf si haz*) it is uncertain whether this statement represents the judgment of Arthur's company as they witness this encounter or whether it is a narrator's comment from his superior position, knowing what they do not yet realise. The former possibility is excluded if we take 780,11f. (*Cundrîe la surziere / wart dô bekennet schiere*) as the point when Cundrie is at last recognised by the Round Table, as is suggested by the use of *wart* and *schiere*, by the fact that only now does the narrator refer to her by name, and by the detail that she has just cast aside the hood which hitherto concealed her features (780,7: *si want mit ir hende / wider ab ir houbtgebende*). Yet this has been denied in the Bartsch–Marti edition[79] with the argument that recognition must have come before this, accompanying the act of forgiveness. This ignores, however, the telling evidence of 780,11f. and forces us to ask whether the narrator would have abandoned his technique of synchronising his naming of a character with the moment of recognition only at this point. Cundrie's request for forgiveness can indeed be read in another way in the light of the topos of an exotic stranger arriving at court, requesting and being granted a boon.[80] If she does not ask this of king Arthur, but only requests him to help her in her request to Parzival (779,15f.), this makes good sense in

---

78. One further hint is available to the Round Table as well as the listeners. In 779,11 the narrator informs us that Cundrie addressed the assembled company in Book XV in French (*en franzoys was ir sprâche*). Although the narrator had said in the earlier scene, too, that she spoke French (312,20f.), this fact was also made available to the Round Table when she addressed Arthur in French (314,20). For the listeners this detail builds on all the other hints which have been conveyed to them, but for the Round Table this is the only link between the two scenes which has been revealed to them. For them it remains a hint as inconclusive in itself and insufficiently particularised as when Parzival comes across Sigune nursing the corpse of Schionatulander (cf. above, p. 114, fn. 89).
79. Cf. the fn. to 780,12.
80. Cf. Désilles–Busch, *Doner*, pp. 19ff.

this context, for Cundrie is about to announce Parzival's call to the Grail, recognises that he is to be her future lord[81] and is therefore anxious to secure forgiveness and favour in advance. Parzival, not Arthur, is the ruler to whom she directs her request, so that even at his own court Arthur is being edged from the focus of attention.

Once Cundrie reveals herself the narrator can mention her name and describe her directly (780,18ff.). At this point he says expressly that she was still as she was on the earlier occasion (cf. 780,15: *noch den selben*; 19: *dennoch*) and reveals openly that the listeners, like the Round Table, know her already (780,18: *ir antlütze ir habt vernomn*). Because the situation is now quite different after her recognition, a final detail about her appearance (780,24: *huot*, cf. 313,10) can explicitly refer to the earlier occasion by mentioning the Plimizœl (780,25), where earlier hints had to be implicit.

The listeners are therefore given hints by the narrator and allowed to suspect the newcomer's identity before it is clear to the Round Table. Where Parzival's moment of recognition falls is left uncertain, but the fact that this newcomer seeks *his* forgiveness must convey more to him than to anyone else, just as the heraldic device of the doves (whether visible before the act of recognition or not) means something to him, because only he has been at Munsalvæsche. In this encounter Parzival can recognise the truth earlier than the Round Table.[82]

Parzival at Munsalvæsche

Under this heading I include two different scenes, one when Parzival accomplishes the healing of Anfortas and the other when, in the presence of Feirefiz, the Grail is the centrepiece of a festive reception. Both scenes are connected, by contrast, with Parzival's first visit to Munsalvæsche and throw light on it retrospectively.

In describing briefly the setting at Munsalvæsche for the first of these scenes the narrator recalls what he told us in greater detail in Book V. One detail (790,7: *sîn fiwer was lign alôê*) is explicitly related to 230,11 (*holz hiez lign alôê*) by a narratorial comment (790,8: *daz hân ich iu gesaget ê*), whilst a similar reminder (794,27: *ir habt wol ê vernomen*) accompanies 794,28f.[83] Since this is Parzival's second

---

81. Cf. 784,15: '*mîn hêrre*'.
82. As with Parzival's combat with Gramoflanz (see above, p. 244, fn. 60) less weight falls on the hero's ignorance in the final stages of the narrative.
83. Although the lines 794,28f. specify two separate details from the earlier scene (*der lente, unt daz er selten saz, / unt wie sîn bette gehêret was*), only the second of

Parzival's success (Books XIV–XVI)

visit, Anfortas recognises him immediately and recalls their earlier encounter (795,4: *'ir schiet nu jungest von mir sô, / pflegt ir helflîcher triuwe, / man siht iuch drumbe in riuwe'*), whilst Parzival, called to the Grail and guided there by Cundrie, similarly has no doubts about Anfortas.[84] Recognition of identity therefore constitutes no problem in this encounter, but instead Parzival faces again the need to recognise how he should behave. Anfortas attempts with Parzival what he has just tried unsuccessfully with his followers:[85] by preventing him from seeing the Grail, it would be easily possible to allow him to die and be freed from torment (795,9ff.); this is how Anfortas conceives the *helfe* he hopes for from Parzival (795,16).[86] In other words, on the brink of his final success Parzival is confronted by a last temptation, the risk of failing to recognise the nature of the *helfe* he is now to bring Anfortas (by allowing him to die instead of asking the redeeming question), just as he had earlier misconceived this *helfe* in taking it superficially as knightly assistance in battle.[87] Parzival's return to Munsalvæsche is therefore no unproblematic folktale gift out of the blue, it still involves him in a testing, in the risk of going as disastrously wrong as on the first occasion.[88]

The narrator takes equal care to connect the second Munsalvæsche scene in Book XVI with Parzival's first visit: he not

these had been explicitly mentioned while Parzival was at Munsalvæsche (230,15ff.), but has been described in greater detail just recently (790,18ff.). The first detail, however, refers back to the same occasion, for it was mentioned after the event by Sigune (251,16: *'Anfortas sîn bruoder lent'*) and then much later by Trevrizent (491,3: *'er lent, âne sitzen'*). Despite the wider distribution of these passages the link constructed is still between Parzival's first and second visits at Munsalvæsche.

84. Anfortas therefore knows Parzival by name (795,11: *'sît ir genant Parzivâl'*), whilst Parzival recognises his kinship with him (795,29: *œheim*).
85. See above, p. 233.
86. In the Bartsch–Marti edition (fn. to 795,13) it is suggested that Anfortas actually wants to prompt Parzival to ask the question, but it is unclear how his tactics could have brought this about. Instead, I take his reference to *warnen* (795,15) to imply the following chain of thought: 'I cannot give you any direct information and I already know, to my cost, that you pay no heed to indirect hints. I must therefore fall back on a solution of despair: help me by letting me die. Here at least I can speak openly.'
87. See above, p. 96.
88. On the actual formulation of Parzival's question to Anfortas (795,29) and its difference from what he had been told by Trevrizent (484,27) see Johnson, *Beauty*, pp. 288f. and Harroff, *Wolfram*, p. 78. In this detail too, Wolfram avoids the more mechanical motivation typical of the folktale. On Parzival's knowledge of how to act on this second occasion see Hirschberg, *Untersuchungen*, p. 161.

merely dwells on details mentioned on the earlier occasion, but reminds us that we have heard all this before. For example, when the Grail is carried in procession in the concluding Book we are reminded how different the auspices are from Book V (807,22: *dô wart der grâl durch helfe ger / für getragen an der selben zît: / Parzivâl si liez in sorgen sît. / mit freude er wirt nu für getragen: / ir sorge ist under gar geslagen*).[89] The effect of the links between these two scenes is to invite us to compare them more closely, specifically to regard Parzival's disastrous behaviour in Book V in the light of Feirefiz's reaction to Munsalvæsche in Book XVI. Neither halfbrother has eyes for the Grail itself (Parzival on the earlier occasion because of a mistaken order of priorities,[90] Feirefiz more drastically because his paganism makes him blind to such a liturgical object)[91] and as a result each wonders only about externals (Parzival about the luxury of the ceremonial meal, Feirefiz about the way in which the vessels magically fill themselves).[92] The significance of this parallel operates retrospectively against the earlier Parzival, it shows up the lamentable state of his insight in Book V, revealing him to have been as blind as a pagan.[93] As the Grail is carried from the hall in procession, it is made clear that Feirefiz has eyes only for Repanse de schoy and that she is all he can see (815,26: *Feirefîz Anschevîn / sach si von im kêren: / daz begunde im trûren mêren. / sîns herzen slôz truoc dan den grâl*), so that he is

89. The conjunction of *sît* with *nu* in this passage relates this scene at Munsalvæsche with that in Book V. Similar links are provided in 808,14ff. (*zeiner zît* refers back to 229,28), 808,23ff. (*ê* and *nu*), and 809,15ff. (where the present narrative task is related to the earlier by *ê*). A more implicit link is provided by the stress on ceremonial *zuht* on both occasions. This was made quite clear in Book V (see above, p. 107, fn. 66), but the allusions in the present scene are just as telling (806,11; 807,14; 808,20; 809,25 (with a negative formulation in v. 19); 815,22).
90. See above, pp. 109f.
91. Cf. 810,9ff.; 813,10ff.; especially 813,15ff. and 24ff. This motivation lies behind the fact that Feirefiz is so frequently referred to as a *heiden* in the context of Munsalvæsche, especially in connection with the Grail itself (793,15; 809,1; 810,3 + 10; 813,4 + 17; 814,3; 818,15. Only after his baptism (cf. 819,9) is he able to see the Grail, 818,20ff.
92. 239,8f. and 810,3ff. On the parallel between Feirefiz and the early Parzival see Hirschberg, *Untersuchungen*, pp. 164f.
93. A further point might be the way in which Feirefiz, rather like a spoilt child, gets angry with his pagan god as soon as he is disappointed in his expectations (810,27f.; 812,28ff.). From a Christian point of view such a judgment on pagan behaviour in religious matters may be fully justified, but the parallel between Feirefiz and Parzival would extend this judgment to Parzival, above all in his angry readiness to accuse God when *he* was disappointed.

Parzival's success (Books XIV–XVI)

blind to the Grail both literally and metaphorically.[94] If Parzival behaved earlier in a similar way, with eyes only for the luxury of the ceremony and not for the Grail or Anfortas, the Feirefiz scene brings it home to us how disturbingly like a pagan he had behaved at his first visit.

Parzival and Trevrizent

Here too the problem is not recognition of identity (for Parzival has deliberately sought out the hermit's cell again, 797,16ff., and Trevrizent recognises him immediately as the new Grail-king), but rather recognition of the circumstances under which Parzival has attained Grail-kingship, involving a recantation by the hermit of what he had said in Book IX. The problem is confined to the lines 798,1–30.[95]

Trevrizent starts (798,2–5) by expressing amazement that Parzival has *ab got erzürnet* the granting of his wish, the acquisition of the Grail. Tax argues convincingly that the verb is connected with *zorn*, meaning not 'anger', but rather 'enmity',[96] so that *ab got erzürnen* means 'to obtain something from God, while in a state of *unminne* or *haz* towards God'.[97] The hermit's choice of verb designates what is for him the characteristic situation of Parzival, this is the state in which he first met him, it sums up the longest and crucial period of Parzival's travels (from the close of Book VI to Book IX) and, in any case, he knows nothing of Parzival's frame of mind and attitude to God after he left him in Book IX (unlike the listeners, who have recently been reassured on this by the narrator, 741,26ff.).

In 798,6–10 the hermit accuses himself of having earlier lied to

---

94. I suggested above (p. 109, fn. 71) the possibility that Parzival's mistaken order of priorities might be seen in the abandonment in his case (236,12ff.) of the 'liturgical syntax' used by the narrator (235,25f.). The same contrast is to be found in this later scene, for when Feirefiz's subjective reaction is described (815,29) the syntax reflects his order of priorities (a human being, the grammatical subject, carries the Grail), as opposed to the narrator's formulation in 809,10ff. (*sich liez der grâl, ist mir gesagt, / die selben tragen eine, / und anders enkeine*).
95. As with the discussion of Book IX above (pp. 185ff.), I owe much to the stimulus of Tax, *Trevrizent*, pp. 119ff., especially pp. 128ff., even where I disagree with him.
96. Tax lists, p. 128, a number of passages in *Parzival* where *zorn* is closely connected, even identical with *haz* or *unminne*.
97. This is after all the state in which Parzival had first presented himself to Trevrizent (461,9: '*ouch trage ich hazzes vil gein gote*').

Parzival, intending to head him off from a fruitless quest for the Grail, and begs forgiveness. Tax is right in arguing that the poet's narrative method is cumulative, adding to earlier information and finally giving a complete, true picture,[98] but if so Trevrizent's words at this point, when he appears in the work for the last time, must embody the truth, we must accept them when he says that he *louc* about the Grail and that this lie served a definite purpose (*durch ableitens list | vome grâl*). To determine the nature of this lie Tax tackles the problem quite literally, even trusting himself on the basis of verbal echoes to pinpoint the section in Trevrizent's long dialogue with Parzival in which he told this lie (he therefore relates 798,6 to 468,22 and 471,29 and suggests that the lie must fall somewhere between these two points in Book IX).[99] I doubt whether Wolfram's technique is as mechanically literal as his interpreter's and think that we must look elsewhere for the significance of Trevrizent's lie.[100]

An alternative answer can be found in Tax's own essay, but only if we recall the different semantic scope of MHG *liegen* and its modern counterpart *lügen*. Both can mean 'to tell a deliberate falsehood, with the intention of deceiving', but MHG *liegen* can also mean 'to say something which, without one's realising it, does

---

98. Tax, *Trevrizent*, p. 129, who bases himself here on Johnson, *MLR* 64 (1969), 77.
99. Tax, *Trevrizent*, p. 129.
100. In the first place, 471,29 is by no means the conclusion of what Trevrizent has to say about the Grail, much more is still to come, so that this line serves rather as a signpost part of the way through his disquisition. Secondly, it is equally dubious whether 468,22 can be seen as a valid starting-point for our search, since Tax himself has to admit that Trevrizent's *ableiten vome grâle* begins before this, already in 468,10ff. (*Trevrizent*, p. 129). Thirdly, Tax pinpoints the actual lie at 471,26ff. (p. 130), arguing that Trevrizent lies when he says, not just that one must be called to the Grail by God (27), but also that this must take the form of an angelic message (28). In other words, Trevrizent deliberately exaggerates the metaphysical conditions so as to bring it home to Parzival that he has no hope of gaining the Grail. Tax sees the justification for this in Parzival 'negating' this angelic motif in 786,5ff., where he repeats Trevrizent's words, but with no mention of an angel (p. 130, fn. 20). But failure to mention something need not amount to its rejection. If it did, we should also have to read 798,25f. as an express rejection by Trevrizent of another condition in his earlier statement, 468,12ff., for in the later passage Trevrizent makes no mention of the necessity of a divine call (468,13) if one is to find the Grail. Since this divine call is the *sine qua non* of the narrative (cf. Tax, p. 130) and since Trevrizent does not mention it on his last appearance, we cannot read failure to mention a detail as a rejection of it, either with the motif of the divine call or with the motif of an angelic message.

not correspond to the truth'.[101] In the light of this second possibility, can we say that Trevrizent, without consciously intending to deceive, spoke an untruth about the Grail in Book IX? An answer lies in the fact that he twice stresses the necessity for a divine call (468,12ff. and 470,21ff.) and that both passages fall in that part of the dialogue where he still thinks he faces Lähelin.[102] What is here said of 'Lähelin' may therefore not be true in the case of Parzival, whilst Trevrizent's ignorance of the situation at this point has no bearing on his later correctly calling his statement, when applied to Parzival, a lie. If the hermit really had been speaking with Lähelin, his remarks about the unattainability of the Grail because of the necessity for a divine call would have been true, because no such call could be expected to reach a hardened sinner like Lähelin, not even a member of the Grail-dynasty, but its enemy.[103] But since Trevrizent was actually speaking with Parzival (and learned this only later), his truth became a lie and he was guilty of trying to head off from Munsalvæsche the knight who could heal Anfortas and succeed him as Grail-king.

It is the confusion between Lähelin and Parzival in the first part of the dialogue in Book IX which removes the apparent contradiction in 798,6f. (*louc* = 'to speak an untruth unwittingly, unintentionally', as against the conscious intention in *durch ableitens list*). The presence of intention in *ableiten* refers to Lähelin, or the knight whom Trevrizent takes to be such, whilst the absence of conscious knowledge in *louc* refers to Trevrizent's ignorance, at the time, that this was Parzival. Trevrizent's lie in Book IX is thus no intentional deception,[104] but an unconscious one, arising from the ignorance which pervades the first part of his dialogue with Parzival.

If we accept the implications of the cumulative narrative method used in *Parzival*, the hermit's statement (798,11–22) that the neutral angels were in fact condemned must be regarded as a definitive truth, as opposed to his earlier suggestion (471,15ff.) that they may after all have been forgiven by God. The question is not why Trevrizent finally admits the truth here, but rather why he con-

---

101. See Appendix B, pp. 337ff. These pages were written before I came across the similar argument of Reither, *Motiv*, pp. 101 and 109.
102. To that extent my interpretation still agrees with that of Tax (p. 129): Trevrizent's 'lie' falls in this crucial part of his dialogue with Parzival.
103. Cf. Tax, pp. 129f.
104. Here I disagree with Tax (p. 131).

cealed it or played it down in Book IX. The answer, as Tax has seen,[105] again lies in how he saw Parzival, taking him to be Lähelin. Even with a hardened sinner like 'Lähelin' Trevrizent is conscious of a pastoral obligation, the need to walk a psychologically difficult tightrope: to head him away from Munsalvæsche, but not to drive him into stubborn despair of salvation. To avoid this latter danger Trevrizent falls back on a white lie, confessing ignorance or the open state of the question about the fate of the neutral angels (whereas in fact he knew that they were lost) in order to prevent 'Lähelin' from identifying himself with them and seeing himself as irretrievably damned. Yet this white lie, told to rescue 'Lähelin', is equally helpful and relevant to Parzival's situation, for Parzival too must be won back from despair. The hermit's conscious lie about the neutral angels is as much applicable to Parzival's situation as his unconscious lie about the unattainability of the Grail was inapplicable to Parzival (but true only of Lähelin). Together, these two points sum up Trevrizent's knowledge and ignorance of the situation at this point in Book IX or, from another point of view, how much Parzival resembles Lähelin and how much he differs from him.[106]

In 798,23–27 Trevrizent again stresses the unheard-of nature of Parzival's success and again refers to his attempt to head his earlier guest away from the Grail.[107] Tax points out that the hermit's words constitute a recantation in which he keeps silent about the nature of his earlier lie.[108] Trevrizent can afford to do this because the facts have overtaken him – his lie concerned the inaccessibility of the Grail to 'Lähelin' (who could expect no divine call), but already in the second part of their dialogue in Book IX he had learned that Parzival had been to Munsalvæsche (so that the possibility of a call existed for him) and now he has just been told that he has been called again, this time successfully (797,19ff.). Quite apart from his embarrassment, the hermit's earlier mistake about his visitor's identity has been rendered irrelevant by what has

105. Tax, p. 132.
106. On this resemblance and also the difference see Green, *Homicide*, pp. 50f. and 57ff.
107. Thus, v. 24 (*ez was ie ungewonheit*) varies v. 2 (*græzer wunder selten ie geschach*), *erstrîten* in v. 26 takes up *erzürnet* in v. 3, whilst the phrase in v. 27 (*gern dâ von genomn*) refers back to *ableitens list* in v. 6.
108. Tax (p. 132).

happened in the meanwhile, by the fact that the Grail has actually been *erstriten*.[109]

The hermit concludes his speech (798,28–30) by stressing the vital importance of humility,[110] suggesting that, without it, what God has given may be taken away again. These lines imply that, in addition to his *erstrîten* of the Grail, Parzival has been granted this honour by God and it is this further dimension which constitutes the need for humility, for Parzival to realise that, although *his* sin of omission at Munsalvæsche may have been forgiven him, not every such sin is pardoned by God (as with the neutral angels). The dogmatic truth which Trevrizent played down to 'Lähelin' (because of the danger of despair) now needs to be stressed to Parzival as Grail-king (because of the danger of pride). The hermit's second encounter with Parzival finishes with him fully conscious of the enormous difference between Lähelin and Parzival, however disturbingly close they may once have been. Only the listeners, assisted by the narrator, can appreciate the full extent of Trevrizent's psychological swing, for we, unlike Parzival, are aware of what went through Trevrizent's mind in the first half of their earlier dialogue.

Loherangrin in Brabant

In this last episode in the work we revert to the question of identity, but an identity which has to be concealed, rather than recognised. When the narrator starts his brief glimpse into the future (824,1ff.) in giving us the story of Loherangrin's marriage, we already know that this story stands under the auspices of a forbidden question, of the need for this Grail-knight to keep his identity and origin to himself (818,26: *swelhen templeis diu gotes hant | gæb ze hêrren vremder diete, | daz er vrâgen widerriete | sînes namen od sîns geslehtes*). The narrator takes account of this by following his usual method. He feels free to mention Loherangrin by name before he starts his brief story (823,27: *Loherangrîn wuohs manlîch starc*), the more so since we already know of Parzival's elder son by name,[111] and then again

---

109. On the use of this verb in connection with Parzival's quest for the Grail see Jones, *Fighting*, pp. 52ff.
110. Cf. Kolb, *PBB(T)* 78 (1956), 65ff. and Henzen, *PBB(T)* 80 (1958), 422ff.
111. We were first acquainted with his existence and name during Parzival's combat with Feirefiz (743,18). He first enters the action himself in 800,20 and from this point the narrator refers to him by name regularly.

after the disaster, after the forbidden question has been asked and Loherangrin departs from Brabant (826,20: *hin fuor Loherangrîn*). In between, however, during the course of the actual story, the narrator refers to him anonymously, reflecting by this technique the ignorance of his wife and subjects. In this short span of narrative he is therefore referred to by nameless epithets[112] and by a variety of circumlocutions: *den si got bewîste* (824,25), *der den der swane brâhte | unt des ir got gedâhte* (824,29f.), *man muose in für den clâren | und für den manlîchen | habn in al den rîchen* (825,4ff.). It is true that Loherangrin's wife may not be given a name either, but then she is unimportant as a secondary character in a secondary episode at the close of the whole work. For her to be called no more than *frouwe* (824,2) or *fürstîn in Brâbant* (824,27) is much less significant than when the named figure of Loherangrin has his name actually withheld for a time.[113]

When Loherangrin gives his prohibition to his wife, more is conveyed to us than can be grasped by her. What he says of his rulership over her land (825,16: *'sol ich hie landes hêrre sîn, | dar umbe lâz ich als vil'*) contains an allusion to Munsalvæsche (*als vil*) which is clear to us, but not to her.[114] When he gives her his warning (825,19: *'gevrâget nimmer wer ich sî: | sô mag ich iu belîben bî'*), we know already from 818,25ff., with its clear link between the conditions of the Loherangrin story and that of his father,[115] why this should be so. In the conclusion to his warning (825,23: *'ob ir niht sît gewarnet des, | sô warnt mich got, er weiz wol wes'*) his last words are a concealed allusion to his being predestined to the Grail which is clear to the listeners at this stage, but hardly to the woman.[116]

More is also conveyed to us by the narrator than Loherangrin's wife can foresee when he hints that the command will not be heeded (825,25: *si sazte wîbes sicherheit, | diu sît durch liebe wenken leit*). This formulation prompts us to ask why her promise should be specified as *wîbes sicherheit*, for the suggestion in the Bartsch–Marti edition

---

112. *Man* (825,8; 826,6); *sîn lîp* (825,10); *fürste in Brâbant* (826,2).
113. There is a notable difference between Loherangrin being referred to as *fürste in Brâbant* (826,2) and his wife as *fürstîn in Brâbant* (824,27). In her case this title really helps to specify and identify her, whereas the corresponding title for her husband has fallen to him only by marriage and therefore tells us nothing particular about his origins or identity.
114. See the fn. to 825,17 in the Bartsch–Marti edition.
115. On the implications of this link see Kolb, *Munsalvæsche*, pp. 51ff.
116. Cf. the note on 825,24 in Martin's *Kommentar*, p. 534.

Parzival's success (Books XIV–XVI)

('Ehrenwort als Frau')[117] simply evades the problem. Instead, I suggest that the addition of *wîbes* is a slight misogynous touch, a hint that, like a woman, Loherangrin's wife would be unable to restrain her curiosity for long and was therefore bound to ask the forbidden question. This is of a piece with Gottfried's comment on woman's inability to resist what has been forbidden[118] or Hartmann's similar opinion in *Erec*,[119] a parallel which the following reference to this work (826,29f.) suggests was also present in the mind of the narrator in *Parzival*. By using such a topos of antifeminism and being able to count on its immediate recognition the narrator is able to make do with a fleeting hint here (the addition of *wîbes* complements *sît*, both suggest that the promise will not be kept), revealing to us a future which is still a closed book to Loherangrin's wife.

This last episode, closing the work with a glimpse into the future beyond the action dealing with Parzival, is brief and, in strict narrative terms, even superfluous. That the narrator should nonetheless have used this last opportunity to treat the problem of identity by the technique of withholding a name suggests that the problem and the technique devised to cope with it preoccupied him so much that he was willing to demonstrate it in a minor episode as well as in main narrative strands of his story.

117. See the fn. to 825,25.
118. Cf. Gottfried, *Tristan* 17925ff.
119. Hartmann, *Erec* 3242ff.

8
Conclusions

In the preceding chapters we have followed the course of Wolfram's narrative, looking at the problems of recognition in individual scenes and taking a broader view only when the narrative suggested this, as in Book IX, when the whole of the hero's past career comes under review. Now is the time to stand back from separate scenes ourselves and to assess the problems of recognition in *Parzival* under a number of wider headings, hitherto only implicit in our argument. These headings include realistic details which may account for success or failure in recognition; the possibilities of recognition; Parzival's gradual process of self-recognition; and the question of Parzival's naming. Although we may start with very pragmatic details, the argument of this concluding chapter will lead us to central problems of the work and thereby show us how close the theme of recognition stands to the poet's concerns.

Realistic details

We may start with those parts of a knight's equipment in the period immediately following 1200[1] which made it difficult or easy for a knight clad in armour to be identified. His chief protection lay in his knee-length chainmail armour,[2] to which was added from the eleventh century a chainmail hood[3] (*härsnier*),[4] slipped over the head to protect it and the back of the neck. This hood was fastened by means of a strip of chainmail (*vinteile*),[5] firmly attached to one side

1. Gamber, *Bewaffnung*, p. 118, reckons with a very rapid spread of innovations in the knight's armour after 1190. In the particular case of the crest on the helmet Schwietering, *Bedeutung*, p. 283, suggests the same.
2. Cf. Schultz, *Leben*, II 42ff. Wolfram's term for this chainmail armour is *halsberc* (e.g. 207,20) or *ringe* for the separate pieces (e.g. 263,28; cf. also *Willehalm* 442,26).
3. Gamber, *Bewaffnung*, p. 114.
4. Schultz, *Leben*, II 50.
5. *Ibid.*, pp. 51ff.

Conclusions

of the hood and hanging loose for ease of breathing and ventilation, but fastened across the chin (and sometimes the mouth) when danger threatened. Since this strip could cover the lower part of the wearer's face, it constitutes the first vital piece of equipment as regards the difficulty of recognising a knight so clad.[6] Another, even greater difficulty was caused by a new type of helmet (worn over the *härsnier*) which appeared towards the end of the twelfth century and afforded greater protection by covering the whole face apart from eye-slits and air-holes (the so-called pot-helm).[7] By contrast with the older style of helmet (conical in shape, covering only part of the face by means of the nasal or *nasebant*)[8] the pot-helm protected its wearer by making his features quite invisible, covering not just his nose but the whole face by a broad armoured plate known as the *barbier*.[9] What we are sometimes told of a knight wearing such a helmet (that it hindered his vision and his hearing)[10] is also true conversely, for it was impossible to recognise his features as long as he still had it on and difficult to recognise his muffled voice.[11]

The need to cover the mounted warrior as far as possible with protective armour (probably arising from the military experiences of the crusades)[12] thus created problems in distinguishing one knight from another, especially as regards his headwear. Wolfram duly reflects the technological facts of knightly equipment in his day and adapts them to the theme of recognition. How he conceives Parzival's knightly headwear is made clear by the realistic details given when the young boy acquires his equipment by killing Ither,

---

6. *Ibid.*, p. 54.
7. Cf. Boeheim, *Handbuch*, p. 28; Schultz, *Leben*, II 64; Gamber, *Bewaffnung*, p. 116.
8. Schultz, *Leben*, II 61f. Wolfram refers to this type of helmet in *Willehalm* 408,5ff.
9. Schultz, *Leben*, II 64f.
10. *Ibid.*, p. 80, and especially the examples given in fn. 4.
11. See above, p. 115, for a discussion of the way in which Sigune, when Parzival comes across her for the second time, cannot see his features because of his helmet, is therefore dependent on his voice alone for recognition, but even so finds this difficult because of muffling. For the same reason in Hartmann's *Erec* 4851ff. Keii has to guess the identity of Erec in his armour, relies on hearing rather than sight, but is careful to imply an element of doubt. If by contrast Gawein recognises Erec's identity without hesitation (4905ff.) this is because of the greater intuitive insight he possesses, as also in the episode in *Parzival* which owes much to this counterpart in *Erec*, the episode of the three drops of blood in the snow (see above, pp. 126ff.).
12. Boeheim, *Handbuch*, p. 28; Gamber, *Bewaffnung*, p. 116.

for his javelin pierces an eye by passing through a hole in the *barbier* of the helmet, worn above the *härsnier* (155,7ff.),[13] or by the way in which the hero seeks to cool himself on leaving Sigune after their second encounter by taking off his helmet and loosening the *vinteile* (256,7ff.).[14] How much concealment was provided by this headwear is suggested by the observation that Clamide was recognised at the Round Table *as soon as* he removed his helmet and hood (219,1ff.),[15] by the fact that, although Cunneware can tell from his heraldic device that the knight sent to her must be her brother, she cannot see whether it is Orilus or Lähelin while he still wears his armour (275,17ff.),[16] or by the way in which Orgeluse *for the first time* looks at Gawan's features once his armour has been taken off him (621,27ff.).[17] The link between these details and the theme of recognition can also be expressly verbalised, as when Jeschute can look at Parzival *erkenneclîchen* (258,2)[18] once he has removed his helmet and loosened the *vinteile* on leaving Sigune, or when Sigune recognises Parzival at their next meeting (440,28: *erkande*)[19] after he has taken the further step of slipping off his chainmail hood.

The problem of recognition was one of contemporary reality, however, and not just of literature, for the more enclosed the knight was in his armour, the more necessary it became to distinguish friend from foe by outward tokens, three of which play a special part in *Parzival*. The most telling of these was the knight's heraldic device painted on the outside of his shield,[20] a practice attested for France, England and Germany from as early as the second quarter of the twelfth century, whilst the literary evidence for this practice offers fairly full indications of the arms by 1200.[21] That the purpose behind this was ease of recognition is suggested by the use of *conoissance* in French to denote a heraldic device from about 1150[22] or by the occasional reference to turning one's shield round, so as to

---

13. Cf. also 748,1ff., where Parzival can only recognise the distinctive features of Feirefiz once the latter has removed his helmet and chainmail hood.
14. See above, pp. 118f. and 121.
15. See above, p. 87.
16. See above, p. 125.
17. When Gawan brings Parzival back with him to the Round Table Cunneware is able to recognise him because he has already removed his helmet (305,21ff., see above, p. 131).
18. See above, p. 121.
19. See above, p. 184.
20. Schultz, *Leben*, II 88ff.
21. Wagner, *Heralds*, pp. 13f. and 17f.
22. *Ibid.*, p. 13; White, *Technology*, p. 33; Gamber, *Bewaffnung*, pp. 115 and 116.

Conclusions

conceal the device, if one wished to remain unknown.[23] Wolfram pays due heed to this established practice in his story of Gahmuret by building his career around a heraldic theme[24] and by taking care to give heraldic details for many of the knights fighting in the collective encounters in which Gahmuret takes part.[25] By working similar topical references into Parzival's career, however, Wolfram created a difficulty for himself. Chrétien's version contained no heraldic details,[26] so that with him two knights can engage in combat without recognising each other, but if the German poet is to retain this motif, as we have seen him do repeatedly, he will be driven to devise a way of neutralising the heraldic signals he has introduced as a reflection of contemporary practice. The same difficulty arises for Wolfram with the other two tokens of recognition. The function of the first of these, the surcoat (*kursît, wâpenroc*)[27] worn over the chainmail, was at first to protect the metal from damp and the wearer from the heat of the sun, but it then came to have stitched on it the same heraldic device as on the knight's shield. The crest on the helmet, attested as coming into use just before 1200 and referred to in literature for the first time by Wolfram himself,[28] served the same purpose of recognition, for it generally depicted the main figure of the wearer's heraldic device[29] and the narrator takes care to specify that Arthurian knights wore their device on helmet or shield *durch bekanntnisse* (383,1ff.).

Wolfram's task is therefore a double one: having introduced these tokens from contemporary practice, he has to show how, as in

23. Cf. Schultz, *Leben*, II 89, and the examples given there in fn. 1.
24. See above, pp. 48f., and Timpson, *GLL* 13 (1959/1960), 88ff.
25. See above, pp. 51 and 55. Cf. also Timpson, *art.cit.*, p. 89.
26. Timpson, *art.cit.*, p. 91, says of the *Perceval* story as recounted by Chrétien that it 'belongs to the pre-heraldic area', a phrase open to misunderstanding. One can only agree if it is meant that the French poet chooses not to make any reference to heraldic devices, but not if it is suggested that Chrétien wrote *Perceval* before these devices were well established. That Chrétien was already acquainted with them is clear from *Yvain* 2243 and *Lancelot* 5773ff. On the same page Timpson talks of a knight in the time of Chrétien and Wolfram being recognised 'even when his vizor is down', but in this period we have to reckon with *vinteile* and *barbier*, not with a visor proper (cf. Schultz, *Leben*, II 53). Timpson also suggests in the same context that Parzival knows perfectly well who his opponent is when he fights with Orilus in Book V. For the reasons why this is unacceptable see above, pp. 123f.
27. E.g. *Parzival* 333,6f.; 756,26ff. Cf. Schultz, *Leben*, II 57f.
28. Cf. Schultz, *Leben*, II 72f.; Schreiber, *Bausteine*, pp. 164ff.; Schwietering, *Bedeutung*, pp. 282ff.
29. Schultz, *Leben*, II 72. Examples of the agreement between crest and shield in *Parzival* are 262,4ff. and 383,1ff.

reality, they allow a knight to be identified, but also how this signal can be lost to view if repeatedly, as in his non-heraldic source, a knight is not recognised. To illustrate the first point the narrator makes a generalised statement about the coat of arms being enough to permit identification, as when Kyot recognises the Grail-knights from their *grâles wâpen*, consisting of *turteltûben* (800,1ff.).[30] Elsewhere, the clue is provided by more detailed pieces of equipment (the shield alone, the banner or the surcoat)[31] or with greater verisimilitude by different pieces on the same occasion (shield and banner thus combine, or crest and shield, or banner, surcoat and crest, or shield, surcoat and banner, or shield, surcoat and horse's coverlet, or shield and saddle).[32] The variety of signals chosen by the narrator thus reflects something of the multiplicity of tokens developed in his day to identify a heavily armoured knight.

To render credible the fact that these signals were not always effective, in other words to allow his story to follow Chrétien in depicting encounters where recognition is hindered, the German poet need do no more than fall back on another well-known experience of knightly warfare, the fact that these signals could have been damaged and rendered unrecognisable in a recent passage of arms. He therefore tells us repeatedly that in combat one knight's shield was hacked to pieces by the other's sword-blows, that the device on the crest of a helmet was badly damaged in the same way, that a surcoat was slashed in an encounter, and he frequently combines such pointers on the same occasion.[33] A knight whose equipment has been so battered about will not be easily identifiable on the next occasion, and the fact that many of these details are

---

30. Conversely, when a knight's travels take him into a region where he is unknown, as Parzival is at Bearosche, his coat of arms, however distinctive, is not enough to identify him (398,5: *bî rôtem wâpen unrekant*).
31. E.g. 320,9 (*sîn schilt unt er wârn unbekant*); 59,7ff. and 341,6ff.; 22,30ff. and 275,21f.
32. 216,16ff. and 793,11f. (shield and banner); 383,1ff. (crest and shield); 377,24ff. (banner, surcoat and crest); 340,18 (shield, surcoat and banner – this negative example presupposes the positive possibility); 14,15ff. (shield, surcoat and horse's coverlet; to these is added the crest in 262,4ff.); 474,5ff. (shield and saddle).
33. E.g. 208,7ff.; 386,24ff.; 537,17ff.; 541,15ff. (shield); 263,17ff. (crest); 81,18f. and 270,11ff. (surcoat); 217,23; 271,16f.; 275,2f.; 283,27ff.; 759,2f. (crest and shield); 756,24 (crest and surcoat). The passage 275,2f. suggests that in some cases we may be dealing not with a crest proper, but with the more old-fashioned, but equally distinctive use of decorative inlay on the helmet (cf. Schultz, *Leben*, II 71f.). As regards the possibility of recognition, however, this makes little difference.

Conclusions

passed on to us on occasions when recognition is not an issue predisposes us to accept without disbelief those cases where a knight is not immediately identified. These details are far from being the only way in which a failure in recognition is motivated, but they are enough to demonstrate that in adopting contemporary heraldic practice Wolfram did not create an insoluble problem for himself.

The realistic nature of such references, involving an up-to-date topicality which has not always been appreciated,[34] is further enhanced when, in order to explain how recognition took place or failed to come about on any one occasion, the narrator finds it necessary to build into his account an accumulation of details to render it more probable. When Ampflise's messengers come across Gahmuret and recognise him in the course of the tournament at Kanvoleis this has to be adequately motivated, especially since the change in his coat of arms renders this even less self-explanatory.[35] The narrator therefore has Gahmuret demand a fresh horse after fighting for some time and, credibly enough, make use of the occasion to take off his helmet and hood for fresh air, so that his features are visible to the messengers, including not just young pages, to whom Gahmuret may mean nothing, but a mature *kappelân* who can recall him from his days in France. We are therefore not just told that Gahmuret was recognised, but how and why this was possible, in such circumstantial detail that the verisimilitude of the encounter is enhanced. This technique of a detailed verbal reconstruction of a precisely imagined situation is taken even further to account for the initial failure of Parzival and Sigune to recognise each other at their third encounter.[36] On the one hand, Sigune is at first prostrate on the floor of her cell, then she appears at the window while Parzival is bidden to sit on the bench by the wall of the cell, but even if she is briefly visible before he sits down his attention fastens suspiciously on the ring she wears rather than on her features. For her part, Sigune cannot recognise her interlocutor for he has laid aside Ither's shield, the rest of his armour is not visible to her within the cell, and although he may also have removed his helmet he still keeps his hood on and is in any case covered in rust. None of these features has to be supplied by our

---

34. It is significant that Schwietering, who devoted several years of his career to 'Waffenkunde', was fully aware of this aspect of Wolfram's interests (cf. *Bedeutung*, p. 283).
35. See above, p. 56.
36. See above, pp. 181ff.

imagination to account for this failure in recognition, all have been carefully inserted by a poet who has envisaged the scene in such coherent detail because he is concerned not merely with the fact of non-recognition, but also with how this came about on this one occasion. Realistic effects are also achieved whenever a situation is explained not just baldly by one reason, but by a whole range of different reasons as in the complexity of everyday life. When Parzival is challenged by Arthurian knights in the scene of the three drops of blood in the snow,[37] this is because he unconsciously grasps his spear upright, in the gesture recently referred to metaphorically by Arthur in warning his followers against combat with Grail-knights, but also because this initial misunderstanding is the fault of an inexperienced young page, but is then carried further by a headstrong Segramors and an aggressive Keii confirmed in his view of an insult to the court by the defeat of Segramors. A lesser poet would have been content with the gesture with the spear as a fortuitous explanation, but Wolfram reinforces this by motivating from the character of each of the three members of the Round Table involved.

Wolfram is also careful not to restrict himself to an oversimplified or stylised one-for-one explanation by at times giving more details in his account than are strictly necessary to motivate a specific point. One of the details which make the Arthurian knights fighting at Bearosche recognisable to Gawan is their distinctive battle-cry (382,12ff.),[38] but if he had left it at that the poet would have been guilty of making his point too obviously, of reducing the complexity of a massed encounter to the one detail required by him. Instead, he scatters further references to *other* battle-cries throughout this episode, so that our task as listeners (to pick out this one cry and realise its significance in motivation) parallels Gawan's in distinguishing the battle-cry *Nantes* from all the others heard on the battlefield.[39] The effort on our part we impute to Gawan himself and are thereby disposed to impute reality to the situation in which he is described.[40] The same technique, rendering the particular

37. See above, pp. 126ff.
38. See above, p. 138, fn. 22.
39. By this technique the listener is put in the same position as Parzival, for example when he first comes to Munsalvæsche (see above, pp. 108f.) or encounters Jeschute for the second time (see above, pp. 119f.), for he is confronted with a wide range of visible details, only some of which are directly relevant to his task of recognition.
40. I owe this point to what Harvey has said of the novel, *Character*, pp. 54 and 70f.

Conclusions

more credible by depriving it of its uniqueness, is employed elsewhere. At Zazamanc, for example, Gahmuret may win the day by defeating the three leading princes, but it is also made clear that he fights not with them alone, but with many others as well, and if the happy chance of Gahmuret coming across precisely these three in the battle seems too much of a good thing, this improbability is reduced by our being told, in the case of Hiuteger and Razalic, that it is their daily habit to do just what they do on the day when Gahmuret encounters them, so that he can hardly avoid combat with them.[41] The same is true of Parzival's arrival at Pelrapeire, for if the defenders at first take him for their enemy Clamide, approaching them with arrogant self-confidence, this is made the more probable by our being told that Parzival is unconsciously doing what Clamide has already done several times himself (181,17).[42]

The more such circumstantial details are elaborated for the sake of verisimilitude, the greater the risk that the narrator will involve himself in self-contradiction or fail to motivate convincingly on all occasions. I have pointed out in the preceding chapters where this seems to be the case,[43] but what needs to be registered is how surprisingly infrequent these relative failures are by comparison

---

41. See above, p. 39, fn. 6.
42. See above, p. 85. L. P. Johnson has shown how a convincing sense of reality is conveyed by the network of personal bonds, especially kinship bonds, leading us in *Parzival*, 'like life itself, to pursue its strands to their very limits and to assume even then that it is our knowledge of the strands that is exhausted rather than the strands themselves' (*MLR* 63 (1968), 612). Cf. also Mohr on 'epische Hintergründe' in *Parzival*, pp. 174ff., especially 177f., and the similar argument conducted by Harvey in the context of the novel, *Character*, p. 55. Examples in *Parzival*, where our knowledge of characters fades off gradually into ignorance, as it does with people in life, and we are therefore prompted to speculate beyond the range of what we are told, would include the intriguing reference to another aspect of Cunneware (284,11f.), the episode of Gawan's pages (428,30ff.), the details of which are unknown to Gawan, but also to us, and above all the way in which Parzival's knightly exploits are graded, ranging from those adventures which are narrated to us in the necessary detail to those which are merely referred to without being narrated (e.g. his encounter with Vergulaht, 434,25ff.) and ultimately to those adventures about which we hear succinctly and retrospectively in his list of victories, 772,1ff.
43. The most obvious case is Gawan's failure to recognise Urians (see above, pp. 147ff.). Other examples include Kaylet's failure to mention the death of Galoes to Gahmuret (p. 57, fn. 68), the change of location between Parzival's first and second encounter with Sigune (p. 116, fn. 92), Parzival's ignorance of Cunneware's name (p. 125, fn. 113), Kingrimursel's belated recognition of Gawan's kinship with Vergulaht (pp. 144f.) and Parzival's encounter with Gramoflanz (pp. 236 and 245f.).

with the large number of recognition patterns successfully carried through from beginning to end. This has not always been acknowledged, as when Schwietering says that Wolfram was perfectly ready to ignore probability in having the knights of the Round Table fail to recognise Parzival, despite his red equipment, when they encounter him again in Book VI.[44] Against this it must be argued that Wolfram does not push aside the claims of verisimilitude in this episode, but rather, as we have seen,[45] builds in a variety of reasons to make it understandable why Arthur's knights are so taken up with their preconceptions that they fail to see what should be obvious. In the same context Schwietering also adduces the combat between Parzival and Gawan and is followed in this by Dewald,[46] who suggests instead a purely symbolic motivation. If there is force to this symbolic argument (Parzival is by now no longer to be simply identified as the red knight, he has passed well beyond this stage), this need not exclude realistic considerations, present to the extent that a number of pointers explain why Gawan is led astray and misinterprets what he sees.[47] In this concern for symbolism reconcilable with realistic details and not simply imposed on the narrative at all costs Wolfram differs from, say, Hartmann who adapts a detail of Erec's knightly equipment to symbolic purposes at one stage, but is later quite ready to ignore this supposedly realistic detail when it no longer suits his book.[48] These

44. Schwietering, *Bedeutung*, p. 283. Cf. also Dewald, *Minne*, p. 68, who argues on the symbolic level exclusively (because Parzival in his vision of the drops of blood in the snow achieves a realisation of his true nature, he is no longer characterised by his red armour and therefore cannot be 'recognised' by the Arthurian knights). Without rejecting this type of argument, I should not accept it because of any lack of verisimilitude in this episode (what Dewald calls an 'Ungereimtheit').
45. See above, pp. 126ff.
46. Dewald, *Minne*, p. 279.
47. See above, pp. 240f. Dewald, *Minne*, p. 275, also questions Wolfram's realism when he has Sigune recognise Parzival by his voice, even though he has just spoken to her twice before. On the grounds for seeing precisely this as a realistic detail, referring to the muffled voice from within the helmet, see above, pp. 115 and 265, fn. 11.
48. Erec's inability to see or hear well while wearing his armour, which means above all his helmet, and therefore his dependence on Enite for warnings (4155ff.) are meant to be read symbolically, as has been shown by Ohly, *Struktur*, p. 72. Yet this realistic level is later tacitly abandoned in Erec's second series of adventures, as when he is alerted to the encounter with the giants by hearing Cadoc's wife himself (5296ff.) or when he is able to perceive Guivreiz and his followers (6872ff.). Hartmann now ignores his earlier statement about Erec's armour impeding him, because for him this realistic detail is less important than the symbolic end to which he puts it.

Conclusions

details are much more closely integrated into his narrative by Wolfram.

Possibilities of recognition

Although the theme of recognition is treated by Wolfram with a frequency not to be found elsewhere it would be wrong to regard the technique he employs as an absolute novelty, for examples are to be found with the two authors to whom he owes much, Hartmann in German literature[49] and Chrétien in French. A clear example from Hartmann's *Erec* is the occasion when the hero and Guivreiz meet for the second time, fail to recognise one another and engage in combat until Enite puts an end to the misunderstanding.[50] To explain how the failure in recognition came about and then was made good Hartmann differs from Chrétien in providing the kind of details which Wolfram adduces in the same type of context.[51] We are therefore told how both came to be riding along the same path in opposite directions and in ignorance of each other, how the moonlit, but overcast night provides enough light for each to see the other, but not so much that recognition is possible, and how their combat begins without a word being exchanged or their names mentioned.[52] This crisis of non-recognition, accounted for in this way, is put an end to only by Enite's intervention who, fearing for Erec, pleads for his life, mentioning Guivreiz by name and recognised by him in turn by her voice.[53] A comparable situation occurs in Hartmann's *Iwein* when Iwein and Gawein engage in combat without at first recognising each other, for here too the poet carefully motivates how and why this should have been possible between two friends.[54] But in this episode Hartmann also employs

---

49. Peil, *Gebärde*, pp. 186f., discusses some of the parallels and differences between Hartmann and Wolfram concerning the theme of recognition.
50. On this episode see Harms, *Kampf*, pp. 123ff., and Ruberg, *Schweigen*, p. 197.
51. Drube, *Hartmann*, p. 70f., stresses Chrétien's lack of motivation at this point by contrast with Hartmann.
52. Cf. *Erec* 6862ff., 6894f., 6899ff. Harms, *Kampf*, p. 125, fn. 16, draws attention however to the limits set to Hartmann's observance of realistic details. Guivreiz fails to recognise the defeated Erec after his helmet has been removed (6937f.), but sees who he is only after the *hüetelîn* worn under the helmet has also been taken off (6988f.) even though the *hüetelîn* did not cover the wearer's features (cf. Schultz, *Leben*, ii 55f.).
53. Hartmann carefully motivates how Enite comes to mention Guivreiz's name, 6946ff. (cf. Harms, *Kampf*, p. 125).
54. See Harms, *Kampf*, pp. 127ff., and Ruberg, *Schweigen*, pp. 218f. Cf. also the assessment of Ragotzky and Weinmayer, *Identitätsbildung*, p. 239: 'Mit dem Augenblick, in dem *unkünde* dem Erkennen weicht, hat der Doppelweg sein Ziel erreicht'.

another technique which we have frequently observed in *Parzival*: previous events have made his listeners aware of the identity of both these knights, but once their encounter begins the anonymity which each combatant has reason to maintain is reflected in the narrator's technique of himself withholding their names until the moment of mutual recognition.[55]

Hartmann therefore employs two methods (detailed motivation and withholding of names by the narrator) which Wolfram also uses, possibly even taking them over from Hartmann. Yet even though Hartmann may go further than Chrétien in details, he owes his essentials to the French poet, for it was he who had originally devised a narrative situation in each romance where the hero fights with a friend without at first recognising him. Even with regard to the naming technique used by Hartmann in *Iwein* Chrétien is still of considerable relevance for Wolfram in composing *Parzival*, for the French author has his own technique with names in most of his romances[56] and in the particular case of *Perceval* has a large-scale example of what Hartmann does for only one episode in *Iwein*: he withholds a name from his listeners (that of the hero himself) as long as Perceval is unaware of it.[57] Yet although both Hartmann and Chrétien may have supplied examples for Wolfram, he goes much further than either of them. He surpasses Hartmann in the frequency with which recognition and non-recognition recur as a problem in countless episodes (this he may largely owe to what he already found in his French source), but he also goes beyond Chrétien, for example in the way in which he converts Parzival's initial anonymity into a problem for his listeners, not simply withholding the name, as Chrétien had done, but also inserting clues which theoretically allow the audience to grasp his identity before his name is explicitly released.[58]

Another way in which to establish how much further than

---

55. Harms, *Kampf*, pp. 129f. Hartmann's *Iwein* is also important as a precedent for Wolfram's *Parzival* in that it treats of the problem of Iwein's self-recognition as he recovers from his period of madness. On this see Wehrli, *Formen*, pp. 177ff.; Mohr, *ZfdA* 100 (1971), 73ff.; Hagenguth, *Iwein*, pp. 90ff.
56. See Green, *Namedropping*, pp. 89ff. and the secondary literature on this problem listed there.
57. *Ibid*, pp. 98f. and 100f.
58. See above, pp. 17ff. Something similar is true of Ither's kinship (quite apart from the fact that this detail of the German romance has no precedent in Chrétien): Wolfram not merely makes Ither and Parzival kinsmen, he also provides clues making it possible for the careful listener to recognise this fact at the moment when they meet (see above, p. 83).

Conclusions

either of his predecessors Wolfram goes in motivating the central problem of recognition or non-recognition is to consider the range within which he illustrates it, the variety of signals available to characters in *Parzival* which they can interpret correctly or wrongly. This problem has been discussed by Hahn with regard to one aspect of the romance (Parzival's beauty) and also in theoretical terms for a whole period of medieval German literature,[59] but in what follows I hope to show something of the size of the problem in *Parzival*, illustrating the variety of Wolfram's treatment rather than aiming at completeness. I follow Hahn's theoretical article to the extent that I discuss the possible signals to recognition or non-recognition under four headings: physical appearance (which may include Hahn's theme of Parzival's beauty, but also goes far beyond it), gestures, words and appurtenances. Under each of these headings examples may be grouped as ambiguous (their significance may be unclear or point in more than one direction), correctly interpreted (so that recognition comes about) and wrongly interpreted.

Appearances are illustrated as ambiguous above all in the case of Parzival, which in view of his early upbringing is not surprising. The discrepancy between his personal appearance, heightened by his knightly equipment, and his behaviour and fool's clothing when he arrives at Gurnemanz's castle calls forth general embarrassment and only one knight there is able to resolve the dilemma by correctly recognising the lofty goal for which he must be destined (164,14f. and 19f.).[60] Soon after this Gurnemanz may be correct in surmising that his guest's appearance stamps him out as a born ruler (he goes further than Karnahkarnanz in correctly seeing in him more than a knight by birth), but this insight is bought at the cost of his inability to grasp that the rulership to which Parzival is destined (at Munsalvæsche) far surpasses what Gurnemanz has in mind.[61] Not even Trevrizent is exempt from the narrator using him as a mouthpiece to express more than he himself means, as when, alerted by the similarity of appearance between Frimutel and Parzival, he

---

59. Hahn, *Schönheit*, pp. 203ff. (the subtitle of this essay is: 'Zum Problem des Erkennens und Verkennens im *Parzival*'), and Hahn, *PBB(T)* 99 (1977), 395ff.
60. Cf. Mersmann, *Besitzwechsel*, p. 128, and Hahn, *Schönheit*, p. 217. Hahn, *PBB(T)* 99 (1977), 405f., rightly sees in this a literary topos which she connects with Cant. 1.4 (*Nigra sum, sed formosa*).
61. 170,21ff. On the interpretation of this passage see above, p. 70, and Green, *Advice*, pp. 67ff.

utters a concluding remark (474,22) in which the word *ouch* is highly ambiguous, meaning both what the hermit intends it to mean and what the narrator implies by it.[62]

If appearances are ambiguous, they will not fail to be interpreted both correctly and incorrectly. Correct examples include Parzival's beauty:[63] although he may not go far enough, Karnahkarnanz is certainly correct in assuming from the boy's beauty that he was born to chivalry (123,11ff.);[64] Sigune correctly reads his beauty as a sign of his future destiny (139,26ff.);[65] both Jeschute and Sigune have been so struck by his outstanding beauty that they are later able to recognise Parzival by this alone (258,3f.; 440,26ff.).[66] Parzival's appearance also tells Cunneware that this must be the one destined for the highest renown (151,11ff.) and enables her to recognise him later despite the stains of rust (305,21ff.),[67] just as what he has already been told of his halfbrother's appearance allows Parzival to recognise Feirefiz (746,22ff. and 748,6f.).[68] Physical appearance also makes it possible to recognise that two people are related to one another by birth: Vergulaht's beauty proclaims him in Gawan's eyes as Parzival's kinsman, indeed almost as his double (400,4ff.);[69] Gahmuret, when he encountered Trevrizent on his knightly travels, knew from his similarity to Herzeloyde that this must be his brother-in-law (497,24ff.);[70] similarly, although Gramoflanz has never seen Itonje he is able to identify her through having met her brother (724,19ff.).[71] On the

62. See above, p. 190, and Johnson, *Beauty*, p. 287. On Orgeluse and the apparent discrepancy between her beauty and her character (at least as betrayed by her words) see Zimmermann, *Euphorion* 66 (1972), 132.
63. This theme has been treated by Hahn, *Schönheit*, pp. 203ff., and Johnson, *Beauty*, pp. 273ff.
64. Ither is similarly struck by Parzival's beauty (146,5ff.). Hahn rightly stresses, *Schönheit*, p. 219, that the conclusions drawn from such recognitions of Parzival's beauty confine him to the context of Arthurian chivalry and *minne* and thus do not go far enough as assessments of his potential.
65. Johnson, *Beauty*, p. 279.
66. See above, pp. 121 and 184, but also Johnson, *Beauty*, pp. 283f. In 47,6ff. the beauty and youth of Killirjacac allow Gahmuret to surmise correctly his reasons for coming to the Middle East, he thus judges character correctly from external appearance (see above, p. 59, fn. 70).
67. See above, pp. 67 and 131.
68. See above, p. 249. Recognition of appearances can also be applied to a place or an object, as when Parzival comes to Trevrizent's cell a second time, 455,25f. and 459,24ff. (see above, p. 185).
69. See above, p. 145, fn. 49, but also Johnson, *Beauty*, pp. 285f.
70. See above, p. 200.
71. Cf. Peil, *Gebärde*, p. 47.

Conclusions

most humdrum level one person recognises another from his appearance because of their earlier acquaintance (Ampflise's chaplain thus recognises Gahmuret, as does Gawan the page he had met at the start of Book VII, or Bene the pages of Gramoflanz).[72]

Failure in recognition of appearance[73] is similarly attributed to various reasons. At Munsalvæsche Parzival is so incapable of piercing to the heart of things that he does not perceive Anfortas's sickness or, if he is aware of it, he fails to appreciate how he should act, just as he remains blind to the significance of the fresh green grass in the courtyard of the Grail-castle or, at the end of the Grail-ceremony, focuses his attention on Repanse de schoy instead of Anfortas.[74] More drastically, unconsciousness can prevent recognition: in Parzival's case when the Arthurian knights approach him in his love rêverie, with Gawan vis-à-vis the queens at Schastel Marveile because of his extreme weakness after combat.[75] Alternatively, a lapse of time can be adduced in the same context, so that these four queens fail to recognise Gawan after so many years, just as Arthur fails to recognise them.[76] Again, the humdrum level of no previous acquaintance is present, as with Parzival and Trevrizent, Parzival at Bearosche, and Parzival when he has to ask which of his sons is Kardeiz.[77]

Gestures can be just as ambiguous as appearances or as deceptive as words.[78] Parzival's gesture of silence before Condwiramurs is at first taken by her as mockery and only later as the tactful courtesy it represents, whilst the façade of polite pleasure in the arrival of a guest shown Parzival at Munsalvæsche is not appreciated as the *trügevreude* which it in fact is.[79] When Parzival wakes up on the following morning and finds his knightly gear laid out ready for him, he takes this as a suggestion to repay hospitality by knightly

---

72. 76,8f. (cf. above, p. 56); 381,8f.; 713,1ff. (cf. above, p. 232, fn. 18).
73. Hahn, *PBB(T)* 99 (1977), 420f., relates this motif with the biblical truth that only God knows the mysteries of the human heart.
74. 225,18 and 227,9ff. (cf. above, p. 94); 236,12ff. and 240,21ff. (cf. above, p. 109).
75. See above, p. 102, fn. 48, and pp. 157 and 160f.
76. See above, p. 157, fn. 86, and p. 170 (with reference to 672,3f.).
77. See above, pp. 185 and 139, and 803,2f. The kinsmen Parzival and Vergulaht can also meet without recognising each other, since we are nowhere told that they were previously acquainted (see above, p. 146).
78. On gestures in *Parzival* see Peil, *Gebärde*. On the ambiguity of a gesture in Gottfried's *Tristan* see Mersmann, *Besitzwechsel*, p. 108 and on the possibility of deceptive gestures Peil, *Gebärde*, p. 84. Peil also discusses in general terms (pp. 297ff.) the meaning of gestures and their interpretation.
79. 188,25ff. (cf. above, p. 86) and 228,25f. (cf. above, pp. 94f.).

service, whereas it is more of an angry reproach, bidding him to pack up his things and be gone.[80] Gestures with weapons are understandably very open to misunderstanding, which is why the members of the Round Table, apart from Gawan, are quick to see in Parzival holding his spear upright when lost in his thoughts what Arthur has recently led them to expect from this gesture, namely a knightly challenge.[81] When Gawan sees Clinschor's knights approaching him from the castle he immediately expects combat and has to be put right on this by Orgeluse, just as Feirefiz reacts similarly when he catches sight of Grail-knights and is corrected by Cundrie.[82]

Such ambiguity does not prevent the correct reading of gestures on occasions. Gawan's general demeanour impresses upon Obie's mother what manner of man he must be (353,13ff.) and what Obilot must see in him (374,21ff.), whilst the same is true, on a more comic level, of the page sent to Gawan by Obie (360,17ff.).[83] To the initiated a person's gestures are enough to reveal whether he is in love, as when Gawan, alone of the Arthurian knights, correctly interprets the significance of Parzival waiting silently in the vicinity of Arthur's camp (301,21ff.), or when Gramoflanz instructs his messengers to observe whether Itonje is suffering the pangs of love on his behalf (709,26ff.).[84] Other examples include Gahmuret's correct reading of the inverted shield carried by the *Anschevîn* at Kanvoleis (80,19ff.),[85] Sigune's recognition, however belated, of Parzival not by what he says, but by his voice (251,28),[86] Gawan's perception, because of the mettlesome quality of the horse he has just mounted, that this must be Gringuljete (540,15ff.), and Sigune's awareness of Parzival's innate virtue (139,25ff.) from seeing his otherwise pathetic gesture of reaching for his javelin (139,9ff.) when he first encounters her and the dead Schionatulander.

80. 246,1ff. and 28ff. (cf. above, p. 96). On the irrelevance of Parzival's belief that knightly service is called for here see Green, *Aventiure*, p. 151.
81. 284,2 (cf. above, pp. 90f.); 287,22f. (cf. above, p. 127); 290,12f. (cf. above, p. 127). Cf. also Peil, *Gebärde*, pp. 22, 148 and 274.
82. 620,24ff. and 621,4ff. (cf. Peil, *Gebärde*, p. 33); 793,3ff. and 7ff. (*ibid.*, p. 34).
83. See above, pp. 136f. Vergulaht's general bearing also marks him out as the ruler to Gawan when he reaches his territory, cf. above, p. 142, fn. 38.
84. See above, p. 128, and Peil, *Gebärde*, pp. 178 and 274; p. 232, fn. 18, and *ibid.*, p. 270.
85. See above, p. 57, and Peil, *Gebärde*, pp. 143 and 272.
86. See above, p. 115.

Conclusions

Even more frequently, however, the true meaning of gestures like these is not recognised. Arnive fails to realise that Gawan's tears at the approach of what he knows to be Arthur's retinue are tears shed for joy (662,3ff.), just as Itonje misreads Bene's tears in the light of her own love for Gramoflanz (697,28ff.), since she does not know what Bene now knows, namely that her lover is about to fight her brother.[87] Cunneware's laugh when Parzival comes to the Round Table, meaningful to the knights there and to us, conveys nothing to the hero (151,11ff.), whilst the inhabitants of Pelrapeire are grossly mistaken when Parzival first comes to them in confusing him with Clamide (181,18ff.).[88] The direction from which someone comes is often enough to bring about a misinterpretation: first Arnive (662,8), then Orgeluse (664,4ff.) misreads the significance of Arthur's knights approaching Schastel Marveile from the direction of Logroys, just as Gawan disastrously mistakes Parzival for Gramoflanz because he first catches sight of him in a region associated with the latter (678,19).[89] Time can also cause confusion in this same episode in that Parzival, having only that morning broken a wreath from Gramoflanz's tree is predisposed to regard the first knight he comes across as Gramoflanz accepting this challenge (701,1ff.),[90] but also elsewhere, since Parzival's unwitting gesture with the upright spear would not have led to dire results so easily if Arthur had not recently warned against the danger of unnecessary skirmishing by referring to precisely this gesture (281,1). A lack of any previous acquaintance is the explanation why Gawan and the knights he encounters at the start of Book VII should fail to recognise each other (342,4f. and 18ff.).[91]

Words, notoriously unreliable even apart from their employment in lying or ironic statements, are a frequent cause of failure in recognition in *Parzival*. The hero registers the need to repay the hospitality given him at Munsalvæsche (a need impressed upon him from the start by his host, 226,5), but goes disastrously wrong in seeing this in terms of knightly assistance rather than a question

---

87. See above, p. 168, and Peil, *Gebärde*, p. 274; p. 231, and *ibid.*, p. 274, fn. 49.
88. On Cunneware's laugh, which is meaningful to the listeners because of the narrator's comment, 151,13ff. and the earlier remark by her brother Orilus, 135,16ff., cf. Peil, *Gebärde*, pp. 278ff. On the situation at Pelrapeire see above, p. 85.
89. See above, pp. 169 and 240f.
90. See above, p. 242.
91. See above, p. 134, fn. 7.

of compassion.[92] Trevrizent's use of a tentative hypothesis when politely questioning whether Parzival has in fact seen anything of the Grail is turned against him by our knowledge that his guest has indeed been to Munsalvæsche (469,5f.),[93] just as the whole of the first part of his dialogue with one whom he at first takes to be Lähelin is informed by a double perspective which escapes both parties.[94] Gawan is similarly the unwitting victim of an unintended double meaning when, on the eve of his combat with Gramoflanz, he expresses the pious conventional wish that God may settle the issue justly (707,26), but lives to experience the ironic truth that this is accomplished when the combat is rendered impossible.[95]

However, words can still be interpreted correctly. This is especially true when what they convey is the identifying mark of a name. Although Parzival can identify himself by no more than the nicknames of his childhood (140,6ff.) these are enough to tell Sigune who he must be and to allow her to name him herself (140,16).[96] Kingrimursel's fame is such that he only has to name himself (324,19ff.) to be recognised at Arthur's court (325,3ff.), even though this had presumably been impossible before he gave his name. Clarification about the combat between Parzival and Gawan is finally brought about only when each names himself (688,5ff. and 17f.; 689,22ff.).[97] From the way in which the narrator reports what Parzival told Gurnemanz about the acquisition of his armour it is probable that he concentrated on what was important for himself (the armour worn by Ither) rather than on his victim's name, but this is in any case enough to tell Gurnemanz of the fate of the red knight (170,1ff.), suggesting that Gurnemanz had previous knowledge of Ither.

Correct interpretations of words still leave ample room for cases where their significance is not seen. If this is to happen and if we are at the same time to be aware that a character is going astray because of his ignorance, then we are approaching very close to the realm of dramatic irony.[98] We witness Parzival's ignorance of the situation when he takes leave of Condwiramurs in order to return to his

92. Cf. Green, *Aventiure*, pp. 150ff.
93. See above, p. 192, fn. 59.
94. See above, p. 188, especially fn. 50.
95. Cf. Green, *Homicide*, p. 32.
96. See above, p. 79.
97. See above, p. 243.
98. Cf. Green, *Irony*, pp. 250ff.

Conclusions

mother for a time (233,19ff.), but also the fortunate ignorance of each other's identity shown by Parzival and Orilus (266,21ff.) and again by Orilus when he is sent to offer tribute to one who is his own sister (267,12ff.), and Trevrizent's unawareness of the full implications of his guest's identity.[99] Ironic implications in a person's words are not seen when Parzival naïvely fails to grasp the sarcastic imports of Keii's invitation to help himself to Ither's armour (150,11ff.),[100] when Parzival is blind to the fact that the boot is on the other foot in his accusing Ither of being another Lähelin (154,25)[101] or when he defends himself against Jeschute's reproach in terms which unintentionally confirm what she has said (258,15ff.).[102] Elsewhere the irony of ignorance can work the other way whenever a remark meant to be ironic is disproved by events and shown to be true in a sense not intended (as in Parzival's sarcastic words about the favours granted him by God, 447,25ff.)[103] or when irony can be mistakenly assumed where none was used (as in the page's assumption that Gawan must be mocking him by pretending ignorance, 324,21ff.).

Appurtenances worn by a character may convey an ambiguous message. The sword presented to him at Munsalvæsche is taken by Parzival as the generous gift of host to guest, at the most suggesting an obligation to repay hospitality by knightly assistance, whereas in fact its symbolic significance is more ceremonial, hinting at Anfortas's abdication and potential transfer of royal authority to Parzival.[104] The same ambiguity underlies the mantle also given to Parzival at the Grail-castle: he takes it as the conventional gift of clothing, generously given to the travel-stained knightly visitor,[105]

99. See above, pp. 70f. and 123f. On Trevrizent's unawareness: 474,18f. (cf. above, p. 190, fn. 55), 485,14f. and 500,28ff. (cf. above, pp. 195f.). On Arnive's unawareness of the implications of Gawan's remarks see above, p. 169, fn. 131.
100. Cf. Schröder, *ZfdA* 100 (1971), 114f. In Chrétien's version it is made more explicitly clear that Perceval failed to see the ironic import of Keu's words (cf. Green, *Recognising*, pp. 15 and 20).
101. See above, p. 68, and Green, *Homicide*, p. 67.
102. See above, p. 122. Cf. also the unconscious irony of Segramors's remark about Parzival (289,27f., see above, p. 129).
103. Green, *Irony*, pp. 186f. and 283. On Trevrizent's words 500,28ff. see Green, *Recognising*, p. 53.
104. On the implications of this sword see Mersmann, *Besitzwechsel*, pp. 135f., and Schröder, *ZfdA* 100 (1971), 111ff., especially pp. 122f. and 125.
105. On this conventional reading of the motif see Mersmann, *Besitzwechsel*, pp. 127ff., and Peil, *Gebärde*, pp. 43, 44 and 64. The conventional nature of this motif means that the listener is likely to react in the same way as Parzival.

whereas later Anfortas reveals that this too was meant as part of specifically royal insignia (500,28ff.).[106] In quite a different context the ring worn by Sigune when Parzival encounters her for the third time is suspiciously taken by him as the token of an illicit love-affair, whereas it is in fact meant as the sign of her marriage, in God's eyes, to her dead lover (439,22ff. and 440,13ff.).[107]

When we come to appurtenances correctly or incorrectly read we find that the examples are almost entirely confined to the heraldic signs, armour and crests discussed earlier.[108] That these should make the act of recognition possible (Belakane's marshal thus recognises Gahmuret from his coat of arms as a knight he has earlier seen at Alexandria, 18,5ff.)[109] is nothing remarkable, since this was precisely their function.[110] Worthy of comment is the fact that these identifying signs can occur elsewhere than on the items of knightly equipment previously discussed: on a tent, for example, or on a woman's cape, or branded on the flanks of knight's horse.[111] Such signs can fail to convey their message, however, for a variety of reasons which go beyond the simple fact that they may have been damaged or made difficult to see by earlier combats. A heraldic sign can after all only serve as an identifier if it is already known, so that Kaylet at Zazamanc, like the *Anschevîn* at Kanvoleis, has no means of recognising Gahmuret once he has adopted a new coat of arms on leaving Anschouwe.[112] Parzival's acquisition of Ither's armour with all its identifying trappings causes much greater confusion, for Clamide's men at Pelrapeire are convinced that it is Ither who is fighting on behalf of the queen (203,27ff.),[113] whilst difficulties are created for Trevrizent when he is confronted by a guest who wears

---

106. Cf. Mersmann, *Besitzwechsel*, pp. 129ff., and Schröder, *ZfdA* 100 (1971), 127.
107. See above, pp. 182 and 183f.
108. See above, pp. 264ff.
109. See above, p. 49.
110. Other examples where a coat of arms explicitly assists the act of recognition include Lahfilirost recognising Razalic (43,11 and 21f.), Gahmuret and the *Anschevîn* (80,11, see above, p. 57), Cunneware and Orilus (275,21f., p. 125), Gawan and the Arthurian knights at Bearosche (383,7, p. 138) and Kyot and the Grail-knights (800,2ff.). A similar example with the crest on a helmet is the encounter between Gahmuret and Kaylet (39,11ff. and 50,4f., pp. 39 and 51).
111. 278,11ff. (Cunneware's tent, cf. above, p. 125, fn. 114). In 64,13ff. Gahmuret's arrival at Kanvoleis is recognised by his tent and the heraldic device on his banners. For the woman's cape see 792,25ff. and for the horse 540,25ff.
112. 50,1ff. (cf. above, p. 52) and 98,19ff. (p. 57). Sigune also fails to recognise Parzival in Ither's equipment, 250,19 (cf. above, p. 115).
113. See above, p. 87.

Conclusions

Ither's red armour and rides a Grail-horse and whom he therefore takes to be Lähelin (474,1ff.).[114] When Gawan meets Parzival at the start of Book XIV, not merely is the latter's shield already damaged, but the task of recognition is made more difficult by his carrying a wreath from Gramoflanz's tree, which convinces Gawan that this must be the latter.[115] Time can also add to these difficulties of recognition. Arnive has spent so long in captivity at Schastel Marveile that she is unable to make the necessary adjustment when she notices the heraldic devices of Arthur's knights: from these she thinks she recognises Isajes, the marshal of Utepandragun, whereas time has moved on by one generation and it is in fact his son Maurin, Guinevere's marshal (662,14ff.).[116] One of the reasons why Parzival should be taken for Clamide when he arrives at Pelrapeire is that his distinctive red armour is not clearly visible to the defenders because night is already beginning to fall (180,20).[117]

The range of explanations adduced to account for success or failure in recognition is thus extremely wide and rich, especially if we add the features of contemporary knightly equipment which Wolfram also exploited for the same purposes and bear in mind that, as with the accumulation of realistic detail, the poet can apply more than just one of the four categories of signals we have been considering to any one episode, showing how the theme of recognition arises from the interplay of many separate details.[118] But he goes much further than this, showing that recognition may be assisted or hindered not just by external factors such as heraldic signs, a gesture or the time of day, but more critically by the psychological predisposition of the person who has to do the recog-

---

114. See above, pp. 187f.
115. 679,13ff. (cf. above, p. 241).
116. See above, p. 169.
117. See above, p. 85.
118. Two reasons thus inform the reaction of the defenders of Pelrapeire to the arrival of Parzival: from the self-confidence of his solitary approach they assume that, as in the past, this must be Clamide (181,18ff.) and the onset of nightfall means that they cannot see Parzival's markings clearly enough to put this right (180,20). Three factors assist Signue in recognising Parzival's identity when they first meet: the beauty of his appearance (139,26ff.), his readiness to help (139,25 and 140,1f.) and his childish nicknames (140,6). At least four details play a part when Trevrizent is approached by Parzival: his guest's outward appearance may unconsciously suggest the possibility of kinship to him (474,21ff.), but other pointers suggest that this might be Lähelin (474,1), neither has any previous acquaintance with the other, and the hermit is ignorant of the vital fact that this is the man who behaved disastrously at Munsalvæsche.

nising. This person's task may be made easier or more difficult by the readiness, previous experience and general awareness he manages (or fails) to bring to bear,[119] and there are occasions when intuitive insight is able to pierce to the heart of the matter and dispense with outward pointers.

Recognition is made possible by what the recogniser himself can contribute to the task in two main respects. In the experience of love it is Obilot's emotional inclination towards Gawan that allows her to recognise the truth about this stranger, to perceive intuitively that he can only be a knight (352,20ff.).[120] To include her sister Obie in this example may seem perverse, especially since it is she who makes the slanderous suggestion that Gawan is no more than a vulgar merchant, but we are allowed to see enough of her motives to realise that her behaviour is dictated by a desperate concern for Meljanz and by her intuitive recognition, just as correct as her younger sister's, of Gawan's true worth and ability to outdo her lover in chivalry.[121] Whereas Obilot's feelings reveal the qualities of her lover to her, Obie's love for Meljanz alerts her to the rival qualities of Gawan. Gawan himself is capable of similar insight, primarily because of his own experience in love (301,8ff. and 21ff.), when he correctly interprets what lies behind Parzival's unmoving stance in the scene of the three drops of blood in the snow.[122] The other context in which this type of immediate or unconscious insight is illustrated is Munsalvæsche. Two important examples show how, despite all signs to the contrary, two members of the Grail-dynasty are enabled to grasp Parzival's identity because their thoughts are already preoccupied with the area in which the truth now presents itself to them. Sigune's belated recognition of Parzival's muffled voice from inside his helmet is unconsciously assisted by the fact that she has just been speaking of the Grail-dynasty to which he belongs (251,2ff.),[123] whilst Trevrizent, previously misled into taking Parzival for Lähelin, has been led by stages into talking of the Grail-dynasty and, subconsciously aware

---

119. Cf. Hahn, *PBB(T)* 99 (1977), 442: 'Der schon in der Didaktik hervortretende Gedanke, daß einer erkennt, insofern er selber etwas ist, genauer, daß man nur das wahrzunehmen vermag, was man in der eigenen Existenz verwirklicht, stellt so etwas wie ein Grundaxiom aller Personerkenntnis in höfischer mittelalterlicher Dichtung dar.'
120. See above, p. 136.
121. *Ibid.*
122. See above, p. 128.
123. See above, p. 116.

Conclusions

of similarities between them and the stranger before him, is prompted into asking him pointblank who he is (474,1ff.).[124] Parzival himself is closely involved in this type of argument, for there are hints that he does not simply come to Munsalvæsche again when providence calls him there, but when he eventually shows sufficient maturity and awareness. Hahn has interpreted the passage 248,6ff. and 14ff. in the light of Parzival's ethical immaturity at the time of his failure at Munsalvæsche, suggesting that Parzival, because he has not yet experienced suffering (*kumber*) himself, is in no position to appreciate the importance of compassion with Anfortas's suffering.[125] This suggestion agrees with Wapnewski's quite independent interpretation of *an rehter zît* (484,3) as meaning subjectively the time when Parzival is suitably equipped mentally, has recognised enough of the situation to be ready to ask the question.[126]

This last example also implies the converse, however, a period during which Parzival will not be mature enough to appreciate the facts of his situation and to act accordingly. Unable to apply correctly what he does know or not even knowing enough on which to base an interpretation, he misjudges situation after situation.[127] This is made clear from the beginning at Soltane in a rather mechan-

---

124. See above, p. 190.
125. Hahn, *Schönheit*, pp. 220ff. In these informative pages Hahn concentrates on the poet's usage of the central word *kumber*, but it is equally important to stress the novelty of Parzival's personal experience of suffering from 248,14ff. on. In this connection it is significant that Parzival's departure from the Round Table and the start of his quest for the Grail should be described by the narrator in terms which stress the novelty of this experience (333,1: *Nu was sîn ors verdecket, / sîn selbes nôt erwecket – kumber* may here be replaced by *nôt*, but the *wecke* of 248,14 is echoed in the *erwecket* of 333,2). On another sense in which personal suffering (and the self-knowledge which it brings) is necessary to an understanding of another's suffering, and hence to the compassion required in Parzival's relationship to Anfortas, see below, pp. 292f.
126. Wapnewski, *Parzival*, p. 102 (cf. above, p. 206, fn. 107). When Parzival is eventually called to the Grail by Cundrie, he looks back on his first experience at Munsalvæsche and sums it up in the words '*done wasez et dennoch niht mîn heil*' (783,15). I take *mîn heil* in a double sense here: objectively it is the favour which God did not grant him on that occasion (cf. 783,10: '*sô hât got wol zuo mir getân*'), but subjectively it implies that Parzival's own behaviour, his inability to see what was required of him, brought this about (cf. 783,13: '*iedoch het ich niht missetân*'). On the interplay between a providential call and Parzival's discovery of his self in eventually coming into Grail-kingship see below, pp. 295f. and 314f.
127. Hahn, *PBB(T)* 99 (1977), 441, has applied this point to Marke in Gottfried's *Tristan*: 'Wieder deckt sich Betrug mit Selbstbetrug, insofern der Betrogene gar nicht erkennen will.'

ical way in order to bring out the humour of the situation (having just been told of God's resplendence by Herzeloyde, he immediately takes the knights in their shining armour as gods),[128] but still underlies the disastrous episode at Munsalvæsche (having recently acquired *zuht* and knightly skill from Gurnemanz, he concentrates on the *zuht* undoubtedly present at the Grail-castle and judges his obligations only in terms of chivalric exploits).[129] This inability to judge a new situation correctly because past experience or a present assumption provides an inadequate guide or even blocks the way to piercing through to a new dimension recurs in numerous episodes. Parzival fails to recognise Jeschute when they meet again because his embarrassment at his earlier behaviour has led to an all too successful repression of this detail from his past.[130] Arthur's knights fail to recognise Parzival and see in him an aggressive challenger because Arthur's recent warning induces them to expect no more than this.[131] The episode with Gramoflanz is rich in such false pre-judgments: Gawan expects to meet Gramoflanz, Parzival expects to be challenged by Gramoflanz after taking his wreath, and Gramoflanz expects an encounter with Gawan, so that in every case the actual situation is misread in the light of what it should be.[132] Suspiciousness, as well as expectancy, can be similarly distorting, as when Parzival's suspicions, roused by the ring Sigune wears, block his way to recognising her or when the same reaction, called forth by Feirefiz claiming to be an *Anschevîn*, jeopardises the recognition of his halfbrother.[133]

These examples should suffice to show that recognition in *Parzival* is not necessarily an intellectual process: it may make demands on perception, alertness and memory, but it can just as easily be brought about by the insight of affection and prevented by the blindness of prejudice. It is Cunneware's *herze* which at once tells her of Parzival's qualities (306,1),[134] the insight of Condwiramurs enables her to assess correctly the thoughts passing

---

128. See above, p. 62.
129. See above, pp. 106ff., and Green, *Aventiure*, pp. 151ff.
130. See above, p. 122, fn. 106.
131. See above, pp. 126f.
132. See above, pp. 240, 242, and 244.
133. See above, pp. 182 and 249.
134. Obilot's mother, won for Gawan by his appearance and bearing, is enabled by this to see immediately whom her daughter has in mind when a request is made of her (374,22: 'er süezer man vil guoter! / ich wæne, ir meint den fremden gast. / sîn blic ist reht ein meien glast').

Conclusions

through Parzival's mind as he sits silently in front of her,[135] Parzival is immediately able to judge the full implications of the blood in the snow,[136] whilst Gawan's intuition in his assessment of Orgeluse is immediate, correct and superior to the under-informed state of the listeners.[137] Accordingly, when a process of recognition is described we can sometimes be shown how eyes *and* heart participate in this joint task. When Lippaut, for example, correctly judges Gawan's chivalric status with the help of *zwei ougen unde ein herze* (364,26) he is doing on the visual plane what Hartmann expects of his listener on the aural plane in urging him to pay attention not merely with his ears, but also with his heart.[138] Recognition is no simple or superficial process: the evidence of the senses has to be reinforced by the insight (intellectual or intuitive) of the heart, or alternatively, as is sometimes implied, a number of senses have to cooperate to bring about a reliable judgment.[139] It is not by chance that a verbal phrase like *ze rehte spehn* can be used of or by the young Parzival,[140] for in the case of a hero who starts life as a *tôre* and whose career is a pathway towards recognition a phrase like this is more than a polite conversational formula, it sums up for us what the ultimate task is of one who is described as *træclîche wîs* (4,18), as is revealed even more sharply when the phrase can be used with unconscious irony as a recommendation by someone who fails to live up to it himself.[141]

---

135. See above, p. 86.
136. This has been analysed by Dewald, *Minne*, pp. 39ff.
137. Cf. Schaefer, *Beobachtungen*, pp. 217f., especially p. 218: 'Wir haben durch unser Wissen nichts vor Gawan voraus, im Gegenteil: wir können nicht wie er Wesen erkennen und mußten daher auf unserer Ebene informiert werden als Menschen, die an der Erscheinung hangen. Seine fraglose Sicherheit hat sogar beigetragen zu unserem Verständnis Orgeluses.'
138. See above, p. 2. Gramoflanz, after having had pointed out to him Beacurs, the brother of the beloved whom he has not yet seen, feels confident that his heart will identify her (722,14: *dô dâhter 'herze, nuo vint / si diu dem gelîche, / der hie rît sô minneclîche. / si ist für wâr sîn swester'*). Cf. also 724,19ff. Cunneware also recognises Parzival by her heart (306,1).
139. Both of Parzival's male mentors are agreed on this point, Gurnemanz with regard to his pupil's future (171,22: *'ir kunnet hæren unde sehen, / entseben unde dræhen: / daz solt iuch witzen næhen'*) and Trevrizent in connection with Parzival's past transgression at Munsalvæsche (488,26: *'dô dir got fünf sinne lêch, / die hânt ir rât dir vor bespart'*).
140. 123,2 (*'ob du ze rehte kundest spehn'*); 147,25 (*'dun sihst des rehten niht'*); 228,22 (*'ob ir mich ze rehte speht'*).
141. Parzival demands Ither's equipment for himself in critical terms (154,10: *'wer mich, ob du bî witzen sîst'*) more properly applicable to himself in behaving with such tragic *tumpheit* (cf. the narrator's judgment of this behaviour as *des tumben*

The Art of Recognition in Wolfram's *Parzival*

Parzival's process of self-recognition

After drawing together these general threads concerned with the theme of recognition we must concentrate on the central problem, Parzival's path of recognition and how it leads him to the discovery of his self. Wolfram not merely illustrates this central problem with many episodes where recognition plays a part in the hero's progress (for he recognises himself in recognising others), he also surrounds Parzival's task of recognition with scenes in which many others are confronted with a similar problem. This technique of having secondary scenes throw light on the major theme is used elsewhere. On the small scale the many battle-cries to be heard at Bearosche highlight Gawan's success in not missing the vital one of the Arthurian knights,[142] whilst on the large scale the variegated depiction of numerous knights killing or sparing their opponents is meant to

---

Parzivâles ger, 161,6). Later Parzival rejects Jeschute's accusation by denying all knowledge of her, but his self-assured tone (258,15: *'frouwe, merket baz, / gein wem ir kêret iwern haz'*) is undermined by the fact that Jeschute is correct in blaming him and by our gradual realisation that it is rather Parzival himself who should pay better heed (see above, p. 122). In the encounter between Parzival and the Round Table both Segramors and Keii are hoist with their own petard, the former by suggesting that it is Parzival, rather than himself, who should have recognised the other's shield and therefore his identity (289,29: *'ober bekande mînen schilt'*), the latter by using a phrase (290,20: *'wær wir alle blint oder toup'*) which he intends as a remote and improbable hypothesis, but which events show us to be no less than the truth. On these two remarks see above, p. 129.

In *Schönheit*, pp. 218ff., Hahn has thrown new light on the theme of recognition in *Parzival* by discussing how others both recognise Parzival and yet fail to recognise his true nature. The Arthurian world, for example, sees through the outer appearances of the *tôre* and perceives Parzival's qualities (Karnahkarnanz sees that he is born for chivalry, Ither that he is born for love), yet remains unaware of his full potential (as Grail-king his chivalry will ultimately surpass the Arthurian ideal, just as his relationship with Condwiramurs cannot be equated with Gawan's experiences in love). Hahn takes her argument an important step further in also applying this point to members of the Grail-world, who like Sigune and Trevrizent recognise Parzival profoundly enough to be able to teach him essential facts about his relationship with the Grail-dynasty (see above, pp. 210ff.), but whose judgment is not necessarily shared by the narrator. Sigune's and Cundrie's criticism of him for *untriuwe* (255,12ff.; 316,16ff.) is therefore undermined by the narrator's express comments (296,1; 319,8). To this extent Parzival not merely surpasses the Arthurian world, he also leaves these members of the Grail-dynasty behind him, as befits one who is to become their king and as is most convincingly and movingly brought out by the fact that even Trevrizent is far from being in complete control of the situation in Book IX and has himself to grope uncertainly towards the truth.

142. See above, p. 270.

Conclusions

show up the unique position of Parzival and how fraught with consequences was his encounter with Ither.[143] The same is true with the theme of recognition, so that we must now consider this problem in the light of Parzival himself.

Just how central Parzival's self-recognition is to Wolfram's work may be seen by contrast with Hartmann's *Iwein*. In the earlier work, too, the hero's crisis (taking the form of his temporary madness) represents symbolically his divorce from society and loss of a sense of personal identity, reacquired not merely by someone else's assistance (in the shape of the healing ointment), but also by virtue of the hero himself reflecting on the question of his identity (3509: '*bistûz Îwein, ode wer?*')[144] and his ethical status by seeing his present position in the light of his past.[145] In quite general terms this structure could be applied to *Iwein* and *Parzival*, but Wolfram introduces radical changes beyond this. Whereas Iwein was immediately aware of the fact of his guilt as soon as the crisis struck him (3221ff.)[146] Parzival has to struggle for recognition of himself over a long period of time from Book VI to Book IX and even in the encounter with Trevrizent has to be guided by several stages to this goal. The longer time required for Parzival's self-recognition reflects the more radical nature of the crisis confronting him, for he is not merely separated from society (like Iwein) after leaving the Round Table, but has also renounced his service of God.[147] Whereas Iwein was able to reflect upon his own past and reconstruct the essential outlines of his present position by his own mental efforts, Parzival's loss of bearings is more thoroughgoing, there are aspects of his past about which he has no knowledge, so that to confront himself successfully and come to full knowledge of himself he needs to be guided once more through his past by someone who knows its implications, by the hermit. The self-knowledge in guilt which struck Iwein immediately at the time of his crisis and the reconstruction of his past which he achieved unaided now take up the whole of Book IX in the case of Parzival, whose task of cognition[148] is infinitely more protracted and made

---

143. Green, *Homicide*, pp. 27ff. and 49ff.
144. On this see Wehrli, *Formen*, pp. 177ff.
145. Hirschberg, *Untersuchungen*, pp. 291f.
146. *Ibid.*, p. 334.
147. *Ibid.*, pp. 100 and 335.
148. Hirschberg, *ibid.*, pp. 316, 334 and 358, talks of Parzival's 'Erkenntnisleistung' in Book IX.

possible only by the hermit explaining his guest's past to him and placing it in the wider context of the history of the Grail-dynasty, of the Grail itself and even, to the extent that Parzival's killing of Ither repeats Cain's deed, of humanity at large.[149] Parzival's task is no longer, as with a typical Arthurian hero, to put things right by means of knightly exploits, for his quest is now for self-knowledge, the acquisition of which allows him to put right his own past when he comes to Munsalvæsche a second time.[150]

In placing the theme of self-recognition at the centre of his work Wolfram grants prominence to a topical concern of the courtly romance around 1200. It has been said of works belonging to this genre that they treat the problem of the hero's alienation from himself and his eventual self-realisation and that the path he follows on his adventures is one from ignorance to knowledge in humility.[151] If the knightly hero's quest is for self-recognition, his departure in search of adventure is to find out, like Hartmann's Gregorius, *von wanne ich sî oder wer*, and the discoveries he makes on his journey will lead him to confess, again like Gregorius: *ich enbin niht der ich wânde sîn*.[152] The widespread concern of the romance with this theme has been compared with the well-attested preoccupation of medieval theology, especially in the twelfth century, with the precept 'Know thyself',[153] a parallel between vernacular literature and Latin theology which is not meant to suggest any particular source for this romance theme, but rather to indicate what it may owe to the intellectual climate of its age.[154] It is in this sense only that I wish now to look at Parzival's process of self-recognition under the three headings under which the precept 'Know thyself' is commonly treated in twelfth-century theology: first, recognition of oneself in the sense of one's own character, but then, because the other helps to define the self and because the self is

---

149. *Ibid.*, p. 335.
150. In *Aventiure*, p. 151, I suggested that knightly exploits were played down by contrast to the importance attached to the question of compassion which Parzival should have asked at Munsalvæsche. In the context of Book IX, however, I agree with Hirschberg, *Untersuchungen*, pp. 316 and 334, that the emphasis is transferred from knightly exploits to the task of recognition. On the possible connection between self-recognition and compassion with others see below, pp. 292f.
151. Haas, *Studien*, p. 12, fn. 45.
152. *Ibid.*, p. 13, and Wehrli, *Formen*, pp. 181f. On this aspect of *Gregorius* see Ohly, *Verfluchte*, p. 14.
153. This has been treated in detail by Courcelle, *Connais-toi*, pp. 231ff.
154. Cf. Haas, *Studien*, p. 13, fn. 45.

Conclusions

not conceived as autonomous, recognition of oneself in relation to society and to God.

We may start with recognition of oneself, if only because medieval theology tends to give it priority, arguing that genuine knowledge of oneself issues in humility, without which it is impossible to proceed to knowledge of God or to a recognition of one's proper relationship to other men. This correlation of self-knowledge with humility is not specifically Christian, for the inscription on the temple at Delphi (Γνῶθι σαυτόν) was far from being a formula of proud individualism, but was meant rather, as a fitting reminder in a holy place, to confront the worshipper with the facts of his own weakness, mortality and ignorance.[155] If this was the function of the formula in antiquity it is not surprising that it should be adopted by Christian thinkers, together with references to its Delphic origin, to stress that the function of self-knowledge is to teach the Christian true humility.[156] Richard of Saint-Victor therefore maintains that man passes from the world to the self, then from the self to God by despising himself,[157] whilst Hugh of Saint-Victor argues that the interior soliloquy of a man with himself leads to the discovery of the secret places of the heart and to contempt for himself.[158] In his treatise *De gradibus humilitatis et superbiae* St Bernard of Clairvaux connects self-knowledge with humility by defining the latter as the virtue by which man, because of an accurate knowledge of himself, reveals his own worthlessness to himself.[159] Elsewhere he suggests that without self-knowledge man can have neither fear of God (without which he can have no hope) nor humility.[160]

The importance of such theoretical equations of self-knowledge

---

155. *Ibid.*, p. 1.
156. *Ibid*, (cf. also p. 5).
157. *MPL* 196, 1077A: *Transi ergo et teipsum, perge in Deum tuum ... Contemne teipsum ... Primum ergo transitum facit contemptus mundi, secundum transitum efficit contemptus sui.* Cf. Courcelle, *Connais-toi*, p. 246.
158. *De contemplatione*, p. 428: *Soliloquium dicitur quia uir se solum alloquitur, id est quando homo interior ab exteriori non turbatur, sed cordis secreta rimatur, mentem et conscientiam, ob sui contemptum considerat et speculatur.* See Courcelle, *Connais-toi*, p. 247.
159. *De gradibus*, p. 17,21: *Humilitas est virtus, qua homo verissima sui cognitione sibi ipse vilescit.* Courcelle, *Connais-toi*, p. 258.
160. *Sermo 36*, 4, 6, p. 8, 1; *Nam si ignoras te, non habebis timorem Dei in te, non humilitatem*; *Sermo 37*, 3, 5, p. 12, 2: *Ceterum si nos ignorantia Dei tenet, quomodo speramus in eum quem ignoramus? Si nostri, quomodo humiles erimus, cum nihil simus?* Courcelle, *Connais-toi*, p. 267.

with humility for an interpretation of *Parzival* lies in the fact that the hero is not merely engaged on a lengthy task of recognition, or more essentially self-recognition, but is also subjected to what has been termed a *schola humilitatis* throughout the narrative. Prompted by the fact that the story of Parzival coming into Grail-kingship is set in motion by the vacancy created by Anfortas's offence against *diemuot* (478,30ff.) and by the equally revealing fact that Trevrizent's last words to Parzival in the work stress the importance of this same virtue (798,30: '*nu kêrt an diemuot iwern sin*'), Kolb has fruitfully interpreted the whole work in the light of this virtue.[161] As regards the correlation of Parzival's self-recognition with humility it is not by chance that Parzival, apprised by Trevrizent at last of the implications of his behaviour at Munsalvæsche and realising now where he stands, should make his final confession to the hermit in terms which demonstrate that he has reached a point in self-knowledge identical with an acknowledgment of guilt and unworthiness (488,9; 488,11ff.; 488,19f.).[162] Moreover, just as Richard of Saint-Victor argued that by contempt for oneself one could come to God, so does Parzival's acknowledgment of unworthiness lead to the hermit at length reconciling him with God by absolving him (501,7). Just as St Bernard suggested that without self-knowledge one could have neither fear of God nor hope, so does Parzival's recognition of himself in Book IX mean that his hatred of God is henceforth laid aside in favour of trust in Him (741,26ff.).

Yet the association of self-knowledge with humility goes much further in application to *Parzival*. This can best be shown from another passage in St Bernard's *De gradibus*,[163] where it is argued that just as pure truth can only be beheld by the pure heart, so the wretchedness (*miseria*) of a brother is felt indeed by the heart that knows wretchedness (*misero corde*). But in order to have a heart full of wretchedness on account of another's wretchedness it is first of all necessary to know one's own condition, so that his state of mind may be found in one's own and so that one should know from one-

---

161. Kolb, *PBB(T)* 78 (1956), 65ff. See also Henzen, *PBB(T)* 80 (1958), 422ff.
162. Kolb, *art. cit.*, p. 107.
163. *De gradibus*, p. 21,8 (cf. Courcelle, *Connais-toi*, p. 258, and Kolb, *art. cit.*, p. 112): *Sicut enim pura veritas non nisi puro corde videtur, sic miseria fratris verius misero corde sentitur. Sed ut ob alienam miseriam cor miserum habeas, oportet tuam prius agnoscas, ut proximi mentem in tua invenias et ex te noveris qualiter illi subvenias, exemplo scilicet Salvatoris nostri, qui pati voluit, ut compati sciret; miser fieri, ut misereri disceret.*

Conclusions

self how to bring him help, following the example of Christ who wanted to suffer (*pati*) so that He could feel suffering or compassion with us (*compati*), and who made Himself wretched (*miser*) so that He might learn how to feel mercy (*misereri*). The argument developed here is relevant to Wolfram's romance in two respects. In the first place, it treats seriously the view that another's experience can only be understood on the basis of one's own, that only one's own suffering can teach fellow feeling with the suffering of another person, and therefore provides medieval theoretical support for Hahn's suggestion, reached by quite a different way, that only Parzival's experience of *kumber* for himself after his departure from Munsalvæsche teaches him to appreciate Anfortas's *kumber*.[164] Secondly, the hinge of the argument is that only by first recognising one's own wretchedness (*oportet tuam prius agnoscas*) can one understand another's wretchedness and thus make the ethically vital transition from suffering to compassion (from *pati* to *compati*, from *miseria* to *misereri*). This argument by St Bernard constructs a bridge from recognition of oneself to recognition of others (in the context of compassion), to the second stage in our discussion of self-recognition.

Both John of Salisbury and the Cistercian Helinand of Froidmont attribute four fruits to self-knowledge[165] and although the fruits listed by one may not tally precisely with those enumerated by the other, both are in agreement in including acknowledgment of one's worthlessness (*vilitatem sui*) and love of one's neighbour (*caritatem proximi*). Elsewhere in his *De gradibus* St Bernard formulates the same idea in different terms, arguing that self-recognition involves contempt for oneself but also, so far as other people are concerned, a flight from justice to compassion.[166] Distinguishing between the three stages of truth, he describes the first as one in which by the exercise of reason we scrutinise ourselves and practise humility, whilst the second is characterised by

---

164. See above, p. 285.
165. John of Salisbury, *Policraticus* III 2, 480b, p. 175,13 (in the context of a discussion of *Scito teipsum*): *Haec etenim contemplatio quadripertitum parit fructum, uilitatem sui, caritatem proximi, contemptum mundi, amorem Dei*; Helinand of Froidmont, *De cognitione sui*, MPL 212,724D: *Haec autem consideratio quadripertitum parit fructum: vilitatem sui, et desiderium coelestis regni, charitatem proximi, timorem judicii*.
166. *De gradibus*, p. 29,28: *Sed cum se ad id sufficere non posse conspiciunt, – cum enim fecerint omnia quae mandata fuerint sibi, servos se inutiles dicunt–, de iustitia ad misericordiam fugiunt*.

feeling compassion with others.[167] How relevant this kind of argument is to Wolfram's work can be seen from the central rôle of the question of compassion to be asked of Anfortas,[168] for when Parzival first comes to the Grail-castle in Book V he has experienced no real suffering himself, hence lacks the necessary self-knowledge and humility to see the overriding need to show compassion by asking the question, whilst by the time he comes there a second time he has been brought by Trevrizent to the necessary degree of self-recognition.

Yet recognition of oneself in relation to others is a two-way process. It involves not merely the extension of self-knowledge to others in a spirit of compassion, but also the possibility that by learning about others, by defining them as similar to or different from oneself, one can learn about oneself. What Goldin has said of the medieval love lyric[169] can be applied to the romance, where the knight achieves self-knowledge by realising that his identity consists in approximating to a pre-existent chivalric ethos. Society is essential to the knight's sense of identity, for without his favourable reflection in the eyes of others he cannot know whether he has realised his potential and therefore cannot know himself. In this respect the situation in *Iwein* is typical, for the hero's loss of his sense of identity (represented by his period of madness) coincides with the loss of his personal reputation and with the withdrawal of his own name.[170]

We have yet to look at the problem of the withdrawal of Parzival's name from long stretches of Wolfram's narrative,[171] but we may apply Goldin's observation to this romance by registering how repeatedly it is said of him that in fighting another knight he has in

---

167. *De gradibus*, p. 30,28: *Cum sint itaque tres gradus seu status veritatis, ad primum ascendimus per laborem humilitatis, ad secundum per affectum compassionis, ad tertium per excessum contemplationis. In primo veritas reperitur severa, in secundo pia, in tertio pura. Ad primum ratio ducit, qua nos discutimus; ad secundum affectus perducit, quo aliis miseremur ...*
168. That what was expected of Parzival at Munsalvæsche was a question of compassion has been unconvincingly denied by Bauer, *Euphorion* 57 (1963), 67ff. It is significant that both Sigune (255,17: '*iuch solt iur wirt erbarmet hân*') and Cundrie (316,3: '*sîn nôt iuch solt erbarmet hân*') see his obligation in these terms. On the spirit of charity which informs Parzival's question when he comes to the Grail-castle a second time see Johnson, *Beauty*, pp. 288f.
169. Goldin, *Mirror*, pp. 237 and 241.
170. On Hartmann's technique in this respect see Mohr, *ZfdA* 100 (1971), 85ff.
171. See below, pp. 298ff.

Conclusions

reality been doing combat with himself. This is said expressly of his encounters with Ither, Gawan and Feirefiz,[172] but to these we could add the near miss of his encounter with Gawan at Bearosche and his actual combat with Vergulaht, not narrated to us.[173] The recurrent symbolism of Parzival's recognition of himself in these opponents operates on various levels. On the most obvious level it is true because of his kinship, close or distant, with each of these opponents, so that in fighting them Parzival is endangering his own flesh and blood quite literally. On another level, however, that worked out by Mohr with reference to the allusion to Cain,[174] this physical kinship does duty for a spiritual bond, so that what is at issue in these combats is the risk, present in any combat, of killing one's brother in Christ. The danger now is that Parzival, in possibly killing another Christian, is endangering his own soul.[175] Finally, on a level which links together all these isolated combats from the beginning of Parzival's knightly career to its conclusion, from Ither to Feirefiz, these combats combine to bring home to Parzival an unwelcome truth about his knightly career, namely that his initial offence in killing Ither is a danger that continues to dog his footsteps throughout the rest of the work,[176] but also the religious truth of his complete dependence on divine grace, on God's intervention if he is to avoid repeating this original sin in the case of his half-brother.[177]

Yet Parzival's recognition of his own position depends on his realising where others stand in a sense far wider than these knightly encounters with kinsmen. More than anyone else in the work he is the centre of a ramified network of dynastic and feudal relationships, so that his growing self-awareness is tantamount to his gradually learning where he stands in this mesh of family connections and what inherited possibilities and obligations define his

---

172. Of Ither the point is made retrospectively by Trevrizent (475,21: *'du hâst dîn eigen verch erslagn'*; cf. 499,13: *'von Ithêr du bist erborn: / dîn hant die sippe hât verkorn'*). On Gawan see Parzival's words 689,5 (*'ich hân mich selben überstriten'*) and Gawan's reply 689,29 (*'dîn hant uns bêde überstreit'*), and on Feirefiz see 752,15 (*'mit dir selben hâstu hie gestritn'*) and Wapnewski, *Parzival*, p. 136.
173. See above, pp. 140f. and 146f.
174. Mohr, *Schuld*, p. 340.
175. Ibid., pp. 342ff.
176. Green, *Irony*, p. 280.
177. Cf. Schröder, *ZfdA* 100 (1971), 112.

position in life.[178] It is significant that when Sigune reveals his name to him (140,16) she immediately defines him further in terms of the feudal rights he has inherited from both parents (140,25ff.), adding however that he has already unwittingly incurred an obligation, since Schionatulander fell in defence of these lands of Parzival (141,2ff.). If Parzival already at this stage learns something of his potential future, confirming what his mother had earlier told him (128,3ff.), this information is still far from complete, he learns more about his mother's feudal realms Waleis and Norgals from Trevrizent (494,15ff.),[179] and, of more vital importance for the goal of his quest, it is only from the hermit that, in addition to being told about his past offences against kinsmen, he is apprised of his kinship with the Grail-family and realises his position as the only possible successor to Anfortas.[180] Although he did not realise it when he departed from the Round Table, Parzival's freely undertaken quest for the Grail (333,27: *schildes ambet umben grâl / wirt nu vil güebet sunder twâl*) is one side of the coin only, the other side of which is the fact that this was his inheritance (333,30: *er was ouch ganerbe dar*). It is the function of Book IX to reveal that Parzival's most intensely personal wish, the goal which defines him and no one else, is one that comes to him from his position within the Grail-dynasty, and that self-recognition is here tantamount to recognition of the wider situation.

Recognition of oneself in humility leads not merely to a compassionate recognition of others, it is also the means to a recognition of God. The Augustinian idea that a man knows himself truly when he knows himself as an image of a divine model[181] was taken up by those monastic writers of the twelfth century, especially the Cistercians, who were preoccupied with the idea that self-knowledge is a path to God.[182] If man is made in God's image, then knowledge of oneself should lead to knowledge of God. For Anselm of Canterbury the more the rational soul seeks to know itself the more effectively it draws near to knowledge of God, since the soul con-

178. Mersmann, *Besitzwechsel*, pp. 116 and 118.
179. *Ibid.*, p. 116.
180. See above, pp. 214ff. Cf. Busse, *Verwandtschaftsstrukturen*, p. 132: 'Mich auf das bisher Gesagte stützend, würde ich die Identität, die Parzival gewinnt, mit dem Ort identifizieren, den Parzival einnimmt, nachdem er sein Doppelziel–Condwiramurs und den Gral–erreicht hat: eine Identität, die das Subjekt in den Relationen der Verwandtschaftsbeziehungen hat.'
181. Cf. Goldin, *Mirror*, p. 225.
182. Morris, *Discovery*, p. 76.

stitutes a mirror in which to contemplate the divinity which cannot be looked at face to face.[183] For Achard of Saint-Victor one of the reasons why man should enter within himself is that without such self-knowledge he is both a stranger to himself and a fugitive from God (*vagus a seipso et profugus a Deo*).[184] This negative phrase, summing up the magnitude of the loss incurred by one who has no knowledge of himself and hence of God, recalls the situation of Parzival during the period of his dissension with God. During these years he is not merely divorced from God, but also disoriented in time and space, remote from human society at large and, to the extent that his name is withheld from him, unaware of his own identity and of where he stands. The heart of Parzival's disorientation is clearly his relationship with God, but the occasion for his dissension with Him is his failure to realise where he stands, what he is and how he may best realise his potential at Munsalvæsche.

As with the relationship between self and others, that between recognition of oneself and God is a two-way process. Not merely does knowledge of self open the way to knowledge of God, but increasing knowledge of self shows that this self is created in the image of God and, however imperfectly, reflects something of God. This truth is put forward by Trevrizent as a moral imperative (462,18: '*sît getriwe ân allez wenken, / sît got selbe ein triuwe ist*'), although how far it is necessary to make such a recommendation to one who is Parzival, rather than Lähelin, is another matter. Yet Parzival is prepared to accept the truth that man best fulfils his identity by following God's example quite early in his career, despite his inexperience and ludicrous incomprehension of the general situation.[185] He goes laughably wrong in taking Karnahkarnanz to be a god (122,21ff.) on the basis of a superficial equation

---

183. *MPL* 158,213A: *Quid igitur apertius, quam quia mens rationalis quanto studiosius ad se discendum intendit, tanto efficacius ad illius cognitionem ascendit, et quanto seipsam intueri negligit, tanto ab eius speculatione descendit? Aptissime igitur sibimet esse velut speculum dici potest, in quo speculetur, ut ita dicam, imaginem eius quam facie ad faciem videre nequit.* See Courcelle, *Connais-toi*, p. 237.
184. *Sermo XV*, 1, 6, p. 205: *In nobis namque hec promissionis terra consistit; et ipsa est cordis inhabitatio, homo noster scilicet interior, qui in semetipso secum debet habitare, immo Christo ibi per fidem cohabitare. Hanc autem inhabitationem pariter illam Dei que ad superiorem promissionis pertinet terram, cum primo peccavit, amisit homo, eiectus a facie Dei et a facie cuiusdam terre interioris, id est cordis proprii, vagus a seipso et profugus a Deo super terram cui maledixit Dominus, in exterioribus quam intus perdiderat querens requiem et nusquam inveniens.* Courcelle, *Connais-toi*, p. 241.
185. See Green, *Irony*, pp. 350f.

between the knight's shining armour and what his mother has told him of God's resplendence (119,19). Parzival takes the knight for God, however, for a further reason, since his mother has also told him that God's nature is unfailing helpfulness (119,23ff.) and what the knight has just said of the abduction of Imane (122,15ff.) convinces even Parzival that the task of this knight must be to set right this wrong. This perceptive intuition may be overlaid by a ridiculous confusion, but at least Gahmuret's son has grasped the truth that a knight best realises his own nature in basing his actions on God's readiness to assist those in need.[186]

The parallels[187] adduced in this section from medieval theology have not been meant to establish anything like direct influences, but only to provide circumstantial evidence that the preoccupation with self-knowledge around 1200, whether in theological theory or in literary practice, was likely to include a number of related themes. In the case of *Parzival* these cover humility, compassion, the hero's relationship with his kinsmen and his dissension with God. There may well be other reasons why the poet was attracted by these themes, but his concern with the problem of Parzival's self-recognition can only have granted them additional importance.

Parzival's naming

A character's name is at once a highly personal feature (it identifies him by distinguishing him from others) and a social one (it is the means by which all others know him). We have seen already how the naming of a character plays a recurrent part in Wolfram's work (Parzival grows up ignorant of his name and learns it from Sigune, a failure of recognition in an encounter can be conveyed by the narrator withholding the name in question), but now we must consider how the overall technique of naming Parzival or leaving him anonymous at certain stages illustrates his process of self-recognition and realisation of his quest for the Grail.

186. When Karnahkarnanz denies that he is God, he adds '*ich leiste ab gerne sîn gebot*' (122,30), thereby implying that his chivalry of assistance freely rendered is ultimately inspired by God.
187. Some of the passages discussed by Courcelle make use of imagery which lies particularly close to the motif of the knightly quest in the romance. The imagery of wandering is present in the description by Achard of Saint-Victor of the soul *vagus a seipso et profugus a Deo* (see above, fn. 184), Richard of Saint-Victor compares a bad conscience with *terra illa deserta, inuia et inaquosa* (Courcelle, *Connais-toi*, p. 246) and the process of self-knowledge can be seen explicitly as *animi exploratio* (*ibid.*, p. 251).

Conclusions

In many respects the technique of naming in the Parzival story seems to owe much to the folktale and thus to be remote from realistic considerations such as contemporary armour with which this chapter began. In Chrétien's version the complete anonymity in which so many of the characters are kept[188] is reminiscent of the world of the 'Märchen' with which the romance genre has so much in common[189] and in which the action is in the hands of characters who are given no names, but are described in terms of their function within the tale ('the mother', 'the younger son', 'the giant').[190] In *Rumpelstilzchen* the motif of knowledge of a person's name as the equivalent of power exercised over him provides the theme of the tale.[191] Ethnological evidence also confirms the magic qualities attributed to names in primitive cultures. A name can thus be felt to incorporate its bearer's essence or character in some mysterious way (just as Sigune's revelation of Parzival's name imposes upon him the obligations of that name),[192] and this essence will be protected by preserving the secret of a name. To do this a childhood nickname will be used until the true name is employed in boyhood, or a common name will be used alongside the true name which is kept secret, or to guard the name intact recourse can be had to protective circumlocutions, especially those describing the bearer indirectly as the relative of a kinsman. Parallels for all these features may be found in *Parzival*,[193] but we have to distinguish between employment of the same motifs and the very different, more sophisticated ends they now serve. Chrétien's anonymous characters in

---

188. Cf. Green, *Namedropping*, p. 89.
189. Völker, *Elemente*; Niessen, *Märchenmotive*; Mauritz, *Ritter*; Nolting-Hauff, *Poetica* 6 (1974), 129ff.; Green, *Departure*.
190. Anonymity as a prevalent feature of the folktale has been established by Junk, *Gralsage*, pp. 139ff., by an analysis of the position in *KHM* (cf. also Lüthi, *Märchen*, p. 25). One does not have to agree with Junk's theory of the derivation of the Parzival tradition from the folktale *Peronnik* to see the value of his demonstration that the characters of this literary tradition, like those of the folktale, were probably originally nameless (*ibid.*, pp. 128ff.).
191. *KHM* 55 (I 254ff.).
192. Cf. Frazer, *Bough*, p. 261 and Pézard, *Dante*, pp. 356 and 361 (on Sigune's revelation see below, p. 305).
193. On the use of a childhood nickname see Clodd, *Magic*, pp. 64 and 73 (see below, p. 304, on the position with Perceval and Parzival); on the common name and secret name see Frazer, *Bough*, pp. 245 and 257 (see below, pp. 306f., on the use of *rîter rôt* in place of Parzival); on circumlocutions see Clodd, *Magic*, p. 55 (for *Parzival* cf. Green, *Namedropping*, pp.127ff., and *Naming*, pp.103 ff.) and on those referring to a kinsman Clodd, *Magic*, p. 52 (for *Parzival* cf. Green, *Namedropping*, pp.133ff.).

The Art of Recognition in Wolfram's *Parzival*

Perceval may remind us of the folktale, but he has at least provided his major characters with names, whilst Wolfram has entirely broken with anonymity by naming as many as 222 characters in his version (as against 36 with Chrétien).[194] By peopling his work with so many more characters, by naming most of them, by linking many of them by bonds of kinship or other ties, and by allowing us to learn more about them only gradually as we move further into the narrative he has endowed his technique of naming with a large degree of realism.[195] Even the apparently stylised feature of having only the defeated knight name himself is not so remote from contemporary practice, where the victor's reputation in society, let alone his hope for ransom-money, depended on broadcasting the names of his victims,[196] whilst Le Rider has also suggested a practice amongst knightly families in naming their male offspring as an explanation of the otherwise so unreal feature of Perceval's initial namelessness.[197]

In granting such an important aesthetic rôle to naming Wolfram was in a position to develop precedents found in Chrétien and Hartmann. Chrétien's romances in particular demonstrate how he came to realise the potential advantages in withholding names for a time and in releasing them only at a carefully chosen point with a particular purpose in mind.[198] The hero of *Lancelot* is referred to by anonymous circumlocutions for the first part of the narrative, so that only in v. 3660 is his name revealed to us, uttered by his mistress Guenevere, who fittingly establishes his true identity for us, both by his name and with regard to his rôle as her lover.[199] In *Yvain* the hero deliberately abandons the use of his name during the period of his guilt and penance, preferring for this stage of his career the anonymous circumlocution *chevalier au lion*. This anonymity is given up only in Yvain's last combat (with Gauvain, an encounter in which Yvain's lion plays no part) by the hero naming himself (6284), so that his readiness to be known by his own name after this symbolic victory is as revealing of where he stands in his ethical quest as was his earlier wish to forgo his name. With *Perceval* the hero learns his name (at a stage later than with Wolfram) imme-

194. See Green, *Namedropping*, p. 113.
195. *Ibid.*, p. 150.
196. Cf. Désilles-Busch, *Doner*, pp. 94f.
197. Le Rider, *Chevalier*, pp. 94ff.
198. On the points raised in this paragraph see Désilles-Busch, *Doner*, pp. 92f.
199. Cf. Green, *Namedropping*, p. 97f.

Conclusions

diately after his failure at the Grail-castle; in guessing it for himself he attains self-awareness, significantly at a point when he has just incurred a new guilt,[200] which leads his cousin to change his name from *Percevaus li Galois* to *Percevaus li cheitis* (3581f.).

The symbolism with which Chrétien invests naming in many of his works concerns a character's position with regard to society at large, which is hardly surprising in view of the double function of the name, personal and social. In *Erec* Enide enters the narrative anonymously, but is granted her name by the narrator at the time of her marriage to Erec, in other words when she acquires the status of the hero's wife and the higher social rank of one married to a king's son, rather than the daughter of a déclassé vassal.[201] The position is similar in *Cligès*, where the daughter of the German Emperor, at first referred to anonymously, is named at the point when she joins the gathering at court and, now proclaimed as the future wife of Alis, the Greek Emperor, has earned the right to her name.[202] Guinevere's naming of Lancelot has been interpreted as the first decisive step towards his acceptance by society,[203] whilst Laudine's immediate recognition of Yvain's name in its social context, her identification of the more than linguistic connection between *nom* and *renomée*, is an important step in the development of her attitude towards him.[204] The link between an individual and society established by his name is illustrated negatively in *Perceval*, where the mother keeps her son remote from chivalry (which means from knightly society) not merely by withdrawing into the solitude of a forest, but also by withholding his name from him and by using only childish nicknames for him.[205] Le Rider has also underlined an unexpected implication of the scene in which Perceval guesses and pronounces his own name in the encounter with his cousin (3575) by reminding us of the literary convention that it is the knight who fails in an adventure who is obliged to name himself, a fact which is true of Perceval in this scene, for he has just left the Grail-castle after his failure there.[206] The disgrace now attaching to his name is soon to be renewed when, after pronouncing his name at

200. Cf. Bezzola, *Sens*, pp. 56f., and Frappier, *Graal*, p. 121.
201. Green, *Namedropping*, pp. 95f.
202. Cf. Schwake, *GRM* 20 (1970), 345.
203. *Ibid.*, pp. 343f.
204. See Duggan, *OL* 24 (1969), 121.
205. Cf. Schwake, *GRM* 20 (1970), 345.
206. Le Rider, *Chevalier*, p. 36.

the apparent peak of renown at the Round Table (4562), Perceval is assailed by the Grail-messenger in terms so violent that the resolution to repair the damage done at the Grail-castle is identical with the wish to remedy the disgrace that has befallen his name.[207]

Wolfram did not therefore lack precedents for the symbolic dimensions to naming a hero or withholding his name, especially since the social implications of this symbolism, as Chrétien had discovered for himself in *Perceval*, made it very apposite to the theme of a character brought up in ignorance of himself and the world and having to discover both. What importance the German poet attaches to names can be gauged quite externally by the regularity, far exceeding what he found with Chrétien, with which he identifies his characters by a name, but also by the transparent meanings he devises for names of his own invention,[208] the conviction that one name, but not another, befits a certain person (Chrétien's Blancheflor thus becomes Condwiramurs)[209] and the care with which he has Sigune interpret the meaning of Parzival's name when she reveals it to him (140,16ff.). In addition to establishing the identity of a person, a name can also sum up the nature and essence of any animate being or inanimate object, so that to know the name is to exercise authority over whatever is so named, a truth from Genesis 2.19f. which recurs in 518,1ff.[210] Power and authority can also be conveyed by a name whenever it is freely uttered by the victor in a combat (as in 38,10: *der sigehafte jach dô sân | 'ich pin Gahmuret Anschevîn'*, after Gahmuret's defeat of Hiuteger), for the victor thereby ensures that his exploit is inseparable from his name, which is thus the guarantee of his renown, the acknowledgment of his superiority by others.[211] This argument is used explicitly by Kingrun after his defeat at Parzival's hands in an attempt to save his skin (198,8: *'got hât dir êren vil gegebn: | swâ man saget daz von dir | diu kraft erzeiget ist an mir, | daz tu mich hâst betwungen, | sô ist dir wol gelungen'*). How effectively this equation of name with

---

207. *Ibid.*, p. 193. Hartmann's technique in naming his characters still awaits systematic treatment (even after Steinle, *Kennzeichnen*), although in the case of *Iwein* some helpful observations have been made by Hagenguth, *Iwein*, p. 91; Mohr, *ZfdA* 100 (1971),85ff.; Ruberg, *Schweigen*, pp. 216f.
208. For examples of this see Rosenfeld, *Gestaltung*, pp. 203ff., and *Herkunft*, pp. 36ff.
209. Cf. Klein, *PBB* 82 (1961), 16f. and 19; Wolf, *ZfdPh* 85 (1966), 82.
210. On Parzival as a new Adam see Deinert, *Ritter*, pp. 51ff. Cf. also Duggan, *OL* 24 (1969), 124.
211. Ortmann, *Selbstaussagen*, p. 19.

Conclusions

renown works in practice is demonstrated by Kingrimursel at Arthur's court, for no sooner does he mention his name (324,21) than we are shown Arthur's knights acknowledging his reputation (325,3ff.). For the victor to name himself first may confirm his reputation, as with Gahmuret's defeat of Hiuteger, but it can also be presented as a token of his generosity and magnanimity, as with the encounter of Feirefiz with Parzival (745,26: *'ich wil mich nennen ê, / und lâ daz laster wesen mîn'*).[212] For anyone not so sure of himself it is more difficult to make the first move, for this would be liable to misinterpretation, as Parzival reveals on the same occasion when he reacts touchily to his opponent's suggestion that he name himself (745,22: *'sol ich daz durch vorhte tuon ...'*).[213] In resolving the dilemma by naming himself first Feirefiz confirms that in the normal course of events this would imply a disgrace, since it would accompany a defeat.

The spread of functions for a name which these examples illustrate tells us how we may best approach the problem of Parzival's naming. At one end of the spectrum the name identifies one person rather than another (Condwiramurs, not Blancheflor) or sums up the essence of a being or object (518,5: *ieslîches art*), but at the other end of the spectrum the name serves a collective or social function, allowing the bearer to be recognised by others. These are the two respects in which Parzival must be seen. As long as he fails to recognise himself and his own nature, his name is not used or recognised by others, so that his place in society is questioned. Conversely, after he has been confronted with himself in Book IX his name is free to be used by others as a sign of his reintegration into society.

The question of Parzival's naming is first raised in the scene in which Sigune tells him his name,[214] if only because the narrator has gone out of his way to avoid any earlier opportunity. There are indeed earlier occasions, especially the point at which the hero's birth is recounted, where we might expect his name to be mentioned,[215] instead of which we are given anonymous circumlo-

---

212. *Ibid.*, p. 20. Cf. also Désilles-Busch, *Doner*, pp. 95f.
213. Ortmann, *Selbstaussagen*, p. 19, and Désilles-Busch, *Doner*, p. 95.
214. See above, pp. 79f.
215. An example of this is Chrétien's *Cligès*, whose hero is named only in v. 2344, at the point in the narrative where he has just been born. Other points in Wolfram's romance where we might have expected the hero to be named are the prologue (on this see above, p. 16) and the start of Book III, where the Parzival action begins.

cutions (112,12 and 17). The same wish not to name Parzival before he encounters Sigune also underlies a revealing change in one piece of advice which Herzeloyde gives her son.[216] Whereas Chrétien has her recommend the importance of inquiring after the name of anyone he meets on his travels, adding that the name tells one about the person (558: '*Ja an chemin ne an ostel / N'aiiez longuemant conpeignon / Que vos ne demandiez son non; / Le non sachiez a la parsome; / Car par le non conoist l'an l'ome*'), the German version talks of the need simply to greet the people one meets (127,19f.) without any mention of their name. By doing this Wolfram has avoided the difficulty, seen by Frappier,[217] that it is astonishing for the mother in the French text to stress the importance of a person's name without also telling her son his own name or without him asking the obvious question himself, but the wish to avoid a situation where the German poet would find it difficult to motivate Parzival's continued ignorance implies an overriding concern to maintain his anonymity beyond this point. How far this lack of a name at Soltane stands in for the absence of society during Parzival's childhood can be seen from another change of detail, concerning the nicknames used of her son by Herzeloyde in place of his proper name.[218] With Chrétien they are *biaus filz* (347), *biaus frere* (350) and *biaus sire* (354), but with Wolfram they have become *bon fîz, scher fîz, bêâ fîz* (140,6; cf. also 113,4). By introducing variation into his adjectives and by keeping the noun *fîz* unchanged the German poet has significantly contracted the world of Soltane in which these names were applied to Parzival, seeing it exclusively in terms of the biological relationship between mother and son, whereas with Chrétien we also glimpse something of the wider human relationships of which not even the boy Perceval is deprived: with his two brothers before their death (*biaus frere*) and with his mother's feudal followers (*biaus sire*).[219] This contraction of scope in the German version (from a society on the small scale to

216. On this see Green, *Advice*, p. 45; Ortmann, *Selbstaussagen*, pp. 26f.; Harroff, *Wolfram*, pp. 99f.
217. Frappier, *Graal*, p. 82.
218. On these nicknames in the French and German romances see Schwake, *GRM* 20 (1970), 345f.; Pickens, *Knight*, pp. 108f.; Harroff, *Wolfram*, p. 44.
219. On Perceval's two brothers see Green, *Departure*, pp. 361f. It is of course true that even in Wolfram's version Herzeloyde is not without some followers at Soltane, but my point is that this incipient social background is not reflected in the childish names given to Parzival, as it is with Chrétien.

Conclusions

the relationship between mother and son) underlines the close connection between Parzival's lack of a name and his complete divorce from society at this stage.

The same connection is established positively in the first Sigune scene. By having Parzival named at this point in his narrative, neither earlier when he was born nor later (as with Chrétien) when he encountered his cousin after leaving the Grail-castle, Wolfram ensures that the hero acquires a name and establishes his identity as part of the process of becoming a knight and entering the knightly world from which his mother had kept him aloof, for it is now as a named individual that he leaves Sigune for three eminently knightly episodes, with the Round Table, with Ither, and with Gurnemanz.[220] At the moment when he enters this wider world, putting the seclusion of Soltane firmly behind him, Parzival also lays aside his earlier anonymity. The acquisition of a name is also tied up with Parzival learning of his social obligations from Sigune, for she tells him more than just his name at this first meeting. By inventing this scene and by transferring forwards to it the motif of naming which occurs so much later with Chrétien, Wolfram has placed this motif in quite a different context.[221] In naming him Sigune also locates Parzival within his genealogy and tells him of the feudal obligations to which he was born (140,25ff.), mentioning only the secular realms for which he is responsible (140,26ff.),[222] but perhaps implying, by the fact that she devotes only the first line to Gahmuret and the rest to Herzeloyde, that his obligations concern the world of the Grail of which he as yet knows nothing. Sigune's disclosure of his name to him thus amounts to a programme for Parzival's future career and the obligations which face him, apparently in the secular, knightly sphere which she mentions, but more essentially in the realm of the Grail about which she is still silent at this early stage. These obligations fall to Parzival because of his kinship relations, so that by being named and placed within the obligations of kinship so much earlier than in the French romance Parzival is given from the start of his knightly career, however little of it he may understand, a prospect of its future course.[223]

---

220. See above, p. 80, and Harroff, *Wolfram*, p. 49.
221. Cf. Ortmann, *Selbstaussagen*, p. 25.
222. Cf. Désilles-Busch, *Doner*, pp. 93f.
223. *Ibid.*, p. 94. Since the argument of the last two paragraphs above has been to stress the differences between the French and German versions of the scene

The Art of Recognition in Wolfram's *Parzival*

How important this naming technique is for an understanding of Parzival's position can be seen from the way in which it is still employed after this scene with Sigune: even though Parzival now knows his name, the fact that he can grasp so little of the obligations it imposes means that he understands little of himself and is therefore not yet fit to present himself to others or to be known to others by name. Whereas before meeting Sigune he knew himself and was addressed by his mother by her childish nicknames for him, now even after learning the proper name to which he cannot yet measure up he continues to be referred to by anonymous circumlocutions.[224] One of the most important of these is also the most ambiguous, for when Gurnemanz, on learning of his young guest's encounter with Ither, is the first to name him with reference to the red armour he stripped from his victim (170,6: *den rôten ritter er in hiez*), this signals at once his victory over an opponent and his brutal killing of him and robbery of the corpse.[225] When Gurnemanz's example in the choice of circumlocution for Parzival is followed by others this means that Parzival is not known by them as himself, but merely as someone who has stepped into Ither's shoes or armour; he is summed up by reference to his first, disastrous exploit and not in terms of the obligations laid on him by Sigune's disclosure of his name. Accordingly, others refer to him pointedly by this long-winded phrase, as when Kingrun pays his respects to Cunneware at the Round Table after being sent there by his victor (206,16: *den man dâ hiez den ritter rôt*),[226] and their usage can be adopted by the narrator as part of his technique of presenting

where Parzival acquires a name, it would be as well to add here two further differences. In the first place, Chrétien's Perceval is able to guess what his name is, whereas Parzival has to be told it (cf. Harroff, *Wolfram*, pp. 102f.). The reason for this change is not, as was suggested by Bezzola, *Sens*, pp. 60f., that Wolfram was unable to appreciate Chrétien's poetic symbolism, but rather that in sketching the progress of one who is *træclîche wîs* he could not depict that character, at a much earlier stage in his career than with Chrétien, showing a degree of intuitive insight such as we might associate with Gawan and therefore not having to be told by someone else. Secondly, although both Perceval and Parzival learn their names in the relevant scenes, only the German narrator has inserted previous pointers making it possible for the perceptive listener to realise the truth before the hero (see above, pp. 17ff.).

224. For a discussion of some of these see Green, *Namedropping*, pp. 127ff. and *Naming*, pp. 103ff. (in the latter article I consider all the circumlocutions used of Parzival in the first four Books of the action devoted to him).
225. Cf. Ortmann, *Selbstaussagen*, p. 24. On this particular circumlocution see Dewald, *Minne*, p. 272, and Green, *Namedropping*, pp. 130f.
226. Cf. also 176,20 and 315,11.

Conclusions

things from an underinformed participant's point of view.[227] Why others should use this anonymous phrase is clear: since they have no idea of Parzival's identity, they have no choice but to fall back on the most obvious identifier (as at Bearosche, 383,24: *ein ritter allenthalben rôt: / der hiez der ungenante, / wande in niemen dâ bekante*).[228] A realistic explanation of this type may be welcome to the narrator, yet it cannot be the whole truth, as is suggested by the fact that some of these circumlocutions imply that Parzival named himself in this way even after learning his name from Sigune (Orilus says of his victor, 276,21: '*der nennet sich der rîter rôt*', and Arthur hopes to find *den der sich der rîter rôt / nante*, 280,9). For Parzival to name himself in this way passes well beyond the realistic explanation invoked at Bearosche[229] and suggests the symbolic implication of the narrator's technique, the hint that Parzival's name is not free to be used as a social marker either by himself or by others at this stage of his career. That Parzival himself is intentionally included in this withholding of his name is suggested by another circumlocution used in the period when he is known to all and sundry as the *rîter rôt*, for he sends the prisoners he has made at Bearosche back to Pelrapeire to pay homage to his wife, instructing them what to say to her (389,8: '*und sagt ir, der durch si dâ streit / mit Kingrûne und mit Clâmidê, / dem sî nu nâch dem grâle wê, / unt doch wider nâch ir minne*').[230] If it made good realistic sense for Orilus to fall back on a circumlocution in referring to his victor at the Round Table (there is no reason why Parzival, as victor, should have told him his name and the Round Table has not yet been informed of it by Cundrie), this is no longer so with knights sent back to Condwiramurs, who of course knows her husband by name.[231] Parzival may well have a positive reason for recalling the way in which he and his wife first

---

227. Cf. 202,21. Alternatively, Parzival can be referred to with a contracted phrase such as *rîter rôt*, both by other characters in the work (218,4; 221,6; 276,4; 278,25; 307,18) and by the narrator (305,11; 309,16; 388,8; 389,4 + 29; 392,20).
228. See above, p. 139.
229. Cf. also the consideration that Gawan, unlike the other participants at Bearosche, knows that the anonymous red knight is in fact Parzival by name (392,28f.), because he had been present at the Round Table when Cundrie addressed Parzival by name (see above, p. 140).
230. On this type of circumlocution see Ortmann, *Selbstaussagen*, p. 33.
231. Although Parzival's introduction of himself by name to Condwiramurs is not actually narrated, see above, pp. 74f., for the suggestion that the narrator's resumption of Parzival's name together with his mention of Condwiramurs's name for the first time at Pelrapeire stand in for the scene of their formal introduction and exchange of names.

came together, but the emotional foundations of their relationship could have been summed up just as effectively by the use of his personal name, so that again it is implied that he still does not know enough of himself to merit the social use of his name.[232]

If, even after Parzival has learned his name from Sigune and the Round Table has been told it by Cundrie, his anonymity lasts well into the period in which Gawan occupies the foreground and Parzival is only fleetingly visible, one of the narrator's tasks will be to show how the hero slowly abandons his solitude and is gradually drawn back into society again. Not surprisingly he again employs his naming technique, plotting this process in the way in which Parzival refers to himself and others to him, by passing from anonymous to named references. Schroedel's analysis of the references to Parzival in the Gawan action (Books VII–VIII and X–XIII) yields the following pattern, based on three layers.[233]

An outer layer consists of three narratorial references to the hero by name (416,26; 520,12; 586,17) to which little importance need be attached (other than their function of keeping *des mæres hêrre* present in the listener's mind) since, as we have seen, what counts in this problem is how characters in the story itself (including Parzival) refer to him. A second layer is made up of three rather more individualising references, in all of which Gawan, present when Cundrie came to the Round Table, is in a position to recall or identify Parzival by name. The first two of these references occur at Bearosche, hence soon after Gawan and Parzival have set out on their quests (370,18: *nu dâhter des, wie Parzivâl ...*; 392,28: *dô dâhter des, daz Parzivâl ...*), whilst the third comes towards the start of the next Book, when Gawan is reminded of Parzival by Vergulaht's appearance (400,13: *Gâwânen des bedûhte, / do der künec sô gein im lûhte, / ez wære der ander Parzivâl*). Together these three references plot how close Parzival remains to Gawan's thoughts soon after their separation, but how he gradually fades into the background the longer this separation lasts,[234] yet it is significant

---

232. Cf. also Parzival's anonymous references to himself in his instructions to the defeated Vergulaht, 425,13f.
233. Schroedel, *Erzählen*, pp. 34ff. and Table I (after p. 208). See also Sauer, *Parzival*, pp. 232ff., who links Parzival's loss of his name with his loss of a sense of time.
234. Steinhoff, *Darstellung*, pp. 47ff., provides more evidence for this from quite a different point of view. On the episode referred to above, fn. 232, Steinhoff says (p. 50): 'Parzival ist anonym geworden und aus Gawans Blickfeld verschwunden, nur Wolframs Zuhörer sollen ihn nicht aus den Augen verlieren.'

Conclusions

that in each passage Gawan recalls his friend in his thoughts (*dâhter, bedûhte*) without voicing them to others. To this extent Parzival as a named character is a stranger to society.

The third layer is the interesting one for our purposes, since it contains utterances about Parzival by various members of society or by the narrator deliberately adopting their point of view. These utterances fall into three classes, both by the type of designation for Parzival which predominates in each and by its chronological position within the Gawan narrative. The earliest class, coming immediately after the hero's renunciation of God and departure from the Round Table, shows him in his greatest disorientation and therefore refers to him in complete anonymity with reference to Ither's armour (e.g. the first example, 383,24: *ein ritter allenthalben rôt*). Five examples of this type of anonymous designation occur in Book VII at the start of the Gawan narrative, one immediately afterwards at the start of Book VIII (but referring back to the action at Bearosche), and there is one solitary example as late as Book XII.[235] The next class is made up of references which designate Parzival not by his own name, but by the name of persons who are close to him in one way or another (e.g. the first occurrence, 389,8: '*der durch si dâ streit / mit Kingrûne und mit Clâmidê*') or by the name of a place associated with a person close to him (in the same context, 389,6: '*sô vart dâ Pelrapeire stêt. / bringt der küngîn iwer sicherheit ...*'). If not by his own name, then at least by the names of those who are close enough to help define him, Parzival is referred to in this class by phrases which permit his identification. The closer definition this implies (by contrast with the complete anonymity of the earliest class), together with the fact that all examples occur in the direct speech of characters (now excluding the narrator who had at times stood in with the first class), suggests that Parzival has now come closer to society. Of these references one joint example occurs in Book VII, two closely related ones in Book VIII, two further related ones in Book XI, and one in Book XII,[236] so that the centre of gravity of these rather more 'social' references to Parzival is noticeably later than with the completely anonymous ones. Finally, the third class of reference restores Parzival completely to society when in Book XII Orgeluse reports how Parzival identified himself

---

235. Book VII: 383,24; 388,8; 389,4; 389,29; 392,20. Book VIII: 398,4f. Book XII: 618,21.
236. Book VII: 389,6f. + 7f. Book VIII: 425,6–8 and 425,13f. Book XI: 559,9 and 559,15. Book XII: 619,8f.

The Art of Recognition in Wolfram's *Parzival*

by name to her and he is referred to by name twice again in Book XIII, still within the framework of the Gawan narrative.[237]

If we take all these three layers together, it is clear that in the sequence of the narrative they plot Parzival's gradual restoration to society, passing from anonymity through an indirect identification by another person's name and finishing with direct identification by his own name. His approach by stages to society is thus registered from the point of view of members of society (or the narrator adopting their position) by means of the various ways in which they refer to him.[238] The society into which Parzival is reintegrated once his quest and Gawan's are brought together in Book XIV is that of Arthur's court, but Parzival's dissatisfied departure from the Round Table at the end of this Book (733,19ff.) makes it clear that he has not yet truly found himself in being restored to *this* society.[239] Arthurian society would suffice for him if Parzival's inheritance were exclusively that of Gahmuret, but it also and more importantly embraces the obligation towards the Grail-realm which he has acquired from his mother, as Parzival realises in this same departure scene (732,19: '*sol ich nâch dem grâle ringen*'). If his restoration to society must take him back not just to the Round Table, but also to Munsalvæsche, then we have to extend our inquiry into Parzival's naming to an area so far excluded. We have to ask, in other words, how members of the Grail-world refer to Parzival.

237. Book XII: 619,10. Book XIII: 645,27; 646,15. As in the second class, none of these is said by the narrator. Although a few other terms are used in these Books by other characters to refer to Parzival (see Schroedel's Table I), these are both infrequent (because Parzival is only rarely visible during the Gawan action) and too general or anonymous (e.g. *ritter*, *helt*) to suggest that Parzival is gradually moving back towards society.
238. Parzival's struggle to find himself and his place in society, reflected in the way in which he can be referred to by name or not, represents another contrast between him and Gawan. Mohr, *Euphorion* 52 (1958), 5, has rightly said that whereas anonymity is almost Parzival's natural element, for Gawan it is something exceptional, so that he can afford to play with it at Bearosche. See also Ortmann, *Selbstaussagen*, p. 22: 'Diese souveräne Gewandtheit im Umgang mit dem eigenen Namen und dessen stilsichere Integration in die Selbstaussage ist überhaupt für Gawan bezeichnend. Sie ist der beredte Ausdruck seines ungebrochen richtigen Verhältnisses zur Welt und zu sich selbst, wodurch er jeder Situation gewachsen ist. Da er sich selbst richtig einschätzt, schätzt er auch die Welt richtig ein und umgekehrt'.
239. Harms, *Kampf*, p. 163, has drawn attention to the way in which, after Parzival's combat with Gramoflanz, other people, including both Gramoflanz's followers and Arthur's, fail to recognise the hero's true goal and nature. Harms discusses the passage 709,2ff., in which Parzival is praised by both parties (*in bêden hern*),

Conclusions

To this question an answer has been given by Ortmann who claims that, by contrast with the Round Table's references to Parzival by anonymous terms like the *rîter rôt*, his true name is used and voiced only by representatives of the Grail-world,[240] so that only they, by knowing his true name, can define his true nature, thereby understanding him on a deeper level than the Arthurian world. Although this is not completely true (Parzival is referred to by name by more than representatives of Munsalvæsche alone), the suggestion is stimulating enough to deserve closer scrutiny.

Three members of the Grail-community refer to Parzival by name at various stages of the work, on every occasion placing him within the context of the Grail and thereby defining him by that context. Sigune does this on three occasions. It is from her that Parzival learns his name (140,16)[241] and if, as we have seen, she nowhere mentions the Grail at this early and unpromising stage of his career, she nonetheless dwells longer on his mother's world and implies that it is here, implicitly in the sense of Munsalvæsche rather than Waleis and Norgals, that his future lies. Sigune's next address to Parzival by name (251,29) comes at their second encounter just after he has left the Grail-castle and when she at length recognises him by his voice.[242] Since she has just been told that he was at Munsalvæsche and revises her initial incredulity on grasping his identity, she follows her statement of recognition by name with a question as to whether he saw the Grail and Anfortas. For the first time, therefore, Parzival's name is associated immediately with the

---

and stresses the concluding couplet (709,11: *dennoch si sîn erkanten niht, / dem ieslîch munt dâ prîses giht*), commenting that neither Parzival's name nor nature is recognised by those who praise him, for they fail to see that this combat not merely stamps Parzival as a praiseworthy Arthurian knight, but is rather to be regarded (like his encounter with Gawan, cf. Harms, p. 160) as a stage on his pathway to the Grail. When Harms suggests that others fail to recognise Parzival's name and therefore his nature, this may well be true of Gramoflanz and his followers (see above, pp. 236f., on their ignorance of his identity). If the Round Table fail to recognise Parzival's nature, this cannot be because they are unaware of his identity at this stage (both Arthur and Gawan have just referred to him as a kinsman, 708,1 + 16). I suspect that the narrator, by associating both retinues in the phrase *in bêden hern*, is attempting to persuade us, against the facts of the narrative, that the Arthurian knights' inability to recognise Parzival's nature can be attributed to the same reason as with Gramoflanz and his followers.

240. Ortmann, *Selbstaussagen*, pp. 24f. A useful supplement (and corrective) to Ortmann is provided by Dewald, *Minne*, pp. 273ff.
241. See above, pp. 79 and 303ff.
242. See above, pp. 114f.

Grail, mention of the one leads without hesitation to the other. The same is true of the third meeting between these two, for as soon as she recognises him again Sigune addresses Parzival by name[243] and without a break then asks him how things stand with his quest for the Grail (440,29f.), thereby implying that to recognise and name him is for her to see him in the context of the Grail.[244] Cundrie addresses Parzival three times by name (315,9 and 26; 316,25) before the Round Table in Book VI, these being the first occasion in the work for the hero to be spoken to by name in public and also the occasion for the Round Table to learn Parzival's name themselves.[245] If the first of these lines merely anticipates the following ones, these two others immediately place him in the setting of Munsalvæsche (cf. 315,27ff. and 316,26ff.). This does not even have to be done when Cundrie appears before the Round Table again in Book XV and addresses Parzival by name (782,5) for the fourth time, for she has already announced his call to Grail-kingship (781,16), so that it is explicitly this office which defines Parzival and underlies his naming. The third member of Munsalvæsche to address Parzival by name (once only) is Anfortas when the hero comes to the Grail-castle a second time – again his name is followed immediately, even desperately, by a reference to the Grail (795,11ff.).

Although Ortmann has correctly seen that in all these passages it is a member of Munsalvæsche who defines Parzival's identity within the setting of the Grail and is therefore able to refer to him by name, she goes too far in suggesting that *only* these characters make use of Parzival's name. There are indeed other occasions where his name is uttered, but even so it is possible to reconcile this with the valuable observation that the Grail-realm is in a special position as regards Parzival's naming. This is already so with the three occasions when Gawan recalls Parzival by name in Books VII and VIII as his friend retreats more and more into the narrative background, for in every case Parzival's name is not actually uttered, it plays no social function but is instead confined to Gawan's thoughts.[246] Three other occasions, however, occur after Parzival's decisive process of self-recognition in Book IX[247] and towards the end of the Gawan narrative, as the hero is returning closer to the society

---

243. See above, p. 184.
244. Cf. Hirschberg, *Untersuchungen*, p. 40.
245. Cf. Dewald, *Minne*, p. 275, and also above, p. 103.
246. Schroedel, *Erzählen*, p. 34.
247. On the importance of this in the present context see Dewald, *Minne*, pp. 276f.

Conclusions

from which he has been divorced. Although the occasion is not directly narrated, but reported by Orgeluse, Parzival's fleeting encounter with her is important in that here for the first time the hero succeeds in doing what Gawan achieves elsewhere without difficulty,[248] he now so far knows himself that he can refer to himself by name (619,8: *'von Pelrapeir diu künegîn, / sus ist genant diu lieht gemâl: / sô heize ich selbe Parzivâl. / ichn wil iwer minne niht: / der grâl mir anders kumbers giht'*).[249] Rather than place emphasis on the fact that it is actually Orgeluse who is speaking here (and Parzival only indirectly),[250] I should rather stress that Parzival defines himself in this passage with reference to his love for Condwiramurs and his quest for the Grail, and that on this latter point he has by now received vital information from Trevrizent and knows where he stands within the dynasty of the Grail-kings. Knowing this much about himself he can now name himself, whilst the fact that this is not narrated to us directly, but only conveyed to us at second hand, is an indication that in Book XII he has still only just begun his return to Munsalvæsche.

The next occasions for Parzival to be mentioned by name both occur at the Round Table: thanks to Trevrizent he has so far established his own identity that Arthurian society for the first time in the work speaks about him in using his proper name. In the first passage Guinevere refers in passing to Condwiramurs as *Parzivâles wîp* (645,27), whilst in the second she calculates the length of time Gawan has been absent by correlating it with Parzival's departure from the Round Table (646,14: *'fünftehalp jâr und sehs wochen / ist daz der werde Parzivâl / von dem Plimizœl nâch dem grâl / reit. dô kêrt och Gâwân / gein Ascalûn, der werde man'*).[251] Guinevere, like Orgeluse, sees Parzival in terms of his quest for the Grail, his identity is by now firmly enough established for him to provide the criterion by which the length of Gawan's absence can be measured,[252] and we know from Book IX that it was Trevrizent who not merely instructed Parzival on his position in the Grail-world, but also provided him with a reorientation in time.[253] After these

---

248. Cf. Ortmann, *Selbstaussagen*, pp. 22ff.
249. Dewald, *Minne*, p. 277.
250. As does Ortmann, *Selbstaussagen*, p. 25, fn. 10. If this point were as important as Ortmann suggests it is, one should have expected the narrator to use indirect speech and thus avoid the first person singular pronoun, used by Parzival.
251. Dewald, *Minne*, p. 278.
252. Cf. Steinhoff, *Darstellung*, p. 55.
253. Cf. Weigand, *Parzival*, pp. 57ff.

two examples by Guinevere and after the Gawan narrative has rejoined that devoted to Parzival it is now the turn of Arthur to refer to Parzival by name when talking of his combat with Gramoflanz (717,29: *'ez ist mîn neve Parzivâl'*).[254] Arthur has known Parzival's name and also that he is Gahmuret's son (cf. 717,23) since Cundrie's denunciation of him, but only now, very shortly before Cundrie's second appearance to call Parzival to Munsalvæsche, has the hero so far found himself that Arthur can refer to him by name. A final example comes slightly before this mention of Parzival by Arthur, but stands apart from it (and all the other cases) in that it is the only passage in the whole work where Parzival refers to himself by name, directly and not simply as reported by Orgeluse. It comes when Parzival reveals his identity to Gawan at the close of their mistaken combat (689,24: *'ich pinz dîn neve Parzivâl'*).[255] At this point the hero has returned to Arthurian society no longer as an anonymous *rîter rôt*, but as one who has subjectively found his place in his dynasty, has recognised his true self and can therefore refer to himself by name.[256]

Parzival is therefore mentioned by name by two classes of characters in the narrative: not merely by members of the Grail-community (as suggested by Ortmann), but also by those more closely involved with Arthurian society (including Parzival himself at the close of his combat with Gawan). It is important to take both classes into account, for the one complements the other. Examples of Parzival's naming by the Grail-community occur from the beginning to the end of his career, they designate his objective position, the vacancy at Munsalvæsche which is waiting for him, whilst the Arthurian examples are bunched significantly towards the end of Parzival's career, after the vital process of self-recognition in Book IX, and illustrate his subjective growth in awareness of himself. This interplay between the objective and the subjective aspects

---

254. Dewald, *Minne*, p. 279. Dewald also includes 695,7 here, since he follows Leitzmann's edition where the lines 695,6f. are taken as direct speech uttered by *die wîsen* of 695,3. I follow Lachmann's edition in regarding these lines instead as a narratorial comment.
255. Dewald, *Minne*, pp. 278f.
256. Cf. Mohr, *Euphorion* 52 (1958), 5, on Parzival's abandonment of anonymity: 'Wenn sich die weltweiten Zusammenhänge, in denen er von Vaters- und Mutterseite her steht, nach und nach um ihn aufklären, dann geschieht wirklich Entscheidendes in seiner Geschichte. Die Lüftung der Anonymität und sein Sich-Besinnen auf sein wahres Selbst, auf seine Schuld und sein Heil, treffen zusammen. Das eine ist die Außenseite, das andere die Innenseite seines Schicksals.'

Conclusions

of Parzival's naming has its parallels elsewhere in the work.[257] It is part of the objective rôle which Parzival is called upon to play in this work that, quite independently of whether he realises it or not, his membership of the Grail-dynasty qualifies him by birth as a possible king of Munsalvæsche, that previous events have created a vacancy in the line of accession to be filled by the son of Herzeloyde, that providential guidance is extended to him on his journey to the Grail-castle, and that the precise astronomic constellation at the time when he arrived there was meant as a tacit pointer to him.[258] Yet Parzival is not just led objectively to the Grail, he also has to qualify himself subjectively for Grail-kingship. The significance of the scene with the drops of blood in the snow (especially 296,5: *sîne gedanke umben grâl / unt der küngîn glîchiu mâl, / iewederz was ein strengiu nôt*) is that Parzival's realisation of the importance of the Grail-quest for him is the first move on his part towards self-discovery,[259] whilst further moves are only made possible by the self-recognition taught him by Trevrizent and by his own experience of *kumber* as the basis for compassion with the suffering of Anfortas.[260] How vital is the subjective contribution which Parzival has to make can be seen negatively in the fact that the wrong reaction on his part to events at Munsalvæsche is enough to bring about a disastrous failure, and positively in the rôle played by his *strîten* in finally coming to the Grail.[261] In short, although Parzival may be called to the Grail, his destiny can only be fulfilled by his recognising its implications for himself and acting upon them. Or to rephrase this point in terms of Parzival's naming: his destiny and his obligations may be summed up in his name, as seen by Sigune and other members of the Grail-community, but

---

257. Cf. Dewald, *Minne*, p. 277: 'Die ihm [Parzival] in den ersten beiden Sigune-szenen von außen angetragene Bestimmung muß er erst subjektiv ausfüllen, um zu sich selbst zu finden' and the quotation given there from Wapnewski, *Parzival*, p. 103: 'Das Erregende am Parzival ist, daß ein offensichtlich Prädestinierter sich zu dieser Auserwähltheit in eigner Entscheidung bekennt!'
258. On Parzival's membership of the Grail-dynasty and on the line of accession in that destiny see above, pp. 214ff., on his providential guidance see Wynn, *Speculum* 36 (1961), 399ff., and on the astronomic constellation see Deinert, *Ritter*, pp. 12ff.
259. Cf. Dewald, *Minne*, p. 271.
260. On Parzival's experience of *kumber* see Hahn, *Schönheit*, pp. 220ff.
261. See Jones, *Fighting*, pp. 52ff., especially p. 70: 'When Parzival and Cundrie credit Parzival's fighting with having earned him election to the Grail while recognizing that it is a gift of God's grace, they accurately reflect the interaction of human endeavour and divine grace which has led to this conclusion.'

these can only be realised once he has recognised this himself and made his name his own.

This connection between a person's name and his destiny may be underlined by one last detail. The act of mentioning a person's name can be expressed linguistically in *Parzival* by the verb *nennen* or, of greater significance in our case, *benennen*. For example, after Kaylet has listed by name many of the knights present for the tournament at Kanvoleis he sums up this information in the phrase *al die ich hie benennet hân* (67,7), just as Gawan, about to specify the various properties he holds from Arthur, says *ein teil ich der benenne hie* (303,17). But this same verb has implications which go much further, since it is used in the particular context of someone being called to membership of the Grail-community. Trevrizent uses this verb of those who are divinely summoned to Munsalvæsche (470,21: *'die aber zem grâle sint benant'*; 473,10: *'wan die dar sint benennet / ze Munsalvæsche ans grâles schar'*) and negatively of the knight who came there and failed to ask the question and who, the hermit assumes, must resemble Lähelin in not having been summoned there (473,12: *'wan einr kom unbenennet dar'*). Parzival uses the same verb in claiming from God that he too ought to be called there (472,9: *'der sol mich dar benennen'*).[262] This is in fact what eventually happens (cf. 781,3f. and 15f., but especially 786,2ff.), but only at a

262. Dewald, *Minne*, pp. 251 and 287f., makes a distinction between Trevrizent's general statement in 470,21ff. (the name and genealogy of those called to Munsalvæsche appear miraculously on the Grail) and his particular reference in 483,19ff. to the knight who came to the Grail-castle and failed to ask the question (he is referred to only as *ein ritter*, no mention is made of his being named). From this contrast in naming Dewald concludes (p. 288): 'Die Namensnennung gewinnt dabei besondere Bedeutung, weil sie auf die wachsende Identität des Helden in ihren verschiedenen Dimensionen zurückweist. So markieren die beiden Ankündigungen auf dem Epitaph symbolisch nochmals den Ausgangs- und Endpunkt der Wesenssuche: Nannte die Inschrift zunächst nur "einen" Ritter, der die Frage stellen würde (483,21), bezeichnet sie beim zweitenmal Parzival namentlich als Herrn über den Gral.' I am not convinced that Dewald's judgment can be accepted as it stands, chiefly because I believe that the Grail-community were aware of Parzival's name when he first came to Munsalvæsche (on my reasons for this see below, Appendix A, pp. 320ff.). We can however rescue Dewald's attractive point if we read the difference in naming between these two passages (the Grail-inscription refers to the name of those called in 470,25, but Trevrizent is silent on the knight's name in 483,21) as reflecting not different facts about the Grail-inscription itself, but rather different facets of what the narrator is prepared to mention at any given point. The fact that the narrator has Trevrizent make no reference to the knight's name in connection with Parzival's disastrous visit is a narratorial hint that Parzival had not yet found his identity at this stage.

Conclusions

time when Parzival's divine summons by name has been complemented by his own discovery of himself and acknowledgment of the obligations placed on him by his name. Parzival's naming and the process of his self-recognition thus go hand in hand, both together plot his gradual approach towards fulfilling his destiny.

To the extent that Parzival's destiny is pre-existent and awaits his fulfilment of it he can be said to be guided towards it. Such guidance is conveyed not merely by narratorial hints that the hero is the recipient of providential assistance,[263] but also by explicit statements, particularly towards the end of the work when guidance reaches its climax, suggesting that now at last his preordained goal will be reached. The terms used to imply the nature of this guidance suggest that it may be good fortune, as in Parzival's encounter with Feirefiz (738,18: *gelücke scheidez âne tôt*),[264] or God may be explicitly invoked, as in Parzival's own statement about being called to the Grail (786,7: *'wan der von gote ist dar benant'*), or Parzival's success is described as preordained, as in a concluding observation by the narrator (827,7: *als im daz gordent was*). But there is more to Parzival's fulfilment of his destiny than that, for this takes place after all within a work of literature, so that, in terms of the common comparison of the omniscient narrator with providence, knowing the outcome and thus standing aloof from his creation like the *Deus artifex* from His masterpiece, the created world,[265] the narrator himself can be said to have guided this character towards his goal just as much as providence itself. This possibility is again made explicit, as when the narrator regards himself as responsible for having brought about Parzival's encounter with his halfbrother (737,25: *ich sorge des den ich hân brâht*) and asks himself how best to extricate the hero from this dilemma (740,14: *wie tuon ich dem getouften nuo?*). The two external forces responsible for bringing Parzival to Munsalvæsche (in terms of the narrative action it is God, but in the context of a work of art it is the narrator) are then brought together in the concluding lines of the poem and shown to be two aspects of the same process when Parzival is said to have been conducted by the narrator to the place for which he was

---

263. Cf. Wynn, *Speculum* 36 (1961), 399ff. and Green, *Irony*, pp. 150ff.
264. Sanders, *Glück*, pp. 55f., rightly associates Wolfram's use of *gelücke* with the Christian concept of providence. This is made clear in this particular instance by the way in which the narrator's wish uttered with regard to *gelücke* in 738,18 is fulfilled by God's intervention in 744,14ff. See also Green, *Homicide*, p. 33.
265. Cf. Green, *Irony*, p. 285.

destined (827,17: ... *Parzivâls, den ich hân brâht | dar sîn doch sælde het erdâht*). This group of lines suggests the same point in yet another way, however, for the verb *benennen*, used to indicate a divine call to the Grail as recently as 786,7, can also be employed in the further sense of 'to recount in detail'[266] and is therefore used to sum up the narrator's task in successfully concluding his narrative (827,15: *sîniu kint, sîn hôch geslehte | hân ich iu benennet rehte, | Parzivâls* ...). The narrator's literary task can therefore be paralleled with God's within the narrative world; both have to bring their chosen hero to Munsalvæsche.

The possibility of this kind of comparison between God and the narrator suggests another parallel, that between Parzival and the listener. It has been said that the trackless forest surrounding Munsalvæsche, penetrated by Parzival only at God's will, is tantamount to the veil of mystery concealing the Grail secrets, lifted for his listeners only at the narrator's will. Penetrating the mysteries of the Grail thus becomes for the listeners what the attainment of Grail-kingship is for Parzival.[267] Yet this second parallel can be taken further. Parzival is not merely conducted to Munsalvæsche by a benevolent providence, he also has to struggle to reach this goal and is only successful because he comes to recognise and understand the implications of the situation in which he finds himself. Something similar can be said of the listeners, or rather of those listeners whom the narrator really has in mind, for it is not the case that they are simply handed progressively more information by a narrator who shows his hand only gradually, they are instead invited to co-operate actively in their own process of recognition.[268] This is after all the point of the many questions to which

266. For this use of *benennen*, applied to the narrator's task, cf. 584,7 and 735,30 (on the use of *nennen* far beyond the restricted sense of 'to give someone's name' see Green, *Irony*, p. 148, fn. 4). There are therefore several reasons for dissatisfaction with Nellmann's short-term interpretation of 241,1ff. (*Erzählkunst*, pp. 89ff., cf. above, p. 113). He sees this narratorial observation only in connection with Parzival's second encounter with Sigune shortly afterwards (251,2ff.), but ignores the wide range of meaning in *nennen* and *benennen* and the fact that so much more information about these names is provided by Trevrizent in Book IX. Parzival and the listeners have to learn not merely the actual names, but what their significance is. The ultimate meaning of *benennen* is likewise not that the narrator should provide names previously withheld, but that he should so conclude his narrative that Parzival is successfully brought to Munsalvæsche (827,15ff.).
267. Harroff, *Wolfram*, p. 59.
268. Cf. Dewald, *Minne*, pp. 362f. It is the merit of Schweikle's article, *ZfdA* 106 (1977), 183ff., especially of his interpretation of the word *stiure* in the prologue

Conclusions

they are given only incomplete answers at any stage, of the constant shifting of viewpoint, of the suggestion that things are not as they seem to be and of the carefully distributed clues which will allow them, if only they follow them up, to attain to an independent understanding of the situation in which they find themselves. Like Parzival the listeners are engaged on a quest for recognition, they too can be described as *træclîche wîs*, for even if the perceptive ones among them may grasp some vital truths in advance of Parzival their overall movement is, like his, one from *tumpheit* to *wîsheit*. If the perceptive listener can be described in terms of what he is not, in terms of the inability of others to *erdenken* the narrator's implications (1,17), then his growing ability to see comprehendingly through appearances parallels Parzival's task in recognising what *sîn doch sælde het erdâht* (827,18). What has been said of the structure of *Parzival* at large ('Die Sinnfindung geschieht bei ihm als Durchbruch durch mehrere Schichten')[269] is a task confronting both the chosen hero and the select listeners, who in their comprehension of the work have to accomplish for themselves what Signune sees as the obligation present in Parzival's name: not to remain content with surface impressions, but to think through to the implications behind them, *der nam ist rehte enmitten durch*. The art of recognition is a skill practised consummately by Wolfram von Eschenbach, but it is also an art which both Parzival and the listeners have to learn to acquire.

(2,7), that he shows the perceptive listener not merely being granted instruction by the romance (2,8: *waz si guoter lêre wernt*), but having to work for it himself by his own contribution (2,7: *welher stiure disiu mære gernt*), which Schweikle expressly sees as 'Einsichtsfähigkeit', as a readiness to 'mitdenken, kombinieren' (p. 187). The narrator demands from such a listener what God expects of Parzival.

269. Haug, *DVjs* 45 (1971), 698. Cf. also what Ragotzky and Weinmayer, *Identitätsbildung*, p. 224, have said of the listener's task in the case of *Iwein*: 'Wer beim Zuhören die Oberfläche der bloßen Handlungsfaktizität nicht zu durchdringen vermag, dem wird sich das vorgestellte *mære* konsequent entziehen.'

Appendix A:
The Recognition of Parzival at Munsalvæsche and by Trevrizent

In this Appendix we are concerned with two problems: the knowledge of Anfortas and the Grail-community in Book V that their guest is Parzival, and Trevrizent's initial ignorance in Book IX that his visitor is his nephew Parzival and also the knight who failed at Munsalvæsche.[1] I return to these problems in an Appendix because they are peripheral ones by comparison with the more vital processes of recognition underlying these Books – in Book V Parzival's failure to recognise what is expected of him, in Book IX his ultimate recognition of his position within the Grail-kingdom. Just as the links between these two Books are close (for Trevrizent explains the mysterious events that took place at Munsalvæsche), so are the two problems dealt with in this Appendix interconnected. Trevrizent's knowledge about Parzival's visit to Munsalvæsche must derive ultimately, by an unspecified channel, from the Grail-community itself. If those at Munsalvæsche were aware of Parzival's named identity when he came there, why, it may be asked, is Trevrizent ignorant of this vital detail? Or conversely: if Trevrizent does not know that his visitor is called Parzival, might this not suggest that the Grail-community were similarly ignorant?

The feasibility of connecting these two episodes suggests the possibility of equating the knowledge shown (or not shown) by Anfortas with that shown (or not shown) by Trevrizent. Weigand and Schirok see this equation positively, arguing that Anfortas and the Grail-community are aware of Parzival's identity at Munsalvæsche, just as Trevrizent realises who his guest is from very early on.[2] The opposite point of view has been taken by L. P.

---

1. See above, pp. 99 and 187ff.
2. Weigand, *GQ* 51 (1978), 444ff. and Schirok, *ABÄG* 10 (1976), 43ff. In his article Schirok is concerned with Trevrizent's knowledge of the situation, but from p. 49 it is clear that he also regards the Grail-community as having been aware of Parzival's identity. On Weigand see below, p. 336, fn. 55.

The recognition of Parzival at Munsalvæsche and by Trevrizent

Johnson, not in a published article, but in repeated conversations and an exchange of written notes in which we have both wrestled with the problem, each seeking to persuade the other. He maintains that Anfortas and the inhabitants of Munsalvæsche are unaware of Parzival's identity in Book V, just as Trevrizent is similarly ignorant at the start of his encounter with Parzival. There are however, theoretically, two other possibilities. First: Anfortas realises Parzival's identity, but Trevrizent does not (I have suggested this in Chapters 4 and 6, and seek to defend my position in this Appendix). Secondly: Anfortas is ignorant of Parzival's identity, but Trevrizent realises it early (I know of no one who has actually maintained this in print).

In what follows I must therefore clarify my position with regard to the three scholars just referred to (Weigand, Schirok, Johnson), but also take into account a recent article by Tax who suggests, not just that the Grail-community failed to recognise Parzival in Book V, but that they actually took him to be Ither because of his knightly trappings and acted on this faulty assumption.[3] This spread of possible answers confirms Weigand's point that we are left very much in the dark on this by the poet if scholars who have worked on *Parzival* for a lifetime can come up with such diverse answers.[4] It also suggests that we are asking questions beyond the range of the narrative which has been carefully motivated by the poet and that no final proof, but only a balance of probabilities, is possible. Some of what follows is therefore based on the text directly, but some on inferences where the text provides no clearcut information. Which is another reason for confining these suggestions to an Appendix.

The two scholars who have argued that Parzival is not recognised as such at Munsalvæsche are Tax and Johnson. Tax goes one stage further, arguing that Anfortas and the Grail-community do not know of Parzival's existence and hence fail to recognise him when he comes to Munsalvæsche. Instead, they take him from external appearances to be Ither and seek a successor to Anfortas from outside the Grail-dynasty by hoping to persuade him to marry into this family. Their bait in this respect, it is suggested, is none other than Repanse de schoy. My reservations about this line of argument are three in number.

My first doubt concerns the view that Anfortas and the Grail-

---

3. Tax, *Kingdom*, pp. 20ff.
4. Weigand, *GQ* 51 (1978), 444.

community know nothing of Parzival's existence. Tax merely claims this point without any argument, saying that to give the reasons would require another paper,[5] so that we are left to take his claim on trust. Furthermore, it is said of Cundrie that she is the spokesman of the Grail-community, especially of Anfortas and his inner circle.[6] As such, however, she knows about Parzival (his name and his parentage) when she denounces him before the Round Table – why should the Grail-community not also be acquainted with this? If Cundrie has a special means, peculiar to her, of knowing this, as is indeed suggested by Tax, we are again given no explanation of how this may be so.[7]

It is also argued (this is my second reservation) that the Grail-community can be seen trying to attract their visitor, whom they take to be Ither, to succeed Anfortas as ruler of their kingdom after marriage to Repanse de schoy by offering him first a royal mantle and then a sword to symbolise the transfer of royal power.[8] In both respects they sail as close to the wind as they dare, tacitly suggesting to the visitor what is at stake without any actual verbal prompting. I have referred to these same points in my own argument and agree that they are to be taken as hints, to Parzival and to us, that a transfer of royal authority is at issue here,[9] but would question the particular force which Tax sees in these implicit suggestions. In other words, the Grail-community see in their visitor a potential successor to Anfortas, but this in itself is not enough to indicate that they take this visitor to be Ither. They *may* do, but this cannot be proved by this detail alone.

Nor do I find the suggestion that Repanse de schoy is used by the Grail-community as a decoy for gaining the visitor they take to be

---

5. Tax, *Kingdom*, pp. 23 and 27. On p. 27 Tax argues that Anfortas would have been acquainted with the Red Knight because his brother Trevrizent had known him. But if we are justified in extending Trevrizent's knowledge about Ither to Anfortas, why should we assume conversely that Anfortas does not share Trevrizent's knowledge about Parzival's existence (that he is the son of Herzeloyde and Gahmuret) and about details of his youth (476,12f. and 25ff.)? It is also misleading to say, as does Tax on p. 27 again, in the context of Parzival's first visit at Munsalvæsche that the reader knows that Parzival is the only possible candidate. On the contrary, we learn this only very much later, in Book IX (see above, pp. 214ff.).
6. *Ibid.*, p. 26.
7. *Ibid.*, p. 32: 'But who had the visitor in the Red Knight's armour been? I could show you how it was Cundrie who found out after some intensive research, but I have to skip this demonstration here.'
8. *Ibid.*, pp. 24, 26 and 28.
9. See above, p. 208, and the further literature given there.

The recognition of Parzival at Munsalvæsche and by Trevrizent

Ither as a successor to Anfortas any more convincing. Tax first makes the point that the narrator describes the maidens in the Grail-procession, leading up to Repanse de schoy, in terms 'to indicate the distinct erotic character of the procession',[10] yet this particular interpretation is hardly borne out by the passages to which he refers.[11] The maidens are rather described in terms of their courtly beauty, their resplendence and radiance, and the colourful impression they create on the beholder.[12] Only in one detail is love hinted at (232,13: *daz si wol gæben minnen solt, / swerz dâ mit dienste het erholt*), but even this I take to be an indirect description of courtly beauty by hinting at its possible effect, applied moreover only to the first two maidens in the procession, not to all of them and least of all to Repanse de schoy. When he makes this point Tax is careful enough to introduce it as no more than a hypothesis, but within two pages this supposition has been converted into a firm fact which is no longer questioned.[13] Finally, in order to buttress his theory of an erotic intention behind this Grail-procession in Book V Tax feels it necessary to play down its presence on the occasion of the second procession in Book XVI.[14] His argument is somewhat perverse at this point since (without the conscious intention he has in mind playing a part) the narrative does now contain an erotic element, since it is as a result of this second procession that Feirefiz falls in love with Repanse de schoy (810,13ff.).

Without going as far as Tax in his assumption that Parzival is taken to be Ither, Johnson also believes that the Grail-community has no idea of Parzival's name or identity when he first comes to them. Against this I suggested above that in the depiction of

10. Tax, *Kingdom*, p. 26.
11. *Ibid.*, p. 36, n. 6.
12. For beauty cf. 232,15 and 20; 233,4; for radiance 232,15 and 20; 233,4; 235,16f.; for colour 232,26; 234,4.
13. Cf. Tax, *Kingdom*, p. 26 ('Let us suppose for a moment that this eroticism leads up to Repanse and that the visitor were to fall in love with her') with p. 28 ('But the Red Knight not only had to ask the question; for dynastic reasons he had to fall in love with Queen Repanse as well' and 'the eroticization of the Grail procession *was* intended to match the Red Knight with Queen Repanse'). Cf. also p. 29: the bed to which Parzival is conducted for the night was 'intended for King Ither and Queen Repanse'. In his interpretation of the Grail-procession Tax nowhere considers the possibility that the narrator's intention may have been simply to stress its courtly splendour and the overwhelming visual impression made on Parzival, diverting his attention from Anfortas.
14. *Ibid.*, pp. 30f.

Appendix A

Parzival's first visit to Munsalvæsche his name was readily used by the narrator (for to withhold it would suggest that the Grail-community were ignorant of his identity), by contrast with the withholding of Anfortas's name (because he is unknown to Parzival).[15] This has been countered by Johnson, who argues that Munsalvæsche must have been ignorant of Parzival's name, for otherwise Trevrizent, when he learned Parzival's identity, would have known that he was the one who failed to ask the question.

In his general observation on those who are called to the Grail-community (470,21ff.) Trevrizent mentions that both their name and family descent (470,25: *'sînen namen und sînen art'*) are given miraculously in writing, in an *epitafum* on the Grail. Trevrizent says this in the context of young recruits of either sex to the Grail-community, but it is a general statement which goes beyond this particular context and is also true of one called to Munsalvæsche to take over kingship of the Grail. This is suggested by the terms of Parzival's ultimate call to the Grail, where *daz epitafjum ist gelesen* (781,15), i.e. his name and family descent have miraculously appeared in writing again. It is also suggested by the way in which Parzival, after now successfully putting the question, is acknowledged as ruler at Munsalvæsche (796,17: *da ergienc dô dehein ander wal, / wan die diu schrift ame grâl / hete ze hêrren in benant: / Parzivâl wart schiere bekant / ze künige unt ze hêrren dâ*). I should argue that what is true of mere recruits and of Parzival in Book XV is also true of Parzival in Book V (or rather that there is no suggestion to the contrary): his name and descent were announced before he arrived at Munsalvæsche.[16]

It is of a piece with this that Cundrie, when she appears before the Round Table, should know Parzival's name (315,9) and also his family descent (317,11ff.; 318,3) and can even enlighten the Round Table on this. Johnson accounts for this knowledge of Cundrie, however, by assuming that she came across Sigune and learned Parzival's identity from her. Yet this involves a number of assumptions (that Cundrie followed the same route as Parzival, that she encountered Sigune, that Sigune passed on this information to her),

---

15. See above, pp. 98f.
16. That Parzival really was *zem grâle benant* on the first occasion is clear, I think, from the supernatural guidance afforded him (on this see Wynn, *Speculum* 36 (1961), 393ff., and Green, *Weg*, pp. 11ff.) and also from the miraculous concatenation of events in his favour, as worked out by Deinert, *Ritter*, pp. 12ff., especially p. 35.

whereas my explanation rests on details that are actually given us by the narrator. After all, only two days separate Parzival's failure at Munsalvæsche from his accusation by Cundrie,[17] who comes to the Round Table fresh from the Grail-castle and therefore knows what happened during Parzival's visit, including his name and descent. Her knowledge agrees with that of the Grail-community, and I see no need to assume that Cundrie, after leaving Munsalvæsche, came across Sigune and acquired her knowledge only from her. I prefer instead to use a good medieval, Ockhamite principle: *entia non sunt multiplicanda praeter necessitatem*.

In support of his view that Parzival's name was not announced at Munsalvæsche so that he could not be recognised there Johnson also refers to Trevrizent's words about this disastrous visit (473,12: '*wan einr kom unbenennet dar*'). We have seen that Wolfram uses the verb *benennen* in two senses ('to name, to mention by name' and 'to call, to summon, to appoint', i.e. to the Grail)[18] and I suggest that this distinction is valid here, especially if we correlate line 473,12 with what is said just before this of those recruited to membership of the Grail (473,10: '... *die dar sint benennet / ze Munsalvæsche ans grâles schar*'). In 473,10 *benennet* has to combine both possible meanings of the verb (to be divinely called to the Grail, but also to be named in the *epitafum*), since such recruits are clearly appointed and if they were not also named, no one would know whom to fetch. When two lines later the same verb recurs in negative form (*wan einr kom unbenennet dar*), Johnson takes this as an antithetical statement, fully contradicting the previous positive statement and therefore meaning 'not named and not summoned.' I agree that a full contradiction of the preceding statement is the least specious reading of 473,12, yet I regard this sense as the one meant by Trevrizent, but not corresponding to the reality of what took place at Munsalvæsche. Trevrizent wrongly infers from the failure to ask the question of Anfortas that the knight was not divinely called to the Grail (just as Sigune conversely assumed, 251,21ff., that if Parzival really was at Munsalvæsche he must have asked the question), and from this in turn he also infers that the knight was not named in the *epitafum*. But the facts of the situation are that, despite his failure, Parzival was divinely called to the Grail[19] – and from

17. Cf. Weigand, *Parzival*, pp. 48ff.
18. See above, p. 316.
19. See the articles mentioned above in fn. 16, but also Green, *Pathway*, pp. 174ff., and *Irony*, pp. 150ff.

Appendix A

this I infer that his name also appeared on the Grail. We have to remember that 473,12 is said by the hermit at a point in Book IX when he is still under the impression that the knight in front of him might well be Lähelin, and there can certainly be no talk of Lähelin having been called to the Grail on the occasion of his combat with Lybbeals. This is in fact mentioned by Trevrizent immediately afterwards (473,22ff.) to suggest the close association, in his eyes, of the knight before him with Lähelin. If Trevrizent still thinks that this knight might be Lähelin and that he might have come *unbenennet* to Munsalvæsche, he is using the verb in both senses (neither divinely summoned nor named by the Grail). We know however that this is Parzival and that he was divinely summoned, so that the implication is that he was also named.

As I see it, then, the members of the Grail-community were aware of Parzival's name and descent at the time of his first visit, since these details had been miraculously announced in advance. Cundrie shares this knowledge with them, but the hermit Trevrizent, because he dwells apart, does not. We have to reckon here with uncertain communications between members of the Grail-family who dwell apart from Munsalvæsche and the events surrounding Parzival. It may well be that Munsalvæsche must have got wind of Sigune's plight (in the world of Gahmuret) after Schionatulander's death and had her brought near to the Grail-castle in order to care for her, but on the other hand Sigune, at her second meeting with Parzival, is still unaware of Herzeloyde's death.[20] Trevrizent is here aware of a detail where Sigune is ignorant, whereas Sigune knows of Parzival's failure at Munsalvæsche earlier than the hermit, because Parzival comes across her just after leaving the Grail-castle. Trevrizent's ignorance of the name of the knight who failed to ask the question means that, when he does learn Parzival's name, this still does not tell him that Parzival must be that knight.

Johnson also asks why, if Parzival's name was announced by the Grail, the knights of Munsalvæsche made no attempt to set out and look for him. Their readiness to sail as close to the wind as possible in giving him the token gifts of mantle and sword suggests that they might have tried similar measures to get Parzival to Munsalvæsche.

20. In 251,11 she refers to the four children of Frimutel who survived him, but her words in the following line (*'driu in jâmer sint'*) include Herzeloyde (cf. Martin, *Kommentar*, note on 251,12) and are significantly in the present tense. Her later words (252,15: *'daz dîn muoter ist mîn muome'*) refer only to Herzeloyde and are again in the present.

The recognition of Parzival at Munsalvæsche and by Trevrizent

Johnson's answer to this question is that Munsalvæsche take no such steps because they are ignorant of Parzival's identity, but two points need to be made about this suggestion.

What is at issue at the Grail-castle is not a simple case of dynastic succession. Grail-kingship is normally an inherited position[21] and does not usually seem to be indicated by an inscription on the Grail, but this kind of designation is called for in this instance because the succession is not so clearcut in Parzival's case[22] and because Anfortas is not dead, but is effectively being deposed in favour of Parzival. Parzival does not simply succeed Anfortas, he has above all to pass a test of compassion for which a measure of maturity and experience are indispensable. It is for this reason that the condition about the time when the question may be effectively asked[23] does not refer to the Grail, but to the readiness of the one who is to ask the question, to Parzival's own maturity.[24] If Parzival is the only possible successor within the Grail-dynasty and if he is about sixteen years old when he comes to Munsalvæsche,[25] then Providence has brought him there at about the earliest possible time when he might be expected to have any chance of passing such a test. Any earlier attempt, brought about by Providence or contrived by the Grail-community sending out for Parzival and enticing him to Munsalvæsche, would have been just as unsuccessful and could not even have been realistically expected to be successful.[26]

The question of dating, implicit in the hypothetical calculation of

21. See above, pp. 214ff., but also Becker, *Recht*, pp. 43ff.
22. See above, pp. 218 and 221.
23. 484,1ff. See above, p. 206.
24. See above, pp. 206f., fn. 107 and 108. Cf. also Dewald, *Minne*, p. 254.
25. For this hypothetical calculation see Weigand, *GQ* 51 (1978), 448.
26. Another reason why any attempt to get Parzival to Munsalvæsche earlier is likely to have been fruitless is implicit in the argument of Deinert, *Ritter*, pp. 12ff. He argues that one of the events providentially arranged for Parzival's benefit so as to prompt him to ask the question at Munsalvæsche *ungewarnet* is the fact that the pain and suffering of Anfortas have reached their climax and should therefore be most obvious, that this has been brought about astronomically by the position of Saturn, that Saturn's influence begins to be decisive precisely at the time when Parzival comes to the Grail-castle (p. 27) and is concentrated on this day in particular (p. 30). If we add to these details the fact that Saturn's power reaches its zenith only because the planet has reached its position after completing a course lasting thirty years (p. 13), it will be clear that the day when Parzival, about sixteen years old, comes to Munsalvæsche is the first possible day in his life when such prompting can be given him in this way. If with even this amount of prompting he still fails to ask the question, how much less likely is it that he would have acted correctly if he had been brought to Munsalvæsche earlier, before Saturn had reached a position favourable to the one who had to ask the question?

Appendix A

Parzival's age when he came to Munsalvæsche, is relevant in another respect, for Johnson also asks *when* all the events in the narrative took place, relative to each other, and wonders whether, if Parzival's name had appeared on the Grail, Herzeloyde could have known about it or even Sigune, when she first met Parzival, and if so whether it is conceivable that neither should have done anything about getting Parzival to Munsalvæsche. Such hypotheses are forced upon us in a case like this, for Wolfram's time technique in *Parzival* is concerned with temporal connections between events narrated,[27] but is justifiably not meant to provide clear answers to questions such as ours which go well beyond the framework of the narrative itself. We are not expressly told when Trevrizent became a hermit or when the inscription appeared upon the Grail, but can only assume that each event occurred some time after the wounding of Anfortas. In other words, we have no means of telling whether Herzeloyde or Sigune can have known of the inscription and therefore done anything about getting Parzival to Munsalvæsche. If I may venture my own hypothetical suggestion at this point it would be to propose that the inscription on the Grail, naming Parzival, could have appeared at Munsalvæsche very shortly before Parzival, guided providentially, was due to arrive there himself. In other words, the inscription could have performed much the same function for the Grail-community as does a narrator's forecast for his listeners (e.g. 435,12 or 734,5ff.), alerting them to what is soon to take place. Neither Herzeloyde nor Sigune (at the time of her first meeting with Parzival) would therefore know of this, so that it is fully understandable that they should make no attempt to get Parzival to Munsalvæsche.[28]

Yet even this alternative hypothesis (which is no more and no less of an assumption than Johnson's) is unlikely to satisfy those who, like him, feel that it is only if Parzival was not named that the full impact of the mystery, of the gradual revelation, of the working out of God's purpose and of the ultimate realisation that in God's wisdom the eventual saviour and new Grail-king is in any case the legitimate heir is really brought out. These are weighty considerations of general aesthetic import and no one would willingly

---

27. On this aspect of Wolfram's technique see Weigand, *Parzival*, pp. 18ff.
28. In the case of Herzeloyde there is the further possibility that her fear of knighthood and its possible dangers for her son may have led her to bring up her son remote not just from Gahmuret's world, but from the equally knightly realm of the Grail. See above, pp. 214f.

dismiss them for the sake of clinging to a particular interpretation of a mere detail. But I would also suggest that the full impact of mystery, gradual revelation and ultimate realisation of God's purpose is not jeopardised by my reading, only this impact is now concentrated on the listeners[29] and, within the narrative world, on Parzival and Trevrizent, the two most important characters at the heart of the work in Book IX.[30] By my reading this impact is lost only in the case of the Grail-community, who know fully what is at stake as events unfold in Book V, but even this is no real loss, since their knowledge that this visitor represents their only chance immeasurably heightens for them the tension and the tragedy of Parzival's apparently irredeemable failure.[31]

In these last few pages we have passed over from the first problem (whether Parzival was known by name while at Munsalvæsche) to the second (whether Trevrizent initially recognised his guest as Parzival). In addressing ourselves now to this second question we must consider the two articles by Weigand and Schirok, each of whom holds that Trevrizent did recognise Parzival early, just as Anfortas had been aware of his identity. In maintaining that Trevrizent did not at first recognise his guest I find myself in agreement with Tax and also, this time, with Johnson. Although Weigand and Johnson hold opposing views about Trevrizent's ability to recognise Parzival, they both make use, independently, of the same argument. Weigand's starting-point is the assumption that the hermit must have heard about what happened at the Grail-castle from Cundrie, the only person who communicates between Munsalvæsche and Sigune or Trevrizent.[32] Assuming that Cundrie communicated this news to Trevrizent, Weigand finds it inconceivable that she failed to mention the name of the luckless knight.[33] For Weigand this constitutes proof without question that Trevrizent knew the identity of the knight before him,[34] but the

---

29. For the listeners the mystery is maintained by their still having to learn whether Parzival will be granted an opportunity to come to Munsalvæsche again, and if so how, and also by their being only gradually informed about his position within the Grail-dynasty.
30. This is reflected in the fact that in the course of Book IX both Trevrizent and Parzival have to undergo a cognitive progress. See above, pp. 186ff. and 197ff.
31. Cf. Tax, *Kingdom*, pp. 32f.
32. Weigand, *GQ* 51 (1978), 444.
33. *Ibid.*, p. 445.
34. *Ibid.*: 'This proves without question that Trevrizent knew the identity of the knight.'

Appendix A

stages by which he arrives at this conclusion are largely made up of rhetorical questions and hypotheses,[35] whilst the fact that Cundrie knows Parzival's identity does not prove that Trevrizent does as well.[36] Equally unconvincing is Weigand's suggestion as to how Cundrie may have communicated this information to the hermit, for by stressing her magic powers he is able to suggest that 'she communicates with Trevrizent at will at, let us say, the speed of a telegraph'[37] and thus prepares him for Parzival's visit. At one point Johnson, too, considered the possibility of Cundrie's supernatural powers, but rightly rejected such an appeal to magic as an unfair shifting of the ground in scholarly debate. To this I should only add that it is equally unjust to Wolfram's art of motivation to assume this of him.

Although he makes use of it for other ends Johnson also finds it incredible that a Grail informant who told Trevrizent what had happened at Munsalvæsche would not also have told him Parzival's name, but from this he draws the opposite conclusion, namely that this name was unknown at the Grail-castle. I argue instead for a discrepancy between knowledge at Munsalvæsche about their guest's identity and Trevrizent's ignorance. When the hermit refers anonymously to the knight who failed to ask the question (483,21 and 484,21: *ein rîter*) these references do not indicate that Parzival was called there without being named, but only that Trevrizent is not informed on this point as the inhabitants of Munsalvæsche are. But we still have to face Johnson's objection. If Trevrizent learned about the inscription and the failure of the knight who came to Munsalvæsche from someone present at the Grail-castle,[38] is it conceivable that his informant would have told

35. *Ibid.*: 'How can we picture that cell to have been built on piles half-way across a flowing brook except by virtue of Cundrie's white magic? Who knows – may she not avail herself of the aid of some of the evil and kindly spirits who live between the earth and the firmament? ... Who but Cundrie La Surziere could be responsible for that disconcerting spectacle? If we accept these wonders we shall be more than ready to assume that she also communicates with Trevrizent.' And on p. 446: 'Could Signe have failed to tell Cundrie ... Is it not likely that Cundrie informed Trevrizent ... A sense of expectation may well have been building up in Trevrizent.'
36. As Weigand's rhetorical questions show, it is after all only an assumption that Trevrizent learned this from Cundrie and there is no actual certainty that she mentioned Parzival by name to him.
37. *GQ* 51 (1978), 464.
38. Johnson assumes that a member of the Grail-community told Trevrizent what happened at Munsalvæsche or that he was there in person when the inscription appeared, and suggests that the most natural reading of 483,19ff. (*'unser venje*

him these vital facts and at the same time suppressed, or overlooked, the equally vital fact that this knight was Parzival, his own nephew? To meet this objection we have to take into account not just the probabilities of consistent motivation, but also the narrator's technique in naming, especially as applied to the hero.

We saw above that Parzival's proper name, as opposed to circumlocutions like *rîter rôt*, was used to define his true nature with regard to Grail-kingship and that his name was used in this sense only by

> *viel wir für den grâl. | dar an gesâh wir zeinem mâl | geschriben, dar solde ein rîter komn*'; cf. 484,9ff.) is that the twice repeated *wir* includes Trevrizent, the speaker. I am not persuaded that this most natural reading is necessarily the correct one. In the first place, the two possibilities suggested by Johnson cannot be alternatives since, however much Trevrizent may have learned while still at Munsalvæsche, he cannot also have learned of Parzival's failure, for he was no longer there at that time. Johnson's second possibility thus does not exclude the first as an explanation of all that Trevrizent knows. More important, however, is Johnson's point about Trevrizent's use of the plural pronoun *wir*, for he ignores the twofold use of *wir* in what the hermit reports about Munsalvæsche. On the one hand it can be used straightforwardly to describe events in which Trevrizent participated while still there, as when Anfortas returns wounded from his disastrous adventure (480,3) or with the vain attempts to heal him (481,18ff.). On the other hand the use of *wir* underlines Trevrizent's compassion for Anfortas, the grief he suffers together with all those still present at Munsalvæsche, as can be shown when the hermit still uses *wir* of events at the Grail-castle when he was no longer present himself. This can be shown with regard to the frost and pain caused by Saturn (489,22: '*nu sag mir, sæhe du daz sper | ze Munsalvæsche ûf dem hûs? | dô der sterne Sâturnus | wider an sîn zil gestuont, | daz wart uns bî der wunden kuont*'; 492,23: *der wirt sprach 'neve, sît noch ê | wart dem künige niht sô wê, | wan dô sîn komen zeigte sus | der sterne Sâturnus: | der kan mit grôzem froste komn. | drûf legen moht uns niht gefromn, | als manz ê drûffe ligen sach*'). In both these passages Trevrizent includes himself by using *wir*, but this cannot be in the literal, physical sense, since Saturn began to exercise such power only on the day when Parzival came to Munsalvæsche (cf. Deinert, *Ritter*, pp. 27 and 30), i.e. at a time when the hermit was no longer present at the Grail-castle. Elsewhere in his dialogue Trevrizent underlines the compassion for Anfortas felt by the members of the Grail-community present (e.g. 481,26–8; 482,10; 483,5), but in using *wir* when he himself is absent he demonstrates by a linguistic detail the fellow feeling between him and them and hence between him and Anfortas which Parzival should have shown at Munsalvæsche by asking the question. In view of these two usages of *wir* in Trevrizent's report about Munsalvæsche I do not regard 483,19ff. as indicating that he was actually present there when the inscription appeared. Nor do I take 484,19 ('*dô zôch ich mich dâ her*') to mean that only now did Trevrizent withdraw from the Grail-castle, after the appearance of the inscription. All that he says in this line is that then he withdrew to his present hermitage, not that he left the Grail-castle. As we saw in the case of Gawan overhearing the report of Clias on the four queens at Schastel Marveile (see above, pp. 153f.), it is rash to assume that a narrator who follows the principle of narrative *krümbe* will always adhere to the *ordo naturalis* and that the sequence in which events are reported corresponds to the sequence in which they took place.

members of the Grail-world.[39] For Sigune to recognise and name Parzival at their third meeting is for her to see him in the context of the Grail[40] and is closely connected with her wish to put him on the right path to Munsalvæsche (442,9ff.). The same link between proper name and Grail is also suggested in the second encounter (251,29: *Dô sprach si 'du bist Parzivâl. / nu sage et, sæhe du den grâl?'*), where Sigune's recognition of Parzival's named identity prompts her to accept that he must after all have been at Munsalvæsche.[41] She soon learns that his mere presence there was not enough and on hearing with horror of his failure she falls back on the distant pronoun *ir* and nameless, insulting epithets (255,13: *'gunêrter lîp, verfluochet man!'*), and abandons all converse with him (255,28: *'iren vindet nu decheinen wîs / decheine geinrede an mir'*). For Sigune therefore Parzival's proper name sums up within itself the prospect of Grail-kingship for him, whilst anonymity is tantamount to his failure. The same is true even of the three occasions when Cundrie addresses Parzival by name (315,9 and 26; 316,25) in her accusation of him before the Round Table, for on each occasion she makes use of the bitter, sarcastic phrase *hêr Parzivâl*. If irony attaches to *hêr* in this phrase,[42] it also informs *Parzivâl*: the hero as little deserves the title as he merits this particular name, for if he has proved untrue to his paternal inheritance (317,14f.) this is even more true of the Grail inheritance he has apparently squandered. Apart from these examples, Parzival's name is not used by a member of the Grail-community again until he is called to Munsalvæsche by Cundrie (782,5) and confronts Anfortas once more (795,11). For the Grail-community to refer to Parzival by name is therefore an indication of his Grail destiny, the promise eagerly expected or about to be realised, whereas anonymity is a mark of his disastrous failure. It is in agreement with this that the Grail inscription announcing his imminent arrival to put an end to Anfortas's suffering should refer to Parzival by name, but that the news of the failure passed on to Trevrizent should insultingly withhold from the hero the privilege of a name which he has not lived up to.

39. See above, pp. 311f. We saw that towards the end of the narrative Parzival could also be addressed by name by members of the Round Table (cf. pp. 312ff.), but these occasions do not define him in the same way in terms of the Grail.
40. 440,28: *do erkande si den degen snel: / si sprach 'ir sîtz hêr Parzivâl. / sagt an, wie stêtz iu umben grâl?'*
41. See above, p. 117.
42. Cf. Johnson, *MLR* 64 (1969), 69f., and Green, *Irony*, pp. 207f.

The recognition of Parzival at Munsalvæsche and by Trevrizent

We come now to the article by Schirok who, although he concedes that most scholars hold the opposite view,[43] argues that Trevrizent realises the identity of the knight before him earlier than has been generally accepted and does not have to wait, say, until Parzival confesses that it was he who failed at Munsalvæsche. Schirok does not touch so much the question how the hermit could arrive at the truth before his guest reveals it to him, but instead interprets the whole dialogue in the light of his own assumption in order to establish its intrinsic probability. I shall accordingly restrict my comments likewise to the dialogue, mentioning some of the points where the assumption that Trevrizent has already grasped the facts of the situation creates obstacles to our understanding.

Henzen has described the manner in which Trevrizent formulates the terms of the question to be asked at Munsalvæsche (484,27: '*hêrre, wie stêt iwer nôt?*') as 'ahnungslos',[44] which is the more convincing since it comes just after the hermit has stressed that the question loses its force if the person concerned is consciously informed about it in advance (483,24ff.). This suggests that Trevrizent still has no idea that his guest had been called to Munsalvæsche and had failed to ask the question. When he therefore reveals the terms in which the question is to be formulated this really is done *unwizzende*,[45] so that Parzival is not *gewarnet* in a sense which would forever disqualify him from success at Munsalvæsche. To assume that at this stage Trevrizent already knew of Parzival's stay at the Grail-castle means accepting that the hermit is here needlessly making things more difficult for all concerned by disqualifying the one person who might still put things right at the Grail-castle. The same is true of this passage in another sense. The hermit has been talking of vain attempts to heal Anfortas's wound (481,6ff.), he then mentions prayers before the Grail (483,19) before giving the message of the divine inscription, apparently promising final relief (484,9ff.). This promise seems to be fulfilled with the arrival of the knight in 484,21, but the hermit then refers to his earlier remarks about this knight and shows that these hopes were dashed, accusing this knight of *unprîs*, *tumpheit* and loss of *sælde* (484,24ff.). Because of his incomplete knowledge of Parzival's

---

43. Schirok, *ABÄG* 10 (1976), 59, fn. 43.
44. Henzen, *Überlegungen*, p. 197.
45. Cf. the Bartsch–Marti edition, fn. to 484,27.

Appendix A

identity Trevrizent's advice has misfired: by so roundly condemning the unknown knight as if he were not actually present he makes it much more difficult for Parzival to broach his confession. If the hermit's pastoral task is made even more difficult by his ignorance of Parzival's complete identity, it is hard to imagine him creating such difficulties if he really knew all the facts. One can also say the same of an earlier passage in which Trevrizent comments on a statement by Parzival as to his two goals in life, placed in their correct order of priorities for him: first the Grail, then his wife (467,25ff.). Out of pastoral tact the hermit reverses this order because he thinks he is dealing with Lähelin,[46] but if this results in the anomaly of recommending what is the wrong order to Parzival, this again suggests that he has no idea of the latter's identity.

Schirok also suggests that Trevrizent recognises his guest as Parzival because of the red armour he is wearing.[47] If Parzival is known by name to the inhabitants of Munsalvæsche and if, in the person of Cundrie, they refer to him as such (315,9), this is in purposeful contrast to the use of *rîter rôt* as a term employed by the Round Table because of their ignorance of Parzival's name.[48] The meeting point for these two ways of referring to the hero is Cundrie's words about Parzival addressed to the Round Table in 315,9ff. Since the phrase *rîter rôt* is never used of Parzival in the context of Munsalvæsche (knowing him by name, they have no need of a circumlocution) it is most unlikely that the red armour alone should serve as an indication to Trevrizent that this must be Parzival. This would only be possible if we were to assume that Trevrizent already knew that Parzival had killed Ither and taken his armour, which is why Schirok is forced to assume that Trevrizent was as well aware of this as Cundrie,[49] but we have already seen that there are grounds for doubting whether what is known to the Grail-messenger, travelling between Munsalvæsche and various points, can be assumed to be known by the solitary hermit as well.

When, again in reply to his guest's statement of priorities concerning the Grail and his wife, Trevrizent attempts to dissuade him from the folly of a hopeless quest for the Grail (468,10ff.), his words make much better sense when mistakenly applied to one whom the hermit assumes to be Lähelin than to one whom he already knows to

---

46. See above, p. 189, fn. 52.
47. *ABÄG* 10 (1976), 49.
48. See above, pp. 306f.
49. *ABÄG* 10 (1976), 50.

be Parzival. By his murderous violence against the Grail-knight Lybbeals as well as by the facts of his birth (outside the Grail-family) Lähelin can have no prospect of a divine call and therefore no hope of attaining to the Grail-castle, so that Trevrizent is right to seek to head off 'Lähelin'. But neither point applies to Parzival. He may have committed *roup* in keeping his Grail-opponent's horse for himself, but this was no *rêroup*, as in the encounter between Lähelin and Lybbeals, since the defeated knight survived the encounter (Trevrizent later seeks reassurance on precisely this point, 500,11ff.), and furthermore Parzival is not merely a member of the Grail-family by birth, he is also the sole available male successor to Anfortas within that dynasty. By later himself repeating these words by Trevrizent that only the man divinely called can attain to the Grail (786,3ff.) Parzival shows how unwittingly they had earlier been inapplicable to himself as an attempt to divert him, as opposed to Lähelin, from a quest for the Grail.

A final reason for doubting the truth of Schirok's suggestion that Trevrizent early grasps the truth of the situation concerns points rather more intangible, but psychologically no less telling for that. By this I mean that at various stages in the dialogue between the hermit and Parzival an unconscious or even ignorant element in the hermit's thought processes is stressed, so that he is not always in such conscious and informed control of the situation as Schirok's argument would imply. We have seen this illustrated in the unconscious associations which allow Trevrizent, when talking about other members of the Grail-family, to stumble across his guest's similarity to them and the possibility which this opens up (474,1ff.).[50] It also underlies my interpretation of Trevrizent's 'lie' to Parzival, which I take as an untruth unwittingly voiced because the hermit thinks he is speaking to someone else,[51] but it also informs his mistake about Parzival's order of priorities, when he reverses what is for Parzival the correct order, again because he thinks he is dealing with someone else, for whom his recommendation would indeed be correct. Rather more intangibly, I have suggested that the narrator makes use of Trevrizent as an occasional mouthpiece, conveying a truth to us from the poet which eludes the hermit, as when Trevrizent makes a number of remarks concerning the knight Lähelin he thinks he is dealing with, but which are also

50. See above, p. 190.
51. See above, pp. 258f., but also Appendix B, pp. 337ff.

Appendix A

applicable, in one sense or another, to Parzival,[52] or in the observation about the quality of the food which Parzival's horse must have enjoyed once at Munsalvæsche.[53] These are all indications that Trevrizent is not fully master of the situation, that the pathway to recognition in this dialogue, although it mainly concerns the hero, is not entirely one-way and that there are important points where even the adviser in this episode, like the *wîse man* in the audience addressed in the prologue, has something to learn. These considerations, combined with the points made in Chapter 6 and in this Appendix, make me doubt whether we can ascribe such knowledge to Trevrizent that he would have recognised Parzival's full identity before the latter's confession.

These are the reasons why, in contrast to the scholars referred to in this Appendix, I incline to the view that although the inhabitants of Munsalvæsche have already been informed of their visitor in advance and are aware of Parzival's identity throughout his visit, the same is not true when Parzival later comes to Trevrizent, for now his host only gradually recognises the truth. None of this can be proved stringently, for we are dealing with questions which go beyond the range of motivation in the work, with questions belonging to what Mohr has called the 'epische Hintergründe'.[54] But whereas the narrative threads which Mohr unravelled in his article were sufficiently intact to permit relatively clear answers to his questions, we are dealing here with a mixture of facts and surmises which amounts at the most to probability, not demonstration. It is typical of Wolfram that the modern reader should be invited to reconstruct such details of his narrative universe with him, but, as Johnson has put it, reading Wolfram is like playing chess against him and we, together with the characters in his work, are all pawns in the master's hands.[55]

52. See above, 188, fn. 50.
53. See above, p. 195.
54. Mohr, *Hintergründe*, pp. 174ff.
55. As this book goes to press I have received a letter from Professor Weigand (1 March 1982) in which he assures me that he has not assumed that Anfortas recognised Parzival's identity in Book V. I stand corrected, but have no need to alter what I have written above, since I am there concerned only with Weigand's assumption about Trevrizent in Book IX. When Weigand says that Wolfram gives us no hint about Anfortas in Book V I can only agree, but would maintain that the poet's persuasiveness prompts us to speculate about this, however hypothetically.

Appendix B: Trevrizent's 'lie'

In Chapter VII, when discussing Trevrizent's final words to Parzival after the latter's call to Grail-kingship, I suggested that the hermit's words about their first encounter (798,6: *'ich louc durch ableitens list / vome grâl'*) could best be understood if we took the verb *liegen* not in the sense of its modern counterpart ('to tell a deliberate falsehood'), but in this context as meaning 'to say something which, without one's realising it, is untrue'.[1] I am suggesting, in other words, that the medieval verb can be used of uttering a deliberate untruth, but also whenever this untruth is not intended or even grasped by the speaker, and that in this latter respect medieval usage differs from modern.

The presence of deliberate intention in the act of lying was stressed by Augustine in his *De mendacio*, for he saw that it was not enough to define lying as saying something other than what one knows or means,[2] since that would make it impossible to distinguish between lying and the use of such sophisticated modes of speech as irony, euphemism and polite social formulas, all of which can be classified rhetorically as allegory in the sense of saying other than what is meant.[3] To make this distinction clear Augustine felt it necessary to add that in the case of lying the conscious intention to deceive must also be present: *mendacium est enuntiatio cum voluntate falsum enuntiandi*.[4] But what was clear to Augustine's trained mind was not always realised in linguistic practice in the Middle Ages, where there are cases of the same verb being used of a deliberate falsehood and also of a statement whose untruth is not grasped by the speaker. In Grimms' *Deutsches Wörterbuch* the first

---

1. See above, pp. 258f.
2. Cf. Weinrich, *Linguistik*, pp. 12f.
3. On the need to distinguish between lying and allegory, specifically irony, see Green, *Alieniloquium*, pp. 150ff.
4. Quoted by Weinrich, *Linguistik*, p. 13.

Appendix B

definition of *lügen* accords with Augustine in stressing the factor of deliberateness ('von personen, eine wissentliche unwahrheit sagen'),[5] but the very first example given illustrates the readiness to ignore this factor (*liegen ist, da ein mensch anderst redet denn er gedenket*),[6] where Geiler von Kaisersberg is content with a definition which did not satisfy Augustine. Despite this, the articles on *Lüge* and *lügen* in the *Deutsches Wörterbuch* do not seem exactly promising for my case. Although it is conceded that, contrary to common usage, *Lüge* can also be used of an unintentional error,[7] only one example is given from so late a source as Sebastian Frank (*Ptolomeus hat hie gefält und ein lugin gesaget*), so that the impression is given that this usage was not common in the Middle Ages.

Common it may not have been, but it was certainly possible, and that is enough for our purposes. In what follows I make no attempt to consider the semantic range of *liegen* in Middle High German at large, since it would not help us in the slightest to establish the use of this word to mean unconscious error by any number of authors, if these did not include Wolfram. For exactly the same reason I shall confine myself to examples from his *Parzival*. In considering these examples, however, I have not restricted myself to *liegen* alone, but have also taken *triegen* into account. This is justified not merely by the semantic closeness of the two verbs, but also because the obvious rhyme they constitute brings them often together in Wolfram's usage where, as we shall see, what is true of the one is also true of the other.

There are admittedly many cases in *Parzival* where it is impossible to tell with certainty whether *liegen* implies a conscious wish to deceive on the part of the speaker (and therefore means what we understand by 'to lie') or no more than a statement made in good faith which happens to be incorrect or mistaken, or whether *triegen* similarly means 'to deceive with intent' or 'to mislead unwittingly'. All such uncertain cases we must classify as neutral from our point of view. To this class belongs, for example, the narrator's assurance about a detail in his account (5,18: *daz sag ich iu für ungelogen*), for we have no means of knowing for certain whether he means simply that he is assured of the truth of what he says or whether he might not be going further and intending no actual lie. The same uncertainty exists with the companion verb, as with the answer given

---

5. *Deutsches Wörterbuch*, vol. VI, col. 1273.
6. *Ibid*.
7. *Ibid*., col. 1269.

Trevrizent's 'lie'

to the question about Gahmuret's identity (64,1: *si sagetenz in für unbetrogn*), for the same reason. When the source from which Nabchodonosor derives his claim to divinity is described as *trügelîchen buochen* (102,6), the Christian attitude to such idolatry makes it probable, but not certain, that this pagan source is being emphatically rejected as 'lying', rather than merely as 'incorrect'. Yet even this degree of probability is lacking when the narrator refers to his own source when mentioning the speed of Parzival's journey after leaving Pelrapeire (224,26: *mich enhab diu âventiure betrogen*), for this could mean that the source contained a lie on this point, but equally that it was no more than mistaken.

Despite these uncertain cases, however, it is certainly possible to determine elsewhere whether a conscious intention to deceive is present or not when *liegen* or *triegen* is involved. When the narrator comments on Gahmuret's words as he prepares to leave Belakane and her subjects (54,16: *mit der rede er si betrouc*), the care with which he conceals his true intention (55,4f. and 12) makes it clear that *betriegen* can only mean conscious deception. Deliberateness can also be conveyed by the addition of a revealing word, such as the adverb *gerne* or the auxiliary verb *wellen*, both implying intention. At his third encounter with Sigune Parzival at first thinks that she is conducting an illicit love-affair from her retreat and is therefore deliberately lying to him[8] (439,9: *dô wânde Parzivâl, si lüge, / unt daz sin anders gerne trüge*),[9] just as at their second meeting she had had grounds for suspecting that he was lying to her (250,17: *si sprach 'swer iu getrûwet iht, / den sult ir gerne triegen niht'*).[10] *Wellen* is just as indicative, as when Gawan is taken to be a proverbially cheating merchant (361,10: *'ein koufman uns hie triegen wil'*) or when the narrator emphatically disclaims any intention to hoodwink his listeners (410,16: *ich enwolt iuch denne triegen*).[11] The fact of intention is even more apparent when *gerne* and *wellen* are combined in the one phrase, as in Gurnemanz's recommendation not to deceive women (172,13: *'welt ir in gerne liegen, / ir muget ir vil betriegen'*).[12]

8. See above, p. 182.
9. The use of *gerne* in conjunction with *trüge* to imply intention suggests that the same is true of *lüge*.
10. See above, p. 117.
11. Although the situation of a narrator claiming the truth of his account is the same, the difference between 410,16 and 224,26 lies in the use of *wellen*, and therefore the suggestion of deliberate intention, in the former case.
12. Here too the use of *wellen* and *gerne* in conjunction with *liegen* is not without its effect on *betriegen*.

Appendix B

We lack such clear pointers when it comes to cases where a conscious intention to deceive cannot be involved, but nonetheless it is still possible to register examples of this, mainly because of what the context tells us. When Scherules reports to Lippaut that Gawan is no merchant he introduces his remark with the words 363,21f. (*er sprach 'hêrre, ir sît betrogen: / swerz iu saget, er hât gelogen'*). That Gawan must be a merchant has been put about by Obie, who has certainly not consciously lied in saying this, but has convinced herself, for psychological reasons which the narrator is careful to reveal to us, that this is in fact the case.[13] Subjectively she means what she says, even if others are quick to disagree with her, so that in Scherules's statement *liegen* means not conscious lying, but saying something which is mistaken. A similar lack of conscious intention underlies the narrator's comment on Orgeluse's reaction on seeing a knightly retinue approaching from the direction of her own realm of Logroys.[14] She is unable to recognise the knights as belonging to the Round Table, toys with the idea that it might be her enemy Gramoflanz with his men or indeed others who have invaded her territory, but is at least certain that they found stout resistance there. With this last remark the narrator voices his agreement, formulating it by using the verb *liegen* in the negative (664,17: *ir munt in louc dâ wênec an*). From our point of view what is telling is the fact that, as the narrator's agreement makes clear, Orgeluse here speaks the truth, but unwittingly: she does not actually know that her men put up a good fight, but correctly surmises it. The use of *liegen* here suggests no conscious wish to deceive on her part (or rather the absence of such a wish), but implies instead that in what she said she unwittingly hit the nail on the head.

The companion verb *triegen* can also be used to convey a similar absence of conscious intention. When Gawan is lying unconscious from his wounds after his adventure at Schastel Marveile and an attempt is made to find out whether he is still alive and breathing (575,23: *ob er den âtem inder züge / od ober si des lebens trüge*), the fact of his unconsciousness (he comes to only in 576,19) is enough to show that literally no conscious intention can be implied by *trüge* (Gawan does not therefore lie doggo!), but instead the possibility of being misled by appearances. The same is implied by the narrator's ironic comment on the young page whom Gawan encounters at

---

13. See above, p. 137.
14. See above, p. 169.

Trevrizent's 'lie'

the start of Book VII. It is made clear to us that the page is bringing up the rear and trying to catch up with the main body of the army (342,9ff.), so that the irony is obvious when the narrator remarks on his 'rushing ahead' (349,22: *ze vorvlüge*) in order to be the first to joust. When this remark is introduced by the words *ich wæn sîn gir des iemen trüge* (349,21), it is not the case that in his eagerness the page might consciously wish to deceive people about his intentions,[15] but rather that they might simply get the wrong impression from appearances.

In all these four cases *liegen* and *triegen* are used to refer to a mistake made or a false impression created without conscious intention being involved. They are enough to show that Wolfram can use these verbs both when such deliberateness is in question and when it is not, so that his use of *liegen* in 798,6, when Trevrizent refers to an earlier mistake on his part, but not to any purposeful wish to deceive Parzival, by no means stands alone. The evidence adduced in this Appendix is not capable of suggesting of itself that we should read Trevrizent's phrase in this way (why we should do this I have suggested in Chapter 7), but is meant to confirm that this reading is linguistically possible.

15. The use of *wellen* and *gern* in 349,22 can no longer be interpreted as implying deliberate deception, for they do not qualify *trüge*, but *die êrsten tjost dâ hân bejagt*.

Bibliography

(1) **Primary sources**

Achard of Saint-Victor, *Sermones*, ed. J. Châtillon, Paris, 1970.
Bernard of Clairvaux, *De gradibus humilitatis et superbiae*, in J. Leclercq and H. M. Rochais, *Sancti Bernardi Opera*, volume III (Rome, 1963), pp. 13ff.
Sermones super Cantica Canticorum, in J. Leclercq, C. H. Talbot and H. M. Rochais, *Sancti Bernardi Opera*, volumes I and II (Rome, 1957 and 1958).
Chrétien de Troyes, *Cligés*, ed. A. Micha, Paris, 1957.
Erec, ed. W. Foerster, Halle, 1934.
Lancelot, ed. M. Roques, *Le chevalier de la Charrete*, Paris, 1963.
Perceval, ed. A. Hilka, *Li contes del Graal*, Halle, 1932.
Yvain, ed. W. Foerster and A. Hilka, Halle, 1926.
Geoffrey of Vinsauf, *Poetria Nova*, ed. E. Faral in *Les arts poétiques du XIIe et du XIIIe siècle*, Paris, 1962, pp. 197ff.
Gottfried von Strassburg, *Tristan und Isold*, ed. F. Ranke, Dublin and Zürich, 1967.
Hartmann von Aue, *Der arme Heinrich*, ed. H. Paul and A. Leitzmann, Halle, 1930.
Erec, ed. A. Leitzmann and L. Wolff, Tübingen, 1963.
Gregorius, ed. F. Neumann, Wiesbaden, 1958.
Iwein, ed. G. F. Benecke, K. Lachmann and L. Wolff, Berlin, 1968.
Hugh of Saint-Victor, *De contemplatione et eius speciebus*, ed. R. Baron, Paris, 1958.
John of Salisbury, *Policraticus*, ed. C. C. J. Webb, Oxford, 1909.
Wolfram von Eschenbach. His various works (*Parzival*, *Willehalm*, *Titurel*) have been quoted from the edition by K. Lachmann, Berlin, [6]1926. Reference is sometimes made to the editions by K. Bartsch and M. Marti (Leipzig, 1929–35) and by A. Leitzmann (Halle, 1928–33).

(2) **Secondary literature**

Footnote references in the text of this book give a keyword which enables the entry in this bibliography to be recognised.

Bartsch, K., 'Die Eigennamen in Wolframs Parzival und Titurel', *Germanistische Studien* 2 (1875), 114ff.
Bauer, G., 'Parzival und die Minne', *Euphorion* 57 (1963), 67ff.
Becker, E. W., *Das Recht im 'Parzival'*, diss. Bonn, 1956.
Bertau, K., *Deutsche Literatur im europäischen Mittelalter*, Munich, 1972.

Bibliography

Bezzola, R. R., *Le sens de l'aventure et de l'amour (Chrétien de Troyes)*, Paris, 1947.
Bindschedler, M., 'Die Dichtung um König Artus und seine Ritter', *DVjs* 31 (1957), 84ff.
Boeheim, W., *Handbuch der Waffenkunde*, reprint, Graz, 1966.
Boesch, B., 'Über die Namengebung mittelhochdeutscher Dichter', *DVjs* 32 (1958), 241ff.
Lehrhafte Literatur. Lehre in der Dichtung und Lehrdichtung im deutschen Mittelalter, Berlin, 1977.
Bonath, G., *Untersuchungen zur Überlieferung des Parzival Wolframs von Eschenbach*, Lübeck, 1970 (volume I) and 1971 (volume II).
Booth, W. C., *The Rhetoric of Fiction*, Chicago, 1967.
A Rhetoric of Irony, Chicago, 1974.
Bosl, K., *Frühformen der Gesellschaft im mittelalterlichen Europa. Ausgewählte Beiträge zu einer Strukturanalyse der mittelalterlichen Welt*, Munich, 1964.
Boysen, J. L., *Über den Gebrauch des Genetivs in den Epen Wolframs von Eschenbach*, diss. Würzburg, 1910.
Braune, W., 'Zu Wolframs Parzival', *PBB* 24 (1899), 188ff.
Bumke, J., *Wolfram von Eschenbach*, Stuttgart, 1964.
Die Wolfram von Eschenbach Forschung seit 1945. Bericht und Bibliographie, Munich, 1970.
Busse, W., 'Verwandtschaftsstrukturen im "Parzival"', in W. Schröder (ed.), *Wolfram-Studien* V, Berlin, 1979, pp. 116ff.
Chaney, W. A., *The Cult of Kingship in Anglo-Saxon England. The transition from paganism to Christianity*, Manchester, 1970.
Christ, W., *Rhetorik und Roman. Untersuchungen zu Gottfrieds von Strassburg 'Tristan und Isold'*, Meisenheim, 1977.
Clodd, E., *Magic in Names and in Other Things*, London, 1920.
Courcelle, P., *Connais-toi toi-même*, Paris, 1974–5.
Cucuel, E., *Die Eingangsbücher des Parzival und das Gesamtwerk*, Frankfurt, 1937.
Curschmann, M., 'Das Abenteuer des Erzählens. Über den Erzähler in Wolframs *Parzival*', *DVjs* 45 (1971), 627ff.
Deinert, W., *Ritter und Kosmos im Parzival. Eine Untersuchung der Sternkunde Wolframs von Eschenbach*, Munich, 1960.
Désilles-Busch, M., *'Doner un don' – 'sicherheit nemen'. Zwei typische Elemente der Erzählstruktur des höfischen Romans*, diss. Berlin (Freie Universität), 1970.
Deutsches Rechtswörterbuch, edd. R. Schröder and E. Freiherr von Künssberg. Volume I, Weimar, 1914–32, volume II, 1935–8.
Deutsches Wörterbuch, edd. J. and W. Grimm. Volume VI, Leipzig, 1885.
Dewald, H., *Minne und 'sgrâles âventiur'. Äusserungen der Subjektivität und ihre sprachliche Vergegenwärtigung in Wolframs 'Parzival'*, Göppingen, 1975.
Drube, H., *Hartmann und Chrétien*, Münster, 1931.
Duggan, J. J., 'Yvain's good name. The unity of Chrétien de Troyes' "Chevalier au Lion"', *OL* 24 (1969), 112ff.
Emmel, H., *Formprobleme des Artusromans und der Graldichtung. Die Bedeutung des Artuskreises für das Gefüge des Romans im 12. und 13.*

Bibliography

Jahrhundert in Frankreich, Deutschland und den Niederlanden, Bern, 1951.
Eroms, H.-W., *'Vreude' bei Hartmann von Aue*, Munich, 1970.
Etzler, G., *Die Komposition des Gahmuret-Teiles von Wolframs 'Parzival' und seine Funktion im Gesamtwerk*, diss. Kiel, 1950.
Fourquet, J., *Wolfram d'Eschenbach et le Conte del Graal. Les divergences de la tradition du Conte del Graal de Chrétien et leur importance pour l'explication du Parzival*, Paris, 1938.
'Les noms propres du Parzival', in the FS for E. Hoepffner (*Publications de la Faculté des Lettres de l'Université de Strasbourg*, 113), Paris, 1949, pp. 245ff.
Frappier, J., *Chrétien de Troyes*, Paris, 1957.
Chrétien de Troyes et le mythe du Graal. Etude sur Perceval ou le Conte du Graal, Paris, 1972.
Frazer, J. G., *The Golden Bough*, London, 1922.
Freytag, W., *Das Oxymoron bei Wolfram, Gottfried und andern Dichtern des Mittelalters*, Munich, 1972.
Gallais, P., 'Recherches sur la mentalité des romanciers français du moyen âge', *CCM* 7 (1964), 479ff.
Gamber, O., 'Die Bewaffnung der Stauferzeit', in *Die Zeit der Staufer. Geschichte – Kunst – Kultur* (Katalog der Ausstellung, Stuttgart, 1977), volume III, pp. 113ff.
Gewehr, W., *Hartmanns 'Klage-Büchlein' im Lichte der Frühscholastik*, Göppingen, 1975.
Gibbs, M. E., 'The role of woman in Wolfram's *Parzival*', *GLL* 21 (1967/8), 296ff.
'Wrong paths in "Parzival"', *MLR* 63 (1968), 872ff.
Gnädinger, L., 'Trevrizent – seine wüstenväterlichen Züge in Wolfram von Eschenbachs *Parzival* (Buch IX)', *Studi di letteratura religiosa tedesca in memoria di Sergio Lupi (Biblioteca della Rivista di Storia e Letteratura religiosa, Studi e Testi IV)*, Florence, 1972, pp. 135ff.
Goldin, F., *The mirror of Narcissus in the Courtly Love Lyric*, Ithaca, N.Y., 1967.
Green, D. H., 'Der Auszug Gahmurets', in W. Schröder (ed.), *Wolfram-Studien*, Berlin, 1970, pp. 62ff.
Der Weg zum Abenteuer im höfischen Roman des deutschen Mittelalters (Veröffentlichung der Joachim Jungius-Gesellschaft der Wissenschaften), Göttingen, 1974.
'Alieniloquium. Zur Begriffsbestimmung der mittelalterlichen Ironie', in the FS for F. Ohly, Munich, 1975, volume II, pp. 119ff.
'On recognising medieval irony', in A. P. Foulkes (ed.), *The Uses of Criticism*, Bern, 1976, pp. 11ff.
'The pathway to adventure', *Viator* 8 (1977), 145ff.
'Homicide and *Parzival*', in D. H. Green and L. P. Johnson, *Approaches to Wolfram von Eschenbach. Five Essays*, Bern, 1978, pp. 11ff.
'The concept *âventiure* in *Parzival*', *ibid.*, pp. 83ff.
Irony in the Medieval Romance, Cambridge, 1979.
'The art of namedropping in Wolfram's *Parzival*', in W. Schröder (ed.), *Wolfram-Studien* VI, Berlin, 1980, pp. 84ff.

Bibliography

'Parzival's departure – folktale and romance', *FMSt* 14 (1980), 352ff.
'The young Parzival – naming and anonymity', in the FS for J. A. Asher, Berlin, 1981, pp. 103ff.
'Advice and narrative action: Parzival, Herzeloyde and Gurnemanz', in the FS for L. W. Forster, Baden-Baden, 1982, pp. 33ff.
Groos, A. B., 'Wolfram von Eschenbach's 'bow metaphor' and the narrative technique of *Parzival*', *MLN* 87 (1972), 391ff.
Haas, A. M., *Parzivals tumpheit bei Wolfram von Eschenbach*, Berlin 1964. *Nim din selbes war. Studien zur Lehre von der Selbsterkenntnis bei Meister Eckhart, Johannes Tauler und Heinrich Seuse*, Freiburg (Switzerland), 1971.
Hagen, J., *Erkennen und Nichterkennen in Wolframs 'Parzival'*, Zulassungsarbeit Erlangen, 1975.
Hagenguth, E., *Hartmanns Iwein. Rechtsargumentation und Bildsprache*, diss. Heidelberg, 1969.
Hahn, I., 'Parzivals Schönheit. Zum Problem des Erkennens und Verkennens im *Parzival*', in the FS for F. Ohly, Munich, 1975, volume II, pp. 203ff.
'Zur Theorie der Personerkenntnis in der deutschen Literatur des 12. bis 14. Jahrhunderts', *PBB(T)* 99 (1977), 395ff.
Haidu, P., *Lion – Queue coupée. L'écart symbolique chez Chrétien de Troyes*, Geneva, 1972.
Hanning, R. W., *The Individual in Twelfth-Century Romance*, New Haven, Conn., 1977.
Harms, W., *Der Kampf mit dem Freund oder Verwandten in der deutschen Literatur bis um 1300*, Munich, 1963.
Harroff, S. C., *Wolfram and his Audience. A Study of the Themes of Quest and of Recognition of Kinship Identity*, Göppingen, 1974.
Hartl, E., 'Verzeichnis der Eigennamen', in E. Hartl's edition of K. Lachmann, *Wolfram von Eschenbach*, Berlin,[7] 1952, pp. 421ff.
Harvey, W. J., *Character and the Novel*, Ithaca, N.Y., 1968.
Hauck, K., 'Geblütsheiligkeit', in the FS for P. Lehmann, St Ottilien, 1950, pp. 187ff.
Haug, W., 'Die Symbolstruktur des höfischen Epos und ihre Auflösung bei Wolfram von Eschenbach', *DVjs* 45 (1971), 668ff.
Heinzel, R., 'Über Wolframs von Eschenbach Parzival', Sitzungsberichte der Wiener Akademie der Wissenschaften (Philosophisch-historische Klasse) 130 (1894), pp. 1ff.
Hellgardt, E., 'Grundsätzliches zum Problem symbolbestimmter und formalästhetischer Zahlenkomposition', in L. P. Johnson, H.-H. Steinhoff and R. A. Wisbey (edd.), *Studien zur frühmittelhochdeutschen Literatur. Cambridger Colloquium 1971*, Berlin, 1974, pp. 11ff.
Henzen, W., 'Das 9. Buch des Parzival. Überlegungen zum Aufbau', in the FS for K. Helm, Tübingen, 1951, pp. 189ff.
'Zur Vorprägung der Demut im Parzival durch Chrestien', *PBB(T)* 80 (1958), 422ff.
Hirschberg, D., *Untersuchungen zur Erzählstruktur von Wolframs 'Parzival'. Die Funktion von erzählter Szene und Station für den doppelten Kursus*, Göppingen, 1976.

Bibliography

Horacek, B., 'Zur inneren Form des Trevrizentbuches', *Sprachkunst* 3 (1972), 214ff.
Huby, M., 'Hat Hartmann von Aue im *Erec* das Eheproblem neu gedeutet?', *RG* 6 (1976), 3ff.
Hunt, T., 'The tragedy of Roland: an Aristotelian view', *MLR* 74 (1979), 791ff.
Huth, L., *Dichterische Wahrheit als Thematisierung der Sprache in poetischer Kommunikation. Untersucht an der Funktion des Höfischen in Wolframs Parzival*, diss. Hamburg, 1972.
Johnson, L. P., 'Lähelin and the Grail-horses', *MLR* 63 (1968), 612ff.
'Characterization in Wolfram's *Parzival*', *MLR* 64 (1969), 68ff.
'Dramatische Ironie in Wolframs *Parzival*', in P. F. Ganz and W. Schröder (edd.), *Probleme mittelhochdeutscher Erzählformen. Marburger Colloquium 1969*, Berlin, 1972, pp. 133ff.
'Parzival's beauty', in D. H. Green and L. P. Johnson, *Approaches to Wolfram von Eschenbach. Five Essays*, Bern, 1978, pp. 273ff.
Johnson, S. M., 'Gawan's surprise in Wolfram's Parzival', *GR* 33 (1958), 285ff.
Jones, M. H., 'Parzival's fighting and his election to the Grail', in W. Schröder (ed.), *Wolfram-Studien* III, Berlin, 1975, pp. 52ff.
Junk, V., 'Gralsage und Graldichtung des Mittelalters', Sitzungsberichte der Kaiserlichen Akademie der Wissenschaften in Wien (Philosophisch-historische Klasse) 168,4, Vienna, 1911.
Kaiser, G., *Textauslegung und gesellschaftliche Selbstdeutung. Die Artusromane Hartmanns von Aue*, Wiesbaden,[2] 1978.
Kellermann, W., *Aufbaustil und Weltbild Chrestiens von Troyes im Percevalroman*, Halle, 1936.
Kelly, F. D., *Sens and Conjointure in the 'Chevalier de la Charrette'*, The Hague, 1966.
Klein, K. K., 'Zur Entstehungsgeschichte des *Parzival*', *PBB* 82 (1961, Sonderband), 13ff.
Kochendörfer, G. and Schirok, B., *Maschinelle Textrekonstruktion. Theoretische Grundlegung, praktische Erprobung an einem Ausschnitt des 'Parzival' Wolframs von Eschenbach und Diskussion der literaturgeschichtlichen Ergebnisse*, Göppingen, 1976.
Kolb, H., 'Schola humilitatis. Ein Beitrag zur Interpretation der Gralerzählung Wolframs von Eschenbach', *PBB(T)* 78 (1956), 65ff.
Munsalvaesche. Studien zum Kyotproblem, Munich, 1963.
Le Rider, P., *Le chevalier dans le Conte du Graal de Chrétien de Troyes*, Paris, 1978.
Lodge, D., *The Novelist at the Crossroads, and Other Essays on Fiction and Criticism*, London, 1971.
Lofmark, C., 'Zur Interpretation der Kyotstellen im "Parzival"', in W. Schröder (ed.), *Wolfram-Studien* IV, Berlin, 1977, pp. 33ff.
Lucas, D. W., *Aristotle. Poetics. Introduction, Commentary and Appendixes*, Oxford, 1968.
Lüthi, M., *Märchen*, Stuttgart, 1962.
Martin, E., *Wolframs von Eschenbach Parzival und Titurel. Band II: Kommentar*, Halle, 1903.

Bibliography

Maurer, F., 'Die Gawangeschichten und die Buch-Einteilung in Wolframs Parzival', *DU* 20, 2 (1968), 60ff.
Mauritz, H.-D., *Der Ritter im magischen Reich. Märchenelemente im französischen Abenteuerroman des 12. und 13. Jahrhunderts*, Bern, 1974.
Meissburger, G., *Grundlagen zum Verständnis der deutschen Mönchsdichtung im 11. und 12. Jahrhundert*, Munich, 1970.
Mergell, B., *Wolfram von Eschenbach und seine französischen Quellen.* II. Teil: *Wolframs 'Parzival'*, Münster, 1943.
Mersmann, W., *Der Besitzwechsel und seine Bedeutung in den Dichtungen Wolframs von Eschenbach und Gottfrieds von Strassburg*, Munich, 1971.
Mertens, V., 'Imitatio Arthuri. Zum Prolog von Hartmanns "Iwein"', *ZdfA* 106 (1977), 350ff.
Mölk, U., 'Das Motiv des Wiedererkennens an der Stimme im Epos und höfischen Roman des französischen Mittelalters', *RJb* 15 (1964), 107ff.
Mohr, W., 'Hilfe und Rat in Wolframs *Parzival*', in the FS for J. Trier, Meisenheim, 1954, pp. 173ff.
'Obie und Meljanz. Zum 7. Buch von Wolframs *Parzival*', in the FS for G. Müller, Bonn, 1957, pp. 9ff.
'Parzival und Gawan', *Euphorion* 52 (1958), 1ff.
'Parzivals ritterliche Schuld', in *Wirkendes Wort. Sammelband* II: *Ältere deutsche Sprache und Literatur*, Düsseldorf, 1962, pp. 196ff.
'Zu den epischen Hintergründen in Wolframs *Parzival*', in the FS for F. Norman, London, 1965, pp. 174ff.
'Landgraf Kingrimursel. Zum VIII. Buch von Wolframs *Parzival*', in the FS for W. Henzen, Bern, 1965, pp. 21ff.
'Iweins Wahnsinn. Die Aventüre und ihr "Sinn"', *ZfdA* 100 (1971), 73ff.
Morris, C., *The Discovery of the Individual: 1050–1200*, New York, 1973.
Nellmann, E., *Wolframs Erzähltechnik. Untersuchungen zur Funktion des Erzählers*, Wiesbaden, 1973.
Niessen, M. H., *Märchenmotive und ihre Funktion für den Aufbau des höfischen Romans, dargestellt am 'Iwein' Hartmanns von Aue*, diss. Münster, 1973.
Nolting-Hauff, I., 'Märchen und Märchenroman. Zur Beziehung zwischen einfacher Form und narrativer Grossform in der Literatur', *Poetica* 6 (1974), 129ff.
Ohly, F., *Der Verfluchte und der Erwählte. Vom Leben mit der Schuld* (Rheinisch-Westfälische Akademie der Wissenschaften, Vorträge G207), Opladen, 1976.
Schriften zur mittelalterlichen Bedeutungsforschung, Darmstadt, 1977.
'Skizzen zur Typologie im späteren Mittelalter', in the FS for K. Ruh, Tübingen, 1979, pp. 251ff.
Ohly, W., *Die heilsgeschichtliche Struktur der Epen Hartmanns von Aue*, diss. Berlin (Freie Universität), 1958.
Ortmann, C., *Die Selbstaussagen im 'Parzival'. Zur Frage nach der Persongestaltung bei Wolfram von Eschenbach*, Stuttgart, 1972.
Peil, D., *Die Gebärde bei Chrétien, Hartmann und Wolfram. Erec – Iwein – Parzival*, Munich, 1975.
Perry, B. E., *The Ancient Romances. A Literary-Historical Account of their*

Origins, Berkeley, Calif., 1967.
Pézard, A., *Dante sous la pluie de feu*, Paris, 1950.
Pickens, R. T., *The Welsh Knight. Paradoxicality in Chrétien's 'Conte del Graal'*, Lexington, Kentucky, 1977.
Poag, J. F., 'diu verholnen mære umben grâl (Parz. 452,30)', in W. Schröder (ed.), *Wolfram-Studien* II, Berlin, 1974, pp. 72ff.
'Gawan's surprise', in W. Schröder (ed.), *Wolfram-Studien* IV, Berlin, 1977, pp. 71ff.
Pörksen, U., *Der Erzähler im mittelhochdeutschen Epos. Formen seines Hervortretens bei Lamprecht, Konrad, Hartmann, in Wolframs Willehalm und in den 'Spielmannsepen'*, Berlin, 1971.
Ragotzky, H., *Studien zur Wolfram-Rezeption. Die Entstehung und Verwandlung der Wolfram-Rolle in der deutschen Literatur des 13. Jahrhunderts*, Stuttgart, 1971.
Ragotzky, H. and Weinmayer, B., 'Höfischer Roman und soziale Identitätsbildung. Zur soziologischen Deutung des Doppelwegs im "Iwein" Hartmanns von Aue', in C. Cormeau (ed.), *Deutsche Literatur im Mittelalter. Kontakte und Perspektiven. Hugo Kuhn zum Gedenken*, Stuttgart, 1979, pp. 211ff.
Rees, B. R., '*Pathos* in the *Poetics* of Aristotle', *Greece and Rome* 19 (1972), 1ff.
Reither, A. K., *Das Motiv der 'neutralen Engel' in Wolframs Parzival*, diss. Mainz, 1965.
Ries, S., 'Erkennen und Verkennen in Gottfrieds 'Tristan' mit besonderer Berücksichtigung der Isold-Weißhand-Episode', *ZfdA* 109 (1980), 316ff.
Rosenfeld, H., 'Personen-, Orts- und Ländernamen in Wolframs Parzival. Gestaltung, Schichtung, Funktion', in the FS for K. Finsterwalder (*Innsbrucker Beiträge zur Kulturwissenschaft* 16, 1971), pp. 203ff.
'Die Namen in Wolframs 'Parzival'. Herkunft, Schichtung, Funktion', in W. Schröder (ed.), *Wolfram-Studien* II, Berlin, 1974, pp. 36ff.
Rosskopf, R., *Der Traum Herzeloydes und der rote Ritter. Erwägungen über die Bedeutung des staufisch-welfischen Thronstreits für Wolframs 'Parzival'*, Göppingen, 1972.
Ruberg, U., *Beredtes Schweigen in lehrhafter und erzählender deutscher Literatur des Mittelalters*, Munich, 1978.
Rupp, H., 'Wolframs 'Parzival'-Prolog', in H. Rupp (ed.), *Wolfram von Eschenbach*, Darmstadt, 1966, pp. 369ff.
Salmon, P. B., 'Ignorance and awareness of identity in Hartmann and Wolfram: an element of dramatic irony', *PBB(T)* 82 (1960), 95ff.
Sanders, W., *Glück. Zur Herkunft und Bedeutungsentwicklung eines mittelalterlichen Schicksalsbegriffs*, Köln, 1965.
Sauer, M., *Parzival auf der Suche nach der verlorenen Zeit. Ein Beitrag zur Ausbildung einer formkritischen Methode*, Göppingen, 1981.
Schaefer, J., 'Beobachtungen zu Wolframs Erzählform im 'Parzival'', in the FS for K. H. Halbach, Göppingen, 1972, pp. 215ff.
Schirok, B., *Der Aufbau von Wolframs 'Parzival'. Untersuchungen zur Handschriftengliederung, zur Handlungsführung und Erzähltechnik sowie zur Zahlenkomposition*, diss. Freiburg, 1972.

Bibliography

'Trevrizent und Parzival. Beobachtungen zur Dialogführung und zur Frage der figurativen Komposition', *ABÄG* 10 (1976), 43ff.

Schmid, E., *Studien zum Problem der epischen Totalität in Wolframs 'Parzival'*, Erlangen, 1976.

Schnell, R., 'Literarische Beziehungen zwischen Hartmanns 'Erec' und Wolframs 'Parzival'', *PBB(T)* 95 (1973), 301ff.

'Vogeljagd und Liebe im 8. Buch von Wolframs *Parzival*', *PBB(T)* 96 (1974), 246ff.

Schreiber, A., *Neue Bausteine zu einer Lebensgeschichte Wolframs von Eschenbach*, Frankfurt, 1922.

Schroedel, M., *Bogenschlagendes Erzählen in Wolframs 'Parzival'*, diss. Göttingen, 1973.

Schröder, W., 'Parzivals Schwerter', *ZfdA* 100 (1971), 111ff.

Schröder, W. J., 'Der dichterische Plan des Parzivalromans', *PBB* 74 (1952), 160ff. and 409ff.

'Kyot', *GRM* 40 (1959), 329ff.

Schultheiss, H., *Die Bedeutung der Familie im Denken Wolframs von Eschenbach*, Breslau, 1937.

Schultz, A., *Das höfische Leben zur Zeit der Minnesinger*, Leipzig, 1889.

Schumacher, M., *Die Auffassung der Ehe in den Dichtungen Wolframs von Eschenbach*, Heidelberg, 1967.

Schwake, H. P., 'Zur Frage der Namensymbolik im höfischen Roman', *GRM* 20 (1970), 338ff.

Schweikle, G., '*Stiure* and *lêre*. Zum 'Parzival' Wolframs von Eschenbach', *ZfdA* 106 (1977), 183ff.

Schwietering, J., 'Die Bedeutung des Zimiers bei Wolfram', in J. Schwietering, *Philologische Schriften* (edd. F. Ohly and M. Wehrli), Munich, 1969, pp. 282ff.

'Natur und *art*', *ibid.*, pp. 450ff.

Speckenbach, K., 'Von den troimen. Über den Traum in Theorie und Dichtung', in the FS for M.-L. Dittrich, Göppingen, 1976, pp. 169ff.

Spitz, H.-J., *Die Metaphorik des geistigen Schriftsinns. Ein Beitrag zur allegorischen Bibelauslegung des ersten christlichen Jahrtausends*, Munich, 1972.

'Wolframs Bogengleichnis: ein typologisches Signal', in the FS for F. Ohly, Munich, 1975, volume II, pp. 247ff.

Steinhoff, H.-H., *Die Darstellung gleichzeitiger Geschehnisse im mittelhochdeutschen Epos. Studien zur Entfaltung der poetischen Technik vom Rolandslied bis zum 'Willehalm'*, Munich, 1964.

Steinle, G., *Hartmann von Aue. Kennzeichnen durch Bezeichnen. Zur Verwendung der Personenbezeichnungen in seinen epischen Werken*, Bonn, 1978.

Tax, P. W., 'Trevrizent. Die Verhüllungstechnik des Erzählers', in the FS for H. Moser, Berlin, 1974, pp. 119ff.

'The Grail kingdom and Parzival's first visit: intrigue, *minne*, despair', in S. Wenzel (ed.), *Medieval and Renaissance Studies* (Medieval and Renaissance Series, 7), Chapel Hill, N. C., 1978, pp. 20ff.

Timpson, G. F., 'The heraldic element in Wolfram's *Parzival*', *GLL* 13 (1959/60), 88ff.

Bibliography

Velten, T., *Der 'Plan' von Wolframs 'Parzival'. Studien zu Verwandtschaftsbeziehungen, Religiosität und Romanform*, diss. Heidelberg, 1956.

Völker, W., *Märchenhafte Elemente bei Chrétien de Troyes*, Bonn, 1972.

Wagner, A. R., *Heralds and Heraldry in the Middle Ages. An Inquiry into the Growth of the Armorial Function of Heralds*, London, 1939.

Wapnewski, P., *Wolframs Parzival. Studien zur Religiosität und Form*, Heidelberg, 1955.

Warning, R., 'Formen narrativer Identitätskonstitution im höfischen Roman', in *GRLMA* IV/1, Heidelberg, 1978, pp. 25ff.

'Heterogenität des Erzählten – Homogenität des Erzählens. Zur Konstitution des höfischen Romans bei Chrétien de Troyes', in W. Schröder (ed.), *Wolfram-Studien* V, Berlin, 1979, pp. 79ff.

Wehrli, M., *Formen mittelalterlicher Erzählung. Aufsätze*, Zürich, 1969.

Weigand, H. J., *Wolfram's Parzival. Five Essays with an Introduction*, Ithaca, N.Y., 1969.

'Spiritual therapy in Wolfram's Parzival', *GQ* 51 (1978), 444ff.

Weinrich, H., *Linguistik der Lüge*, Heidelberg, 1970.

White, Jr., L., *Medieval Technology and Social Change*, London, 1978.

Wolf, A., 'Die Klagen der Blanscheflur. Zur Fehde zwischen Wolfram von Eschenbach und Gottfried von Strassburg', *ZfdPh* 85 (1966), 66ff.

'Die "Adaptation courtoise". Kritische Anmerkungen zu einem neuen Dogma', *GRM* 27 (1977), 257ff.

Wolff, L., 'Die höfisch-ritterliche Welt und der Gral in Wolframs *Parzival*', *PBB(T)* 77 (1955), 254ff.

Kleinere Schriften zur altdeutschen Philologie, Berlin, 1967.

Wynn, M., 'Geography of fact and fiction in Wolfram von Eschenbach's *Parzival*', *MLR* 56 (1961), 28ff.

'Scenery and chivalrous journeys in Wolfram's *Parzival*', *Speculum* 36 (1961), 393ff.

Wolfram von Eschenbach's 'Parzival'. On the genesis of its poetry, to appear shortly.

Ziltener, W., *Chrétien und die Aeneis. Eine Untersuchung des Einflusses von Vergil auf Chrétien de Troyes*, Graz, 1957.

Zimmermann, G., 'Untersuchungen zur Orgeluseepisode in Wolfram von Eschenbachs *Parzival*', *Euphorion* 66 (1972), 128ff.

Kommentar zum VIII. Buch von Wolfram von Eschenbachs 'Parzival', Göppingen, 1974.

Zips, M., 'Einige Zeugnisse aus der mittelhochdeutschen Epik zur Beziehung zwischen dem ritterlichen Helden und seinem Wappensymbol', *JHGG* 8 (1973), 155ff.

Zutt, H., 'Parzivals Kämpfe', in the FS for F. Maurer, Düsseldorf, 1968, pp. 178ff.

Index

The name of Parzival, which appears very frequently in the text, is included in this index only under a number of major headings. Similarly, the name of Wolfram von Eschenbach is included only when reference is made to works of his other than *Parzival*. Names of fictional characters are generally given in the form used in the text, so that a distinction is made, for example, between Gauvain (Chrétien), Gawan (Wolfram) and Gawein (Hartmann).

Abel 197ff.
Abenberg 7, 94
Achard of Saint-Victor 297f.
Adam 219, 302
Addanz 83
Alcuin 69
Alexandria 41, 49, 282
Alis 301
ambiguity 13, 66, 70f., 84, 90f., 190, 192, 197, 207, 213, 226f., 246ff., 275ff.
Ampflise 44ff., 49, 56, 143, 269, 277
Anfortas 6, 10, 28ff., 70, 90, 92ff., 97, 99, 101, 109ff., 115, 117ff., 157, 164, 174, 179, 190, 193ff., 197, 200f., 203ff., 212, 216ff., 229, 233, 254f., 257, 259, 277, 281f., 285, 293f., 296, 311f., 315, 320ff.
angels, neutral 203, 205, 259ff.
Annore 42
anonymity 9, 11, 15ff., 47, 53, 55, 61, 73f., 88, 98, 102, 113, 120, 125, 135, 138, 142f., 150, 186, 234, 237, 246, 249, 274, 298ff., 304f., 308ff., 314, 330, 332. *See also* circumlocutions *and* epithets, anonymous
Anschevîn 41, 45, 47ff., 57, 62, 249, 278, 282, 286
Anschouwe 38f., 44ff., 51ff., 282
Anselm of Canterbury 296
Antanor 26, 72
Antikonie 142ff.
Arnive 150f., 153ff., 160ff., 165ff., 173, 231, 279, 281, 283
Arthur 12, 16, 61, 63f., 67, 72, 75, 80, 82f., 102, 104f., 125ff., 143, 152, 154, 158, 165ff., 173, 202, 226ff., 231f., 235, 239, 242ff., 251, 253f., 270, 278f., 283, 286, 303, 307, 310, 314, 316. *For* Arthur's court *and* Arthur's retinue *see* Round Table
Ascalun 141f.
Astor 137f.
audience *See* listeners
Augustine 296, 337f.

barbier 265ff.
Beacurs 17ff., 72f., 97, 287
Bearosche 133ff., 141ff., 145, 147, 174, 187, 228, 244, 268, 270, 277, 282, 288, 295, 307ff.
Belakane 41ff., 49f., 83, 238, 282, 339
Bene 157, 173, 230ff., 234f., 277, 279
benennen See nennen
Bernard of Clairvaux 291ff.
bîspel 31ff.
Blancheflor 302f.
'Blutstropfenszene' 13, 90, 162, 236, 242, 270, 272, 277, 284, 287, 315
'Bogengleichnis' 12, 24, 28f., 31ff., 98, 113, 180, 216
bow 31ff.
Brabant 240, 261f.
Brandigan 85
Brizljan 116
Brobarz 9, 74, 84f.
Brumbane 94, 123

Cadoc 272
Cain 189, 197ff., 290, 295

Index

Calogrenant 2, 16
Castis 38, 202, 215, 220
Chrétien de Troyes 7f., 14ff., 19f., 22, 42, 267f., 273f., 300f., 305
   Cligès 81, 301, 303
   Erec 15, 73, 81, 301
   Lancelot 16, 55, 75, 81, 267, 300
   Perceval 4f., 17, 79f., 141, 267, 274, 281, 299ff., 304, 306
   Yvain 2, 16, 73, 81, 251f., 267, 300
Cidegast 10, 164
circumlocutions 16, 43ff., 53, 72, 74, 76, 92, 98ff., 104, 125f., 131, 135f., 139f., 216, 224, 232, 236f., 240, 246, 248, 262, 299f., 303f., 306f. *See also* Red Knight
Clamide 64, 66, 68, 72ff., 84ff., 97, 104, 125f., 147, 158, 266, 271, 279, 282f., 307, 309
Clias 153ff., 160, 165, 168, 175, 331
Clinschor 150, 152, 162, 278
compassion 290, 293f., 296, 298, 315, 327, 331
Condwiramurs 9, 14, 35, 54, 62f., 67f., 70ff., 84ff., 205f., 227, 230, 233, 277, 280, 286, 288, 296, 302f., 307, 313
Cundrie (Gawan's sister) 153f., 157, 162, 171
   (Grail messenger) 7f., 11, 54, 89, 91, 95, 97f., 103, 105, 132, 146f., 152f., 155f., 158, 177, 179, 203, 205f., 210, 212f., 215, 239f., 247ff., 255, 278, 285, 288, 294, 307f., 312, 314f., 322, 324ff., 329f., 332, 334
Cunneware 26, 67, 71f., 82, 97, 101ff., 121, 123, 125f., 128, 130ff., 136, 266, 271, 276, 279, 282, 286f., 306

Delphi 291

Ehcunaht 145
Ekuba 98, 103, 249, 251
Enide 301
Enite 272f.
epithets, anonymous 16, 45ff., 53, 72ff., 76, 88, 98ff., 104f., 139, 146, 149, 156f., 160ff., 171, 180f., 186, 235ff., 239, 249, 262
Erec 4, 75, 265, 272f., 301

Famorgan 145
Feirefiz 11, 23, 45, 98, 103, 198, 212, 226, 228ff., 233, 237ff., 245ff., 250, 254, 256f., 261, 276, 278, 286, 295, 303, 317, 323

Florant 170
Frank, Sebastian 338
Frimutel 92, 98, 111, 190f., 199ff., 216ff., 220ff., 229, 275

Gahmuret 17, 19, 37ff., 60, 71, 73, 75, 78, 83, 91f., 96f., 103, 121, 135, 138, 143, 145f., 172, 186f., 190, 197ff., 202f., 212, 215f., 218, 220, 228, 230, 246ff., 267, 269, 271, 276ff., 282, 298, 302f., 305, 310, 314, 326, 339
Galoes 39, 42, 45ff., 57ff., 75, 81, 146, 184, 271
Galogandres 71f.
Gandin 43, 48, 83, 146, 198
ganerbe 92, 193, 215f., 218, 222f., 296
Garschiloye 212
Gaschier 43, 51f.
Gauvain 141, 300
GAWAN 8, 10, 18, 21, 23, 25f., 37, 54, 59, 64, 72, 89, 97, 101ff., 128f., 133ff., 176, 179, 198, 205, 226ff., 230ff., 239, 244ff., 266, 270f., 276ff., 286ff., 295, 306ff., 316, 331, 339f.
   I at Bearosche 23, 134ff.
      Schanpfanzun 141ff.
      Schastel Marveile 4, 7, 50, 151ff., 174, 277
   II encounter with Gramoflanz 134, 158, 162ff.
      Kaylet 51
      Lischoys Gwelljus 4
      Parzival 23, 158, 173, 179, 226, 234ff., 240ff., 272
      Urians 133, 147ff.
   III kinship with Parzival 5
   IV surprise by 8, 165ff., 174
Gawein 4, 265, 273
Geiler von Kaisersberg 338
Geoffrey of Monmouth 73
Gottfried von Strassburg, *Tristan* 2, 22, 34, 263, 277, 285
Graharz 85
GRAIL 17, 23, 27ff., 71, 92, 107ff., 140, 164, 176, 178, 180, 189, 191ff., 197, 200, 202ff., 220, 224, 230, 251, 254ff., 280, 290, 296, 311f., 315ff., 324ff., 332ff.
   castle *See* Munsvalvæsche
   community 94, 99, 108, 110, 190, 193, 208, 215, 311, 314ff., 320ff.
   family 12, 29, 92, 116ff., 160, 174, 184, 186f., 191f., 200, 202f., 211, 214, 216ff., 259, 288, 296, 313ff., 321, 327, 329, 335

Index

horse 187f., 190, 195f., 198, 203, 242, 283
king 10, 30f., 70, 90, 93, 98, 112, 117f., 127, 175, 190, 193, 201, 205, 217ff., 221ff., 229, 234, 250, 257, 259, 261, 284, 288, 290, 313, 315, 328
kingdom *See* Terre de Salvæsche
kingship 8, 10, 36, 79, 97, 160, 190, 193, 212, 215f., 218ff., 257, 275, 292, 312, 315, 318, 324, 327, 331f.
knight(s) 115, 127, 178, 180, 187f., 190ff., 196, 203ff., 211, 233f., 242, 261, 268, 270, 278, 282, 335
messenger *See* Cundrie
procession 28, 106ff., 204, 256, 277, 323
Gramoflanz 150f., 158, 162ff., 169, 171ff., 227, 230ff., 240ff., 244ff., 254, 271, 276ff., 283, 286f., 310f., 314, 340
Gregorius 290
Guinevere 167f., 170, 283, 300f., 313f.
Guivreiz 4, 272f.
Gurnemanz 9, 25, 60f., 63ff., 68, 70, 72ff., 76ff., 80, 83ff., 95, 122, 142, 195, 198, 208, 275, 280, 287, 305f., 339

härsnier 264ff.
Hardiz 42f., 55
Hartmann von Aue 14f., 19, 22, 40, 75, 95, 273f., 287, 302
Büchlein 2
Erec 4, 75, 83, 142, 251f., 263, 265, 272f.
Gregorius 290
Iwein 2, 83, 180, 273f., 289, 294, 302, 319
Helinand of Froidmont 293
heraldic device 39, 48ff., 55ff., 80, 85, 87, 115, 125, 134, 138ff., 148, 168f., 182, 187, 189, 205, 245, 252, 266ff., 272, 282f., 321
herze 2
Herzeloyde 17, 19, 38, 40, 42ff., 52ff., 61f., 66f., 69, 71ff., 75, 78, 82, 92, 96, 103, 197, 199f., 202, 212, 214ff., 220ff., 276, 286, 304f., 315, 326, 328
Hiuteger 43, 271, 302f.
hôchvart 189, 200f., 203, 205
Hugh of Saint-Victor 291
humility 290ff., 296, 298
hyperbole 18f., 120, 163

identifiability 55, 265ff., 309f.

identity concealed 142, 261ff.
loss of 289
sense of 294
unawareness of 20, 22, 74f., 297, 307
Imane 298
INFORMATION by instalments 9, 12f., 19, 83, 117f., 121, 124, 163, 174, 203, 210ff., 222, 246ff.
fed to actor 5f., 50, 81, 154, 158, 165ff., 174
fed to listeners 3ff., 9, 11f., 14, 18f., 30, 39f., 57, 66ff., 75, 77, 81ff., 90ff., 110ff., 114, 118ff., 127f., 148, 153, 174, 178ff., 189ff., 195, 197, 208, 210, 213ff., 223, 230ff., 241f., 246ff., 250ff., 262f., 306
withheld from actor 6f., 9f., 14f., 17, 30, 39, 57, 64ff., 71, 82ff., 90ff., 98, 110ff., 114, 118ff., 127f., 148, 174, 178ff., 189ff., 195, 197, 208, 210, 213ff., 223, 241f., 246ff., 252f., 262f., 306
withheld from listeners 7ff., 14f., 17, 28, 30f., 46, 50, 64ff., 69ff., 77, 98, 151, 153ff., 158, 174, 177ff., 229f.
inscription on the Grail 204, 316, 324f., 327f., 330ff.
irony 1f., 11, 20, 121, 127ff., 134, 163f., 169f., 176, 184, 192, 196, 227, 232, 242f., 279, 280f., 287, 332, 337, 340
Isajes 169, 283
Isenhart 41, 43
Ither 12, 61, 67f., 72, 75f., 80, 82f., 85, 87, 103f., 115, 122, 125ff., 129, 135, 138, 140, 145, 147, 173, 179, 182f., 186ff., 191, 197ff., 202, 220, 224, 244, 266, 269, 274, 276, 280ff., 287ff., 295, 305f., 309, 321ff.
Itonje 153ff., 162ff., 171ff., 230ff., 234f., 276, 278f.
Iwanet 61, 76, 104
Iwein 4, 273f., 289

Jeschute 5f., 11, 20f., 23, 54, 61, 66, 69, 71f., 75, 77f., 81f., 97, 100f., 118ff., 161, 185, 207, 252, 266, 270, 276, 281, 286, 288
Joflanze 167f., 170ff., 174, 227
John of Salisbury 293

Kahenis 178, 180, 186
Kanvoleis 39, 41, 44ff., 52ff., 62, 75, 103, 121, 138, 145, 157, 214, 228, 269, 278, 282, 316
Kardeiz 35, 228, 233, 277

Index

Karnahkarnanz 18, 61, 63f., 69f., 72, 75, 275f., 288, 297f.
Kaylet 17ff., 39f., 42, 44, 46f., 49ff., 53, 55ff., 72, 138, 271, 282, 316
Keii 3f., 72, 82, 90f., 97, 101f., 104f., 127ff., 265, 270, 281, 288
Keu 281
Killirjacac 43, 50, 59, 276
Kingrimursel 91, 97, 141, 143ff., 271, 280, 303
Kingrun 66, 72f., 75ff., 87f., 104, 125f., 158, 302, 306f., 309
kinship relationship 5, 221, 295f., 298, 305
    Antikonie with Gahmuret 145
    Gahmuret with Kaylet 39, 46, 50
    Gahmuret with Killirjacac 50
    Gawan with Arthur 144
    Gawan with the queens at Schastel Marveile 7, 11, 153ff.
    Gawan with Vergulaht 144
    Herzeloyde with the Grail-family 30
    Parzival with Anfortas 197, 200f.
    Parzival with Arthur 83, 144
    Parzival with Feirefiz 198
    Parzival with Gawan 5, 144
    Parzival with the Grail-family 11, 14, 23, 29, 31, 92, 96, 199, 214ff., 220, 223, 296
    Parzival with Ither 12, 61, 83, 191, 197ff., 274
    Parzival with Sigune 78, 96, 217
    Parzival with Trevrizent 197, 199f., 224f., 283
    Parzival with Vergulaht 144ff., 156, 276
    Sigune with the Grail-family 29
kiusche 205, 209
Klingsor 1
krümbe 32, 34f., 331
kumber 285, 293, 315
Kyot (source) 17, 29f., 92, 218, 220f., 223
    (von Katelangen) 72, 221, 268, 282

Lachfilirost 43, 282
Lähelin 42, 63, 68, 71, 77, 79, 81f., 123ff., 186ff., 196ff., 200f., 203ff., 224, 228, 259ff., 266, 280f., 283f., 297, 316, 326, 334f.
Lambekin 43
Lancelot 16, 301
Laudine 180, 184, 301
Liaze 63, 67, 69, 72
Liddamus 144, 146f.

lie, by Trevrizent 257ff., 335, 337ff. *See also liegen and triegen*
liegen 258f., 338ff.
Lippaut 136, 287, 340
Lischoys Gwelljus 4, 150, 159, 170
LISTENERS attentive and inattentive 1f., 12, 24, 227, 319
    equated with Parzival 14, 19, 30, 62ff., 85, 100, 108, 113, 119, 177ff., 196, 203, 213, 217, 222, 228, 230, 238ff., 246, 270, 281, 318f.
    qualities of 24, 31, 34f.
    recognition by 3, 8, 15, 21, 65, 241f.
    task of 1f., 10ff., 18ff., 24f., 52, 90, 185, 229, 250, 274, 318f.
Lit Marveile 153, 159
Logroys 64, 151f., 167ff., 171f., 279, 340
Loherangrin 229, 233, 240, 261ff.
Lot 17f., 73, 103, 163, 172
Lucifer 189
Lybbeals 188, 191, 197f., 204f., 326, 335

Manpfilyot 72
Marke 285
Maurin 169, 283
Mazadan 145
Meljahkanz 75, 139
Meljanz 136f., 139ff., 284
Munsalvæsche 6f., 13, 21, 23, 28, 30f., 33, 35f., 59, 66, 70f., 80, 86, 92ff., 106ff., 115ff., 151, 153, 157f., 160, 164, 174, 177, 180, 186, 191ff., 201ff., 213, 215ff., 219ff., 224, 227, 230, 233f., 240, 242, 252, 254ff., 259ff., 270, 275, 277, 279ff., 283ff., 290, 292ff., 297, 305, 310ff., 320f., 324ff.

Nabchodonosor 339
NAMING 3, 14ff., 20, 274, 298ff.
    1 delayed 5, 15, 43ff., 74, 81, 274
    of Ampflise 44
        Anfortas 97ff., 324
        Clinschor 152
        Condwiramurs 9, 73f., 84f.
        Ekuba 98
        Galoes 44
        Herzeloyde 44f.
        Kahenis 186
        Parzival 15, 17, 35, 61, 65, 72f., 78ff., 298
        Schoette 44
        Titurel 97
        Urians 149

Index

II immediate 15, 42f., 50, 71f., 74, 82, 97, 102, 142, 150, 162f., 261
III of Parzival 298ff.
IV temporary abandonment of 9, 15, 274, 298, 303
  with Clamide 88
  Cundrie 239, 253
  Feirefiz 237
  Gahmuret 45f.
  Gawan 158, 235
  Gramoflanz 236
  Jeschute 100f.
  Loherangrin 262
  Orilus 101
  Parzival 72, 74ff., 88, 234ff., 303ff.
  the queens at Schastel Marveile 171
  Sigune 100, 181
  Trevrizent 186
narrator 2f., 6, 8ff., 16f., 24ff., 36, 39, 62f., 76f., 86, 98, 112f., 114, 118, 122f., 178, 190, 196, 200, 203, 217f., 228, 230, 232, 234, 240, 262, 306, 309f., 316ff., 328, 335, 338ff.
nennen 28, 113, 192f., 222, 316ff., 325f.
nickname 79, 280, 283, 299, 301, 304, 306
Norgals 79, 215, 228, 296, 311

Obie 135ff., 278, 284, 340
Obilot 135f., 139, 278, 284, 286
ordo artificialis 34
ordo naturalis 5, 331
Orgeluse 7, 10f., 14, 149f., 162, 164ff., 172f., 187, 201, 205f., 221f., 266, 276, 278f., 287, 309, 313f., 340
Orilus 5f., 20f., 42, 66f., 71f., 75, 77, 81f., 90, 97, 101, 104, 118ff., 125f., 128f., 184f., 266f., 279, 281f., 307

PARZIVAL
  I at Bearosche 23, 179, 277, 295
    Munsalvæsche 6f., 70, 89ff., 106ff., 158, 220, 233f., 254ff., 270, 277f., 320ff.
    Pelrapeire 74ff., 84ff., 271
  II beauty of 17ff., 78, 121, 131, 145, 184, 200, 275f., 283
  III called to Grail kingship 8, 99, 192, 229, 251, 254ff., 260, 285, 312, 314f., 317, 324, 332, 337
  IV encounter with Condwiramurs 62, 75, 86, 277
    Feirefiz 11, 23, 198, 229f., 237ff.,
245ff., 261, 295
Gawan 23, 135, 173, 187, 226, 234ff., 240ff., 272, 295
Gramoflanz 227, 232, 236f., 244ff., 254
Gurnemanz 76
Ither 12, 82f., 295
Jeschute 21f., 77f., 100f., 118ff., 161, 207, 270
Keii 3, 101f.
Orgeluse 10, 164f., 313
Orilus 5, 101, 123f., 267
Sigune 65, 78ff., 100, 113ff., 177, 179ff., 194, 210ff., 216f., 265f., 269f., 303, 305
Trevrizent 29, 185ff., 257ff., 320ff.
Vergulaht 146f., 277, 295
  V guidance of 13, 66, 93, 96, 99, 118, 177, 192f., 208, 214, 222, 315, 317, 324, 327f. See also providence
See also NAMING, delayed, of Parzival; RECOGNITION, failure in, by Parzival and of Parzival; RECOGNITION, by Parzival and of Parzival; Red Knight; NAMING, temporary abandonment of, with Parzival
Pelrapeire 9, 60, 64, 67f., 74ff., 84ff., 88ff., 95, 104, 139, 147, 158, 162, 208, 271, 279, 282f., 307, 309, 313, 339
Perceval 4, 16, 79, 274, 301f., 306
Peronnik 299
pet-name See nickname
Physiologus 247
pilgrim-knight See Kahenis
Plimizœl 8, 134, 251, 254, 313
Plippalinot 153ff., 158f., 165
point of view 3ff., 20, 28, 55, 62ff., 91ff., 106ff., 113, 119, 133f., 140, 151ff., 168, 186, 202f., 207, 209f., 229ff., 234, 239ff., 307, 310, 319
pot-helm 265
Presterjohn 229
providence 36, 113, 118, 177, 179, 192f., 208ff., 214, 285, 315, 317f., 324, 327f. See also PARZIVAL, guidance of
Punturtois 148

question (at Brabant) 261f.
  (at Munsalvæsche) 112, 206ff., 211, 213, 220, 255, 290, 294, 316, 324, 327, 331, 333

Razalic 41, 43, 271, 282
reception 3, 7ff., 15, 20, 31

355

Index

recital, subsequent 7, 39, 91
RECOGNITION 3, 20ff., 77, 103f., 265ff., 273ff., 283ff., 315f.
  I and naming 15, 17, 79, 224f., 280
  II of God 296ff.
  III of place 185, 276
  IV of self 23, 65, 74, 274, 285, 288ff., 298, 312, 314f., 317
  V of situation, by Condwiramurs 86
  VI of Anfortas, by Parzival 255
  of Arthurian knights at Bearosche, by Gawan 137f.
  of Clamide, by Kingrun 87, 266
  of Cundrie, by the Round Table 8, 253f.
  of Feirefiz, by Parzival 237f.
  of Gahmuret, by Kaylet 53f.
  of Gawan, by Parzival 130f., 235, 243f.
  of Jeschute, by Parzival 6, 21, 122f.
  of Kaylet, by Gahmuret 51
  of Orilus, by Cunneware 125, 266
  of Parzival, by Anfortas 255, 321ff.
  of Parzival, by Gawan 101, 131, 139f., 243
  of Parzival, by Jeschute 21, 101, 121
  of Parzival, by Sigune 78f., 101, 115f., 184
  of Parzival, by Trevrizent 186ff.
  of the prince of Anschouwe, by Gahmuret 57f.
  of the queens at Schastel Marveile, by Gawan 153ff., 161
  of Sigune, by Parzival 116, 181, 183f.
  of Trevrizent, by Parzival 197ff.
  VII failure in 20, 22, 144, 277, 279ff.
  of Clamide, by Kingrun 87f.
  of Cundrie, by the Round Table 239f., 250ff.
  of Gahmuret, at Kanvoleis 53ff.
  of Gahmuret, by Kaylet 51f.
  of Gahmuret, by the prince of Anschouwe 57f.
  of Gawan, by Parzival 135f., 138f., 242
  of Gawan, by the queens at Schastel Marveile 157, 171
  of Jeschute, by Parzival 21, 122
  of Orilus, by Cunneware 125
  of Orilus, by Parzival 123f.
  of Parzival, by Clamide and Kingrun 76f.
  of Parzival, by Gawan 139, 240
  of Parzival, by Gramoflanz 244f.
  of Parzival, by the inhabitants of Pelrapeire 74
  of Parzival, by Orilus 123f.
  of Parzival, by the Round Table 101
  of Parzival, by Sigune 114, 182f., 265, 269f.
  of Parzival, by Trevrizent 185f., 329ff.
  of Parzival's intentions, by the Round Table, 91, 126ff.
  of the queens of Schastel Marveile, by Arthur 171
  of the Round Table, by Parzival 130
  of the situation at Munsalvæsche, by Parzival 89ff.
  of the situation, by Sigune 117f.
  of Trevrizent, by Parzival 185f.
  of Urians, by Gawan 147ff.
Red Knight (reference to Parzival) 76, 80, 91, 104f., 126, 129, 131, 139, 242, 272, 299, 306f., 309, 311, 314, 331, 334 *See also* Ither
Repanse de schoy 92, 97, 107ff., 112, 196, 201, 203, 208, 211f., 217, 220, 228, 256, 277, 321ff.
rêroup 76, 188f., 191, 198f., 335
revealing while concealing 3, 11ff., 19f., 40ff., 92f., 112f., 176f., 216f., 227f.
Richard of Saint-Victor 291f., 298
ritter rôt See Red Knight
Round Table 8, 67f., 75f., 82, 87ff., 98, 101ff., 121, 125ff., 140, 146f., 152ff., 158, 162, 167f., 172, 179, 203, 232, 236, 239, 242, 245, 249ff., 266, 270, 272, 278ff., 285, 288, 296, 302f., 305ff., 322, 324f., 332, 334, 340
Rumpelstilzchen 299

Sabins 240ff.
sælde 194, 211f., 219, 318, 333
Sangive 153ff., 162, 171
Saturn 204, 209, 327, 331
Schafillor 43
Schanpfanzun 133, 141ff., 162, 174
Schastel Marveile 4, 10, 50, 133, 150ff., 165ff., 174f., 226, 231, 277, 279, 283, 331, 340
Schenteflurs 9, 73, 84f.
Scherules 134, 136, 138f., 340
Schionatulander 5, 61, 67, 69, 71f., 81, 100, 177, 184, 253, 278, 296, 326
Schoette 44f.
Schoysiane 92, 217, 220f.
Secundille 211, 247f.

Index

Segramors 91, 97, 101f., 104f., 127ff., 270, 281, 288
Seville 200
sicherheit 76, 87, 104, 124ff., 147
Sigune 6, 15ff., 19, 23, 28ff., 36, 61, 67, 69, 71ff., 78ff., 82, 92, 94ff., 100ff., 110, 112ff., 118, 121, 123, 148, 153, 158, 177, 179ff., 186f., 191f., 194, 200, 203, 206, 209ff., 216ff., 220f., 223, 225, 252f., 255, 265f., 269, 271f., 276, 278, 280, 282f., 286, 288, 294, 296, 298f., 302ff., 311f., 315, 318f., 324ff., 328f., 332, 339
Soltane 13f., 18, 60ff., 70, 77, 185, 217, 285, 304f.
stiure 318f.

Tampenteire 73
templeisen See Grail knight(s)
Terre de Salvæsche 28, 89, 95, 98, 117, 176, 194, 204, 210ff., 215f., 234, 242, 252, 305, 310ff., 320, 328
Terre Marveile 153, 159
Thabronit 247f.
Thasme 247
Titurel 28f., 97, 118, 190, 202, 204, 209, 216, 218, 220f., 223
Trevrizent 10, 12, 23, 28ff., 36f., 42, 54, 59, 67, 92ff., 98, 113, 116, 153, 158, 177f., 180, 185ff., 216f., 219ff., 240, 244, 255, 257ff., 275ff., 280ff., 287ff., 292, 294ff., 313, 315f., 318, 320ff., 337ff.
Tribalibot 247f.
triegen 338ff.
triuwe 79, 114, 201, 233
tump(heit) 1, 19, 21ff., 61, 64, 67, 189, 193f., 196f., 213f., 287f., 319, 333
Turkentals 188, 197

unprîs 194, 333
Urians 133, 147ff., 162, 166, 174, 271
Utepandragun 83, 103, 169, 283

venje 181, 183
Vergulaht 54, 140, 142ff., 156, 173, 179, 228, 244, 271, 276ff., 295, 308
vinteile 264, 266f.
Vridebrant 41, 43

Wâleis 65, 102f., 215, 228, 296, 311
warnen 194, 255, 333
Wartburgkrieg 1
Wildenberg 7
wîs(heit) 1, 19, 23ff., 61, 65, 213, 287, 306, 319, 336
Wolfram von Eschenbach *Titurel* 26
  Willehalm 3, 32
wunsch 205, 211ff., 219

Yvain 16ff., 300f.

Zazamanc 39, 41, 43, 45f., 49ff., 53f., 56, 58, 62, 90, 172, 271, 282
zuht 86, 107, 183, 209f., 286

OHIO UNIVERSITY LIBRARY

Please retur~~n thi~~s book as soon ~~as you~~
have finish~~ed with~~ ~~it.~~ ~~Recor~~d